With many grateful thanks to all who have contributed to this book in any way whatsoever, I dedicate this book to my dear friend Nigel, to whom "The Lord gave the word" – and great has been "the company of the preachers" – in every sense!

So Nigel, this comes with love and gratitude, to one who always sees the glorious 'potential' of the Lord, from one who has so often been astonished by it, but in the certain knowledge that every year in March, I shall forever remember your words, "It's the latency I love Jules, the latency!"

Julie

Contents

A smile from Thea Hoelscher

There's new life in Jesus!

Singers in the Pantheon

Sam Openshaw and Catherine Swinford-White soloists

Contented conductor

Cellist and alto soloist Hannah Cawston

Introduction

Only be careful, and watch yourselves closely so that you do not forget the things your eyes have seen or let them fade from your heart as long as you live. Teach them to your children and to their children after them. Deut. 4:9 (NIV)

IN my heart of hearts, I always suspected I would one day attempt to put down my own memoirs as a private project, probably in retirement (supposing that happy state ever arrives!). However, in the light of the many wonderful stories involved in this ministry of over forty years, it seemed appropriate to try and write something during this final year of the NEO as we consider the legacy of this remarkable 'act of God'.

I met Nigel in my late teens, in the days before NEO began, and worked with him and a group of friends for a wonderful, formative period in all our lives. I returned to work with him in what had become the New English Orchestra, in 1985, and so from that point on have seen the unfolding of the story, and experienced much of it from the perspective of Central Administrator.

As is explained within, I actually left the group in 1976 for a few years. There are understandably therefore, great swathes of those early experiences of which I only knew second-hand, or in the case of the opera, *The Hiding Place*, from being part of its privileged audience for one performance. Many early stories are of course covered very adequately by the memoirs of Chris Bell, who was specifically appointed by Nigel to the emerging need of a 'General Manager' at the time of the production of the above opera. However, where I felt there were significant tales to be told which I missed, I have requested accounts from others as indicated, and we are so grateful to all contributors for taking the time to share those memories.

The collection begins then, with the writings of Chris Bell. I need to clarify that those memoirs appear thanks to Keith Buckler, who actually took the initiative and booked appointments with Chris, and, armed with only a cassette recorder, interviewed him until all this wonderful material was suitably captured. What followed leaves me utterly lost for words, since I know how much time it would have taken me, even as a speedy touch-typist, to have transcribed all those recordings, presumably without a transcribing machine! For Keith it must have been a simply heroic effort! Therefore I must begin by honouring him for this feat of endurance which has left us with a treasured account, spanning everything from the poignant to the absolutely hilarious events of those early days of NEO!

I do hope that everyone who reads this account will forgive any inaccuracies and omissions – there is an unbelievable amount of material about which I could write, but I fear I would have to echo the Apostle John's sentiments at the end of his wonderful Gospel as rendered by J.B. Phillips: John chapter 21 v 25:

Of course, there are many other things which Jesus did, and I suppose that if each one were written down in detail, there would not be room in the whole world for all the books that would have to be written.

A major reason however, for making this attempt, is to provide what I hope will be a catalyst for other NEO members to use this as a springboard for their own memories and perhaps for anyone who reads this, to consider leaving their loved ones a record of God's interventions in their own lives.

I anticipate that for NEO folk there will inevitably be more than a few cries of "Oh, she's left out so and so, and that was so amazing!" or, "Oh yes, I remember... that was when such and such happened, but that doesn't seem to be in the book!" Those I hope will be the moments when pen is put to paper to write for future generations of family or friends. In the coming years, I believe such testimonies will be hugely encouraging to them as (in the words of Graham Kendrick) we see the 'clouds gathering', and in the light of all we have encountered of the astonishing grace and mercy of God, we, and they in their turn, look in hope for the final return of our Saviour.

Julie Fry
2016

Dimples

Dotted around these pages, you will find little comments entitled **'Dimples'**! These are humorous comments made by Nigel at odd moments – so named for a certain aspect of his personal physiognomy when amused!

1

Kicking the ball off the spot

Memoirs of Chris Bell, the first official Central Administrator of the NEO

As originally dictated into a cassette recorder and transcribed by Keith Buckler, and subsequently edited by Julie Fry and Nigel Swinford.

Early singers group, Chris Bell third from right on back row

I'D like to start by saying why I think it is important for this book to be written. Looking at Scripture one is struck by the way the Israelite nation repeatedly recounted, and indeed were enjoined to recount, God's blessing and His deliverance of them from a never ending variety of situations. Indeed, that practice persists today, so that if you go into a synagogue you will find that they are still praising God for deliverance from Egypt at the Exodus three and a half thousand years ago. I venture to suggest that no other nation on earth has such a wholesale and accurate view of its history as seen through its major incidents, and there is a benefit for us in that we need to recount God's blessings much more regularly and frequently than we actually do. If

we fail to do that, they get lost and forgotten – even the most important ones, never mind the rest of them, and therefore we lose an opportunity to build up our faith for the future. And it is for that reason that I think this book ought to be written, before what happened in the early days of the NEO fades into the distant past.

Vision

Talking now about the origins as I recall them: my first contact with Nigel Swinford was in about 1974 when he was Director of Music at the Jesus Centre in Birmingham, and in that position was responsible for the organisation of a

Massed choir that toured throughout the Midlands region, presenting the Jimmy Owens' musical *Come Together* for some considerable time, and subsequently *If my People*. In both cases this included the television broadcast productions of both musicals throughout the country, I was not involved with *Come Together* but many of the choir of about one hundred and twenty people who did the first of those two musicals did do the second one as well. I joined in time for *If my People*. That ran through 1975 and overflowed into the earlier part of 1976, culminating in a televised broadcast from a church in Bordesley in the spring of 1976. That was the Midlands Choir under Nigel's direction. Both these musicals required a core group of singers for some numbers which involved quartets or octets etc., and some of the people that Nigel selected for that role subsequently became founder members of a group which he called the Jesus Centre Singers. I was not one of those, but I did join the Jesus Centre Singers a little later in 1977, mainly because Nigel and I were attending the same church – St John's Anglican church, Harborne, (I was dying for him to ask me) and one Sunday morning after a service he turned round and said, "You've got a voice like a bona fide purist", and so I joined.

In the interim, Nigel had had this vision from God about the founding of an orchestra. I use the word *founding* advisedly, because there was no sense of permanent founding – it was rather bringing a group of Christian musicians together to do a particular thing. As I understand it, this was all God told him to do. There was no sense of ongoing ministry for this group. Indeed, Nigel himself would I think admit that he was not even aware at that time that there were that many Christian musicians of a professional standard anywhere in the country. But he shared the vision that he felt God had given him with David MacInnes, Colin Day and Nick Cuthbert. As a foursome they regularly met week by week to pray, not only for the needs of the Jesus Centre with which they were all involved, but also for the needs as they saw them for the city of Birmingham in a spiritual capacity. That group effectively became, I suppose, the group that checked out his vision if you like and backed him to carry on and do it.

The first event and the Feast of Praise Orchestra!

So, Birmingham Town Hall was booked in the name of the Jesus Centre, for this concert on January 2nd 1976 – so you will appreciate therefore, date-wise, there is a slight overlap between the continuing and not yet complete ministry of *If my People,* and this concert. The last performance was the televised version from the church at Bordesley in March/April of that year. I will go into some detail about how that founding concert, on January 2nd 1976 took place. As I said, Nigel had no real knowledge that there were sufficient musicians of a professional standard who were Christians in the country as a whole, and he just had to start with the few contacts he had, and hope and pray that one would lead to another, as in fact it did, and by an incredible miracle – and miracle indeed it was – this orchestra came together on New Year's day in the evening, and rehearsed fast and furiously, never having for the most part met each other, never mind ever having played together before. Nigel himself had never conducted – at least nothing significant – he did in fact share the conducting with Noel Tredinnick of All Souls, Langham Place, some of whose arrangements of hymns and choruses were used, and also with somebody else whose name I have forgotten, but it is on the sleeve of the record that was made.

So we did this concert. Now I think I should say in that in terms of the spiritual life of the city of Birmingham it was quite a landmark. The folk who had been singing "If my People" were now becoming, I think it's fair to say without boasting, fairly seasoned warriors in terms of knowledge of spiritual warfare. We had quite a lot of training in this respect in terms of some very helpful Bible studies from Bob Dunnett, a lecturer at Birmingham Bible Institute, and we were getting a bit used to the battling of the enemy when we did things that were spiritually important.

So we had prayed particularly hard about this, that it would be a landmark in the city of Birmingham, and not only would those who attend be aware of it but that in some way God would so affect the city that people who hadn't come would know something distinctive had been going on at the Town Hall, or that it would be a distinctive memory. And indeed it was! It was of course a sell-out. There wasn't a spare seat to be had for love nor money. It was a *wow* of an occasion. Word Records got to hear about this, and asked to be allowed to record it. So the stage was not only filled with musicians and singers but with Masses of microphones and recording equipment and they subsequently produced an LP called *Feast of Praise,* which was the title of the occasion and which I think I can also say was the first time that title had been used for such an event. It was subsequently used quite widely all over the country. But I think the title was more or less invented by us. The record that Word produced was a best seller in the Christian market for many months after this, but has long since gone out of production, though I have one. It includes an interesting welcome speech by Nick Cuthbert which is worth hearing.

It was a tremendous time of worship in which everybody really got involved – a real roof-raiser. Having prayed for the Lord's special blessing on this event, outside a tremendous storm was blowing through the city, though we were quite unaware of it. This type of experience was new to us then, but we became much more familiar with this in subsequent work. We came out of the Town Hall afterwards and there was this incredible scene of devastation, right across the city. Huge plate glass shop windows had blown out, trees were down, vehicles had been upturned – there was wreckage everywhere. It was simply incredible. It was like a whirlwind had hit the place, and one could not but think about Acts 2 and the first Pentecost. Indeed, I can now say with hindsight that when the great storm hit southern England in October 1987 and the press were looking up their records as to when anything similar had previously happened, it was this occasion and Birmingham specifically, that they referred to as the nearest thing comparable to the more recent experience.

Anyway, that's all I think I can say about that occasion. We did have, apart from the orchestra and the Massed choir, two soloists in the shape of Anne Linstrum who had been involved with *If my People*, and who was, of course, a professional opera singer. Anne had been converted only less than two years previously. She sang a number of Nigel's own songs. The other soloist was Graham Kendrick who then was still fairly new on the Christian music scene – he wasn't as well known as he is today. He made his contribution as well.

The Salzburg Music Festival...?

After the televised presentation of *If my People* at Bordesley which I mentioned previously, Nigel called the singers together and explained that a way had opened up for the orchestra and singers to go to Salzburg that summer during the Music Festival. If anybody felt they would like to come, or were called to come, they were to have a word with him afterwards. It was so casual in those days. There was no sort of heavy letter writing or anything like that. There was thought to be some cost involved, I can't remember whether a figure was quoted, but at all events I personally did not feel, after some reflection, that I was so called. I can't even remember what my reasons were. I wish I had gone but a group did in fact go and the whole thing was a pretty hair-raising and not particularly organised experience from start to finish, *literally* from start to finish. I mean there were weird things that happened on the motorway in this country before they even got across the Channel. They were charging down the M1 behind schedule, to get to somewhere for the boat. They were in a very ancient coach which was towing the musical instruments on a trailer behind, because they couldn't get everything in, and I can't remember whether it got a puncture or whether it came off its tow-bar or whether the wind took it, but they suddenly looked behind and saw this thing sort of coming to pieces in some way. It looked like everything was going to fall apart on the M1 before they even started. I think the coach broke down and they had to get another coach, all sorts of things.

Anyway, they did make it to Salzburg and they stayed in a horrendously primitive youth hostel fairly near the city centre. There were bars on the windows and doors were locked at night which frightened everyone in case of a fire. They were bitterly cold in the hostel and the food was atrocious. David MacInnes, who went with the group, for reasons which I'll come back to in a minute, had nearly been arrested because he was selling *Feast of Praise* LPs, and they marched him up to the police station in Braunau, Hitler's birthplace. He was released after questioning!

The background to all this goes back actually to about the time of the founding concert, or maybe even earlier, when a man named Jim Goldie was out in Salzburg doing a chaplaincy through the Commonwealth and Continental Church Society at the English speaking church, and he decided he wanted to advertise the English- speaking services to try and get a few more people along. He couldn't speak a word of German, but he set forth round the city trying to put up notices, and by chance finished up at the Cathedral, the *Dom*. He went in and found somebody who looked like a verger wandering around and tried to make this man understand he wanted to put up a poster. It was pretty rash of him I think to go into the Roman Catholic cathedral and ask such a thing, but anyway he did. The man he spoke to couldn't speak a word of English and so they had total failure to communicate, and in desperation the man hauled him off to someone higher up, where there was a further failure to understand. Eventually Jim was given a piece of paper with something written on it which he didn't understand, at which point he gave up and went away. He then went and talked to Tony Pokorny whom he knew as the Austrian/English founder and sole worker of the Austrian Bible Mission.

Tony Pokorny looked at this piece of paper and said, "You've got an appointment with the Archbishop." So Jim Goldie said, "That's no good – he doesn't speak English and I don't speak German, we're still no better off", and Pokorny, having the sense to realise what a chance he would miss, said, "I'll come along as your interpreter."

So in due time they both presented themselves at the Archbishop's Residence, and the way I've heard the story is this: that when they went into the room Pokorny and Archbishop Berg realised that they knew each other from donkeys' years ago, before the war, when Berg had been a seminarian training for the priesthood, and Pokorny had at that stage joined the Hitler Youth Movement. So their paths had diverged and they had become enemies. I think they had known each other in boyhood but when they got to the stage of taking these respective courses, obviously they had nothing much more to say to each other. So Berg didn't know that Pokorny had become a Christian and had gone to England before the war broke out. Anyway, when they

worked this out they had a good old rabbiting session and eventually the Archbishop realised that there was another fellow in the background, so he said, "What do you want?" Jim, who had been silent all this time, said, "Please sir, all I want is to put up a poster in your cathedral."

Apparently at this point the Archbishop did a sort of double backward somersault and laughed his socks off! But then sobering up he said, "Well, this seems to me a wonderful opportunity because we Catholics can teach you Protestants a thing or two about decency and order and tradition and worship and that sort of thing, and you can teach us about the Holy Spirit." So not only was Jim able to put up his poster, but he was given a bit of paper which effectively gave him authority to go into any Catholic church in the province of Salzburg. In fact it was actually a sort of permission to preach, and Jim found that whenever he presented it to a Catholic priest he practically got a royal salute! It was a mandatory introduction which said, "You shall give this man every help and assistance he wants", and nobody could gainsay it!

Anyway Jim finished his chaplaincy in Salzburg, and came back to England. I think the situation was that David MacInnes was due to go out on a chaplaincy in the summer of 1976. When Nigel heard of this, he realized that the *Feast of Praise Orchestra*, which by then had had its founding concert, would be a wonderful vehicle for outreach in Salzburg at the time of the summer Music Festival. So that's how our first contact with Salzburg came to be.

Early events

I'll talk now a bit about the early days of the singers – and I'm thinking here in terms of 1976. I wasn't a member of the singers then. I assume that the singers first became an identifiable group after April 1976 when those who decided to volunteer and respond to the invitation to go to Salzburg must have been called together by Nigel to rehearse for that purpose during the summer of that year. After they came back from Salzburg, I assume that they continued to meet at the Jesus Centre in the autumn. I actually joined them in the spring of the following year, 1977, after Nigel invited me to do so. We used to meet every Thursday night in the top room at the Jesus Centre in Ethel Street,

Birmingham. We sat in a circle on these enormous scatter cushions, corduroy covered scatter cushions, which were absolutely hopeless from the point of view of attempting to sing or do anything except fall asleep really. The room was huge and incredibly cold. It didn't seem to matter though, because the Lord was building a fellowship. I would be inclined to say, as a generalisation, that over the next two or three years it was normal for a rehearsal to consist more of praying and deeply personal sharing plus a bit of Bible study, than actual singing.

I recall a number of events which we did after I joined. I have records of what was, I think, the very first thing I participated in, called *The Festival of the Holy Spirit,* which was at St Mary's Anglican Church, Leamington Spa, on Saturday, 28th May 1977, when the singers made an input into that festival celebration. I think it was a *Festival of Flowers, Music and Worship* – that's how it was billed. Very much a mixed bunch I think! I should make it clear that at this stage we were not even called the Jesus Centre singers. It was either later in 1977 or else not until 1978 that we began to give some consideration to giving ourselves our name. I remember the discussion waxed some considerable time, where we thought about clever names like 'Icthus', all these sort of Greek derivations most of which we realised had been thought of by other people previously, and it was only when we had exhausted just about everything else that we settled for what some of us thought a bit of a mouthful, namely the Jesus Centre Singers. So I think at this stage, early summer of 1977, we were just a group of singers who happened to meet and be based at the Jesus Centre, Birmingham. We didn't really have a proper label.

Another thing we did – I haven't got with me the records of everything the singers did – but I have got a note here that we were involved in the *Jubilee Harvest Flower Festival* at the end of September/beginning of October 1977 at St Martin in the Bull Ring. I can't remember any of the details of it. A little later we started to get involved in providing musical input into some of the weekly Tuesday talks which took place at lunch times at St Philip's Anglican cathedral in Birmingham. I have got a note here of one on 29th November 1977 which was labelled *Praise – and Glory celebrating the Cross of Christ with Bread and Wine.* Again I

have a note of another of these Tuesday talks at St Philip's Cathedral on 14th February 1978, entitled *The Love Feast – thanking God with Bread and Wine,* another one about a month later on 21st March 1978, *Celebrating the Cross with Bread and Wine,* a note of something at Bearwood Gospel Hall on 12th April 1978 – I've got it in exact detail here what we actually did. Linda Isgrove sang 'I wonder as I wander', we all sang, 'Father we adore you', and then there were selected worship choruses in which everyone was involved. We sang 'My Jesus I love Thee', 'I will sing', 'We really want to thank you', 'Therefore with joy', 'Jesu priceless treasure' and Stella Jones introduced 'The Queen of Sheba'. Then we did 'Ho everyone that thirsteth', 'The Oil Song', a sixteenth century anthem by Orlando Gibbons, 'O Lord increase my faith', something we called 'The Joy Song'. We finished up with 'Fear not, rejoice and be glad'. I've also found on the other side of this piece of paper something we did at Kidderminster. If I remember rightly that was at an Anglican church the previous month, Saturday, March 18th. We sang most of the same songs, but this time including 'When the Roll is called up Yonder', 'The Carol of Praise', 'The Joy Song', 'Roger's Song', 'Alleluia, glory to the Lord'. Stella Jones did a solo, I don't know what it was. We sang 'Jesus is Lord' and Roger did another solo. All the pieces had a similar flavour and the repertoire was fairly tightly limited. We were doing much the same few songs, a lot of them were very straightforward, they were simply worship songs anyway, which nowadays one would expect whole congregations to join in, but we did them as our item.

Getting a "Handel" on 'classical' repertoire!

And so we proceeded like that. There's another one at Stourport on 31st January 1979. By now we were doing choruses from the Messiah, we concluded with 'Lift up your heads' and 'Worthy is the Lamb' and we had also added 'For you and me' to our repertoire. There's also a printed programme for a Community Carol Festival organised by the Church of Christ at Goosemore Lane and by the Goosemore Lane Residents' Association. By then we were being referred to as the Jesus Centre singers, and were obviously into Christmas carols.

I think it's time now to refer again to what had happened to the Feast of Praise Orchestra since that first founding concert on 2nd January 1976 and the visit to Salzburg in the summer of that year. The Jesus Centre felt, (and when I say the Jesus Centre felt, I think what I probably mean is the core prayer group of David MacInnes, Nick Cuthbert, Colin Day and Nigel Swinford), that such had been the success of that opening concert in the Town Hall at the beginning of 1976 that it should be repeated. So at the beginning of 1977 we did a similar event, this time called *The Trumpets are Sounding*. I haven't got any details of it at all, except that it was a programme that involved the orchestra, and this time not a Massed choir but just a select group of about twenty singers who rehearsed at the Jesus Centre. This was held in Birmingham Town Hall and it was also done at Manchester Free Trade Hall. It was then again felt by the same group at the Jesus Centre that something similar should happen at the beginning of 1978, and so they did in fact do something then, although in actual fact it was the 30th December 1977 to be precise, but it was intended as a sort of New Year 1978 thing. It was called *Let my people go* and the programme, which I have, was repeated at Solihull Civic Hall. It's interesting that the singers are referred to here as the Jesus Centre Choir! There was a piece by Dvorak to start with, then an introduction by Nick Cuthbert. Everybody sang 'All hail the power of Jesus' name', followed by a time of worship with choruses. Everybody sang the hymn 'Our God reigns'. The Jesus Centre Choir sang 'Ding dong merrily on high', Roger did his song, we did 'The Oil Song', the Gibbons Anthem 'O Lord increase my faith', 'Therefore with joy', 'The Joy Song', and 'Bind us together'.

Then Bradley Creswick, who by 1989 had become the leader of the Philharmonia Orchestra and was already, back in 1977, an extremely brilliant musician and was leading the orchestra, (still called the Feast of Praise Orchestra if it was called anything at this stage). He did a solo by Wieniawski. Anne Linstrum was also involved and sang Nigel's song based on Psalm 9, and the first half ended with the hymn 'At the Name of Jesus'. After the interval there were more choruses for everybody, Anne Linstrum did Nigel's song called 'Gypsy Song', and also one called 'Take me with you', Nick Cuthbert spoke, Anne sang 'Marriage at Sunrise',

another of these songs which were written by Nigel with lyrics by Colin Day. The orchestra did a piece by Vaughan Williams, Nick spoke again and the programme ended with 'Let all the world in every corner sing.'

Now in fact those concerts were called *Let my people go* at the end of 1977/beginning of 1978 – though there wasn't quite the feeling about them that there had been about *The Trumpets are Sounding* at the beginning of 1977 or about the *Feast of Praise* at the beginning of 1976. I think I would be right in saying that there was a feeling that perhaps the slight mistake had been made of presuming that because something had worked the first time it ought to go on more or less forever. The concerts were quite well attended, not so much in Solihull, better in Birmingham, but I think that there was that slight uncertainty, and consequently when the orchestra dispersed after that, it was not to meet again for eighteen months.

Heavy schedules!

Bear in mind that until then, from its founding it had met once a year, almost exactly to the calendar month. This prolonged gap was actually quite interesting as there was real searching as to what God was saying. But meanwhile the singers, as I've said, were continuing. Accordingly, at the beginning of 1979 the orchestra was not called upon to do anything, the singers however were, and it was decided to do something which we called *Rejoice Greatly*. This was basically a programme of choruses from Handel's 'Messiah' interspersed with, as I recall it, Scripture readings and other simple worship songs in which of course the audience could join. It represented quite a major advance for the singers in terms of repertoire, moving from relatively simple stuff to rather greater complexity, and we therefore decided to have an intensive period of rehearsal and spiritual retreat, so we all went down to the West Midlands Baptist Association Conference Centre in Malvern over the New Year of 1979. I see from the bills that there were twenty adults and seven children present, which shows you that the Jesus Centre Singers had not grown substantially numerically, and I don't think from memory the membership had changed particularly over the two or three years at this point. So we did that, and then we did this programme *Rejoice Greatly*, initially on January 6th at Manchester Free Trade Hall, and then on January 13th and 14th at St. Philip's Anglican Cathedral, Birmingham, then on January 18th at Hume Street Gospel Hall, Cape Hill, Smethwick. This was in fact to be the prelude to what I am inclined to say was by far the busiest year that the singers had ever had, though we didn't know it at the time, (which was just as well, as otherwise we would probably have all run a mile). And indeed, even by more recent levels of time commitment, I would still rank 1979 as unprecedented. To illustrate that, I actually have a sheet listing every rehearsal and every event we did throughout the year of 1979, and it's quite long.

I've already mentioned the four presentations called *Rejoice greatly* in January. Bear in mind apart from what I am going to read out now we were rehearsing every Thursday evening for two and a half hours, and this was how it went:

January 31st: Concert with Anne Linstrum, Stourport Civic Centre

February 3rd: Bowley Park Baptist Church, Kidderminster

February 11th: Westbury Chapel, Wolverhampton

February 17th: Flat warming party for Ruth Miller (at the time Ruth Hyatt) in Harborne and the unveiling of Nigel's proposed musical *The Hiding Place*, about which more later.

March 3rd: CYFA Rally at Carrs Lane United Reform Church, Birmingham

March 23rd: Extra rehearsal (I don't know why or what for)

March 31st: An event at City Road Methodist church

April 7th: We began interspersing our normal singers' commitments with extra rehearsals in relation to *The Hiding Place*. That day we had an all-day rehearsal for *The Hiding Place*.

April 27th: The basic singers group did something at St Martin in the Bull Ring, Birmingham, in connection with a visit by Juan Carlos Ortiz.

April 29th: Something at Shirley Baptist Church. (In connection with the Ortiz thing – I think it was evangelistic

– we were supporting cast, we weren't running the whole thing. In those days we were sometimes in that supporting cast role but the amount of singing was just as great).

May 19th: Extra all day rehearsal for the musical

May 26th: We all went off to a huge camp that was organised at the Agricultural Showground at Stafford – that was a whole weekend thing. The Jesus Centre had organised this enormous camp, it wasn't the first such camp there had been actually, there had been another one either the previous year or two years before at Tamworth I remember – that's just reminded me of it – I've no written record of it but I remember there was one. This one was at Stafford and there were two to three thousand people there, and we not only went on the Saturday 26th, but in the middle of the proceedings most of us charged off to go to Loughborough where Val and Ernie were getting married and we sang at their wedding and then we rushed back to Stafford camp again and stayed over till the Sunday. I remember I slept in the back of the estate car I'd hired for the purpose to go up there, that's all I had.

June 2nd, 16th and 30th: All three all-day rehearsals for the musical.

July 3rd: An extra singers' rehearsal

July 8th: An open-air service in Sparkbrook

July 11th: Further extra rehearsal

July 14th: All day rehearsal again for the musical

July 17th: An extra rehearsal

July 19th: The normal Thursday night rehearsal was cancelled. Why? Because by then we were about to depart for the Salzburg Music Festival for our second trip, again about which more later and we departed the following day, July 20th, returning on August 4th.

As I recall it we did not have a break during the rest of August, although I haven't got any dates written in for the rest of August. Maybe we did allow ourselves a couple of weeks or so to recover. But then with the musical pending in October, and by this stage the theatre was booked and so on, we were really at it in earnest and the basic singers group who were doing all these individual gigs I've mentioned, were for the purposes of the musical expanded to a group of about forty-five singers. Bit like forming the orchestra – one person led to another, one dragged up everybody one could think of. I think we picked each others' brains a bit about people we remembered singing in *If my People* and *Come Together,* and tried to get some of those people involved.

Anyway so here we are back from Salzburg on August 4th.

September 5th & 7th: Extra rehearsals this time specifically for the musical

September 8th: an all day rehearsal

September 10th: extra rehearsal

September 11th: extra rehearsal (all these for *the Hiding Place*)

And then, would you believe, just when we thought we might have a spare day, the singers had a commitment made about a year previously to do something at Rugby Town Hall. I have a particularly vivid recollection of this occasion because we were so tired with all the singing we were doing, and it was booked as a Gospel outreach occasion – in fact it was called a SOON weekend, whatever that means. I have the original ticket for it and we did the Hallelujah chorus to the accompaniment of two guitars! And I recall this as the most embarrassing musical occasion of my life! I don't know, other people might not remember it, but for me it was absolutely atrocious.

It was a fairly sort of peculiar thing to do the 'Hallelujah chorus' to two guitars, played respectively by Ruth and Val, at opposite ends of the front line of singers, We sang it so atrociously badly, it was out of tune, we missed leads, we forgot things – you know, I don't know how we got to the end really honestly – and yet the Lord certainly taught me a wonderful lesson through it, because afterwards we went down (I don't know how we had the nerve to) and mingled with the audience, and this chap came up to me, practically with tears in his eyes and said how wonderful the singing had been. He picked out the 'Hallelujah chorus' as the thing that had really sort of hit him. And I thought yes, I'm

not surprised it hit you and I really thought he was being sarcastic! Then I realised he wasn't actually being sarcastic, so I thought perhaps he was just dim when it came to music, but as the conversation continued I discovered to my amazement that I was in fact talking to someone who really knew his oats where music was concerned. He knew just what he was talking about, he had plenty of experience of good music and he had not heard anything duff coming out. He had really enjoyed our rendering of the 'Hallelujah chorus', It was a tremendous lesson to me that God can do this miracle of transforming what you are quite sure is an archetypical dumb performance, into something which ministers to someone who is musically extremely adept. And I have never forgotten that. Anyway I digressed slightly there.

But exhausted as we were, I see we came back and had two more extra rehearsals on September 11th and 19th for the musical, and then the next weekend, Saturday 21st September, we had committed ourselves to a gig at Worcester Cathedral. And so we went down there. No rest for the wicked! I'm almost sure that was a Saturday, and then the next day, 22nd, we had a third event which was quite separate from the musical. So on 22nd September, the day after Worcester Cathedral and all this week of rehearsals, we did a thing called *Hosanna 79,* which was a sort of festival in Handsworth Park with a heavy emphasis on the West Indian community – hence that venue.

We are now within a couple of weeks of the opening night of the musical so at last our attention is undivided.

September 25th, September 28th – extra rehearsals, all day rehearsal on the 29th, extra rehearsal on October 1st, 2nd and 3rd. Extra rehearsal with the orchestra for four hours on the 6th and ditto on the 7th, dress rehearsal on October 8th, evening performances on October 9th, 10th, 11th, 12th and 13th. Even then we hadn't come to an end because we had got long term bookings. So we had a party for the whole cast on October 18th which was a relaxation. We then allowed ourselves the incredible luxury of cancelling two of our normal Thursday night rehearsals on October 25th and November 3rd, but after that it was business as usual. November 10th we were at Bromsgrove Baptist Church, November 13th at Pheasey Evangelical Church. On November 24th I see I organised a party for the production

After a performance of 'The Last Sea' (Swinford)

New English Orchestra & Singers

Principal Conductor Nigel Swinford

A very young Nigel at the first concert in 1976

Feast of Praise

The cover from the LP of the first ever concert

staff of the musical, which was nice. December 18th we had a cathedral lunch time carol service, then a carol service in Erdington on December 20th – and we cancelled the last possible rehearsal of the year on December 27th.

But there we are, there is a list of about 60 things and it's in addition to the fact that almost every Thursday, night the core group of 20 singers was meeting, so that's why I say I think 1979 was an unprecedented year. Looking at it now I can't begin to think how we did it. Looking at that record now, I realise how big a keystone it must have been because we must have learnt a tremendous amount about depending on the Lord for all manner of things. In particular for sheer sustaining strength day by day because nearly all of us had full time-jobs. As far as I know everybody had. For example, Roger Beasley, a travelling salesman, could be three hundred miles away, hammering back after a day's work to a rehearsal, then going to the next day's work and back again in the evening to the next rehearsal! We must have had a lot of long suffering spouses too, or some people did, and the Lord must have sustained the children too in all sorts of ways, because it was really crazy when you look at it. If we had known that was how the year was going to be at the beginning, none of us would have started. No way!

In general terms the year 1979 was a very busy year, so now I am going to be specific about two particular things in that year – one is the visit to Salzburg in the last week of July/first week of August, the second is *The Hiding Place* musical, which was played in October.

In effect, as far as I personally was concerned, the two projects ran more or less side by side, because in the January of that year approximately, Nigel asked me if I would take on some of the responsibility for the organisation of the trip to Salzburg – the preparation work in terms of the fixing of travel and all the sort of administrative work relating to accommodation in the hostel, and so on and so forth. I was already working on that when in mid-February, Ruth Miller (Ruth Hyatt as she then was) held a flat warming party in Harborne, to which all the singers went, at which Nigel unveiled to our startled gaze his concept of a musical

based on *The Hiding Place*. Subsequently he rang me and said, "Look, do you think you could investigate this theatre... or that church hall" and so on, and kept asking me to do things until in the end it was becoming quite a considerable commitment. So I said, "Are you really asking me to be the business manager for this production?" and he looked at me and said, "Well yes, I suppose I am. Do you mind?" and I said, "No, I just want to know!" Fool that I was – that was it for the next seven years!

So from then on my commitment was not only to the singers but also in an administrative role. I had daily contact with Nigel at great length, and I'm sure Carolyn would recall how the two of us would speak for an average of 45 minutes to an hour almost every day on the telephone if we didn't actually meet. Fortunately we were both in Birmingham then. I was teaching, Nigel was still working at the Jesus Centre and I used to rush to the telephone every time I had a break or a free period. Yes, there were other people who peripherally made their contribution in various ways, but in those early days it really was, I think it's fair to say, just Nigel and myself liaising together and taking courses of action. Behind Nigel of course there was the group that I previously mentioned of David MacInnes, Nick Cuthbert, and Colin Day, who continued, as far as I know, at that stage to meet every Monday night to pray together about the work of the Jesus Centre and so on. Because Nigel was working for the Jesus Centre, both the proposed Salzburg tour in the summer of that year and *The Hiding Place* were regarded as projects of the Jesus Centre.

Anyway, all that by way of preamble, you will have gathered from what I have said, and the list I gave of all the events and rehearsals, that the two projects ran side by side through the summer. As well as normal rehearsals of the singers in preparation for the Austrian tour, there were extra rehearsals beginning for *The Hiding Place* musical. For that purpose the singers were augmented to more than double their original strength of about 20 people, because the total cast for *The Hiding Place* was about 45-50 people. We have a programme of that, to which I will refer soon.

Second trip to Salzburg – 1979

Anyway in the fullness of time, we left to go to Salzburg, and I don't want to sound as though I am blowing my own trumpet here, but those who had in 1976 experienced the relative disorganisation and inadequate hostel conditions, felt that this was quite a transformation. I had no responsibility for picking the hostel – that was done at the Austrian end. Indeed, almost all the work at the Austrian end was done by Pastor Pokorny of the Austrian Bible Mission, who effectively had taken over (at our behest) all that considerable area of organisation. He therefore fixed the hostel, arranged for the publicity and its distribution and also booked many of the venues to which we subsequently went. So I think it's right and proper to make that clear at this stage, as it was the same hostel we have continued to use ever since – Eduard Heinrich Haus. They didn't know what we were going to be like that first time, and they were as suspicious of us as any hostel management is of a group of foreign musicians landing on the door step. However, once they realised that we weren't going to paint the town red and that we were responsible and nice people, they rapidly warmed to us and relations have continued to blossom ever since. Over the ten years since, I think most of the staff has changed, though there may be one or two of the domestics who are still there.

Anyway, we flew out to Salzburg and our travel arrangements, though complicated, were uneventful. We did twelve concerts and some open airs. All this was in the space of a fortnight, in and around Salzburg. When I say "in and around", we did, that first year, extend beyond the confines of the actual province of Salzburg, because one of the concerts was at Kufstein, which is actually in the Tyrol. Another was at Gosau which is quite a long way to the south east, and Bad Hofgastein which is a considerable distance to the south.

But we began the tour by going to a little village called Pfarrwerfen. This has since become a village that those of us who have been going a long time have really grown to love, not least because of the warmth of the welcome they have always given us from that very first time. When we got off our coaches the Mayor and half the village were there assembled to meet us, and there was some formal speech-making and then the Mayor boarded our coach and took us on a tour of the whole area of the village, not just the buildings in the centre, but up the mountains into the remotest parts of the area which his domain covered. It is a very mountainous area and extremely dramatic scenery. It was really beautiful. Then he brought us down to the swimming pool and there was a certain amount of tom-foolery around. It seems that whenever the New English Orchestra get near a swimming pool, they take leave of their senses as well as their clothes! Then we were taken back down to the village for tea before the concert and afterwards we thought we were going home but they said, "Oh no, you must come to the village hall, we have a reception for you." We were treated to Wurst and beer with great liberality, and a good time was had by all. So it was a wonderful opening, bearing in mind that this was the first concert of a tour and a few people were on that tour who could remember the conditions of 1976, three years previously. One really felt, and I suppose those people felt it particularly, that we had got off to an excellent start. It was a lovely welcoming way in. I guess the invitation came about through Tony Pokorny and certainly the next concert the following day at Kufstein was through him. That was (I think) a Lutheran church, whereas Pfarrwerfen was certainly a Catholic church, and it was a very different kettle of fish. We found Kufstein very hard. We've only ever been there again once, some years later, and it was equally problematic that time as well. The concert was not well attended, the atmosphere spiritually was difficult, and later I think we came to realise that as a broad generalisation our ministry in Salzburg was likely to develop more and more in the Catholic frame, not merely because the country is 85% Catholic, but because in fact there was this hardness and resistance in the Lutheran churches. There was a superficial welcoming, but one didn't feel that anything was going further than skin deep. I'll come back to that again a little later in reference to another concert.

The following four days we were in Salzburg. We did our first concert in at the church of St Blasius – a very ancient church at the end of the Getreidegasse right under the Moenchberg – quite a difficult place to play in actually, a very low ceiling, but interesting. Then on the following three days we did three concerts in the Aula, which is the large hall of the University of Salzburg. Audiences were not at all bad and they improved successively through the three nights to the point that on the third night we were doing very well. The format of those three concerts was very much along the line of the *Rejoice Greatly* concerts that we had done back at the beginning of the year in Birmingham and Manchester, using a sort of skeleton structure of 'Messiah' choruses interspersed with other things, which went down very well. I think it would be fair to say that it was at those concerts that we began to sense the Spirit moving, which was quite an encouragement.

We then did a concert at a place called Oberndorf, which is right at the very north point of the Salzburg province on the German/Austrian border, and is of course the town which is most famous for the church where the carol 'Silent Night' was composed. It wasn't that church however that we sang in. A couple of days later we went south, (down what has since become a very familiar route to Bad Hofgastein), to a place called St Johann im Pongau, and there we gave a concert in a very large civic hall. It was incredibly hot that day, the hall was very stuffy, the singers if I remember rightly had quite a lot of difficulty in getting their tuning right – perhaps because of the weather conditions and the long drive in the coaches, and so it wasn't particularly easy.

The day after that we were supposed to go to a little church up in the mountains not very far from Salzburg, a similar situation to the Pfarrwerfen thing, at a place called Strasswalchen, but when we got there we discovered that the church was closed for repairs. I don't know whether it's fair to describe it as an organisational error, but the concert had been transferred to another church in a neighbouring village called Irsdorf, but no one had remembered to tell us. When we got to Irsdorf it was an absolutely tiny place, I mean if you think Pfarrwerfen is tiny, Irsdorf is about a quarter of that, really ridiculous, into which we had to pour the whole company of forty-five piece orchestra and about thirty singers! I don't know how we did it, but the incredible thing was that the congregation was huge. Where they came from I don't know because I don't recall a significant number of dwellings. There must have been some small

community around the church but it wasn't even a big village, yet people flocked in. Well I suppose they would, I mean how often does a village that size get a symphony orchestra? The church was absolutely packed, so much so that there were people quite literally standing on the lower mouldings of pillars and clinging to the higher mouldings with their hands, just to be able to have a vantage point. As one looked down the church from the sanctuary through the nave and under the tower at the west end one could see that not only was the aisle packed with people standing shoulder to shoulder, but it was packed right through under the tower and out into the church yard and so far as one's vision allowed, one could just see a solid Mass of people standing out in the churchyard gazing in. This was amazing because in fact it had rained quite hard just before the concert, but it didn't rain thankfully during the concert itself, and people stayed and there was a tremendous spiritual atmosphere that night. I've got the whole thing on cassette, not with me, but it's very special because I remember it clearly to me as the concert par excellence of what was, for me, the first trip to Austria, when the Holy Spirit really came down on people.

Nick Cuthbert was with us that year as a sort of evangelist-cum-compère, although he didn't speak German so everything had to be translated by Pokorny. And I recall – well it's on the tape if you want to hear it – Nick sort of comparing the coming of the Holy Spirit with the rain coming and soaking everything, you know, and God wanting us to be so bathed. It was one of those occasions too when there was an element of spontaneity. We had prepared chorus sheets which we used in those early days (we had translated a lot of well-known worship choruses into German) and the congregation had participated to some extent, but after we had run out of our programme, there was just this tremendous atmosphere which took the form of a silence. Nobody clapped, nobody did anything. It was just that everybody knew this was a holy moment and it lasted for what seemed like an eternity. It was actually about thirty seconds because it's running on the tape, and I recall at the end of it Linda Isgrove just quietly started singing, 'Be still and know that I am God' in German, totally unaccompanied, and again after that there was another silence after people felt a sort of release. Then there was spontaneous applause. It was a very, very special night. That was the 31st July, 1979.

By way of extraordinary contrast, two days after that we went a very long way to the south east of Salzburg to a place called Gosau. I referred earlier to our work with Lutheran churches (this was a Lutheran church) I mean initially and superficially the welcome was quite warm, but there was a very, very hard atmosphere and it persisted the whole way through the concert. It was quite well attended. I remember it particularly because there was one man present who had previously heard us in Salzburg and evidently been very impressed. He was sitting in splendid isolation in the gallery and we were sort of unaware of him being there, because there was nobody else up in this big gallery and we were just concentrating on the people we could see down below. All of a sudden, when the applause had died away at the end, this figure leans over the top of the gallery and demands in stentorian tones, "I want the 'Hallelujah chorus'!" in a sort of tone that brooked absolutely no argument or demur. It was quite funny in one way, but if one thinks it over seriously, it was almost symptomatic of the hardness which we continued to experience in subsequent years when we attempted to work with the Lutherans. They were superficially pleasant but one never really felt that one got through to them particularly, and gradually our work was focused more and more on the Catholic church to the exclusion of the Lutherans (not that we didn't want to work with them) but I think that we were looking for some movement on their part, and there was much more readiness and openness in the Catholic church.

The last concert was Bad Hofgastein, which is a spa town. We were very struck by this place because there were so many analogies between the Gospel and the situation of the people in that town. We were largely I think unaware of this, but in Austria and southern Germany people go to the spa to take the waters almost as a matter of course. It's a sort of national fetish – you don't have to be ill or elderly to do it, though if you are, you are more likely to go. Nevertheless, people who are young and healthy also do it – it's almost a religious observance, part of normality to do it at some time during the year. That's one aspect

of it, but the other aspect is that people who are sick and elderly take it very seriously indeed. They put a lot of faith in taking the waters, and it requires no imagination at all to draw the analogy between that and the pool of Siloam, for example in the Gospels, and we were doing a lot of songs that year like, 'Ho, everyone that thirsteth, come ye to the water, and he that hath no money, come ye, buy and drink'. It was a very obvious invitation to people through the music to consider another kind of water which was far more efficacious than anything they could get in the town. We didn't know it then, but that has proved to be one of the most fruitful places we've been to outside Salzburg, and it's one of the few places outside the city of Salzburg that we have continued to visit for ten years although we didn't actually fit it into the tour in 1989. For some years now, they have had a prayer group, and quite an enlightened priest, so things are happening there. It's very encouraging and this has happened as a result of the way the Lord has used the New English Orchestra in that place.

We were based that year at the Eduard Heinrich Hostel and we just went out in coaches each day. It was our first introduction to Erich Reischl and the firm of Esterbauer Reisen, and what wonderful people they have proved to be over the years! A firm of coach drivers who would gladly lie down and let us walk over them – nothing was ever too much trouble, and they rejoiced in showing off their country to us, and, despite the hairy stories you will sometimes hear, all were brilliant drivers who put their buses through the most impossible places.

Also it would be well worth looking at the newsletter of the Austrian Bible Mission, a yellow one dated autumn/winter 1979, and seeing the considerable detail that Tony Pokorny wrote about each of the concerts we did that time. There is quite a lot there, and it's fairly accurate I think it would be fair to say. The only tape recording which was publicly available in 1979 which had actually been produced for public consumption at that stage, was of the Austria tour in 1976, recorded, I think, by Roger Beasley on a good quality portable cassette player with a couple of microphones.

On the 1979 and at least the three subsequent tours (possibly on the preceding 1976 tour), at every concert we handed out an A5 leaflet which had on the front a picture of the NEO and an insert picture of Nigel. Inside in both English and German was an interview with Nigel which was to explain to people what we were, why we were there, and basically gave the Gospel in a nutshell. On the back cover there were details of all the concerts and the repertoire for that particular year.

The Ten Boom shop sign from The Hiding Place

The Hiding Place Musical – Birmingham Hippodrome, autumn 1979

Returning to *The Hiding Place* musical, the other major project in 1979: as I said previously, this was unveiled to the unsuspecting company of singers at Ruth Miller's flat warming on February 17th that year. Subsequently Nigel asked me if I would start investigating possible venues. At this stage I don't think any of us had any grand ideas about this, certainly neither Nigel nor I had. I remember Nigel was talking about a church hall somewhere – we talked about

St John's, Harborne because that was our church. As we talked about it and as Nigel explained the scale of things he had in mind, it became rapidly apparent that there was no church hall anywhere that could possibly stage a show of this scale – not if you wanted to have an audience inside as well! And so we had to start looking at secular theatres, and we pootled down to Bournville I remember, and had a look at the Cadbury Theatre, which is used by a number of amateur groups in south Birmingham. That didn't appear to fit the bill – we were unhappy about it because the dressing rooms were about a million miles from the stage and were not very adequate. In any case we didn't quite see how we would persuade people from a wider area than just Birmingham to come to a theatre that was out in the sticks.

Already it was becoming quite clear that we were going to have to market this show over a wider area than just the city, and if we were going to do that people wouldn't budge if they thought it was just a local thing. The image was wrong. So then I think we made a brief enquiry about the Rep but obviously because it is a Rep there was no chance there. We did try the Crescent Theatre but it was far too small and was less adequate even than the Bournville Cadbury Theatre. We suddenly realised that by a process of elimination we were being forced up-market, and we were slightly appalled at ourselves when we found that we were left with nowhere to go except either the Alex or the Hippodrome. The other place we did look at was the old Rep in Station Street, but that wasn't on either, it was a non-starter. So by elimination we found ourselves faced with the prospect of tackling the biggest theatres in town. There was a problem with the Alex, I've forgotten what it was. I think it had been temporarily closed for refurbishment and the Director had gone away for an extended holiday, and we couldn't make any contact initially and so that forced us to investigate the Hippodrome. At that time the Hippodrome was not owned by the city of Birmingham, it was owned by the largest West End theatre management company, Moss Empires Ltd, and I have on file a letter from them in response to an enquiry I had made about hiring the Hippodrome. It's dated 21st March, so apparently it would appear that in the space of one month from Nigel unveiling the musical, we had moved very fast. I am astonished looking back, but the evidence is there in the date on the letter. I thought it took much longer than that, but that was just the first response, so we must have eliminated the others quite quickly, and we hadn't even started rehearsing or casting or anything at this stage.

Keith: *Had Nigel finished writing it?*

Chris: *Oh no, he'd only finished writing it about an hour before! That's only a very slight exaggeration!*

Where does one begin to talk about this? I mean for a start, the whole idea of doing a musical on a story like the *Hiding Place* seems an extraordinary concept – hardly the sort of subject matter one would think of turning into a musical. Musicals are essentially things you tend to associate with a slightly fantastical story line (all happy laughter stuff really) but this was the real live gory side of one of the most appalling things in the history of mankind. I think our amazement that there should be even an attempt to turn it into a musical was certainly shared by John and Elizabeth Sherrill who had written the book with Corrie ten Boom's co-operation. All our contacts were with the Sherrills, who gave their permission. There are letters on file from David MacInnes, as Chairman of the Jesus Centre, asking for permission to use the material, which they gave without charging any fee. Later they got very enthusiastic and said they wanted to come over and see the production and indeed they did so. They flew over especially from New York to be at the theatre. I'll come to that later. When Nigel did actually start to let us get to work on what he had produced it became apparent that as is invariably necessary in musicals, there had to be a considerable eliding of the total story. The first Act in the space of about thirty-five to forty minutes moves from the hundredth anniversary party of the founding of the Ten Boom watch-making business, (which actually took place in the early 1930s I think), moving through to the arrival of the first Jews at the end of the party, claiming refuge, to the betrayal and arrest of the family at the end of the first Act. All that happens in the space of forty minutes and so it's a considerable elision of the true timescale of the facts. So things moved at a remarkable pace.

The musical opens with a very happy celebratory tone, in a song based on Psalm 150. Then moves to the pain and disruption caused by the beaten up Jews arriving to seek sanctuary, and on to the ominous threat of one of Hitler's Nuremburg speeches being played on the radio. When Corrie switches on the radio, she hears a stentorian voice, and the whole audience hears it as well. So the first evil omen casts its shadow, and then it becomes apparent that there's somebody spying outside the window, and Jews are cowering in terror, and the final denouement with the betrayal and the soldiers arriving smashing the place up and so on.

The second Act is quite a lot longer – it runs for about an hour. Whereas the first Act is entirely set within the home of the Ten Boom family, the second Act, except for the brief finale, is entirely set inside Ravensbruck concentration camp. Again there is a jump there, because the Ten Boom sisters didn't go straight to Ravensbruck, they were in prison elsewhere for some time before they finally finished up there. But the Act opens in Ravensbruck with an off-stage voice singing, 'Behold and see if there be any sorrow like unto my sorrow', as the women are shuffling around, zombie-like, shovelling dirt, you know, and the whole stage set is very sombre. This is constantly interrupted (scene changes were heralded invariably by a klaxon) the German prisoner of war camp type klaxon siren sounding, and this always heralded a major scene change where suddenly the camp commandant and some soldiers would come into the scene, throwing their weight around and being generally objectionable and downright sadistic. It also varied between scenes of the women actually working or inside their huts. We had reversible scenery and dimmed the lights for about five seconds flat, while the stage crew spun things round so we could then transfer the scene indoors and there were the women railing at the Ten Boom sisters "How can you believe in God in a place like this, can't you smell that smell? That's women like you and me being set alight like a pile of garbage and you talk about God. I hate your hymns and Bible readings!"

There was no overt violence portrayed, but at the same time the subject wasn't shrunk from and when the camp commandant lashed out at Betsy with her whip we actually depicted that, and jolly dangerous it was too doing it. I think Anne Linstrum, who played the part of Betsy, was very courageous actually because the whip came close to reality

– it was a real whip. In some ways the climax comes not at the end with Corrie's unexpected release, which after the war was found to be due to a very unusual German clerical error, but in some ways the climax actually comes halfway through the Act when, in response to the objections of other prisoners, Corrie and her sister remember times past in their family, and the Christian upbringing they had. They recall an old hymn they used to sing, 'The crowning day', and in it they sing, "Our Lord is now rejected and by the world disowned". It's a very old hymn which you can find in really old hymn books like Moody and Sankey, and by the time Nigel had orchestrated it, and Anne Linstrum had given it every last decibel she could (and she can give more decibels than most), it was an absolutely enormous hit. Every single night the audience was on its feet, and those that weren't were weeping. It was very, very dramatic.

The whole of Act Two featured only women, and so the men in the chorus were singing into off-stage microphones and watching Nigel through closed-circuit TV, and I think we found it just as moving. Then of course the scene does change just at the end when Corrie is released. We did have a finale in which Corrie returns to Haarlem, the war is over and the family foregather and say, "What are you going to do now?" and she says (Betsy of course has died in the camp) "I am going to go everywhere and tell everybody that there is no pit so deep that He is not deeper still, and Jesus is the answer and forgiveness is the key." So we then effectively do come to a sort of happy ending, but with loads of poignancy on the way.

We were very careful indeed to be accurate and truthful in this representation. We did in fact make contact with somebody who lived in Birmingham who had herself been a victim, I don't know whether of Ravensbruck, but of one of the concentration camps – and she felt able to come and see the production, which was a very hard thing for her to do, but she felt she could. Afterwards she said it was extremely true, the way we had represented it, the way Nigel had written it and the way it was acted out she felt it was a very accurate representation of what she remembered, and she was hardly likely to forget. The Birmingham Post did a full-page interview with this woman at the same time. Michael Hart was the director, a producer at ITV. I think he'd only been a Christian for two or three years at most, but it was lovely to have him as a very professional person directing such a bunch of bungling amateurs as we were, because apart from Anne Linstrum, who was a professional obviously, having worked for Opera for All and Glyndbourne, the rest of us were all rank amateurs. Some of us may have had reasonable voices, but I don't think any of us had done any real drama. I'd done some stuff at school and I expect some other people had, but that was all. None of us were members of drama clubs or operatic societies in the locality, or anything like that. So he was starting with some pretty rough material, was Michael Hart.

Miracles....

There are just so many extraordinary miracles and stories about this whole production, it is difficult to know quite where and in what order to put them. We had no money. None at all, and I recall that Moss Empires Ltd appeared to want a huge sum of money to secure the hire of the theatre. In the end I think it whittled down to £750 up front. Well I mean that's peanuts here in 1989 with such a high level of inflation, but in 1979 it was an enormous sum of money. I can't work out an exact equivalent, but, if you've got nothing, well that's it. We eventually found somebody to put up that money. He knew Nigel, he knew me, he knew the Jesus Centre, but he didn't half take a risk. A man of great faith!

We acquired the services of a girl called Jill Douglas, who was a member of St Michael's Church, York. She was a professional stage designer, and other than Anne Linstrum and Michael Hart, they were the only professional people involved really. Jill Douglas designed this really fantastic stage set. I have to say it was rather on the lavish side which was a bit worrying, but then we were pretty ignorant about what the cost of things was, and what she did was so good. She did a tremendous amount of research on what the Ten Boom clock-makers' house looked like. She met somebody who had actually been there or knew them or the family or something, and she designed this incredible set which was what I referred to earlier. There were things that spun round, and whole sections of the set which could be reversed to become something quite different. These were on something like giant casters, so it only needed virtually one man spin it round in 5 seconds flat. Something that appeared to be the wall of the camp, or something, could then become the bunks that the women were lying in at night inside a hut. It was very cleverly done, and in the first Act the stage set was very true to what the Ten Booms' house looked like inside. The staircase had an upstairs platform that was Corrie's bedroom, with a panel behind the bed which led to the hiding place through which the Jews escaped when the time came. They came charging up the stairs and went through this panel. What the audience couldn't see was what they went through to! I kid you not, it was a platform about five feet square and fifteen feet above the stage with no hand rails round it, and the only way down was a ladder which was held steady by one of the stage staff from below! Trying to get down that ladder fast, because it was urgent obviously with soldiers at the door, we had to get twenty-five people up those stairs, through the bedroom, through the trap door, down the ladder

and out the other side without making a mess of it and destroying the scenery... and without making undue noise. It was hairy! We only ever succeeded in getting everybody out of sight, we never got everybody down the ladder, so there were always about 10 people still standing on the platform with their arms around each other, holding on for dear life because if anyone had moved, someone would have fallen off the edge! It was absolutely crazy!

But I digress – it was actually a fantastic stage set. Therein lies another miracle. You see, there was nowhere to build the set. We had no facilities whatsoever. You couldn't have built a stage set of that magnitude inside the Jesus Centre, which anyway was up two flights of stairs before you even got to it. We also had no money to buy the materials, and again we had another miracle of God's provision, I think it was a relative of the man who actually put up the money for the theatre, who had a timber business in Stafford. We had the timber from him at less than cost price, though the bill was still over £1,000. So you could imagine from this that we are talking about a big stage set and a lot of other money involved too.

Now what actually happened, in logical sequence, was that we were progressing quite nicely, but certain things hadn't been resolved like where and when the set would be built, and by whom. At the same time the singers were partly pre-occupied preparing for the Austria tour, and indeed we went off to Salzburg with these questions unresolved. The only thing that did happen before we left for Salzburg was that Michael Hart was forced to stop work because there was a strike at his ITV company. He didn't personally wish to strike but because it was 'one out all out' he was locked out. Nobody worked at his company for some weeks, and we came to realise that this was God's provision because Michael Hart was therefore free to give his whole and undivided attention to *the Hiding Place* project. He had nothing else to do and whilst we were in Salzburg, he was faced with the prospect of receiving a lorry load of £1,000 worth of timber for building the stage set and nowhere to receive delivery of it because we hadn't yet found anywhere to build it. But somehow or other while we were away in Salzburg he came upon through devious channels the fact that there was a redundant church in Smethwick, St Albans, that was half closed down, and we obtained permission from the Vicar to use that church as a warehouse effectively. The only part that the congregation used, was the chancel.

So the timber was duly delivered to this church in Smethwick. We then acquired one Mr Lewis, master carpenter, and his son Dave, who was a regular member of the Jesus Centre. Basically they gave themselves unstintingly to this project. We also acquired one or two other people – there was a retired man from Wolverhampton, I can't remember how we heard of him, but he had been a craft teacher so he knew how to work with wood, and he came and got involved, travelling down from Wolverhampton every day at his own expense. He just worked, and all sorts of other people did likewise. So we returned from Salzburg to find it was all happening! What actually they were doing was building a concentration camp inside this church! Well, you know, it's one of the basic tenets of good marketing that if you want to succeed in selling something to the media you have to be able to answer the question, "What's so special about yours that makes it different from fifty-five others of similar ilk?" Answer: "Who else is building a concentration camp inside a consecrated church?"

It was exceedingly newsworthy, and remained so, and again that was an unlooked- for benefit that I'm sure God had His hand on. It was a lovely occurrence, because once a week on a mid-week morning the Vicar said, "Well, we do have a mid-week Communion, do you mind?" and Michael Hart said, "Not at all, we'll join you", and so the whole stage crew, dressed as they were, downed tools and had Communion with the few parishioners that were left in the chancel once a week, which was really lovely. I think it was quite important too, because we have learnt over the years that if you are going to deal with evil, either by representing it or playing it, singing about it or dancing, you are under threat, and I'm sure that the people who were building this representation of evil (as part of the set certainly was), were under threat too. So it was very lovely to be doing this in such a place – and of course it was all free, there was no charge for the church.

Job's a good 'un!

One disadvantage of having a master carpenter was that there is a great difference between his work and that of a stage carpenter. A stage carpenter does not use great bulks of timber, he uses 'clap trap', you know, it's sort of held together with string and glue, and it's built to last two or three weeks or whatever, after which it can be taken out and burnt. But Mr Lewis and his son were not wont to build things like that. They were building for eternity when they built this set. There were very few nails and screws in it, it was all morticed and jointed and it was absolutely immaculate. There was only one problem – when they had finished it they apparently couldn't get some of the pieces out of the door! They hadn't reckoned with the fact that the only exit from the church was a relatively small door, so we had to do a small demolition job at the very last minute when it came to transferring the stuff to the Hippodrome. But in the interim it meant also of course that we had a very adequate place in which to rehearse. When the stage set was sufficiently advanced it was actually possible to go and rehearse on set in the church, which was again a tremendous bonus. Following on that line a little further, I asked the Hippodrome whether we would be able to get in a day or two before, because I was getting quite concerned about how much time it was going to take to erect this set, having demolished it, and put it up again, and to my amazement the Manager said "Yes, well the theatre is dark for several weeks in September, so you can come in about mid-September and start rehearsing if you want to", and again there was no charge for this.

Strike me pink!

Since those days, the Hippodrome has been taken over by the City. It has had several million pounds spent on it and there is never a day when that theatre is dark. It is, outside London, one of the prime theatres in the country. But there we were in 1979 being offered it for nothing, so we were able to go into the Hippodrome and use the real stage that we would be performing on and rehearse, night after night after night. It was quite amazing. Michael Hart continued to be on enforced strike, so he continued to be available and give it his undivided attention. There were just so many things like that that went on, and so many people just got the whiff of what was going on and were eager to help. We didn't have to work particularly hard as I remember it, to find people to do various jobs. We had a chap who designed our publicity for us. He was a professional designer who worked for the 'What's On' free magazine for the City and he was a Christian. It was his wife, together with someone else, whose name I can't remember, who took on the whole responsibility for the costumes. When it came to the actual production Michael Hart simply went and laid hold upon a professional make-up artist, who was also on enforced strike, and pulled her down to the Hippodrome to do all the make-up for us. So we had professional expertise in that area as well. And this went on and on and on. There were several women, who formed themselves into an ongoing prayer group. They were praying constantly every day, and in the theatre and during the actual performances, they were up in some spare room praying, and that was another very valuable thing. There were just so many miracles of God's provision. It seemed to go on and on and people volunteered their services in so many areas.

There were miracles too I think in the way God enabled us to get to grips with the actual learning of the stuff because again, as I said earlier, none of us were experienced in this sort of thing. We were not professionals nor even experienced amateurs and there was a lot of music to be learnt before we even began to act. It was astonishing how God enabled us and encouraged our faith into the bargain.

One strangely relevant feature of that time, which in one sense had absolutely no relevance at all, but in another sense seemed to impinge very strongly, we became very closely welded together as a Christian unit, sharing in prayer – not just in relation to the production, but sharing our personal needs. A lot of rehearsal time was given over, as it still is with the singers, just to prayer. And we would often break off in mid-rehearsal to pray about something which was proving to be problematic. It was quite unlike anything you would think of in normal life. I remember one of my brothers was taken seriously ill very suddenly with what was thought to be a brain tumour. He was rushed into Plymouth Hospital and then he was transferred to the neurosurgical unit at Exeter with all the symptoms, in very dire pain and very ill indeed. This was shared, and a tremendous amount of prayer went up for him by all these people, who only knew him because he was my brother. He was miraculously healed. He was never operated on, it just went away. The whole problem disappeared and he has never had any recurrence. That event proved to be extraordinarily encouraging.

Manager required – no previous experience!

Another area in which I was very encouraged, was that I had very little experience of publicity at this stage. Like everything else I was doing, I was learning as I went. For instance, Nigel had asked me to administrate the Austria trip. I had no experience of organising groups to go anywhere, least of all abroad. Foreign travel – I knew nothing about that. He asked me effectively to take on the business management of this production and I'd never done anything like that before. I knew nothing about the whole business of publicity. As with everything else I was doing at this stage, I just tried anything that seemed a good idea. I felt that it was obviously going to be necessary in order to fill a two thousand seat theatre for five nights, to have to work jolly hard on the publicity over a much wider area than just Birmingham. And so I picked the brains of anybody who could conceivably be of use, to try and obtain contacts in other towns and cities within 100-mile radius. It was totally arbitrary and actually quite ridiculous. However, it was astonishing how many contacts I actually finished up with – people in other cities, who on the basis of a telephoned approach and occasionally just a letter, were quite prepared to either give me their complete mailing list of all the churches in their area, or were prepared to accept publicity and insert it themselves into their next mailing. By this means I was able to canvas Oxford, Bedford, Northampton, Sheffield, Stoke-on-Trent, Shrewsbury and Chester. Those are the ones that I can remember. Obviously Birmingham was done very thoroughly and I have letters on file from most of the people involved in all those places.

We had an article in 'Crusade' magazine, with Anne Linstrum on the front cover, featuring a substantial article with her as 'The Hiding Place star'. Meanwhile all the cast made contact with their local rags, which covered several areas. We also invited the Mayor and local Bishops to our opening night, and they came.

Give me a ring!

One other little miracle has occurred to me. We had to have a telephone bell and it had to be the kind you would have heard in a Dutch household in 1939/40. We couldn't just go to theatrical suppliers and get the traditional, or even an ancient British one. It wouldn't do. Now we knew that there was somebody who had one of these things so the stage manager arranged to go and collect it. When he got there they had gone home early and the place was closed. This was a matter of hours before the performance, and then it was Michael Hart himself, who remembered he had got a contact in some museum or something like that, and he rang whoever it was and lo and behold they had got the exact thing we wanted. I think he went himself an hour before the opening night, I don't know where, Evesham or somewhere, to get this thing. He was due to be standing in the Foyer of the theatre in a line-up for the VIPs at seven o'clock. He missed that – he arrived in the theatre about thirty seconds before curtain up, handed the bell to the technician, who had no opportunity to test it. He wired it up and put it in place and at the critical moment in Act One pressed a button. To his enormous relief it did what it was supposed to do! Talk about cliff hangers – that was just extraordinary.

"Increase the recipe!"

Every theatrical production has its funny story – the funniest one that I can recall from the week of this production related to the need to represent bombs falling when the Jews were cowering in terror in the Ten Boom household. To do this we used standard stage thunder flashes which you drop into a dust bin and they make a nice loud hollow report which is supposed to produce the desired effect. Well, on the first night Doug Brown, the stage manager, chucked what he thought was an appropriate amount in, and after the performance Nigel said, *"What happened to the bombs tonight? I didn't hear them"*. The cast just about heard them but nobody else did. It was just pathetic. So Doug said, *"Well*

I suppose it's a very big stage, I'm not used to doing productions on this sort of scale, perhaps I underestimated". So Nigel said, *"Well increase the recipe tomorrow please"*. So the next night he doubled it and Nigel said, *"Doug, I thought I told you to put more in it"*. Doug: *"I did, I doubled it."* Nigel: *"I didn't hear anything."* And it was true it was still not very loud.

Well this went on every single night until after the penultimate performance. Nigel was really quite irritated about this. So it came to the last night, and Doug thought, *"Blow this for a lark, we are going to get it right once."* He got a virtual armload of this and packed the dustbin, as you would gelignite into an IRA bomb or something, lit the blue touch bar at the right moment and retired. There was this almighty explosion! Half the audience leapt from their seats, and the funniest thing was a dead pigeon descended from the rafters above the stage where it had presumably been resting for some years, and landed fortunately off-stage because it would have ruined the drama of the moment, it was meant to be terribly intense with all these Jews cowering. If it had actually landed on stage at that point, we'd have to close the show! The offstage staff members were absolutely doubled up, reeling like drunks, holding their sides, quite incapable of doing anything for the rest of the Act!

Another miracle of God's provision related to the cyclorama, if you know what one of those is! A cyclorama is a huge sort of screen – it's almost like a net curtain for want of an amateur description of it, which is hung across the back of the set and is almost transparent. It can be used for all sorts of lighting effects as well as a general mask. The Hippodrome stage is really vast, and I can't quite recall whether we had just overlooked the need for this item because we thought the back wall of the Hippodrome stage was the right colour anyway or something. It may have been that we had been let down about where we were going to get it from, but at all events we discovered that need on the Saturday before the show. The dress rehearsal was due on the Monday and the opening on the Tuesday. We were faced with the fact that within a matter of hours we had got to lay hands on a cyclorama that was big enough for that stage, which meant that it had got to be at least sixty feet wide and about twenty feet deep.

Michael Hart went deep into his past and spent hours researching every conceivable contact he had once had in the theatrical profession around London, ringing up people at home and tracking them down to see if he could find anything. In the end one thing led to another and we finally tracked down one which was at the Arts Theatre in Cambridge. We rang this Theatre and explained that we had absolutely got to have this thing, and to our amazement (because we had previously found one or two in London and they wouldn't let us have them – obviously they weren't going to let something that was used on a West End stage just be handed over to a bunch of bungling amateurs in Birmingham who they'd never heard of) the people in Cambridge said, *"Yes, we've got one. It's currently on a stage set which we will be striking after the last production of this show at ten-thirty tonight, you can have it then."* So I drove through the night to Cambridge and collected this thing at two o'clock in the morning, and drove back to Birmingham just in time for the get-in, because being the sort of thing it was, it's one of the first things that has to go up. You can't put everything else in and then try and fix it. The get-in was bright and early Sunday morning because our master carpenter had built this fantastic set which was going to take all day to rebuild, so again we had another wonderful example of the Lord's provision.

Timber!

There came a night about the middle of the week, during Act One when, as I told you earlier, the Jews escaped up the stairs through Corrie's bedroom, through the trap door into what to the audience seemed like the hiding place, but was actually this miserable little platform fifteen feet above the stage, accessible only by a step ladder. Most of the 'Jews' had managed to get down the ladder and disappear, but I and about four or five others were stuck on the platform, and all of a sudden, as the play was proceeding and the audience was gripped by the drama, I suddenly saw this huge piece of scenery start to sway. It was just about four feet away from me, at the back of the platform on which I was standing, and it had obviously become detached from its neighbour, at which point I saw it start to move! To this day I can remember it – it was like a perpetual slow motion

film. It was an enormous thing built as though for eternity and I knew if it wasn't stopped it was going to go crashing down and was going to rend that cyclorama from top to bottom. It was also going to demolish part of the stage set and stop the show at a very bad moment. I can remember leaning off this platform trying to reach this piece of scenery, and I couldn't lean very far because I had nothing to hang on to. Just at the moment when I thought all was lost and the thing was about to go, and I think one or two people in the audience could see it swaying by that point, one of the stage crew just happened to come by. He grabbed it and held it, but we were a split second from disaster that night, and cycloramas are very expensive things. We had got this for nothing so we would have had to pay to replace it, as well as having that night's show ruined. Such is life in amateur dramatics I suppose.

Reactions to the production were excellent, as seen at the time by the press reviews and the comments from people who wrote in. It also became a hot topic of conversation at the Jesus Centre when people called in for lunch. It was a very substantial talking point for a lot of people for a long time.

Shall we dance?

I was just reminiscing about certain aspects of the dance in the first Act. We had a choreographer named Anne Harris, who was a very gifted girl, a member of St John's, Harborne (her husband was in the cast). They were both from New Zealand. Very sadly, Anne, having done all the work on the choreography, was taken ill with an ectopic pregnancy shortly before the production and was very upset and very low after she came out and quite unable to take part at all. I think if I remember rightly she did come along and sit in the audience one or two nights and we dragged her on the stage on the last night for a bow. She was credited in the programme, but it was a great sorrow to us – and also to her – that she couldn't actually be a part of it and dance with us. The dance included a clog dance which was done by a solo dancer, a girl – I don't know how we came by her but she knew a clog dance and I think she was the only girl in Birmingham that could do it. There was another dance that involved four men and four women doing something dramatic, and I recall being one of the men selected for this dubious privilege.

The thing ended with a very dramatic piece of music, the final chord on which the girl standing with her back to the man did a little spring and the man had to get the girl up on his right or left shoulder. In order to achieve this gymnastic feat I had to go and practise with Sue Hill in the garden of her home out at Kingswinford to the great delight of the neighbours and the consternation of her parents! I may say, with considerable trepidation on my part, because Sue made it quite clear that there was no possibility of getting it wrong, because she said dressed as she was, if I threw her too high she would go over the top and disappear and break her neck landing upside down over my back. On the other hand, if I didn't get her high enough and hung on, she would slide gently down her front and display her underwear to two thousand people in the audience. You know, the prospect of either was so terrifying that I absolutely had to get it right. We spent days and days and evenings and evenings of that summer on her back lawn practising this business of her jumping and me just using the right amount of lift to be secure, and thankfully got it right every night. But it was close!

There was another occasion in the first Act when there was a bit of fooling around, and a chap called Pete Nichols, who was one of the founder singers, was supposed to fall backwards and I was supposed to catch him just before he hit the ground. Well we rehearsed it and it was just a bit of deliberate tomfoolery, very carefully staged, and as inevitably with all such moves you deliberately err on the cautious side. So at first Pete hardly got ten degrees from the vertical before I was propping him up again. It didn't look real, so as the week wore on we perfected it and on the last night we perfected it so much that he actually bounced. He came back absolutely rigid because he'd learnt to trust me and I left it a little bit too late, so he hit the stage and came up on to my arms and this sort of reflex action caused me to fall over so he also got my knee or my foot in the small of his back as well for his pains. It stretched brotherly love a bit, that did!

The MU cometh!

One thing occurred about the Musicians' Union (MU) in relation to *The Hiding Place*. Just before the dress rehearsal a little man from the Birmingham branch arrived at the theatre and was very upset and objectionable, because he reckoned that we were in a professional theatre using musicians who were not members of the MU and thereby depriving hard pressed professional musicians of a livelihood by using non-union labour. It was the days of the 'closed shop'.

We pointed out that most people we were using were either professional musicians or musicians in training for such, which of course was not a 'let out' as he immediately wanted chapter and verse. So we were very green and we didn't see any other way out but to be very humble about it. We had an orchestral meeting immediately and the official addressed the assembled company. We had secretly said to them before we let him loose on them, that if it came to the crunch we would pay their annual fees. He said that unless everybody joined, he would see that the theatre was blacked. If that had happened then the management would certainly have stopped the show. Everybody did in fact join barring one person, who was a conscientious objector and they accepted that.

The Gospel of Reconciliation

Just a little word more about *The Hiding Place,* in terms of the effect of the musical upon the audiences on successive nights: I have already referred to how moved people were, particularly in the second Act, by the depiction of the Ravensbruck concentration camp scenes. Night after night it was the climactic rendering of 'The Crowning Day' with Corrie and Betsy singing and everybody else joining in the chorus, both on and off-stage, that brought the audience to their feet. But I think at a more sensitive spiritual level, one would want to say that we were aware that there were people in the audience who were moved in quite a different way, because the essential message of *The Hiding Place* was the message of the Gospel of reconciliation. No matter what one man may have done to another, nobody has the right to retain an unforgiving spirit. In Christ we must be able to forgive those who have abused us, which is the lesson Corrie had to learn, and is the lesson that perhaps supremely, was the one that Nigel wanted to portray through the story as he depicted it. This was clearly a message that went right home to some people. There were people in the audience who broke down and wept. There were people who were clearly convicted about unforgiveness and there were people I think who were converted and altered their lifestyle as a result of coming to *The Hiding Place* musical.

I think whenever a group of amateurs have got together and done a show like this, especially when it has been so well received, there is an inevitable sense of euphoria that follows it. I think however in the case of this particular production, it was something a great deal more than mere human euphoria. There really was a tremendous wellspring of thanksgiving to God for what He had done for us and through us, and for what He had taught us all, both collectively and individually, through the experiences we had had together. Obviously we did thank the people. There was a party not only after the last night but later another party for all the acting personnel. We also had a production staff party.

I should say at this point that I had felt it right to give up my teaching job at the end of the summer term. The pressure was so great on me for the Austria tour and *The Hiding Place.* I felt I couldn't go into the new term in September free enough to do what was required in relation to the week of *The Hiding Place* production and all that led up to it, because I was the focus for the administration. Whenever the stage designer wanted some money to go out and buy costumes or bits and pieces, it was through me every time. There were things going on every day and I was dashing hither and thither. Ruth Miller also felt it right to give up her teaching job (I think in an infants' school). As far as I can recall, that was at the end of the summer term, but she may have stopped before that, because she was playing the part of Corrie. I think she felt it was a sufficiently great calling that she really needed to prepare herself spiritually as well as vocally. She had singing lessons, I think from Anne Linstrum actually, to prepare herself for the production.

The New English Orchestra!

Significantly, from the time of the 1979 Austria trip, we took the name The New English Orchestra and Singers and ceased to be known as the Jesus Centre Singers except for *The Hiding Place.*

Third visit to Salzburg 1981 – NEO on the move...

or not ...as the case may be!

Moving on now to the Austria tour of 1981: Tony Pokorny of the Austria Bible Mission had persuaded us to expand our sphere of activities and to include a period of time in the southern province of Austria (Carinthia) based in a youth hostel in the town of Villach. We had had quite a lot of difficulty in getting people out to Austria by aeroplane in 1979, on two separate flights. The airline wouldn't do a deal on the tickets for the party because they could fill the plane anyway at that time of year. This caused the complexity of having different groups of people arriving at different times. So we decided to give the train an opportunity to prove itself as a means of transport to get us all there. Apart from the few hardy souls travelling independently in their own cars, the bulk of the party (about ninety people) were due to travel by boat train from Dover to Ostend and on across Europe by train right down to Villach. It shouldn't have been too difficult. It is a through train all the way from Ostend to Villach with no change. However, we were tried, I think it is fair to say, tried very severely – although those of us who were coming from Birmingham to meet the rest of the party at Victoria Station in London, had left Birmingham in ample time by any stretch of the imagination (allowing over four hours) – it just proved an absolute nightmare from the very start. The motorway was exceptionally crowded (this was 1981 remember, long before motorways became permanently crowded). We were incredibly late getting to London.

Once we hit London the whole of the West End seemed to be fused up solid. In retrospect it may have been that it was less than a week before the Royal wedding of Charles and Diana and a lot of people were drifting around London on the chance of spying the happy couple or something. I don't know what it was, but at all events we finally hit Victoria railway station fifteen minutes after our boat train had gone! There was general consternation on the part of the orchestra who were wondering why we hadn't come. I was on the coach and I had all the tickets, so nobody could travel. So everybody stood firm on the concourse at Victoria Station and I went off to see what I could sort out from what seemed to be a disastrous situation. I mean, it's one thing for an individual to miss a train, he or she gets the next one, but when you've booked a party of ninety and you've booked couchettes right across the European continent you don't just get on the next one!

British Rail comes up trumps!

I went up into the Continental Enquiries section of Victoria Station and was quite amazed. I mean I started off at some enquiry desk downstairs and they quickly found the whole thing far too big to handle and I was directed to some private office upstairs. A very genial middle aged man came to the rescue, took me behind the counter, sat me down at his desk and gave me a cup of coffee, and everything was sweetness and light. Nothing was too much trouble. He listened to the explanation. He didn't bat an eyelid, didn't make any recrimination or say what an idiot I was not starting from Birmingham earlier or anything like that. He simply accepted it as a situation that had to be resolved.

In fairness, one has to say, this was not the sort of service one expected from British Rail! Well, it was an amazing experience. For an hour or two I sat at his right hand while he simply directed. He shouted orders, and minions came scuttling to and fro', telephones rang, telexes were sent, telex machines chatted and spouted tape back to acknowledge reservations and cancellations and everything else 'ations'! Eventually when it seemed like the whole of the Continental Department had been put into reorganisation for the NEO, he said, "Right, well what I have done is this: you can get on the boat train at ten o'clock tonight (or something like that), and get your night crossing to Ostend. I have had your couchettes put into a siding at Ostend and they can be used as far as Cologne, but after that they will be required, so you will have to change trains there and get an ordinary train down to Munich and then another one from Munich to Salzburg. That will get you as far as Salzburg at nine p.m. I can't get you any further than that. That's the best that I can manage. Will it do?"

Well of course Salzburg is the other side of the Hoehe Tauern mountain range from Villach, which is about four hours' drive away, but I remembered our tame coach

company – Herr Erich Reischl and Esterbauer Reisen – so I said, "Well, we do have a coach company that we use when we go to Salzburg" (to make it sound like we do it all the time) "and we will be using them when we come back to Salzburg for the second half of our tour. Initially we are not using them for the first ten days that we are down in the south." So he said, "Do you want to phone them?"

I thought, "Pinch me, I'm dreaming! Here's British Rail having done all this, now offering me a free phone call to Austria!" So I thanked him, and there and then I picked up his phone and I rang Erich. I said, "Erich... disaster! We have missed our train. We aren't going to be able to get to Villach on time and the best we can do is to get to Salzburg. We need help to get on to Villach!" And he didn't beat about the bush. Erich was absolutely wonderful! Quite uncharacteristically, because Erich normally likes a good chat, he said, "What time are you arriving at Salzburg?" I said "Nine o'clock, Saturday night." This was still Thursday afternoon or something. He said "I'll be there" and put the phone down. No argument – that was all he wanted to know. He already knew how many people were involved. Now I don't know how he did it, because he is not a big coach company and this was the peak holiday weekend of the year when the whole of Europe decides to get up and move. How he could whistle up enough coaches and drivers just like that at that time, was a miracle of the Lord's provision.

Oh, yes, before I go on to the sea crossing, I should explain that whilst I was up being dealt with so graciously by British Rail, the orchestra and singers were just loping around on the station, getting pretty bored and fed up. Some of the orchestra had been waiting for some time before we even arrived. Some of them had the wit to start praying and praising. It began with somebody getting a guitar out of its case and someone else got their violin out, and in no time at all about half the orchestra had got their instruments out and started having a praise session on the concourse. They sang the 'Hallelujah chorus' – an absolutely amazing and spontaneous rendering of it, without anybody sitting down or being organised or laid out as an orchestra – just there and then! I am sure the Lord was really honoured by that, and I didn't know they were doing this, but as they were singing, the whole of the travel situation was being resolved! Subsequently having got it resolved and obtained the tickets and so on, we all trooped off. Somebody had made contact with The Well (a Christian restaurant) just up the road from Victoria station, and hearing of our plight, they had kindly agreed to open up especially for us. They were due to close at the end of the day and they agreed to stay open and effectively gave us private shelter. Ninety people, with children! So we rested there for four or five hours and had some food until it was time to go back to the station.

We had a rough sea crossing which was unfortunate, unseasonal obviously for July, and we were all pretty shattered when we staggered off at Ostend. The train from Ostend to Aachen and on to Cologne was extraordinarily slow and kept stopping. We had not proper couchettes they were these sort of things where you pull a slide out from under the seat and it meets in the middle, to create a continuous bed and you put your feet up, head to toe, but a lot of people were tired enough to go to sleep. Nobody got much sleep on the boat, least of all me. I sat opposite a woman who kept giving her child crisps and pop and as often as she gave it to him, ten minutes later he brought it back up into a bag. But she still kept feeding him, it was quite disgusting! But anyway, I digress.

The Celebration Mass ('Salzburger Festmesse')

The train from Ostend to Cologne kept stopping for protracted periods and then it would go on at a sort of walking pace, and it became quite apparent that on top of everything else we were not even going to make the connection that British Rail had arranged for us to make at Cologne, go on to Munich and thence to Salzburg. I was particularly worried because we were about to feature the brand new Celebration Mass that Nigel had written. It had never previously been performed. The singers had rehearsed it but the orchestra had not even seen the parts, yet we were due to do this as the very first item of the tour in the Dom at Klagenfurt on the Sunday morning.

Nigel had only just finished writing it. I think the ink was scarcely dry on the orchestral parts. The copying out of the parts had been finished the night before or something. Anyway I kept going to Nigel and I said, "Look, when this train gets to Cologne we have got to get a message to Klagenfurt to cancel that Mass." Well, typical Nigel, he said, "We can't do that, Chris." I said, "What do you mean, we can't do that – we must! We won't even be there, and even if we are we will be absolutely knackered and nobody will have had time to even look at the parts." Nigel said, "Well we can't do that". I said, "Well why not? Surely it's perfectly obvious we must." He said, "Well, God hasn't told us".

'Oh bananas!'

It seemed to me God was shouting it loud and clear – how much clearer can the Almighty make something? You miss your train, the subsequent train runs late, everyone is ill, you have a rough sea crossing, you're not even going to make it till the eleventh hour if you make it at all. All this seems to be ample reason, but anyway I just thought, "Oh, bananas, if he wants to be in Klagenfurt, so be it! I resign!"

We got to Cologne eventually, and of course we were miles too late and the train we were supposed to catch had long since left. So we all got out on to the platform and everybody looked at me and said, "Well, what do we do now Chris?"

I mean, I began to discern how Moses felt – it was a terrible situation. I said, "I don't know. Stay here. I will go and find out" (thinking, "Oh dear, here we go again but this time I've got to do it in German!") I was just about to move off and find out, when this German railway official came up, all sort of spluttering efficiency and gold braid. He said, "New English Orchestra?" I said, "Yes" (thinking "How does he know who we are?") He said, "Wait here please, your train will be here in a moment." And I opened my mouth to say "Don't be stupid, you silly old trout", you know, "the thing went about two hours ago, we know we're late, we've missed it!" But he didn't stop. He just rushed off in a cloud of efficiency, and I was so tired by then I would have believed flying saucers, anything, so I just sort of shrugged my shoulders, waved my hands in the air and said to everybody, "Do what the man says. Stay here." I just folded my arms and waited to see what happened. What actually happened was that within two minutes, literally, a train came puffing in on the opposite platform, consisting of a locomotive and two coaches. I took no notice of this at first. I thought it was a local 'push and pull' or something.

The Mystery Train

Back came the said official. "New English Orchestra – this is your train. Board please". I started to say, "Where's it…" I thought, no, don't even ask. Who cares if we go on a mystery tour? I don't care if I go to Moscow now, I'm so fed up and tired and irritated and worried. So I said, "Do what the man says, get on it".

So we all piled in and found first, that it consisted of only two first class coaches, second, that we were the only passengers, third, it was not a scheduled service and fourth, it had the same kind of seats as the previous train, where you could pull out the thing from underneath where you sit and it made a bed. However, being first class, it was more 'plush'. The luggage just went on the rack, or under the seats, wherever. We could see down the Rhine valley, it was a beautiful summer's morning. We were mostly too tired to appreciate it but not quite too tired to look out because it was absolutely idyllic, very picture postcard, all the way down the Rhine valley. There weren't any refreshments, the one thing the German railways had not managed to rustle up – but they perhaps didn't realise the need. I have never been able to find out since, (and I have back-tracked very thoroughly, including with the man back at Victoria, in case he had had a hand in it. But he swore that he didn't even know.) Somebody however, was monitoring our progress, somebody knew it was important we reached our destination at a given time, somebody realised that we weren't going to because of the train running late from Ostend to Cologne, somebody organised a special train for us for which we had not asked and for which we were not charged anything. No explanation was ever given and I've never been able to find out how or who was involved! It's fundamentally an absolute miracle story because no human official that I could track down could explain it to me. The bloke at British Rail was flabbergasted! We invited him to one of our concerts later.

Anyway because it was a private train we didn't stop anywhere and we caught up all the lost time. We were in Munich in ample time not only to make our connection to Salzburg, but also to visit the refreshment stall. By that time we were all ready to turn cannibal, so as I have repeated on many occasions since, the best thing about Germany/Austria is the Wurst!

So – on to Salzburg where Erich met us and put us into his three or four coaches. Then we had a four-hour drive over the Alps. We had an overland vehicle which was ahead of us by then for the large instruments. We didn't have much on the overland vehicle, driven by Trevor and Ernie. But there was an American chap who was a very fine double bass player, who had an instrument that was worth £20-30,000 even then. He said, "I'm sorry, wherever I go my double bass goes". (It was like the story of Ruth – *where you go, I will go*). It was hilarious actually, because when Peter got up into a bunk in the train, he insisted on taking his double bass with him! Sleeping with your double bass! He wouldn't even have it in the corridor or the guards' van or anything. It went with him – incredible!

We finally made the Villach hostel at 1.30am and were absolutely bloodshot, we really were. We had basically been travelling since Thursday afternoon. There had been very little proper sleep for three days, and yet we were due to do the Mass the following morning. By the time the last of us were in bed it was 2.30am. We were up for breakfast at six o'clock, on our coaches by seven o'clock and we were in the cathedral rehearsing by eight o'clock. The singers had never heard the orchestral version of the Mass, they had only heard Nigel thumping it out on the piano. The orchestra had never even seen the dots – they hadn't even had them – it was so late copying the parts out there was no question of being able to send them out by post to enable them to practise in advance, so there was a rehearsal of sorts. It was fantastic! You know when you rehearse something just with the piano and then you hear the orchestral version, it does sort of hit you, especially with Nigel's music. But there wasn't time even to go through the whole thing, and basically about half of the Mass was played and sung at sight. There was a recording of that occasion, and for quite a long time afterwards, Nigel swore that that was the best recording of the Mass. It was exceedingly good. There were all sorts of rough moments but the audience wouldn't have the first idea of that. Well there it is – amazing!

"Life's like that"!

There was a sequel to this. Fifteen months later in October 1982, the Readers' Digest of that month, in their regular feature *Life's like that*, published the following story, contributed by a reader in Rochester, Kent: *It was a busy Friday afternoon at Victoria Station, and the members of a choir standing near me on the concourse had clearly decided to do some practising while waiting for their train to arrive. As the strains of Handel's 'Hallelujah chorus' filled the air, I heard a passing commuter ask, 'What's up? Has a train arrived on time?'!*

So Austria 1981 began in adverse circumstances indeed. I think I should say also in relation to that first Mass in Klagenfurt, that as the orchestra began to rehearse, the Dom Kapellmeister came to me in absolute amazement. He had heard about all our travel problems and he just couldn't credit that we would be rehearsing despite them. He said, "That's fantastic! Our professionals in this country spend their time asking how long the rehearsal will last, but as for your people, they live their music, it's part of their life." And after the concert he requested that we should do a further engagement.

There was one other aspect of the Klagenfurt Mass at the opening of the 1981 tour that was to some extent rather amusing. We had no knowledge of this of course until we arrived, but when we got to the cathedral we were confronted with some white and purple posters headed *Festlicher Kirchen Musik in Dom zur Klagenfurt*. Basically it was a list of all the special music at the Sunday Masses for seven or eight weeks through July and August, and if one looks down the list of the composers which was in very bold type down the left side, with, in smaller type, the title of the work that was being performed at each Mass, it went like this: *Mozart, Haydn, Nigel Swinford, Haydn, Mozart, Schubert, Dvorak!* So it would appear that at least there was an element of considerable faith on the part of the Dom

Kapellmeister that he was quite prepared to put Nigel Swinford in the same sort of company as the rest! Just as well we turned up!

Swinford in excellent company!

There is just one other thing I would say about Austria 1981. Again it refers to the first half of the tour, the ten days we spent in Carinthia. We found that our time in Villach coincided with the annual *Villacher Kirchetag*, which basically is a sort of carnival. Kirchetag means literally 'church day', but in fact one couldn't see much evidence of anything religious about the occasion. It was a huge carnival and beer festival. I don't think I have ever seen such a big carnival procession, and because Villach, like Salzburg, is a border town, people came from across the border from Italy and Yugoslavia, Czechoslovakia, Hungary and places like that, all in their distinctive national costume. There were also people from every conceivable area of Austria, each one in their distinctive costumes – because in Austria they have costumes for different regions. If you are expert enough, you can tell where someone comes from by the different feathers in their hat, or the braid on their jacket or the beading on their dress, and you can distinguish between a mile or two where people emanate from. This was an enormous procession – it took about an hour and a half to pass through the town. We were invited to be part of this, because we happened to be there at the time. We hadn't got any national dress with us, so we all dressed in our T-shirts (it was blisteringly hot, the temperature was in the nineties) and we took our overland vehicle and plastered it with posters advertising who we were and where we were going to be performing. We put some of the children on the van roof, armed with loads of our throw away handbills, and the brass section, who obviously were the sort of people who were accustomed to marching along playing their instruments, came along behind. Tony Pokorny managed to get hold of a large Union Jack banner which we marched along with, in a horizontal rather than vertical position, singing worship choruses with the brass doing odd bits of whatever they felt like doing. It was a totally informal rabble and we were definitely the scruff-end of the procession compared with everybody else who was dolled up to the nines, but people were thrilled to pieces that folk from as far away as England were participating in their carnival.

It turned out to be actually the biggest events of its kind in the whole of southern Europe, a regular annual thing. It was the first year we had NEO T-shirts and just about everybody had one. In addition, we'd also bought red, white and blue stripy boaters for some of the brass for another occasion, so they were all wearing these plastic bowlers and boaters on their heads as well, and I think it was important that we did that. Then in the evening there was this enormous beer festival. It simply closed the town off to traffic and all the streets were laid out with trestle tables. We could smell the beer the next morning half a mile away at the hostel and the gutters were still running with it, I mean I shouldn't think there was a sober person within a hundred miles of the place! I can't believe how they got through so much beer – I've never seen anything like it in my life, and I don't know that I particularly want to again. But I think it was good that we were there and did that – it was a very distinctive feature

of the tour and certainly an incredibly public Christian witness with maximum exposure. We had given a concert that same morning in the Rathausplatz which had been very well attended too, with crowds of people in town for the carnival, though Villach is not a big town.

Back home in the UK...

The next NEO event was at Christmas 1981 when we did a concert in Birmingham Town Hall on December 19th entitled *Celebrate Christmas with the New English Orchestra & Singers*. This was the first event we had done in Birmingham Town Hall since the beginning of 1978 as far as the presence of the orchestra was concerned. We did of course do the *Rejoice Greatly* thing in January 1979 but that was just the singers, so it was quite an important occasion for our 'home territory' in a sense. We gave a mixed programme of carols and Christmas music, interspersed with readings. There was a time of worship and chorus singing as well as carols for everybody.

There was also some input by Birmingham Cathedral choir boys, conducted by Hubert Best, who had become quite closely involved with us. Later on he did actually sing with us on a number of occasions, but at that stage he was just a friendly associate, not least because the two Mole boys (Andrew and Jonathan) were both cathedral choristers. We gave away such profits as we made from that concert to a local charity caring for homeless people and to the Austrian Bible Mission. I don't think there is anything else to say about that, except that it was the first occasion apart from Hiding Place when we succeeded in attracting the attention of the press (admittedly only at a local level) but they were very complimentary. I think we particularly liked the bit which said "enjoyment and enthusiasm were the key notes of this concert presented by a strong orchestra" and Nigel was particularly pleased that the reviewer said, "Although the players included members of orchestras from other parts of the country, there was the style and confidence about the performance which often comes only after months of playing regularly in the same group." Nigel felt that was a wonderful testimony to God's ability to do what humanly speaking wasn't possible, and wonderful too that the reviewer could see it. The lady who did the review went on to say that "Nigel Swinford obviously has the ability to bring people together and to encourage them to give their best to the glory of God".

The next thing the orchestra did was in February 1982 when we went to Nottingham for the first time, not to the Royal Centre which then had not been built, but to the Albert Hall, which in fact was the sort of central Methodist church of Nottingham – a huge place, not altogether dissimilar to Central Hall, Westminster. We did a concert which was fundamentally for Christians and not evangelistic. It consisted of a praise time. All the details of this are on file. I don't recall quite why we decided to go to Nottingham. Anyway this was the first occasion when we did a bit of jazz in the programme. There was a jazz group that did two or three songs with Liz Sheppard and Roger Beasley as soloists.

Just four days later, on 17th February, the singers were involved in a little thing for ITV (I don't recall the title of the programme) it was probably one of the late night epilogues, produced by Michael Hart and the title of the occasion was *Come close through the Good News*. I think it must have been an early Easter that year, because I notice that we sang at least two Easter hymns. Several of the singers gave their testimonies (Iris, Graham and Carol Corpe, Janice Taylor and Roger Beasley) Roger also sang a solo, I think it was one he composed himself called *Trumpets are Sounding*, but yes, basically the theme of it was Easter so it may be that we were simply recording it in February for transmission at Easter. I simply don't recall now.

The Ecumenical Orchestra

Our next event was in January 1983. This was quite an important set of three concerts, on 1st January at Dudley Town Hall and then on 3rd at Birmingham Town Hall and on the 4th at the Royal Centre, Nottingham. It was the same concert in each of the three places and it was entitled *Mass Celebration*. The purpose was primarily to speak to Christians I think, about the shame of our disunity. There were two halves to the programme – the first was a fairly typical NEO concert programme, mixing orchestral and choral items, but after the interval we did Nigel's 'Celebration Mass', interspersing the fundamental sections of his Mass with

worship choruses and Scripture readings, so that effectively we created a liturgical service, recognisable to Catholics, Anglicans and also non-conformists.

There was a programme note Nigel wrote at that time, which included the following: "The purpose behind this work is to help pave the way for the time when all true believers in Christ, both Catholic and Protestant, are able to take communion together, that they may all be one. The composer fully realises the weighty theological problems involved at this point but notes that there are true believers in Christ on both sides of the divide. Whilst this is the case he believes it is a dreadful thing they should be-unable to break bread together. He in no way advocates that truth should be compromised but believes that all real Christians who are walking sincerely with their Lord, and not consciously holding to evil, should be free to celebrate communion as one."

To emphasise that point, in the middle of the orchestra, during the interval, we set a table on which were placed a cup and a patten with a loaf of bread on. They were spot-lit and remained untouched and un-referred to and un-interfered with throughout the second half, so the audience could not fail to realise that we were talking about something that we could not actually legitimately fulfil, and it underlined the point.

The programme for this was significant also because there is on the inside back cover, a page given over to the first public statement (and the only public statement we ever made) about the proposed West End production of *The Hiding Place*. It includes extracts from reviews from the local press, as well as personal comments from John and Liz Sherrill and from Noele Gordon of course, who was a well-known Birmingham actress, and basically reminds people of what the story was about and says what we were trying to do in attempting to get it into the West End. It welcomed people to express their interest if they wished. We had pamphlets about this available at the cassette sales point in the foyer, so that people could do so. I think it is quite important to note that we did actually say this publicly in January 1983. There was again a very good press review of these concerts, for which we assembled what I think may have been the biggest orchestra ever – with between eighty-five and ninety players, and both the Birmingham Evening Post and the Birmingham Mail wrote very complimentary reviews.

The next occasion when the orchestra came together was in Ripon. This was an occasion to which we had been specifically invited by the local Christians, and in particular by one man, a farmer. I can't quite recall how he had come to hear about us, but he was really fired up and keen to invite the orchestra to his area. He worked extremely hard at getting people together in his local Council of Churches. We were invited to come and do a concert in Ripon Cathedral on 9th April and we also did a Mass in the Cathedral as the normal liturgical service on the Sunday morning.

That was the first time that Nigel's Celebration Mass had been done as a liturgical service in this country at all, and of course we were doing it in an Anglican cathedral as distinct from the Catholic setting in Austria. Not that that made any difference as of course the basic sung parts are the same in both liturgies. Ripon was a wonderful occasion, it was jolly cold up in North Yorkshire but that was more than compensated for by the warmth of the welcome we received. This farmer had done a fantastic job and had really stuck his neck out in faith as far as the cost was concerned too, which the Lord honoured. As far as I know, all was cleared at the end of the day – there wasn't much to spare but that didn't matter. It was virtually the only time we have been anywhere near there, though back in 1977/1978, when David Watson was at St Michael le Belfrey, there was a Christmas event involving a collection of Christian musicians and input from the Jesus Centre Singers, but it certainly wasn't under the NEO label. So this stands out as the greatest visit, even now six years on, that the NEO has made into the frozen north (east anyway – we did do Kendal!).

A broken cello, a mended heart.

There was one very dramatic incident in the middle of Communion at Ripon Cathedral (Saturday 9th April 1983), when it came to the giving of the peace. Everybody got up as bidden, to go and share the peace with one another and the orchestra did likewise. There was a very enthusiastic priest who was going to and fro and shaking people warmly

by the hand, and to this day I don't know exactly how he managed to do it, but as he moved towards somebody in the orchestra, he knocked a cello belonging to Juliet Merz and there was a split second of frozen horror as this cello went bowling over and the whole neck snapped from the body. Even when one thinks back to it now it sounded like a deafening explosion. It obviously wasn't but it was such a loud, distinctive noise even above the people greeting each other. Everybody froze. Juliet collapsed in tears and had to be led away and I remember Jo Garcia and myself both ministering to Juliet behind a pillar, out of sight. The cello was more or less in pieces. It was a valuable instrument. It was very devastating – this was only Juliet's second time out with us, she played in the Mass Celebration concerts at the beginning of the year, I think, so she was very new and she was the principal cello because Nigel had a high opinion of her playing. So it was really very devastating for her, poor girl. Subsequently it was found that it could be repaired. The priest of course was filled with utter consternation. He was devastated, poor man, he hadn't even been unduly clumsy, it was just one of those – I was going to say 'incredible accidents' but of course it was the devil trying to destroy right at the supreme moment when there should have been peace. The cello was repaired and was, if anything, better than ever. Juliet recovered from it all and continued to play with us.

About this time we were approached by a retired colonel from the Westminster Charismatic Catholic Association. I have forgotten his name, but he was responsible for the group and he had heard of us and wanted us to participate in one or two of the days of renewal that they regularly held for charismatic Catholics in the Westminster diocese, which were normally at Westminster Central Hall. So we went and made an input into two of these occasions in 1983. The first was on 23rd April and the second on 1st October. I don't have a programme as such, but we weren't responsible for organising the whole evening, we merely provided a musical input into it with orchestra and singers.

Somehow or other we also were invited, to do Nigel's Mass (which we were very pleased about because we were going to play it again in Austria in the summer so it was good practice to use it) at the Catholic cathedral at Clifton, Bristol, on the Sunday morning June 5th. That was our first contact with Christopher Walker, who was at that time the organist at Clifton Cathedral. It was a great joy to meet him and work with him. It was quite a full cathedral – not a building I must say I particularly like, rather Spartan, plain concrete and modern, but nevertheless a very interesting event to have been able to do.

The next occasion of what was proving to be an extremely busy year for the orchestra and singers, was in Birmingham just a couple of weeks later, 18th June, when we did what we called a Midsummer Prom. To some extent I suppose we were cheekily stealing the thunder of the Prom season of the CBSO (City of Birmingham Symphony Orchestra) which started a week or two later, so we billed our concert as Midsummer Prom, and it was very well attended. I think it could fairly be said that on this occasion we were out to get the non-Christians in to this one so the programme was, I think, what you would expect of a Prom concert – a mixture of orchestral and choral items. We had Anne Linstrum singing with us for this as a soloist, and she did a number of spirituals as well as one or two items from *The Hiding Place*, one of which was the celebrated item 'The crowning day'. The concert also featured the first English performance of a new composition by Kevin Jones, 'Concerto for Three Trumpets', which we had previously performed in Austria in the summer of 1981. I guess the reason why we put *Hiding Place* items in, was because at the time the programme was designed, the West End project was still live, but by the time the concert came into being, that was no longer the case. The programme notes do not therefore feature any detail about the project, as had the concert at the beginning of the year.

Fourth trip to Salzburg 1983

And so we come to Austria 1983, the fourth trip to Austria by the New English Orchestra. Again, as two years previously, we decided to have the tour for three weeks rather than two weeks and to include Carinthia as the first half of the tour, ten days in Carinthia, followed by 10 days in Salzburg. At this stage, working from my memory, the total complement of people going on the tour had risen to about one hundred

and twenty. In 1981 it was about one hundred, in 1979 about ninety, so the numbers kept going up, partly because people had the temerity to get married and have children (!), but partly because we were taking more performers. From the publicity file, here we have fifty-six in the orchestra and thirty-two singers, whereas back in 1979 it was forty-five in the orchestra and thirty singers. We had dance of an informal nature only at this stage. We experimented with dance for the first time on this tour, which consisted of nothing more than three girls, namely Sue Hill (as she then was, now Sue Castle), Lizzie Swinford and Heather Bromley, who was both a flautist and in theory also a member of the singers. She got to do everything, with just a very small dance input on one or two occasions. The rest of the time Heather either played her flute or sang and Sue sang, and Lizzie was just Lizzie. It seemed to go down well.

We didn't attempt to go by train again this time, for fairly obvious reasons! We went back to the aeroplane business and two or three different flights – I think actually what we had to do in the end was fly everybody out to Munich, stay overnight, and then travelled by coach on the following day to Carinthia. Anyway we began our tour in Carinthia and the first event on the Sunday morning was Nigel's Celebration Mass at a place called Lilstadt which we hadn't been to before. Here they have an international music festival which is obviously not as famous as the Salzburg Festival. Nevertheless it is one of the more important ones in Austria certainly, and is something a bit 'a cut above the average' as music festivals go. It was billed – because the Austrians don't separate the secular and the sacred to quite the degree we do in this country – as a Mass, and it was the liturgical service in the church (the Kirche) but it was billed in the festival programme as well. So I dare say that meant there were some people present who came purely for the music. But in a country that's substantially Catholic anyway there wouldn't be much of that. We were allowed to put one or two extra bits into that too. We began with the introit 'Come before the table of the Lord of Hosts' which we used in our *Mass Celebration* concerts earlier in the year. As on the cassette, Roger sang 'I am waiting for the dawning' just before or during the administration and it was a lovely start to the tour.

Regarding the rest of our time in Carinthia it became borne in upon us that whenever we went to Lutheran venues (and most of them in Carinthia were) we had a very poor response. The reception, if warm, was rather formal, and the audiences were numerically pathetic, in some cases down to about a dozen people, quite ridiculous. We were becoming concerned about the whole publicity machine in Austria in general but particularly in Carinthia. One or two of the places were return visits to venues like Schloss Wolfsberg, the castle, where we played in this wonderful enclosed courtyard set right up on the hill above the town, a fantastic thing to do in the evening light. We also visited an Abbey in Eberndorf, which had been a very special place to us the previous year. We visited Klagenfurt Dom and did the Mass again, and another very special place too was the Dominican monastery at Friesar. This was the last place we went to on this first half of the tour. It was very special because we didn't perform in the Abbey church at all, but in the open air, in a sort of enclosed garden. They had built an amazing stage for the performance of open air plays, amazing because it was permanent. It was a huge long stage, the whole thing was built in a long rectangle with tiered seating for the audience. If you were sitting at the far end it wasn't a lot of good. You needed to be fairly central although the stage extended a good way as well, so you could get some of the action wherever you were. But there were Tudor-type houses, with overhanging balconies very much of the Romeo and Juliet style stuff – in fact some of us lost no time in clambering back inside and pretending to do this, fooling around before we started, and there are some wonderful photos of people being Romeos and Juliets! They actually had real trees growing through the stage, and had built the stage round them, so instead of having a cardboard cut-out, there was the real thing! It was a magnificent setting, with permanent floodlighting and good sound reproduction so there was no problem. It was a wonderful place. I must say that was a rather lovely ending to what had otherwise been in some respects a rather dubious time spent in Carinthia.

Up until then at least, we always had quite a significant number of new players for the Austria tours. This presented us with a problem of sheer integration, not only musically but also into the whole spiritual unity of what we were about, and this year 1983 I think proved particularly challenging in this respect. We moved on up to Salzburg via a trip up the Grossglockner where we stopped and had time to skate around on the glacier – by kind permission of Erich Reischl and his coaches. He took us all the way this time.

Getting the act together!

Nigel had a feeling that the company was not settling down and was not taking things seriously enough. There was too much, he felt, of a holiday atmosphere, which is not what we are all about. And I think also he was struggling considerably too with this issue of obtaining real integration in the orchestra alone, never mind anybody else. I remember when the breakthrough really occurred – I couldn't tell you which day it was – but one day down in the rehearsal room in the hostel in Salzburg he was really frustrated. In fact he had said privately to me the night before how upset he was feeling about the way things were going, or not going and he didn't know what to do. I think the Lord gave him a real inspiration because he made the orchestra stand up, and then he made them face inwards in groups of three and four. The only ones who were allowed to remain seated were obviously cellos and double basses who couldn't physically play standing up, but they had to face inwards in groups of three or four. He then said to them "Right, you are now in a position where there is only one of you in each group who can actually see me conducting. The other people in the group will therefore have to depend on the one who can see me for getting their act together."

To the best of my knowledge nobody has ever done that before, and it was an absolute transformation. Someone gave me the whisper that it was happening and I rushed down the stairs and peered round the door, and I couldn't believe what I was seeing. It was quite amazing! They were all standing there you see and it began to come together. I remember very distinctly half an hour later when the orchestra broke for lunch and came upstairs there was a tremendous buzz, because they had suddenly realised they had not been where they should have been, and something had happened. I don't mean it solved all the problems immediately, but it was a minor breakthrough and I really felt the Lord had given Nigel an extraordinary inspiration to do that little experiment at that point. As I say, I don't think it solved all the problems immediately but it was a turning-point and things did begin to get a bit better.

The singers meanwhile were better integrated through working together more. The one thing I particularly remember as negative in the second half of the tour, was that having found this place difficult in 1979, it remained very difficult. We arrived, and they had had a Mass beforehand in which we were not involved and they didn't seem to be expecting us, or no attempt was made to sell our presence, and even though we were all there waiting to get in, the people all walked out past us and away. It was very discouraging. That was on the Saturday evening, 6th August and I remember having real problems that night, such that I had to receive ministry from Nigel's friends, David and Muriel Knight, who had come from the Chawn Hill Church, Stourbridge, which the Swinfords attended.

A double booking and a fabulous venue!

But I think the biggest problem was at the very end of the tour. Our final concert was due to be at St Blasius Church, (again somewhere we hadn't been since 1979). We discovered at the last minute, I don't know how, that for some reason or other the place had been double booked and we were to be the losers. I don't know whose responsibility this was, whether it was Tony Pokorny, or the priest in charge, or the priest who should have been in charge but wasn't, I haven't a clue. It's one of those mysteries that you don't really quite get to the bottom of, but it's immaterial. The point was we were double booked and it looked like we were going to end the tour on an anti-climax, having that same afternoon done an Altermarkt open air without a concert to continue on to in the evening. However, what actually happened was an amazing miracle (again whether this was via Tony Pokorny or someone else, I can't remember) but by some means or other we were able to secure the monastic church of St Peter's, which really I don't think any of us knew much about at all. It was 'tucked away' in Salzburg and you have to be looking quite hard to find it.

The high altar of St. Peter's Stiftskirche

distinctly is arriving there, walking into that building and being absolutely bowled over by the sheer beauty of the interior. I have never seen, except in Belize, such a beautiful church in my life and I think a lot of other people felt the same about it. It is not only beautiful, but also beautiful in a spiritual sense, because there was a tremendous atmosphere of centuries of the praises of God, even though the monks told us that not many people attended the normal liturgical services. There was a tremendous sense of privilege in God giving us a real jewel at the end when all seemed lost. So we set up to do a concert and before we started, the Father Prior appeared, a little white haired, frail-looking man, and announced to the very large congregation that had assembled that there must be no applause, which we were perfectly happy to respect. He didn't know us and we didn't really know him, but he was entitled to make the rules. As we went through the concert, there was no applause – and that was really good. At the end there was a silence and then a spontaneous burst of applause which was led by one or two of the monks who had crept in and who felt evidently compelled by the Spirit to do so!

During the concert we had seen one or two of them watching through a glass window high up, but one or two more had crept down and I think they just felt compelled to give the Lord praise in that way and it was very lovely. It was actually a turning point I think, because of the way the tour had gone in general, or Nigel felt it had gone, both musically and spiritually too. I think we might have become discouraged enough to question whether we should have gone back to Austria, and it was at that moment that God stepped in and made it quite clear at that final concert that the work was not finished. On the contrary, as it turned out, all that was happening was the end of a chapter and the end perhaps of the 'seed time'. Although I don't think we knew that then, either, that became apparent nearer to the 1985 tour. St Peter's is a Festival venue so it was precious in that respect too, and we were conscious of being acclaimed in a church that was frequently used by some of the Festival ensembles, the first such venue we had been able to get into.

Julie: *It was actually Roger Beasley and Guenther Reinthaler who liaised with St. Peter's Stiftskirche. Nigel recalls that this tour had felt very stark up until this astonishing night, when the Holy Spirit fell, and at the end of the evening as he was standing at the back of the church, he encountered what he believes may have been an angel sent to tell him, as they watched the crowds, that this had been 'pleasing to the Lord'. This was the critical turning point which led to NEO's work in the centre of Salzburg from that time on.*

One of the problems of taking a party of more than a hundred people anywhere, particularly abroad, is that inevitably their diet and their habits are by force, changed slightly, with the risk that they don't entirely adjust. Working under pressure as we were all doing, the old body may protest, and we have found by experience that generally in these Austria tours, we experienced some degree of illness. The enemy has often tried to attack the body as a whole by laying out a considerable slice of personnel with, if they are singers – sore throats, or others with tummy bugs or something. The worst occasion that I think I can recall, was on the 1981 tour when we certainly had a very virulent tummy bug upset which assailed quite a number of the party during the first half of the tour down in Carinthia. It

was very acute, and so bad indeed that one or two people virtually slept on landings so that they could run into the loo – they didn't dare even sleep further away from a toilet than that. Of course once you get something like that going around it can spread very rapidly. It's not at all pleasant but fortunately it's usually short and sharp.

More miracles!

1983 was worse however, because the bug that came then was more debilitating. It was very severe. People just couldn't cope with it at all, and were in considerable pain and discomfiture with high temperatures as well. I recall that as we came towards the end of the tour we were really wondering if some people would even be able to travel back, and it was basically a gastric upset of some kind, with not much to be done except grin and bear it. One found that it passed in about forty-eight hours. But at the last minute, just before the St Peter's concert, it assailed the principal clarinet – a little girl called Marion Orchard – and the programme as such really required that we should have both the clarinettists. It wasn't a case of being able to' get by' with one really, it was too critical and I don't know what we would have done if she hadn't reacted as she did. She asked for prayer, hands were laid upon her and then she was told, "Well, the decision is yours. We are not going to tell you you've got to play, but we will support you." She decided to come, even though physically she was quite unable, and because of the configuration of St Peter's, the singers were sitting quite close to and at right angles to the orchestra in the choir stalls, and I was able to keep close tabs on her. I was worried because I thought she might keel over, frankly, if the Lord didn't do a miracle for her. We prayed for her right up to the last minute, she played an absolute blinder of a concert and you could tell she was enjoying it. She was really laying into all the passages she had got that were exposed solo bits, you know, and you could tell by her face that she was okay.

I went up to her afterwards and said, "Are you alright?" She said, "Yes, fine, not a twinge, the Lord just switched if off like a tap, just before the concert." That again I think has been our experience, and the experience of many individuals, on so many occasions when the enemy has tried to get at us through our bodies. You do have to sense that it is right before the Lord to do so and it generally is. I suppose there could be occasions when it isn't, but when people have refused to accept their being laid aside and God has called them to do something and He is not going to cancel it through illness, and they have persisted, then the illness has been removed and they have been able to carry on. I think that has been an important lesson we have learnt through the Austria tours.

Chris Bell

2
Earliest beginnings
"Has cambiado en danzas mis lamentos"
"You have turned my mourning into dancing"

Come Together: 1st June 1974, Birmingham Bull Ring

AS these are my personal memoirs as well as our corporate experience, I thought it would be appropriate to begin by mentioning my own journey into NEO. There must be hundreds of our stories of how the Lord brought us all together! I do hope more will be recorded.

My parents had always taught me to believe in the existence of and to have respect for God. So there was actually never a time when I didn't believe He was there. I just felt that He was always watching me, probably not very pleased with how I was getting on sometimes – and I found myself saying 'sorry' very often. I knew absolutely nothing about salvation until 1971, when a school friend had a crush on a sixth form

lad, whom she heard attended the local Methodist church youth club (for which one also had to attend the church). She dared me to go with her – I accepted. We were sixteen. There, eventually, I met the young man, Pete Fry, who was to become my husband. He, along with a number of his friends, disappeared over the summer holidays to various camps, jobs etc., and returned in September, all having had quite dramatic personal encounters with Jesus, and together they were incandescent in their faith. Pete used to help run the evening youth club, and began using the 'cellar', an area beneath the stage, to set up evangelistic Sunday evening meetings to lead Gospel songs on his guitar (others brought their own instruments) and give some simple Bible teaching. At its height, this regular event attracted a crowd down there (including a bunch of local young 'skinheads' as they were called at the time) and it was beginning to be fruitful and exciting. Sadly, at that point it was closed down by our Minister (a liberal theologian) who didn't see the potential at all and wanted to use the space to store the church's gardening equipment!

Pete and I began going out together, and through him, his friends and the teaching I was privileged to hear at various meetings we attended, I came to understand what it meant to be able to have sin forgiven, and that in putting my trust in Christ's death and resurrection, I could be literally clothed with His righteousness and made totally acceptable to God! On February 18th of the following year I stopped 'running with the herd', gave my own life over to Jesus and began the lifelong process of being taught to grow in Christ. I felt as though I had been given wings and was learning to fly!

The Lord was at work in the West Midlands and by various means, was bringing through our midst a fresh outpouring of the Holy Spirit. One of these came via the winsome character of Arthur Blessitt, an American evangelist who carried a large cross through the UK, gathering crowds and preaching in his own inimitable way. His testimonies to the power of God came from encountering His miraculous work among the broken lives of the people who nightly inhabited the notorious 'Sunset Strip' in West Hollywood, California. Many young people turned to Jesus as a result of Arthur's meetings all around my home area, and suddenly there became a need to feed and nurture these folk at a time when some local churches were struggling to survive, while others had slipped into liberal thinking and were unable to understand or help in the circumstances.

Meanwhile, Rev. David MacInnes had become Precentor of Birmingham Cathedral, having arrived in the city in 1967 to work under Bishop George Sinker. Bishop Sinker was himself a man filled with the Holy Spirit and had obviously seen the Lord's gifts in David. David, for his part, saw a growing need for work with the young people in the West Midlands, especially those who had recently come to Christ. He wrote to Nick Cuthbert, a vivacious young man headed

for a career in medicine whom God had stopped in his tracks and appointed to be an evangelist instead! Nick married Lois, (who had been working as a nurse) in April 1972, shortly after they stepped out in faith to come to Birmingham and found themselves charged by the Lord with addressing this new situation! A young man named David Saunders also came for a while to help with this work, and was eventually replaced by Colin Day, a gifted and enthusiastic person. Together they formed an incredible team! They decided to create a meeting place every fortnight on a Saturday evening in Birmingham Cathedral, where young people could come to be given Bible teaching, learn how to live the Christian life on a day to day basis, and experience the joy of worship 'in Spirit and in truth'. The work continued to flourish, such that around five hundred of us were meeting in this way for a number of years. This gathering seemed to me unique, in that the sense of warmth and love made it a welcoming and safe place for anyone, whether they knew the Lord yet or not. By this time I had left school and was studying at college for a London Chamber of Commerce Private Secretary's qualification. I found no problem taking fellow students along with me to these meetings. They were always moved by what they encountered.

One night there was an appeal for a music group to lead the worship times at what had become known as *Youthquake* (apparently from a comment by Mary Quant that society was encountering a *youthquake* at that time) – anyone interested in singing or playing was encouraged to sign up and meet together to see what could be done. About a dozen of us responded. I can recall vividly the moment that I suddenly felt moved to ask Jesus if I could be allowed to sing for Him. This open invitation seemed an opportunity for this, and so, with some trepidation and quite honestly with very little confidence at all, I took it, and gave in my name.

That first gathering (in a room at St Martin in the Bull Ring) was a highly significant event. After the initial introductions and chat, Nick Cuthbert started by asking who played the piano. Two people responded; Geoff Hill, a lovely Welshman, soon to become a much loved friend of us all, and Nigel Swinford, about whom we learned very little that first evening. Geoff played, confessing he played largely by ear and it was absolutely fine. Later, as we began to meet, it transpired that Nigel was a music teacher working in Stourbridge, who had trained as a concert pianist at the Royal Academy in London (where Carolyn his wife also trained as an oboist). Quite quickly his gifts became apparent of course, marking him as the one who would bring, arrange, teach and conduct the beautiful songs we used. These were largely written by a wonderful musical community group known as the Fisherfolk, and consisted mainly of scripture verses set to music. They were so memorable I can recall many of them even now, and they still help me to remember specific Bible verses!

Carolyn (Caro) would join us when possible and play her oboe. Over the next year or so, things began to happen rather fast. Back in 1973, Jimmy and Carol Owens had brought their musical *Come Together* (aimed at restoring Christian unity in the Spirit, and hugely popular with its audiences) from California to the UK, under the auspices of an evangelist named Jean Darnell. (Jean worked here in the UK quite extensively and had written a very influential book called *Heaven Here I come*. I remember being totally blown away when I first read it.) Pat Boone (a popular American Christian singer at that time) acted as both narrator and soloist, and some of us here in Birmingham were able to sign up to form one of the local choirs who would join with the American nucleus group when they arrived to perform this event in the Methodist Central Hall, Birmingham. There were other performances all around the country of course. To my amazement, when the time came, we were actually trained by members of the Fisherfolk, and Pete and I had the privilege of being in a group taught by Diane Davies, one of their wonderful composers and soloists.

After that first successful tour, it appeared there was a move to do a much more local and widespread tour and by now there was quite a connection between the leaders of *Youthquake* (now joined by Nigel), and the Owens family. Nick Cuthbert remembers the evening at *Youthquake* when Jimmy had brought along their daughter Jamie (who looked very young) and had told Nick that she would like to sing. Nick wondered what on earth the outcome would be, but they allowed her to have a spot, thinking she would at least do no harm. I recall the moment she took up her guitar and

approached the microphone. The first melodious notes sent everyone into ecstasy! She single-handedly took the place for Jesus and stilled the atmosphere completely. That left a huge impression on me. The Owens were, and still are, a very talented family of artistes.

Our little group used to meet regularly to rehearse and to learn new material, and of course to pray together. I remember one evening as we prayed (when I think I had probably missed the previous meeting for some reason, I know there was a sense of having been away) I encountered a spiritual 'picture' unfolding in my mind, the first that I can remember. As I sat with my eyes closed, I saw what might be a picture frame – with blackness or darkness within, and from the centre there grew rapidly a bright, living, tree, shooting up and dispelling the darkness. It produced many branches which extended all around it, and immediately grew fruit. Then, encircling the tree, appeared a ring of people, reaching up to pick the fruit, but they then each turned back, whereupon a second line of people appeared, who took the fruit and in turn passed it back and in a few seconds, I saw more and more people in ever-increasing circles, taking the fruit and passing it ever on to more and more people. Then, as quickly as it had appeared, it all vanished.

I felt I had to try and tell everyone about this, and Nick was so tuned in to the Holy Spirit, that he stopped and encouraged us to share anything, and I was able to describe what I had seen. When I had finished, I recall seeing what appeared to be a significant look pass between Nick and Nigel, as though they knew something we didn't. When the time was right, they released the news that the musical *Come Together* was to be continued through the UK in its next phase, and instead of the American team, home-grown nucleus groups were to gather folk from local regions around them and our own group, with Nigel as its director, was to become the nucleus for the West Midlands! Looking back, it's quite clear that this period, which must have been very hard work for Nigel, was a doorway into the plans the Lord had in store for him. Also, looking back on forty-odd years of NEO history, it's clear that the picture the Lord painted for me in that brief moment was even more significant than we could possibly have dreamed!

I guess this entire section could have been entitled *Long hair and jeans* (not to mention some rather extraordinary 1970's style jumpers!) Looking back now at the photographs, one cannot help but smile! However, leaping forward, we spent the next two years doing fifty-two performances throughout the West Midlands, Staffordshire and Shropshire. The Lord did many wonderful things. Nigel pressed me into singing a few of the solo parts, despite it being the time of my finals in college – and I had to sing a few notes to Jimmy Owens at the piano as he auditioned some of our people. Jimmy graciously passed me, but was not impressed with this nucleus group we later heard – he thought we were the worst in the country! We had no vocal training – some of us didn't even read music (and still don't incidentally!). But we did it, and I remember being thankful that maxi skirts and long dresses were all the rage, as I was so nervous that on one occasion when I wore a knee-length dress, I was sure everyone could see my knees trembling! We actually had the most fabulous time seeing all the Lord did in people's lives, as congregations were literally brought together again after having split over disagreements, marriages were restored, people came to Christ, and new initiatives were inspired. I have a report in the memorabilia here in my office, which logs the fact that even at the half-way mark in this series of events as many as three hundred and fifty people had already come forward to commit their lives to Christ. One of my most touching and hilarious memories, is of receiving 'fan mail' from children who attended with their parents. One of the songs I had the privilege of singing, was one of Jamie's, entitled 'May I introduce you to a Friend?' and was the point at which those on the stage behind me would pray together, as people listened to this invitation to come and meet Jesus. So it was with a huge smile that I received a letter from a five or six year old girl one morning, saying: "I luvved that song called May I enterdruce you to a Fiend".

Further projects however, were in the Lord's vision to be born out of the leadership of the *Youthquake* team. There were many wonderful ministries which sprang from this fertile soil in those early years. By June 1974, I had left college and begun to work as personal secretary to a Christian solicitor named Anthony Collins, who had set up his practice just the previous year. (At my interview I met

Ivan Jackson, Sylvia Wallace, Kim Hancock and Julie Fry (née Such). TV still.

his other new staff- member, only to find she had been singing in the local choir with us in *Come Together* and was to become a precious lifelong friend and one of my bridesmaids – a favour I returned for her a while later.)

Through other Christian businessmen who also met at Birmingham Cathedral each week for the lunchtime *Tuesday Talks*, instigated and often led by David MacInnes and others, a strong core of believing men and women had the vision and God-ordained audacity to purchase a building in Ethel Street known as the 'Midland Club', above what was then a cinema. It was to become The Jesus Centre – a vibrant, multi-faceted project designed to a high spec, to facilitate businessmen's lunches, and an alternative nightspot for young people in the evenings. I remember going into the building for the first time with Colin Day, armed with a heavy, leather-cased tape measure, to take the first measurements of the various rooms in preparation for ideas to be made visible as plans were drawn up. I also remember Anthony being thrilled to find a portrait of one of his ancestors hanging on the wall! It was a classically styled interior of its time, with heavy furniture, and even a billiard/snooker room on one floor, together with full-sized table. For me it was like stepping into a history book.

By this time, Pete and I were engaged, and he had returned from a year at Cliff Bible College in Derbyshire to become part of a small building team under the auspices of Colin Hickling, one of our singers. Over time, they gutted this building, creating a lecture theatre with tiered seating, a very 'modern' room where meals could be served, and an upper room – destined, had we foreseen it – to become the home of many, many singers' rehearsals as the future unfolded.

The Jesus Centre

The project was complete and fully operational by the time that Pete and I were due to marry on May 1st 1976, and we held our wedding reception in the Jesus Centre, with an evening concert by another of Nigel's projects, the 'Jesus Centre Jazz' group! Pete's parents kindly arranged for coaches into the city centre for our guests. One of the building team, Colin Shields, devoid of his paint-covered overalls, acted regularly as MC for these occasions, amid much hilarity! At our wedding, Nigel and Carolyn played, and Roger Beasley came to sing also. He had joined the *Come Together* nucleus as a soloist for the local tours, and he and wife Dawn were to become great friends and later extended family, as their eldest daughter married our son! Nick's wife Lois and others (including David and Linda Isgrove, part of our original meeting in St Martin in the Bullring and big workers in all the projects mentioned at this time) all came too and sang or played. It was a blessed service and a wonderful day in our lives. We still love listening to the recording of the music, and David MacInnes' wise sermon!

However, Pete and I were members at a small church which we felt needed more input from the younger generation, and so rather sadly we made the decision that I would pull out of the group at that stage. Unknown to us, it was to be several years before our paths were to properly converge again! We stayed in touch and attended performances, and prayed for our dear friends. All that occurred in those years for Nigel and the team is related wonderfully in Chris Bell's account in Chapter 1.

We meanwhile, went on to buy our home, be blessed with two children, Luke first in February 1981 and then Lucy in December 1982. Throughout these years, my father had suffered angina and various heart problems, so it was no real surprise when one October afternoon in 1984, he incurred a heart attack which caused him to be rushed to hospital, and which was quickly followed by two further attacks which ended his life. I mention this because in his will, Dad bequeathed to Pete the large amount of professional audio-visual equipment he had amassed as a hobby, which at that time included two large and very expensive reel-to-reel tape recorders. (Believe it or not, these were high-ranking technology then and much sought after!) The will stated that Pete could keep all he could use and sell what he felt he could not. We both thought immediately of Nigel and the team – which by then functioned under its new name of the NEO – New English Orchestra.

So Pete rang and subsequently visited Chris Bell, who lived a few roads away from us. We were astonished to hear that that very morning, Chris had been instructed by the NEO's leadership team (the Prayer and Planning Group – or 'P & P') to purchase some professional recording equipment!

It was during this conversation that, unbeknown to me, Pete had asked Chris whether there were any openings for singers, as he felt I was missing singing. It turned out there were two soprano spaces required for the forthcoming tour to Salzburg that summer. Chris had sent us a copy of Nigel's glorious 'Celebration Mass' ('Salzburger Festmesse') on cassette tape, and though I had previously sung with an alto voice – I suddenly found, as I learned the Mass through singing along with this recording, that I was singing soprano and had no trouble reaching all the top 'A's! This was a revelation! So that's how it came about that I arrived, with a sore throat and a cold obviously imminent, to Ruth Miller's home one evening in early January 1985, to be auditioned for a soprano part, by what I found to be a room full of people, many I knew and one or two I didn't. I stumbled through the audition, we caught up with each other after the long separation, and wonderful fellowship was renewed.

I don't recall hearing any heavenly trumpets blowing in the distance – but they should have been heralding, not just for me, but for many of us who were as yet completely ignorant of the fact, that a life-calling was being placed upon us. This was to be one of those ministries that would take precedence over most of our future existence! Here's a note or two from my diary at that time:

Friday, January 18th, 1985

"At 7.30pm I had a lift to my first ever NEO rehearsal at Brian and Ruth's: wonderful time of prayer and lessons. I was so moved that Nigel was in the middle of writing the South American movement of the 'Symphony of Nations'. He had just brought to us the lovely piece: "Has cambiado en danzas mis lamentos, me has quitado el luto y me has vestido de fiesta! Te cantare' hymnos de alabanza!" It grew faster and more exuberant with every repeat! "You have changed my mourning into dancing and have exchanged my mourning clothes for garments of joy (fiesta). I will sing to You songs of praise!" – so relevant for me such a short time after Dad's death. They will accept me if the Lord says yes! Need further singing lessons from Elaine. Memo – phone Elaine!"

This was Elaine Evans, a friend from those early years at the Quinton church, who is presently vicar of a church in Staffordshire – she was also an excellent singer! Her husband used to play viola with NEO in early days.

It had been quite an evening! I had so enjoyed the learning! I remember being huddled on the crowded floor in Brian and Ruth's lounge. I met Linda Cooper, Alison Hawcutt and Roz Gane, who had joined around three weeks previously. There were also two almost identical twins, Faye and Andrea Hogg, who had their auditions on the same evening as me. The twins were already worthy of becoming future opera singers for the high notes and volume of which they were capable at the age of only fifteen!

I do remember noting down the following scriptures, which I believe had been shared at the time, as they were certainly relevant to Nigel's new composition of 'Symphony of the Nations':

Isaiah 25 vv 6-9: *On this mountain the Lord Almighty will prepare a feast of rich food for all peoples, a banquet of aged wine – the best of meats and the finest of wines. On this mountain he will destroy the shroud that enfolds all peoples, the sheet that covers all nations, he will swallow up death forever. The Sovereign Lord will wipe away the tears from all faces, he will remove the disgrace of his people from all the earth. The Lord has spoken. In that day they will say, "Surely this is our God, we trusted in him and he saved us. This is the Lord, we trusted in him, let us rejoice and be glad in his salvation.*

The Sovereign Lord had in fact wiped the tears from my own face – He gave me the most unutterable joy and purpose in bringing me into the NEO Singers at that point in time. As we rehearsed for this particular section of the symphony, I found myself being thrilled that I had chosen Spanish at secondary school – though German would have been immensely useful for all those Salzburg tours that were to feature throughout this ministry. But that night gave me such an overwhelming sense of comfort and joy, and a definite thrill of 'Fiesta'!

Then came **Isaiah 52 vv 13-15**: (headed, "The Suffering and Glory of the Servant")

See my servant will act wisely; he will be raised and lifted up and highly exalted. Just as there were many who were appalled at Him – His appearance was so disfigured beyond that of any man and His form marred beyond human likeness – so will He sprinkle many nations, and kings will shut their mouths because of Him. For what they were not told, they will see, and what they have not heard, they will understand.

Many, many years later – this second reading featured in the last tour to Rome during our *Recreatio* events in the Pantheon, and was read beautifully by Daphne Ryland. We could never have foreseen such a forty-year period of grace outpoured on this still 'new' ministry.

Daphne Ryland

Monday, January 28th 1985: *Ruth phoned to say it's a yes.*

By this time I felt I had had a clear indication from the Lord as I had prayed, that I should join NEO 'as a Singer and a Servant', which seemed strangely specific. Of course as time went by, it soon became apparent that the servant role comes first and the singing role second and this proved to be a principle of NEO for every one of its members. Whether it took them a long or short while to realise it, it was all about their own walk with God. As time went on, it also became apparent that singing wasn't by any means the major reason for my being called to NEO.

Wednesday, January 30th 1985: *Found number of chap in London re: South American instrument.*

It seems I was doing more than singing right from the start! I have absolutely no memory of this entry but this must have involved one of the several genuine South American instruments which were played during this piece.

Friday, 1st/Saturday 2nd February 1985: *My first full NEO rehearsal!*

I loved every minute and record being tired after it! This was to be the first of hundreds of such days of rapt concentration! On the Friday I had recorded notes "About dancers". I recall I had noted the need for someone to make all the 'Symphony of Nations' costumes for our newly appointed dancers. We had a sewing project at the time at City Road Methodist Church, and eventually I did put the two together and the folk there made the

costumes. Amazing – God's working and timing! The Saturday ran from 10am to 3pm and records: *'Symphony S/A' pieces/'Resucito'/'Behold the Man'/'Praise Him, Alleluia'/'Between the Singing Mountains'. Dancer came too.*

Tuesday, April 9th 1985: *Travelling to Devon.*

Rehearsals for this challenging project involving singers, players, enablers and umpteen dancers were arranged at a college in Devon. We stayed from the above date until the Saturday, to rehearse with the orchestra and then perform two concerts, all of course in preparation for the new repertoire for Salzburg. This was an amazing time for me, as I had never met or heard the instrumentalists before. They were such wonderful and talented people. Being able to hear the 'Symphony of the Nations' fully for the first time was totally incredible. Sometimes one is vouchsafed the experience of suddenly knowing "This is what I was made for!" For me that was the moment!

Friday, April 12th *Concert – St Mary's Bideford*

Saturday, April 13th *Concert – St Peter's Barnstaple*

Sunday, April 14th *Mass at S. Peter's – returning home.*

Julie & Pete, with a fund of memories to treasure!

I remember this whole experience as a hugely formative week as the music developed. Back home, it was Pete's first taste of babysitting and holding the fort whilst I was away. Again that was to end up being a regular experience years later when I was to go off on events and later still 'recces' with Nigel, without him! What a long and amazingly faithful ministry Caro and he have contributed in that respect!

It was a wonderful week though, involving my first live concerts, and of course deepening friendships and experiencing the wonderful worship times then led by Richard Williamson and various others. I found them memorable.

And so it all began, what was to be for many of us, forty years or more of working together in this series of exciting adventures, learning to hear the Lord's voice and doing what He told us. It has involved, as anything worthwhile does, its own share of tough times, but oh, the joy and the fun we've had!

Bull Ring Come Together

An interview with the building team

Come Together! And they did!

THE JESUS CENTRE
Birmingham B2 4B?
TEL: 021-643-1984/5

LUNCHES 12.30-2.00pm   WED, THURS, FRI.
OPEN EVERY FRI & SAT 7.30-11.00pm

music   refreshments

Fri 4th 8.15pm   FISH CO.

TICKETS 60p   LAST SIGHTED IN THE 'JESUS CENTRE' APPEARING IN CONCERT WITH JAMIE OWENS.
(members 45p)   THIS BRISTOL DUO ARE BECOMING INCREASINGLY POPULAR WITH THEIR MUSICAL
ABILITY AND PARTICULAR STYLE OF ZANY PRESENTATION.

Fri 11th 8.15pm   Teach-in: "LISTENING & RESPONDING"

CLARE MacINNES continuing her series on understanding ourselves and others
around us - and also giving those with reservations the opportunity to
express their doubts.

Sat 12th 8.15pm   London rock group making a rare visit to
Birmingham. Much travelled around the South
of England, they recently changed their line-
up and are just moving into full swing again.

TICKETS 55p   (members 40p)

REALLY FREE......in concert

Film Night "THE GENERAL"   ONE OF THE FUNNIEST FILMS EVER MADE,
AND WIDELY ACCEPTED AS BUSTER
KEATON'S MASTERPIECE. ORIGINALLY
MADE IN 1926 AS A SILENT FILM, THIS
Fri 18th 8.15pm   VERSION RETAINS THE ORIGINAL TITLES
BUT HAS AN ORCHESTRAL SOUND-TRACK
ADDED.

TICKETS 55p
(members 40p)

"Tom & Jerry"   WHO CAN SAY MORE?!!

Fri 25th 8.15pm   Teach-in: "LISTENING & RESPONDING"

CLARE MacINNES concluding the series.

**Sat 26th
8.15pm   WATER INTO
WINE BAND**

RETURN VISIT OF THIS EXTREMELY ACCOMPLISHED BAND. BASICALLY FOLK MUSIC AND FUN.
IF THEIR PREVIOUS VISIT WAS ANYTHING TO GO BY, THE POPULARITY OF THIS GROUP WILL
MEAN A FULL HOUSE.   TICKETS 65p (members 50p)

MEMBERSHIP   **JUNE**   **LUNCH-TIME TEACH-INS**
ANNUAL: from £2.50   WEDNESDAYS & THURSDAYS
DAILY : 15p   1.10 to 1.30 pm

Events at the Jesus Centre

Bull Ring from rear of platform

Ethel Street as it used to be

Geoff Hill

Ivan Jackson
& Kim
Hancock

Julie & Roger

Julie singing
May I introduce
you as people pray

Left to right Guy Hordern Pete Fry Colin Shields Colin Hickling Colin Day Ivan Jackson Maggie Hinton Rev Canon David MacInnes Jill Gooderidge Sue Allchin and Pauline Wright (centre front)

Linda Isgrove far right

Malcolm Muggeridge Festival of Light, London

Pete the electrician re-wiring building

Pete Fry

Roger Beasley

Praise and worship in the old Birmingham Bull Ring!

Rev. Canon David MacInnes

Roof top

Sonia

The club room

Room used for rehearsals

Sound check

Televised Come Together at St. Agnes Cotteridge

The club room

Typical events at the Jesus Centre Birmingham

The Ethel Street building

The Jesus Centre Club Room

Worship

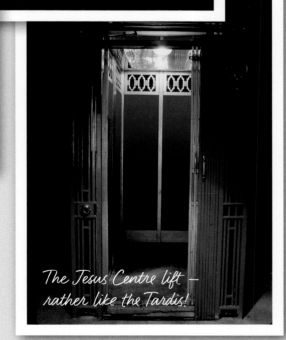
The Jesus Centre lift — rather like the Tardis!

Colin Hickling by the sound system in the Bull Ring

3

Of mountains, thunder and lightning and semmel buns... the NEO in Salzburg!

Salzburg at sunset

WHERE on earth do I begin on this vast subject, spanning nearly forty years and twenty-four separate trips? Well, Chris Bell thankfully told the story of the very first events which led up to the brand new Feast of Praise Orchestra being invited to Salzburg back in the summer of 1976, as the result of the collaboration between one Jim Goldie and Tony Pokorny, founder of the Austrian Bible Mission. I loved that story from the first moment I heard Nigel tell it! Chris himself was not part of that particular team however, so I asked Val Dalton if she would be kind enough to give her own memories of that first tour. There were myriad other people I could have asked – I have a suspicion that everyone who took part recalls it vividly!

Val Dalton

1976 – Such a pivotal year in NEO history and for me a year that changed my life! It had begun with stormy weather and very high winds. I was at my parents' house at the time and vividly remember having to tie the garage door shut with ropes

Val at the Folk Festival in Villach

as the wind had battered them so hard that the lock had broken. I heard that the weather had been just as bad back in Birmingham when I returned after the holidays.

A young teacher at the time, and a young Christian, I was a member of St John's Church in Harborne, Birmingham. The previous few years had been very exciting with the whole charismatic renewal movement, new ways of worshipping, new music, and the gifts of the Spirit being used in prayer and worship. I'd heard and been very moved by 'Come Together' and 'If my people', and had been astonished and thrilled when the Fisherfolk came to St John's for a weekend and ran worship workshops. All very exciting, but what was God saying to me?

In the middle of the city of Birmingham was a building called the Jesus Centre. I didn't know very much about it, but was taken there for lunch by a friend one day in the summer holidays of 1976. She got talking to a man called Colin – she thought he had been the lead in a play that she had seen the previous week. He wasn't, but he stayed chatting and told us about the 'Feast of Praise Orchestra' (I hadn't heard of them!) and how they were going to Salzburg in just a couple of weeks time. Colin went on to say that they were having trouble finding viola players, whereupon my friend told him that I played the viola. It appeared that they had no percussion players either, so my friend told him that I was a percussionist too. I agreed to give Colin my contact details and then my friend and I left. Two days later a young man named Nigel Swinford appeared on our doorstep and after a preliminary chat, asked me if my passport was up to date and invited me to join the Salzburg

tour playing viola and percussion. Incidentally, I had heard of Nigel Swinford as he was named on the Teacher Training College music notice boards as the timpanist for the college wind orchestra … although I never saw him at rehearsals.

_____ Dimples _____
I'm conducting in 2s if anyone's interested!

A very busy two weeks followed as I contacted my former college to see if I would be able to borrow some timpani and other percussion instruments. They agreed and transport was arranged: they were to travel to Salzburg in a large trailer which was to be towed by the smaller of two coaches which would carry the orchestra to Salzburg.

That journey proved very interesting. While still on an English motorway there was a problem with the trailer and all the equipment had to be transferred into the small coach – except for my timps which had to be left at the side of the road! Apparently the heads had been badly damaged too and would need replacing. The first I heard of this was when we arrived in Dover as I had been travelling on the larger coach. To say I was worried is an understatement, but I was assured that someone would pick them up and take them to be repaired.

The other memorable thing about that long coach journey was the catering. Some lovely people had prepared sandwiches for the journey for everyone but when we opened them, there were maggots everywhere!

We finally arrived at the Youth Hostel in Glockengasse, and what a place that was. Girls in one dormitory, boys in another as you would expect – but those dormitories were huge with uncomfortable metal bunk beds and nowhere to put things. There were a few toilets for each dormitory and a row of washbasins for our washing facilities. Showers could be booked and paid for – they were in the basement of the building and the temperature of the water depended on how many people had their shower before you did! We discovered that we were locked in to the hostel one evening when one of the girls dislocated her knee … and one of the boys had to climb out through a window to get help. It was a grim place and when I went to see it on subsequent trips to Salzburg it looked just as grim as I remembered it.

I don't recall much more about the hostel, but I remember that it was quite a walk from there to our rehearsal base in St Elizabeth's church, and that it poured with rain most of the time so we were cold and damp too – and of course, there was nowhere to dry our wet things.

But it was wonderful, and as I write this the words of an old worship song come to mind: "Turn your eyes upon Jesus, look full in his wonderful face; and the things of earth will grow strangely dim in the light of his glory and grace." I probably wasn't singing this at the time, and the 'things of earth' – the rain and all the discomfort were there every day, but somehow they disappeared as we shared fellowship, prayed and worshipped together and used our music to bring glory to God.

This was something I hadn't experienced before: I had been brought up in a very traditional local church and sung in the choir as a child, then gave my life to Christ as a student, and I enjoyed the 'new' worship of the Fisherfolk etc., but it never really occurred to me that 'classical' music (as different to 'worship' music) could be used in worship, and that classically trained musicians could focus all their hard-won skills on praising and worshipping God. What an astonishing revelation.

I also learned a lot about fellowship and the business of living and working in close proximity with other Christians. We had two excellent teachers in Nick Cuthbert and David MacInnes, and while I don't remember much, one thing that has stayed with me is Nick's talk about being a living sacrifice ... and how living sacrifices have a tendency to keep crawling off the altar! That has stayed with me throughout my life and every now and then the Holy Spirit will (gently) point out to me that I've crawled off the altar!

The concept of being broken by God so that he could use me was another piece of teaching that was new to me and has stayed with me throughout my life. I've lost count of the breakages and am sure there are many more to come, praise God.

St Elisabeth's was a big church and we were able to use various rooms for fellowship and rehearsal and over the two weeks we played concerts in various churches – but I don't remember very much about that. As I said earlier, I was there to play viola and

timps/percussion, but you may remember that the timps had been left at the side of the motorway back in England. I don't recall where they came from, or who found them, but a pair of timps was borrowed from somewhere – I don't know where – and they were, I think, ones that Mozart might have been familiar with. Octagonal in shape, cast bronze (I don't think they were copper) and with a single tuning mechanism but no way to tune them until Graham Corpe, who had travelled to Salzburg in his camper van, produced an adjustable wrench. We had a lot of fun with those timps!

Cymbals too bring vivid memories: I remember asking Nigel if I could put some cymbal crashes towards the end of 'Behold the Man' – it just had to be done! I've always found something particularly liberating about worshipping with cymbals: I love the well-tuned ones, but the loud ones are spectacular! I also have vivid memories of the leader of the viola section being so startled that she literally jumped off her chair.

Postscript:

I said at the start that 1976 was a year that changed my life. When I got back from Salzburg my house-mates said that I had changed – they weren't sure how, but they knew that I had changed. I knew that God had called me to this amazing ministry and I joined the Jesus Centre Singers which became the NEO Singers. I continued as principal percussionist for several years and as an assistant to various young professionals to this day, alongside singing alto.

I was reunited with the newly-repaired timps and kept them and other borrowed instruments safe until the college reopened in the Autumn. Before that, I cleared it with the musicians and clergy at St John's to use cymbals in the Harvest celebrations. There's something glorious about playing cymbals to the Lord. After the service, I (with the cymbals) was offered a lift home by a friend of a friend. This friend also offered the use of his car to return the timps and other instruments to college. The friend's name was Ernie Dalton and we were married two and a half years later, returning to Salzburg in 1979 as newly-weds of six weeks. Ernie became the 'Sound Guy' first to the Jesus Centre Singers and then to the NEO – for not quite 40 years!

Thanks to Val for this account, which bears out both the difficulties first encountered on this tour, but also the burgeoning growth in practical experience and spiritual wisdom, which was all part of this very first essay into Salzburg.

Here is another account from Brigitte Furze, who also explains the life-changing nature of working with the Lord in NEO!

Brigitte Furze

Val & Ernie, Wedding day May 1979

Brigitte Furze:

For me, NEO hasn't just been about playing some wonderful music with lovely people to God`s glory! NEO has literally changed the course of my life.

I had already been a post graduate music student at the Guildhall for two and a half years when I went on a concert tour with the All Souls Orchestra. During a long coach journey, my friend Jane told me that she was in a tricky situation – earlier in the year she had agreed to take part in a three week trip to Austria with the New English Orchestra, but now she didn't feel anymore that this was the right thing for her to do (as it turned out, Jane got engaged during that summer instead!). Would I consider taking her place?

Of course the trip to Austria sounded exciting – there was only one sticking point, and that was money: I was studying in London on a grant from my Swiss conservatoire, and however generous that was, it didn`t quite run to financing three week trips abroad. But I gave Nigel, whom I had never yet met, a ring anyway. And if my memory is correct, the NEO paid for me to go and play instead of Jane.

But three days before our departure, I received a letter from the Home Office, outlining that I had studied in this country long enough, please would I now go back to Switzerland. There was a deadline for my last legal day in this country – three days after the NEO was due back in England! Somehow I did not have time to go and sit on a hard bench in the Home Office for hours, to try and convince somebody in a uniform that I really very much wanted to stay in England, especially now that I was engaged to a wonderful young man. Or maybe I was just very young and naive, but I simply left the country together with all the other NEO members and arrived in Villach hugely excited. At some stage I told Nigel about my 'problem', and his simple response was, "We'd better pray about this." And so we did. A small group of six or eight people met, I told them about the letter from the Home Office and some people prayed – until one member announced, "We can stop now, I have seen the green light".

Being a fairly young Christian, that 'green light' didn`t mean much to me, but I just kept enjoying NEO`s way of making music, and didn`t think too often about what might happen at the end of the tour.

When we finally arrived back at Gatwick, all the people with burgundy-coloured passports joined a very short queue, but with my bright red Swiss passport I had a long wait behind people from every country under the sun (that was in 1979!).

Maybe, deep down, I thought they would let me back in just for the remaining couple of days to pack my bags...... I certainly had no plan in my mind about what might happen: so I simply presented my passport, only to be told very firmly that I had no right to do so, and that "over there" was a Swiss aeroplane to take me back home. I knew there was nothing I could say, so I didn`t say anything; nor did the man behind the desk. This went on for a long time (I heard later that it had been one hour!!), but suddenly, the official took his stamp and printed, 'twelve months' into my passport. I was far too surprised to ask any questions – I simply walked through the control and past the screens, where, to my big surprise, the whole group of NEO people stood praying!

So I was back in the country, able to do what I loved doing: playing the violin. But, on a twelve-month visa, I couldn't get a work permit; I tried, other people tried on my behalf, but (not surprisingly!) I could never prove that no British person could do the jobs I wanted to apply for. But two months after the Austria trip, NEO asked me whether I would once again play with them, this time for a week of performances in the Hippodrome in Birmingham. Everything was wonderful until, at one of the rehearsals in the theatre, the man from the Musicians Union came, to check up that all the orchestral players had their MU cards.

This time I wasn't the only one without the correct documents, and the officer was clearly unsure about what to do, since we were fairly close to opening night. Then he had a brainwave: "Well, if everybody is willing to join the MU that would solve the problem, wouldn't it?" It certainly did for me!

I have had several opportunities to ponder the question how my life might have turned out if I hadn't met the NEO; I will never know the answer, and I don`t need it, because I am convinced that God was in control all along.

Chris also covers beautifully, the tours of 1979 (at which point the orchestra first officially took the name 'New English Orchestra') and 1981, which were, to say the least, rather phenomenal accounts displaying the extraordinary

hand of God on the first outings of this ministry to this beautiful city, which at that time represented the epicentre of classical music in Europe.

New experiences!

My own memoirs of Austria however, begin in 1985, the fifth visit of the orchestra, when Pete and I and our children (Luke aged five and Lucy three) flew out with the team for the first time. I had been well prepared by the week of full rehearsals in Devon and the couple of concerts which gave the music an initial airing. Dawn and Roger Beasley had also invited us round for a Sunday lunch and given us the low-down on how we needed to prepare ourselves and what it would be like. We were deeply grateful for all those hints!

I remember thinking that I would never manage to remember everyone's names! There were so many who came on those early trips. My first and overall impression, from reports I had heard of previous tours (including some of the things Chris relates) was that I had walked into this outfit rather like the man in the parable Jesus told, who was hired 'at the eleventh hour' and yet paid the same amount as those who had worked through the heats of the entire day! (*Matthew 20 vv 1-16*). Though we had our battles with weather and health (see Chapter 5 – *Whatever the weather*) and our poor kids emerged looking as though they had measles on their faces after the first couple of nights being devoured by mosquitoes, I went through that fortnight for the most part, walking in a dream! It was rather like being able to pass through a gate that someone else had laboured to force open for you.

I was aware that the whole Salzburg experience was no walkover – it was a place of spiritual battle, often intense and unsettling. It was also of course a place where NEO members deepened their experience of God and of fellowship with one another. Nige always used to describe these times as having a 'greenhouse effect' upon us all, i.e. they were times of rapid spiritual growth. This was not only true for the adults and teenagers, but these tours became a vital core of the memory banks of our children. Yes those memories may have been slightly chequered – one moment having the thrill of being featured perhaps in a large scale performance, the next being kept back at the hostel, the tiniest ones in tears as the child-carers let them wave to their parents through the window, watching their Mums and Dads disappearing on yet another coach to yet another evening concert! They had their own times of teaching and worship and a whole range of fun activities however, thanks to the myriad people who gave up their holiday leave and a lot of money, to come and look after them – often missing many of the events as a result. Dot Goodliff (née Pearce) and Judi Newman, are two of these exceptional people who for years gave their time and expertise to our NEO families and kept us all amused by their fabulous personalities too!

The famous Helbrunn Water Gardens...

But for our children, these were seminal times, when they learned that it wasn't just their parents who went to church and worshipped God, but that there were lots and lots of other families who loved Jesus, enjoyed music and used their talents for Him and wanted to share Him with people who didn't know Him yet, and that doing this could be the most enormous fun! They also saw first-hand, that when a crisis hit, prayer would be the natural response throughout the whole party, and they would see the answers come.

For a child too, Salzburg had a number of rather lovely attractions, like the *Helbrunn Water Gardens*, which would spout water all over you when you least expected it, or the chocolate bars one could buy at Reception in the hostel (and everywhere else), the *Manner* wafers and the little packs of *Maoam* fruity sweets! I think most of the kids, certainly our Lucy, soon developed a big love of the morning breakfast 'semmel buns' which had to be spread with the amazingly rich 'teebutter' and lashings of jam! This could be a lengthy process, especially with tiny toddlers, and usually ended

up with them in a complete mess before breakfast was even over! As the tour progressed, the semmel buns often became rather *harder* we noticed. In fact by the end of the first week one could have used them as missiles worthy of the *Drones Club* of P.G. Wodehouse fame! Eventually, I recall Brigitte Furze took one home and fixed it to her wall as an ornament! She may have varnished it, I know not, but it stayed pretty much the same in appearance for a very long time!

...Good job they moved!

On this particular occasion in 1985, my husband Pete had been asked by Nigel to act as an enabler, helping the team rig up the huge stage in the *Kapitelplatz*, which was to be built under the supervision of Dave Vernon, who worked for a scaffolding company. This was in preparation for our first performance of Nigel's new *Symphony of the Nations* with dance. He and his wife Maggie (who sang with us in those days) ended up being key figures on that tour: Dave for his knowledge of how to assemble the whole rig, including two twenty-foot lighting towers, and Maggie, for being prepared to release him to do it while she worked away with us in the singers! Pete's main jobs on that tour, included being the lighting technician (he had some experience of being an electrician in earlier years having worked on the Jesus Centre building) and, for the rest of the time, child-care, mainly of our own two, but taking a hand with the others as well! Ernie Dalton and Trevor Wright were, as far as I could see, the core members of what eventually became known as the 'Technical Enabling team', and worked like Trojans for most of the time!

However, for all the technical enablers this was quite an experience! The staging and towers were set up in blazing sunshine (108 degrees – Fahrenheit in those days) and they had to wear gloves to be able to even touch the metal poles. Then, because of the wilful Alpine climate, there would be periods of great prayer and anticipation as dark clouds blew across the tops of the ring of mountains surrounding the plain on which Salzburg is built, depositing at frequent intervals, the most incredible downpour of rain I had ever witnessed. The heat and humidity were pretty amazing too between storms. So by the time Pete had spent ages attaching the spot-lights, which together made up a pretty scary voltage – and, I add, he did this by shinning up the towers in his shorts, wearing gloves and holding in one hand the instruction book! – he then found himself and the rest of the enablers having to rush to unroll huge lengths of plastic sheeting to cover the whole lot in the ensuing storm! I can vividly remember the enablers desperately trying to keep people away from the towers, just in case a lightning bolt should suddenly come down in the wrong place! More specifics on the weather front in the chapter mentioned above!

―――――――――――― **Dimples** ――――――――――――

In the middle of a tour: "If you tell yourselves you're tired you'll be tired!"

On this my first tour, I was caught up in a whirlwind of new experiences – not just getting used to the climate, having to cope with two children's needs, plus a very different timetable from Pete, who was working with the enablers, but 'hostel life' with the whole family living in one dormitory, new foods to encourage the children to eat (!) and not much sleep on the thin foam mattresses!

On some of those tours we were served up the delight of whole trout, I recall – but the delight soon turned to dismay as parents realised they not only had to bone their own fish but all their children's too – and what a time consuming palaver it was! Children varied in their ability to cope with their dinner giving them a glassy stare from the plate! We learned as time went by, to 'filter' the menu so

that local dishes involving dumplings created from slices of unmentionable offal were definitely excluded!

We were involved in no less than sixteen performances during this particular stay, including some extremely ground-breaking ones. The tour is very well documented by Pastor Tony Pokorny's Austrian Bible Mission Newsletter (Autumn/Winter 1985) and Ruth Miller's prayer letter reporting back afterwards. She begins by telling the faithful prayer warriors (as we have done ever since in our prayer letters, guides and bulletins) the outcome of their prayers on the run up to and during this tour!

- all gaps in the party were filled with two weeks to spare

- after various cross-continent phone calls it seemed that God was telling us our resources were among us and so to hire an extra vehicle to transport staging and lighting equipment provided by local contacts

- Chris Bell had a most profitable week in Austria in early July, preparing the way

- through using the Austrian Bible Mission newsletter many are more aware of Tony Pokorny's work and we have a closer bond with him

- in very good travel arrangements we were all kept safe despite three breakdowns on various vehicles

- there were few trips to the doctor, only one minor accident, and the two usual ailments, (throat infection among the singers and a stomach upset) were contained, for although some were ill, no one was prevented from performing.

(To interject at this point – I do recall being one of the patients who had to be taken to the doctor, and I was thankful to one of Susan Mole's two sons (I am having difficulty recalling whether it was Andrew or Jonathan) who spoke such good German that he kindly accompanied me. A number of us had decided on our day off, to go up the Untersberg using the cable car, to explore. But whilst up on the top, a thick mist had come down and whether or not there was any actual connection we don't know, but somehow most of us on that particular trip ended up with throat infections and coughs. My doctor's visit was rather an odd one, in that I found myself handed a packet of dried

A brilliant way to advertise NEO!
With the Octopus man!

A budding conductor on the ceiling of the
Grosser Saal, Residenz Palace

A special public meeting during the
Festival of Spiritual Music

A cool moment in the cloisters
for Catherine & Pete White

Banner for one of our
innovative tours!

A selection of glorious NEO youth in Salzburg!

A trio of tenors! Jonathan, Roger and Nick!

Composers together, Pelecis and Swinford!

Brass practice in the car park at Aigen Hostel!

Concerts in the hot Altermarkt over the years!

Doug Gallaher on duty!

Dancers getting their 'pointe' across!

Enablers leafleting on the Octocycle!

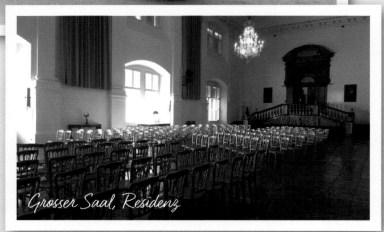

Grosser Saal, Residenz

Franciscan Church chancel — the only time NEO ever sang in a cage!

The team on the steps of Eduard Heinrich Haus, Salzburg

Jamie Dalton and Chris Young with one of our Salzburg banners!

How did he conduct in the heat we wonder ..

Kiddies now grown up but Brenda Lowe looks much the same!

Lisa and Su dance Fantasia on Greensleeves at the Residenz 1987

Our own Dr. Flo' with the amazing smile!

Luke & Maria Fry with the very young Corrie & Hannah Gerrard!

Luke (bottom right) and some of our amazing NEO enablers!

Sierning 1993 Dr. Walschofer & Tony Pokorny distributing gifts!

One of our wonderful brass teams in Salzburg

Precious day off at the Gaisberg with Brian and Ruth Miller

Our dear friend Sister Marie Christa, a faithful prayer supporter!

Singers balance on benches at Sierning!

Finale of the South American Movement in UK tour

Talented maestro János Czifra with Brigitte Furze and Martin Lowe

The Church of St. Michael, Mondsee Sound of Music wedding fame!

The 'Pofflemeister' shares wisdom over a picnic!

The Dom, Salzburg

The crafty wit of our NEO youngsters!

The children and their carers!

The dove of the Holy Spirit in the cupola of the Dom

The glorious venue of St. Peter's Monastery Church Salzburg

The huge crowd in the Domplatz 1987

sage, and told to cover a certain amount of it with boiling water, and then inhale the steam at regular intervals! – (This was my first experience of European alternative medicine!).

– children were happy and settled, with great skill and willingness expressed by the babysitting team, especially in the varied weather conditions

– the teaching from Matthew Baynham and Richard Furze fed the party sensitively, leading us to greater devotion and obedience

– we have been encouraged and thrilled by people's generosity and financial sacrifice

Tony Pokorny writes enthusiastically – he had worked hard, presumably with Chris Bell, to set up the venues for this tour. This is a long extract (despite my edits here and there) but stay with it, because it gives a rare insight into why this particular tour had such a feel of 'breakthrough' about it, and led to new opportunities which were set to continue and develop the work over following years:

This has been an eventful summer, particularly the period of 27th July – 7th August, the Salzburg Music Festival, during which the New English Orchestra and Singers gave sixteen concerts. We were even invited to perform in the Residenz and in the presence of the Governor of the Federal State of Salzburg! The 'Salzburger Nachrichten' one of Austria's national papers, had an article about our visit and a photo of the Governor with the orchestra. Another grand occasion was the invitation to Schloss Mirabell where we performed before the Deputy Mayor of Salzburg and where Nigel Swinford presented a copy of 'Symphony of the Nations' to him. After the concert, Nigel and several of the NEO committee were invited to the Mayor's parlour where we spent an hour with him, being served with drinks and sandwiches. He was most interested in our orchestra and told us how much he appreciated that we gave our concerts free of charge. He gave each one of us an illustrated booklet of Salzburg and a silver pin with an angel's head, the badge of Salzburg. He asked me to let him know in good time of our visit in 1987 as he would like to arrange a concert at Schloss Mirabell to which he would invite special guests. We also had a meeting with the Archbishop Berg, who showed keen interest in what we were doing though he was not able to attend any concerts.

However, he sent a delegate to our last concert at the church of St Andrae, who recorded our performance for the Archbishop. On this, our fifth Concert Tour since 1976, we finally got the highest official recognition both from secular and ecclesiastical authorities. It is a thrill to play and sing to large enthusiastic audiences and we always have full churches, usually between four hundred and six hundred. The highlight of the tour was the privilege to play in the Dom (Cathedral) for the first time in our five visits to Salzburg. The Dom was filled with people singing in the aisles and the 'Salzburger Nachrichten' reported that the Italian conductor Riccardo Muti was also in the congregation which applauded at the end of the service. The sense of praise and sharing was tremendous and many came to talk to us.

(Julie: He certainly was, it is now the stuff of NEO legend that one of our players, David Naylor, looked up whilst playing the Celebration Mass, to find the great man peering over his shoulder at the music!)

As a result of having been to Pfarrwerfen and Bad Hofgastein several times, they both now have prayer and Bible groups.........

This summer we entered into two new areas; Mondsee and Sierning. Mondsee is about fifteen kilometres from Salzburg, now famous through "The Sound of Music" as the wedding ceremony took place in the Abbey Church. I had been trying in the past to get our orchestra into this church, but there seemed to be no interest. And then in 1983 after the morning service in Vincent Palotti Church in Salzburg, I was approached by a young lady, a member of the Abbey of Mondsee, inviting us to her church. She said they had recently formed a prayer and Bible group as well as a small music group and our visit would help them very much in their witness. She was sure enough she could get her parish priest to invite us. When I asked her name it was Elisabeth Pokorny! No relation, though now a sister in Christ. A week before our concert I visited Mondsee to meet the folk responsible for the arrangements and I got another surprise when meeting Mr and Mrs Landgraf. Mrs Landgraf is an English lady, a Roman Catholic, who was converted at Sheffield University. She came to Mondsee to teach English and fell in love with an Austrian English teacher and became 'Mrs Landgraf' (We all know her as Jo and she and Frank have helped us on many occasions since to renew fellowship in this lovely venue right up until our last Salzburg tour!)

Tony continues:

...A typical reaction to a concert came in a letter from Mondsee: "There are often concerts at Salzburg in the Festpielhaus, but we have never heard one like this. It was not only the performance which impressed us but the atmosphere you created by your joy and enthusiasm. You expressed your love to Jesus and let people feel it." On many occasions this 'atmosphere' led to members of our party being able to pray with individuals, including leading musicians, about their personal needs.

Tony went on to explain that he had also been approached by the wonderful figure of Herr Walschofer, who introduced himself as the leader of the Catholic Education Movement of Sierning and Headmaster of a school in Bad Hall. He tells of the church being full (as I remember it too) with around four hundred people. I also remember us having to negotiate the rather cramped performance space, which meant the singers had to stand in two single files, on either side of the orchestra, which was itself squashed into the chancel area! Not for the first time were we ladies called upon to hoist ourselves as delicately as possible, without treading on our skirts, onto some bench or other. (I recall that in Pfarrwerfen, most of the soprano singers in fact ended up squeezed into the pulpit!) In the afternoon the NEO was given a wonderful meal in the church hall at Sierning, and on this and all subsequent visits, the particular hallmark of this host, was the plethora of gifts which were bestowed upon us before we left. To some were given candle lanterns, to some Austrian posies (beautifully crafted), to most a red wax plaque depicting some scene or saint, and for the coach loads en route home late at night (it was often, as Tony recalls here on the first visit, after midnight before we got back to the hostel in Salzburg), crates of beer and bananas! Why? I have no idea, but they were very welcome!

To this day I believe that Nige and Caro still exchange Christmas cards with Herr Walschofer, and on at least one occasion I recall Nige relating how the 'English' he used had set Caro laughing so much she almost ended up on the floor in hysterics! He is a truly memorable man and we are all very fond of him!

Taking time to show a little of the inner workings of the 1985 tour I hope helps to show how very many opportunities could arise not only prior to a tour, but during it. Ruth's Prayer letter following states this:

Before we left for Austria, we were given a promise that our visit would be like a tree coming into blossom. Whereas previously the seed had been faithfully sown and the ministry planted, this time there would be the more noticeable, fragrant blossom. We experienced this in three ways. Firstly, because of the more frequent concert appearances in central Salzburg, especially Symphony of the Nations, we were recognised in cafés etc., which gave further opportunities for witness.

Secondly, we had contacts with all the highest authorities in Salzburg. Since our last visit two years ago, a new British Consulate had opened and the Proconsul, Dr Steigenberger and his secretary Frau Danmayr, did everything they could to help and promote our tour. We were also grateful to have the services of a Christian journalist, Peter Jennings (see Chapter 15 – To the Saints in Rome) as part of our party. Through these contacts we were summoned to an audience with the Governor of the Salzburg Province. He had so arranged this that our short performance before him formed the prelude to a meeting of the entire Festival Committee, to discuss their financial problems. As a devout Catholic, he was encouraged by our music and impressed by the self-financing basis on our fifth visit.

Thirdly, we found many of our contacts with those in authority were much easier than usual, as if God had gone before and prepared the way. Doors opened with a gentle push where we had anticipated using muscle!

I love that last quote and have since referred to it in one of our many NEO prayer bulletins. So often we have had a strong sense of the Lord having done just that – preparing the ground for us before ever we set foot on it. I recall mentioning in one of our much more recent bulletins, that we felt as though we were walking in pre-trodden footsteps.

Perhaps it's clearer now why I felt so blessed, and why my *late* entry into the ministry in Salzburg at this particular and crucial moment in its development, made me feel overpaid for my efforts!

The Residenz building

The only time Nigel ever used a megaphone!

The stunning Grosser Saal of the
Residenz Palace Salzburg

Thea & Georg Hoelscher's performance of
Nevertheless by Georgs Pelecis

Time out for a table tennis match!

Untersberg in the snow Salzburg

Nigel's minimal conducting with a biro when wearing a jacket in the heat!

Who could resist a leaflet from our ladies!

Getting used to the feel of the city, not just its beauty, the fabulous buildings, the Austrian way of life, the elegance, the culture etc., but that extraordinarily penetrating sense of the spiritual realm just behind it all, hidden by a thin veil, was an overwhelming experience for me.

Nigel was incredibly anointed in his portrayal of Austria's particular need in Symphony of the Nations. It was depicted by the use of dancers moving along the floor inside what appeared to be bags made of a stretch fabric, painted with sombre colours, reaching out to envelop and subsume, warp and destroy. In Chapter 5 – *Whatever the weather,* where I mention spiritual warfare, there is reference to the responses which came from Austrian people who understood what lay behind the vulnerability of their nation – they saw so clearly in this particular movement, the truth of whom they were battling.

In subsequent tours, we would often meet people such as one lovely lady whom several of us came to know and admire, who was the daughter of a Jewish family torn apart by the war. She was obviously still coming to grips with the things she had had to live through, such as when, as a fifteen year old girl, she ran to stand in front of her uncle, who had been pushed against a tree in their garden to be shot by the Gestapo. She succeeded only because a female member of their number faltered in the raid and her uncle was allowed to live. The infamous *Eagle's Nest* over in Berchtesgarten, just over the border in Germany, was Hitler's headquarters, and Himmler apparently took over the beautiful home in Aigen, which had once belonged to the real Von Trapp family. Happily, when Nigel and I visited it at the behest of a member of a Catholic brotherhood who acquired the building for a time, we found a most beautiful chapel had been created, where we were invited to stand for a moment and repeat the Lord's Prayer in English, as our host spoke it in German. It was an emotive moment, because the room, which still maintained the heavy leather padding on its doors, had been the secret meeting place where so many death warrants had been signed and so many direful decisions made. Our host explained that the great table on which such documents had been officially stamped, had been taken out and burned.

Another aspect of this city however, is the ever present influence of the Festival itself, which we could not help but notice brought the great, the rich and the elegant to parade before the doors of the *Festspielhaus*, chatting at small tables and drinking champagne – the women displaying their remarkable designer gowns and the men their sharp suits (which I tried to echo in my mannequins later on in 1991 for the Feast of Trumpets, as you will read in Chapter 7 – *Solemn Feasts and Laughter in the heavenlies*). But for the people of Salzburg themselves, many of whom could not afford the ridiculously priced seats (anything up to three hundred and fifty or four hundred Euros these days I believe) many were ashamed of the type of performance portrayed, which could at times be avant-garde and risqué in interpretation. The larger ecclesiastical buildings in Salzburg also felt the force of this annual event, as one by one we found them used as Festival venues and as such, they became bound up in the business of receiving Festival money, much needed to maintain these edifices, but also in receipt of artistic projects of which they might not fully approve. I shall never forget the day we entered the huge University Church in the middle of the city, to rehearse in readiness for an evening concert, only to be met by a great cubic scaffold erected inside the building, from which were hanging bandaged 'bodies' with severed parts. Obviously these had some ghastly significance in the production for which they had been created – but I recall it was one of those moments where the NEO team, undaunted, gathered to pray and clear the air before doing anything else!

Somehow these aforementioned elements of Austrian life seemed to me a great intrusion into the beauty of the country itself and its rural people, complete with their lederhosen and dirndls, their *Maibaum* (May tree) celebrations and *oompah* bands, their beautiful horses with champagne-coloured manes and tails, and their cattle roaming the mountain meadows wearing large cow bells round their necks! The Austrian Movement of the symphony then, blew like a fresh wind of hope for those who had eyes to see and ears to hear, as it depicted Christ coming in His glory to break chains, to redeem, to forgive, to set captives free and to release people into laughter, praise and dancing, first to the beautiful melody of the traditional 'laendler' (with the words 'I will sprinkle clean water upon you, and you shall be clean' from Ezekiel 36 v 25 ff) and then rounding off with an 'Alleluia Polka'!

I think one of the most challenging aspects of this 1985 tour and of all others which followed it in Salzburg, was the need to be incredibly alert and versatile. One moment there would be outrageous hilarity among friends relaxing over a drink between rehearsals, the next there would be intense prayer and vital teaching which would send one's thoughts soaring into faraway places. Swiftly following would be the practicalities of leaving that mode to address the very real needs of small children who had been without you for several hours, and would be again in the evening – finding energy to go shopping, and to feed them, before desperately trying to freshen up from the humid heat, change into concert gear and be ready at the sound of the trumpet (literally!) to dash for the coach, after bidding numerous farewells to the little ones and handing them over to the amazing team of babysitters. Here and there one might just be able to catch up with one's husband on the enabling team, who had one moment been drenched by a thunderstorm, the next rendered hot, sweaty and filthy after building or de-rigging a stage and loading a lorry. (Had he eaten anything?)

On the various years which involved travelling overland by coach, so that we could save costs not only on flights, but also on expensive coach travel inside Austria (which did occur in later years when we had lost the wonderful services of Erich Reischl's company), there was the added exhaustion factor of being on the road for around twenty-seven hours 'fore and aft' of a tour! There was one such occasion, when I had incurred an infected mosquito bite on one ankle and it had blown up to a ridiculous size and become extremely painful. As we all sat, trying as we might to find any kind of comfortable position to sleep during those long hours en route home after a very busy tour (and none who were in any way 'wounded' having any real space to stretch out an offending limb) I remember thinking, "I literally feel as though I've been in a battle!" I wasn't the only one on board who felt like that.

Oh, but the sense of working with the Lord of all Creation, and of really being a small part of His *awful patient purposes* (a phrase of C.S. Lewis) as He specifically led and guided us over the years, is indescribable! None of the above difficulties were to be compared with it – it's just that it's definitely easier to write that now in retrospect, than when right in the middle of it all! Nigel had described in his original vision of the work in this city, as a 'tower of praise' arising. Many years later, I too saw a picture in which all the previous NEO tours appeared rather like smoke rings rising up from the city and becoming solidified one on top of another – which I took to mean that it was the persistence of this ministry, so blessed with longevity, which was making the difference. Each tour had a purpose of its own, but together over the years there was an increasing spiritual impact on the city, its people and its 'atmosphere'.

Romance! Romance! (in defiance of Rule 10!)

As an aside to all the above, I must say that many of the surnames I found in the original lists for the Devon rehearsals and the 1985 tour were destined to change as people paired up and were married! I was interested when we received a very wise and instructive letter from Nigel before the next tour in 1987, which comprised a list of bullet points with some great headings! Some of these I have

NEO youth in Rome 2015

included in Chapter 5 – 'Whatever the weather...', as they are so relevant there – but others encouraged us to take care of one another, see that no one was left out; reminded us to check whether individuals could manage financially to be part of say, a special trip out on a day off. We were warned about 'super-spirituality', which Nigel indicated that the Bible terms 'self-righteousness'; we should avoid a) trying to achieve righteousness by our own efforts and b) trying to show others how 'spiritual' we are – both, Nigel pointed out, objectionable to God! His advice; "Go for a strong, simple faith in Jesus which avoids all artificiality and play-acting and yet expects great things from Him at all times." (Advice for our whole lives not just an NEO tour to Salzburg!).

We were given hints on being flexible and adaptable – especially if the piece we had rehearsed so exhaustively, ended up being taken out of a programme at the last minute! The orchestral players incidentally, had to cope with *very* last minute guidance coming to Nigel via the Holy Spirit, and often from Nigel by means of a mouthed whisper to the rest of us – heralding the entrance of what became known as *the NEO dive*, as each player leaned out of his or her chair to fumble in their music bag for the piece Nigel felt needed to come next! Sometimes we only learned what was to be performed that evening whilst we were on the coach en route! We were, therefore, also advised in one bullet point to, 'Be prepared' – especially musically! Then, came the notorious Rule 10!

A refreshing moment with Brother Virgil and Pater Benedikt!

shortly before or after the tour that it isn't the real thing. It has happened to most of us sometime or other. However, people can be hurt by this and it can be a serious distraction from our calling. So my advice is – mix freely but try to avoid crushes.

This incidentally, was also followed by a note about moderation in terms of alcohol consumption – to be moderate in all things, so that our witness would not be damaged. All of these points were of course hugely relevant once we were actually out there, and there were just odd instances of having to deal with one of these situations, happily very rare – hence the wisdom of this preparation. However, over the years we have had some notable romances leading to beautiful weddings and successful marriages of course. In the very best cases, then, even the very best rules are only there it seems, to be broken!

Theology of Place

I will always remember Nigel using this phrase when describing certain scenarios in Salzburg as we walked around on recces. He would talk about the particular importance of the place where we were going to work, either in history, or in terms of the significantly great blessing of the astonishing size of a site we had acquired, its centrality, and its value for the Gospel. But he would speak of it in terms of the Lord's viewpoint, and likewise also that of our spiritual enemy. I found this helpful.

—————— **Dimples** ——————
We must be homogeneous in our naughtiness (band & singers!)

Don't get crushed!

Yet more practical advice! The enemy has many ways of deflecting us from the job in hand and also from the blessing God has lined up for us. One of these is that well-known phenomenon – "the holiday romance". We can be tricked into thinking we are in love with someone, only to discover

For example, Chris Bell outlines the moment in NEO history when a double-booking propelled NEO into St Peter's Monastery Church, where no doubt it took a while to realise where they had landed! This was the oldest abbey in the German-speaking area, founded in 696 by St Rupert at *"the site of a Late Antique church stemming from the first Christianization of the area in the days of Severinus of Noricum. It was meant to forward missionary work in the Eastern Alps. Until 987 the office of Abbot was joined in fact to that of Archbishop of Salzburg; the two were always held by one man."* (Wikipedia)

This was actually the Arch-abbey of the Benedictine order, the church's most recent refurbishment taking place in the Rococo style, hence the exquisite beauty of which Chris speaks in his memoirs, which held him spellbound after first entering the building. However, much later on, Nigel happened to embark on a quite intensive period studying the works of Luther, and found in passing, that Luther's spiritual director, Johannes von Staupitz, (of the Augustinian order) had himself once been Abbot of St. Peter's and had died and been buried there! Luther had joined the Augustinian order as a friar rather than a monk, thereby able to take active service in church and society. He is quoted as saying *"If it were not for von Staupitz, I would have sunk into hell."* (Wikipedia) Such was his inner torment in trying to confess every single sin he had ever committed! When a theology faculty was established at Wittenberg, von Staupitz was given the chair, but after seeing the various trials under which Luther was labouring as he struggled with the whole Catholic practice of confession and indulgences, von Staupitz decided to resign the chair, and appointed Luther in his place in a masterstroke by which Luther would come to study in depth the word of God, and find greater understanding of the glorious grace which was his and is ours, through the blood of Christ. Eventually difficulties arose again however, and Luther's teachings became seriously controversial, to the point at which the Pope ordered von Staupitz, as head of the order, to silence him. Creatively, von Staupitz rather chose to release him from his vow – keeping peace within the order and allowing Luther freedom to act as he wished. Eventually however, von Staupitz himself resigned the order and was allowed to

St Peter's Clocktower on a perfect Salzburg day

join the Benedictines in Salzburg, where he quickly rose to the post of Abbot. He eventually died there in 1524.

We found ourselves then, in a historically and very theologically important site where, given the individuals the Lord brought across our path, we were enabled to continue sharing the Gospel in very significant ways and to build up the people of God in the city. This was a great privilege.

Turning to the glittering world of music however, at the very beginning of NEO's visits, Herbert von Karajan was still the Festival Music Director and Principal Conductor. I have newspaper cuttings in my memorabilia, from the Sunday Times July 23rd 1989, following his death:

When music luminaries assemble in Salzburg cathedral tonight to hear Riccardo Muti conduct Mozart's Requiem in memory of

Herbert von Karajan, music will be the last thing on their minds. Karajan's sudden death and midnight burial have left a power vacuum that reaches deep into the entertainment industry.

I remember reading this and wondering why on earth this man had left instructions to be buried at midnight? Norman Lebrecht, who wrote the above, continued by detailing the 'dismantling' procedure which lawyers would have to embark upon, of Karajan's 'media empire'. This empire included a private film company, which was 'sitting on a mountain of '*definitive concert videos*' he had directed over the previous 10 years with both the Berlin and Vienna Philharmonic orchestras. It seems he had invested the equivalent of £6 million of his own money *into a scheme which would perpetuate his image for all eternity.*

Karajan, in his final moments, had apparently collapsed into the arms of the president of Sony, the Japanese company which, Lebrecht informs the public, had.. *built a compact disc factory virtually at the bottom of his (Karajan's) garden and relied on him to endorse innovatory devices.*

The Festival, with all its ups and downs, had and still has, a major impact on the city and its economy, certainly in terms of being a major centre for western classical music. It appears that both it and Karajan had been at the centre of a huge and complex web of commercial interest. We came to appreciate quite quickly (See Chapter 5 – *Whatever the weather*) what was involved in engaging with institutional power. The above article also mentioned the following:

Salzburg faces a more immediate and intractable crisis. The festival opens on Thursday amid demands by Austria's cultural minister, Hilde Hawlicek, for an inquiry into its organisation and finances. The festival receives £5m of public money and has been criticised for profligate opera productions, high ticket prices, and providing a showcase for untested record stars.

An international impresario, Dr. Hans Landesmann, was destined to rectify this situation – he comes into the story further on in Chapter 17, *The Phenomenon of the Recce*!

My times are in your hands Psalm 31 v 15:

The timings of NEO events and tours were also hugely relevant and this then, was a particularly strategic point to

The Dom, 1989

be visiting Austria – as NEO actually did in that crucial year of 1989. My family did not however, as I had just given birth in May of that year, to our third child. I acted instead as a prayer contact for other folk who could not go that year, keeping them updated as Ruth Miller rang me at given times. I prayed with another singer, Jenny Sheldon, by agreement one evening after a meal at our home, and received some very specific and incredibly clear prayer pointers as we

The wonderful 85–87 dance troupe

prayed, all of which were confirmed a couple of days later by a call from Ruth to keep us up to speed. One concerned a health issue, in which I saw clearly a passport-sized photo of a player whom I later learned had had to be taken to hospital with a threatened miscarriage (all was well on that occasion). Another concerned poisonous insect bites: our soloist Lesley Thompson had been very perturbed to hear that one of the possible creatures which had given her a painful, swollen bite, could carry botulism! Thankfully even though we had prayed against bites and she was still bitten, the outcome was 'safe'! I recall Ruth saying, "You don't know what might have happened if you *hadn't* prayed!"

In view of the dramatic changes which were occurring in the Salzburg Festival following Karajan's sudden death, it was fascinating to read Ruth's report in the prayer letter that September:

———————————— **Dimples** ————————————

I need more soprano – more Boadicea than Twiggy!

So far as the concerts and services are concerned, the key word this time was freedom. Everywhere we went we had a greater sense of liberty than ever before. It was as if something had snapped and barriers had been broken down. The authorities in the Dom elongated the Mass so as to include extra worship, and in most of the venues the orchestra spread out among the audience in spontaneous worship at least once during the concert, giving an amazing sense of the Holy Spirit filling the building. I don't think I have ever heard such sounds in my life before. The sense of the Spirit seemed almost tangible. As usual there was much weeping to be seen. You only had to look at the faces of our audiences to see the effect the ministry was having. Attendances were consistently large – the police estimated three thousand in the Jedermann stage concert. The weather for that was perfect and there was a great sense of proclamation about the event. We were indeed preaching the Gospel. The dance that night was particularly beautiful. An Austrian fellow believer who watches our work carefully said: "There was a new tenderness, calm and freedom about the ministry this time which was quite fresh – it came from heaven. There was a greater depth and gentleness".

More detail occurs elsewhere as promised, but my initial imagined picture of the beauty and peace of the mountains and pastures, the quaintness of the church spires and the delights of the national dress and customs, was definitely only half the story! Here we had to (as Matt Baynham suggests in Chapter 5 – *Whatever the weather*) keep our 'tin hats' on at all times – and our music-making was a definite act of powerful proclamation as well as worship!

It would be entirely impossible to draw such detailed pictures of all our tours to this beautiful and challenging city, though there are veritable encyclopaedias of NEO history to be shared from them, but for now, just imagine having gone through such a tour, and then arriving home, knowing one has to steel one's self to find the most innocuous response

Mary Burton (née Corpe) and Annie Routley wearing their dirndls

to the inevitable question which will be asked through pleasantly smiling lips by at least some of one's friends on Sunday morning:

"Oh! Hello! Did you have a lovely holiday?"

On an open palm

Vigil

Vigil at Bristol Cathedral

THE *Vigil* genre was to become a major aspect of NEO's work for many years, covering so many issues as they emerged here in the UK or overseas. I remember it all began, funnily enough, when Nigel had come to our home on January 21st, 1988, to ask me if I would join the Prayer and Planning group as Singers' Secretary, whilst Ruth Miller was on sabbatical with her third pregnancy. We fell to reminiscing about those early days of *Youthquake,* and the incredible warmth of fellowship and sense of God's love which surrounded us all on those occasions.

At the time of Nigel's visit, the UK was in the midst of a period of great national unrest in the light of the troubles in Northern Ireland and the IRA bombings that were a major feature of the news on TV, radio and in the press. By early 1993, bombings had occurred in both Warrington

and Liverpool and the stage was set for further disruptive acts, causing injury and death as the violence stepped up in the following months. We had met again at my home and our conversation several years previously, now took on a more poignant relevance. We talked about the vigil that had been held in memory of those who had recently died in one of these bombings. People were gathering in churches or cathedrals and lighting candles, as they mourned and interceded. We wondered if this could be a way forward for NEO? Could we simply provide a place for people to come and meet with God? A place where the Lord could come and say 'Hello' to them, and a place which had that same atmosphere of warmth, safety and love that we had known before the vision of NEO had been given. What would He do with such an opportunity?

NEO therefore launched its first tour entitled *Vigil for Great Britain*, in January and February 1994. We felt that the time was ripe to provide an opportunity for ordinary people to gather together in expression of their mutual concern for the nation. We did not want to create a massive prayer or preaching rally, nor did we wish to spread doom and gloom – but rather to share the hope of the Christian, that even in the most difficult circumstances, God really is there.

The *Vigil* took a simple pattern of beautiful church music, based around the main movements of the Mass, including presentations of spiritual songs, orchestral pieces, both traditional hymns and modern songs of worship, and sometimes Dance. These were interspersed with Bible readings and times of silence (the watching and waiting of the true vigil), and prayers of confession and supplication.

For our first tour we visited Bristol, Birmingham, London and Manchester (both Anglican and Catholic venues), and we played to surprisingly large audiences for an event that was the first of its kind. People were ready for this. The response was quite overwhelming. Though there was no 'emotional' aim involved, many were weeping in the congregation at various points throughout the evening. Though there was no preaching, many met with God, some finding faith for the first time, we later learned, others receiving answers to their questions or comfort and direction in their own life struggles. It seemed to be the solution to the space people needed in such a busy lifestyle – time simply to sit for ninety minutes and take stock of their national and individual life. Those who had no faith at all came without pressure or embarrassment; people from all walks of life came, from the unemployed to those in high-level positions in society, people who regularly went to church and people who never did.

It was not a time for arguing or debating rights and wrongs, but rather for taking in the situation as a whole, and for those who felt able, offering it all back to God, and asking for His mercy. Problems in those days and more so today, are rather too intrusive for people to close their eyes to them, or for anyone in leadership to solve easily, whatever their policy may be. We often made these events civic occasions as the genre developed welcoming people who held positions of responsibility in the cities we visited.

The overall tone of the evening was hope. It gave people something fresh to think about and be inspired by. For those who had eyes to see it, there was a portrait in music of the life and redemptive work of Christ in the first section of *Proclamation*. In the second section, *Confession*, we highlighted the basic issues of concern in our prayers, pointing the finger at no one. In the third section, *Supplication*, we prayed simple, positive prayers together for our nation.

That tour of 1994 concluded with Allegri's beautiful 'Miserere', sung by torchlight in the darkness of the cathedrals, as people pondered the words (sung in English) of the Penitent's Psalm (51) the heart cry of King David after his affair with Bathsheba. People found this deeply moving. The blessing was pronounced, and in the stillness, by torchlight, the Singers recessed, quietly singing a simple song, 'Purify my heart', (freshly arranged by Nigel for four part harmony) which summed up what was felt to be in most people's minds at that point. Many did not want to leave straight away. Many we spoke to afterwards could find no words, no ready terminology to express what they really felt. It was obvious that this event was meeting a need in the nation.

This then, was to be the first of many series of Vigil services around the country and of course in Salzburg. I recall that in 1994, Nigel's daughter Catherine gave her debut in Allegri's 'Miserere' as the soprano of clear and pure top Cs! The quartet section with Martin Lowe bass, Matthew Baynham tenor, and Elizabeth Davidson (now Llewellyn) alto sang beautifully and many were deeply moved. I can recall thoroughly enjoying singing the choral parts of the piece and feeling able to offer it as sincere and pure worship.

This psalm of David had meant a great deal to me personally. In my own early journey, immediately prior to rejoining my friends in NEO, I had experienced a number of occasions when fears and problems had encroached on my normally happy life, including an experience of post natal depression, and living through the trials of a church which was beginning to fall apart at the seams through various disagreements. This had left me feeling inadequate, unholy and less able to come before the Lord with a bright and shining faith! So it was highly relevant that in the two weeks between my audition for NEO in January 1985 and my actually joining, the Lord had moved me to read this psalm and I found I had a strong rapport with it. I came to the place where David cries in verse 15:

O Lord, open Thou my lips, and my mouth shall show forth Thy praise. For Thou hast no delight in sacrifice; were I to give a burnt offering, Thou wouldst not be pleased. The sacrifice acceptable to God is a broken spirit; a broken and contrite heart O God, Thou wilt not despise.

My diary reflects that the prospect of the Lord opening my lips that I could show forth His praise, was very important to me at that time. Little did I know how often that was destined to be the case!

My 1994 diary logs that people in those Vigil audiences had seen visions. For example, one person had seen an arch of lit torches, showing the face of Jesus, and then the arch opening out as He walked through with His arms outstretched – He was laughing during the word *hosanna* in the Sanctus from Fauré's 'Requiem'! Another lady saw the face of Christ almost like a sixth century icon above us the whole evening.

Significant times, significant Vigils

1995 had seen an incredible year packed with activity. This next *Vigil Tour* visited no less than six cities, Winchester, London, both Anglican and Catholic Cathedrals in Birmingham, then Manchester, Clifton (Bristol) and Bradford. My records show that we also invested around £1500 per night in those events! They were given free to all who wanted to come.

In May we launched a *Connoisseur Tour* of three venues, with an investment of a further £11,000. We held a summer concert in Hereford Cathedral, and then in July/August we were off to Salzburg for the shock of our lives when we almost lost the use of the *Everyman Stage (Jedermmanbuhne)* in the Domplatz, for our spectacular performance of the *Dance Messiah*! This had left us with a rift in our relationship with János Czifra – and yet I find an entry in my journal: *"We returned finding money in the bank!"*

Julia rehearses Wise and Foolish Virgins for ITV's 'Good Morning Sunday'

There was a deal of broadcasting! A recording of *Sunday Half Hour* at the Black Country Museum took place in September, then at the end of the month, Nigel had been on a Holy Land Pilgrimage with live broadcasts and recordings for a *Songs of Praise*; Nigel and I went on a recce back to Salzburg in the autumn half term, for a meeting at the *Festspielhaus* to discuss our recent horrific experience (!); next, we had *The Wise and Foolish Virgins Jazz Parable* featured on the *Good Morning Sunday* programme. We then contributed an eight-piece band to a *Songs of Praise on Ice* at the Blackpool Arena and finally charged into one of the most successful Christmas tours we had ever held – our *Grand Christmas Gala* in Symphony Hall, Birmingham, Colston Hall, Bristol, Free Trade Hall, Manchester and Westminster Central Hall, London.

Phew! I mention that astonishing list because it was typical of the sort of schedule we experienced during this decade when we were so busy giving out in all possible directions! No surprise then that we declared a sabbatical for almost eight months at this point to wait on God for future guidance.

As mentioned in Chapter 5 – *Whatever the weather*, these times of waiting upon the Lord were always so vital to the health of the NEO family and its work. We needed to come to a full stop and prioritise hearing the Lord, no matter that everything we were doing was proving a huge success. Usually these periods were hugely informative and this was no exception.

We embarked on 1996 with our sister ensemble, *The New European Orchestra (NEuO)* ratified in Switzerland under the leadership of Brigitta Hofer, with oversight and conducting by Nigel. We then decided to form regional prayer and planning groups in Bristol, Manchester and London, which were to prove a terrific help in our outreach work in those cities which was happening now on a regular basis.

Nigel experienced Africa for the first time in June and July as he went to record the programme for Radio 2 Arts also mentioned in Chapter 5 – *Whatever the weather...*

That was also the autumn when I first accompanied Nigel and Carolyn to Austria for a part holiday/part first ever recce to involve myself! We had much to discuss and plan for in Salzburg following our last encounter the previous year! But apart from these few events which did not include everyone, we waited on the Lord.

A much loved NEO venue, Hereford Cathedral

Our media work continued then on September 3rd with the thirty-fifth anniversary of BBC *Songs of Praise*, held in Symphony Hall, Birmingham – NEO providing the core music. We visited Hereford Cathedral again on December 5th, and finished the year with a further *Songs of Praise* broadcast with Nigel conducting the *NEuO* in Vienna in December. This involved only the European players. The programme was successfully received when broadcast on 29th December.

By 1997, we were well prepared for a longer tour of *Vigils*, spanning the first three months of the year in five venues, with various fellowship meetings and two further *Songs of Praise* programmes (Bournville and Clitheroe) in between. My diary comment records: *A great success, with all new groups functioning well in admin. Cathedrals were all full – Birmingham to overflowing. Need to rethink this for the future.*

These times were wonderful for NEO personnel too, as it gave us the space *we* also needed, despite the fact we had much to keep in mind as we performed our music. The times of silence were such a blessing to all present – even then silence was a rarity – these days it is almost impossible to find in the general day to day bustle of life. I was often called upon at that time, to write and deliver the prayers of intercession and supplication, and always found this an enormous privilege. The *Vigils* were I think, not only our gift to the people, but God's gift to us, fuelling our other engagements with His peace and renewing power.

That year saw us make new strides in Salzburg, as we not only held weekend events for Christians in the *Kapitelsaal*, but managed to celebrate our twenty-first birthday in the beautiful *Mozarteum* that summer, with a capacity audience. It was a brilliant evening, and actually a tribute to the restorative grace of the Lord, as we had felt this had been given to us at no cost, because of the debacle of 1995!

I do remember in one of our P & P meetings, where we shared the concept of the *Vigils*, that we commented how they were always going to be related to what was happening around us. By the August of this particular year, the nation was in shock at the death of Diana, Princess of Wales, and the church meanwhile, was rumbling with the various viewpoints coming out of the new 'Toronto Blessing' era!

We, meanwhile, launched our wonderful 'Vigil!' CD, which still comes up fresh every time. It was a very apt offering to the public at that moment in history. We also planned to have a *New Year Vigil* series in three cathedrals to open 1998, and to follow them up with one for *Shaftsbury Sunday* in Southwark Cathedral, London.

Centenary Square, Birmingham 19th July 1998

I had no idea at that time, but the next largest *Vigil* we would undertake was going to provide an interesting challenge the following year! (We had absolutely no clue then that the next decade would contain the eighty-thousand-strong *Papal Vigil* in Hyde Park in 2010!) By September 1997, I had held a site visit at Coventry Cathedral with a view to our first ever open-air national *Vigil* with fireworks! As it happened, we found, almost at the last moment when we could still feel we had a sensible 'lead time' for such an event, that we could not achieve this after all in the grounds of the ruin of the old Coventry Cathedral. I recall having a couple of weeks in which I asked the P & P to let me see if I could re-site it in Birmingham. The Lord answered our prayers, and I managed to hold a meeting with Birmingham City Council representatives, and was allowed the use of the enormous Centenary Square, which would hold up to ten thousand people! In fact around five thousand came – and it still seemed like a huge number. We had two covered stages erected, one for the NEO main performance area, and the second for our dancers. Fireworks were launched from the rooftops of the International Convention Centre, and a brilliant time was had by all! I still have a large sheet of paper on which I mapped out the event, which included not only our own performance needs, but the plethora of arrangements for security guards, information going out to local churches to invite hundreds to come, (bringing folding chairs, and their umbrellas just in case), police coverage – and so on! Looking back at this, it was like a micro-version of what Nigel, Martin Lowe (NEO Orchestral Secretary) and I were later to experience on the Standing Committee of the *Hyde Park Vigil*!

The stages at the International Convention Centre Centenary Square.

Vigil for the Nation Sign

1999

At the end of this year, we had felt we must hold Vigils again in preparation for the rather mind-blowing entry into a new millennium. *Vigil for the Millennium* then, happened in Bradford, Bristol and Manchester, followed by other events. It was an exciting and phenomenally busy period in all our lives.

2001 – '9/11'

This fateful year saw the awful and never-to-be-forgotten day of September 11ᵗʰ in the USA, and I happened, unusually, to have the television on at the point at which the breaking news switched to this cataclysmic series of events. It was like watching a nightmare happening. I rang Nigel and told him to put on his TV as this was 'history in the making'. We and the rest of the nation stared in disbelief as the two planes flew straight into the twin towers, and after the huge fires had roared through the buildings, eventually one by one they crumbled, with the attendant loss of so many lives and the ensuing grief of people all around the world. The landscape of that city was forever changed, but it was as though the whole world had shifted too.

2002

We responded to this with a series of *Vigils* for which we were joined by our dear friend Rev Bob Dunnett (formerly tutor at Birmingham Bible Institute and at this point in time worshipping at St John's Church, Harborne). We enlisted him to write and offer the prayers at the cathedrals of Rochester and Bradford, St Mary's Church, Watford, St Philip's Cathedral Birmingham, followed by those of Worcester and Manchester. These prayers were truly apt and written 'in the mirror of God's word'.

As I write this particular chapter, our nation is in the midst of its community celebrations for the ninetieth birthday of Queen Elizabeth II, which prompts me to recall that Bob included one item in the prayers of supplication which had been a private prayer of Queen Elizabeth I:

O LORD God everlasting, who reigns over the kingdoms of men, so teach me your Word and so strengthen me with your grace that I may feed your people with a faithful and true heart, and rule them prudently with power.

I acknowledge, O my King, that without you my throne is unstable, my seat unsure, my kingdom tottering, my life uncertain.

Therefore, O Lord, create in me a new heart, and so renew my spirit that your law may be my study, your truth my

delight, your Church my care, your people my crown, your righteousness my pleasure, your service my government.

So shall this my kingdom through you be established in peace.

Bob went on to complete it thus:

Grant, O Lord, that the sentiment and desire of this former Queen of ours may become the sentiment and desire of all those who currently rule us, in whatever sphere of office. Grant also, that among those who rule the nations of the world, the same sentiment may increase.

As I read those words today, my heart responds with a loud *Amen*! How we need to pray for our leaders. Along with the privilege of democracy comes the responsibility we all share in the governance of our nation.

We used what Nigel, in Newsletter No. 10 of that year described as *musical flavours from several continents including the sound of the tabla, the tambura and African drums mingling with traditional classical strings and wind instruments. Some of the poignant yet joyful music of Sting and Paul Simon (Graceland) stood beside Duke Ellington's Psalm 150, together with beautiful modern European church music, and special dances were composed to enhance the occasion.*

Similarly, in our Friends' magazine of the time, *Opus 15*, Nick Gerrard records the following comments contributed by people present:

This is theology. (David Ford, Regius Professor of Divinity at Cambridge)

I met God

God's presence was very much tangible throughout the whole evening.

The intense beauty of the violin solo forced me to cry with amazement. It was such a privilege to hear such an arresting clear tone. It made my heart dissolve.

Duke Ellington's 'Praise God' – shockingly outrageous vocal elaboration, brilliantly executed.

We did of course, always involve the clergy of the venues we visited, and here are some of the wonderful reactions from our archives from that time:

From Bishop Peter Selby, of Worcester, who incidentally, was also Bishop to HM Prisons. He wrote:

The NEO Vigil held in Worcester Cathedral was a very inspiring and thought-provoking event, in which I was glad to take part. The quality of performance was very high, and as a result the message of the occasion was conveyed in a direct and attractive way. I do hope such vigils can be held elsewhere and in particular that the NEO can be given the opportunity to put on a vigil in Westminster Hall.

(Such had been our hope – but in fact it did not come to pass.)

From Bishop David Smith, of Bradford:

I have now had the opportunity to be present at an NEO Vigil on two occasions and have been a participant in the event. The standard of production is of very high order indeed and is coupled with a sensitivity of approach which was much appreciated in a city such as Bradford. I am by temperament a little wary of some large religious events, but I was so impressed by the NEO that I commend their work without reservation. This is an evening of high quality and I came away feeling that I had been respected as a person and had been greatly encouraged in seeking to relate my faith to life.

From Bishop Christopher, of Manchester:

The New English Orchestra led a remarkable Vigil in Manchester Cathedral in March 2002. It was a wonderful occasion. People came from all over Greater Manchester – people of different ages, of different ethnic groups, of different faith communities. We came together to share our concern for God's world and its people, to contemplate and to pray with hope for the transformation of sadness into joy, war into peace, and poverty into healthy living.

The whole event was conceived, planned and led by the dedicated members of the New English Orchestra and its Choir. It was a hugely inspirational occasion that has led to the development of many new friendships.

I have a particularly hilarious memory of this Vigil series actually, the event in Bradford Cathedral in particular (despite the fact that for others it had been an incredibly difficult time). I had been responsible for organising a few acceptable refreshments for a small reception for our guests. These included representatives of various local faith groups. We were, as mentioned, featuring some Indian instruments, played beautifully by talented Indian Christian musicians we had encountered. (Their offering was a delight, particularly when merged with a simple Mass written years before, by the Fisherfolk. The affect was arresting!) However, for this particular buffet, I knew I would also be entertaining a couple from a local synagogue, and so was challenged to ensure I had Asian food, English food, *and* Kosher food available. I was eager to explain to the Jewish couple that in fact there were some rather nice mint chocolate creams I had introduced into the array as something sweet after the savouries. "Have you found them?" I asked, "They *are* Kosher!" The husband smiled at me and replied, "Thank you so much, but my wife is diabetic!"

One account in our Birmingham Cathedral report in Nick's Opus magazine, which I found fascinating, was written by Steve Adams, (husband of one of our dancers) who served as one of our NEO enablers for these events:

A man of Jamaican descent had been sitting in Birmingham Cathedral for an hour watching the rehearsal. We struck up a conversation and he explained he had come to Birmingham from overseas several months before to work on a youth project looking at curriculum for youths of Caribbean descent. He said he loved the space the cathedral provided and the sound of the music – though he was an atheist. He said that I was the first member of the public to have spoken to him since he arrived in Birmingham. We sat together in the performance – which he found stimulating, and to date, one month on, we are in weekly email contact, talking about our lives, experiences, space, God and hope. Clearly the Vigils were a sparking point for this relationship, a place where someone who was lonely and missing Jamaica found some light.

I believe such encounters have been a huge part of this ministry to individuals. So many important conversations have occurred over the last forty years, miraculously even across the barriers of language!

Jo Wright wrote for her church newsletter in Bristol, that she was *so taken by the occasion that I cried in certain pieces (Sanctum Nomen and Glory to God). Thankfully I had stuffed my pockets with Kleenex tissues before I left.*

Canterbury Cathedral ensemble

2009

The last actual series of this genre, *The Canterbury Vigils*, took place between June and November of this year, beginning at St Saviour's, Guildford, on June 13th, moving on to Wye Parish Church, on 4th July, St Luke's Church, Maidstone (*The Maidstone Vigil*) on 10th October, then Holy Trinity Church, Margate, on 7th November and finally Canterbury Cathedral, on 21st November.

I remember we were encouraged to look for the sign in the grounds of Canterbury Cathedral, which indicated the start of the Pilgrim route to Rome! We had in fact just completed this journey in reverse, having visited Rome in September, and October (see Chapter 15 – *To the saints in Rome...*)

This was an unforgettable tour for many reasons, some of which are not mentioned herein! However, we felt we must address the national concern about the financial crisis which was then occurring – and Nigel was inspired to view this from the stance of the nation's young people, who would of course be sufferers in any crisis, but who were definitely being affected in myriad ways. The prayers needed to deal with this carefully and I recall being deeply challenged in writing them. One of the venues had encountered particular problems with child abuse cases, and there was a discernible need to bring the powerful love of God into these areas through our worship and intercession, our instrumental music and our own personal demeanour. We were billeted with some wonderful families and shared much fellowship across this tour.

My husband and I stayed with a delightful couple who ran a Christian book shop. We were introduced by them to the ministry of Ffald-y-Brenin and the book written by Roy Godwin, "The Grace Outpouring". We tried subsequently to get hold of it, but everywhere had sold out. However, a good friend from around the corner popped one through our door a few months later, not knowing we been trying to acquire it. That started off another whole series of incidents which ended in us sharing this book with one of our number on a Rome tour, and it travelling right through her church as a result! Another common spin-off of our work together is what Nigel often calls the 'intricate lace-work' of our fellowship. It is truly creative, beautiful and inspiring – delicate and yet strong. Almost like a spider web: a touch in one place will resonate in another, as the Lord uses our own 'in house' conversations and experiences as well as our 'outreach' to others.

Rehearsal in Canterbury Cathedral

The final event in Canterbury Cathedral became particularly memorable, as an elderly man, visiting as a tourist with his daughter I believe, was taken ill with a heart attack at the back of the building during our rehearsal for the *Vigil*. While the paramedics were awaited, we were urged to continue singing, as he had apparently been so enjoying hearing us. Sadly, we later heard that the man had passed away. However, it seemed appropriate that we were there and worshipping the Lord with beautiful music at that particular moment. It was a poignant reminder that at every single point in our experience, the Lord is present.

Stunning Wells Cathedral exterior

Dr. Florence Odonga dancing!

Nigel with presenter Carol Vorderman on stage at Hyde Park

Vigil for the Nation, 1998. The now non-existent 'Forward' statue!

Vigil team at Hull

Andrew, Pete, Russell and Tim on brass with Andrew Whettam Hull

Fireworks!

Chrissie Townsend rehearsing a solo at Hereford Cathedral

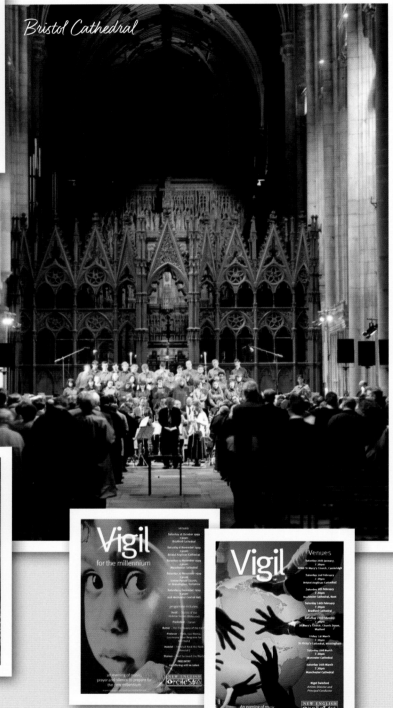

Bristol Cathedral

5

Whatever the weather, and whether or not we're well

I cannot omit from these memoirs some reference to the myriad occasions when we found ourselves up against it! *Up against what?* Well, that's the question, and one which I guess depends on one's point of view, seed of faith, experience of the workings of God and most important of all, knowledge of His word.

Thankfully, Nigel had been sufficiently trained in all the above, both prior to and throughout the years of this ministry, to recognise a contest when he saw it. Like the prophets of the Old Testament and also St Paul in the Acts of the Apostles, Nigel would see no problem in linking events on earth with those in the 'heavenlies'. He would sum up such occurrences, as did Paul, in terms of the effect of the principalities and powers the latter writes about in Ephesians 6 vv 10-12. Here is the excerpt, from the J B Phillips version we so often use in NEO:

In conclusion be strong, not in yourselves but in the Lord, in the power of His boundless resource. Put on God's complete armour so that you can successfully resist all the devil's methods of attack. For our fight is not against any physical enemy: it is against organisations and powers that are spiritual. We are up against the unseen power that controls this dark world, and spiritual agents from the very headquarters of evil.

In any overview of forty years of NEO, I think it could be said that in this ministry, we encountered elements of spiritual warfare under four main headings:

- Weather events
- Illness and threat to family or personal possessions
- Communications
- Encounters with 'institutions'

Nigel often chose to refer to such principalities and powers, as 'systems of thought' prevalent in society, and particularly active in terms of the various institutions whose judgements and regulations have such an impact on our lives. He frequently repeated this teaching, particularly during our away tours. It was always valid! However, those of us who had been involved with NEO from its earlier days, (especially abroad in Salzburg), learned first-hand and very quickly, that heavenly battles can have a particularly devastating effect on earthly weather! Nigel often reminded us not to be surprised that such contests have an effect on the cosmos.

As mentioned, I joined this ministry at the beginning of 1985, and my family and I were to take part in the summer tour to Salzburg, (the fifth of its kind, but our first experience). We were told to expect both hot sun, pelting rain and high levels of humidity, because of the alpine climate. The city itself sits on a plain, but mountains surround it so that currents of air will rise over them, developing impressive clouds, which then disgorge all over Salzburg, often at highly inconvenient moments!

I was soon to learn however, that there was more to this than met the eye in this gloriously beautiful country of Austria. Nigel had composed his wonderful 'Symphony of the Nations', which imagined what might happen at Christ's return – what would be the particular issues from which each nation had suffered, and which Christ would heal? How would they each express their rejoicing in music, song and dance? Austria appeared to have a fascination with the occult and with superstition, particularly in the mountainous areas, which had held sway over many years. This almost certainly affected its culture and history and contributed to a vulnerability both in terms of church and state. Its borders were constantly assailed in the startling events which have taken place since the days of the Austro-Hungarian Empire. As I write, this is of course very much still the case, with the huge movement across the world of hundreds of thousands of refugees from the Middle East, many of whom have found their way into Austria.

One of the first sights I noticed when walking through the Old City of Salzburg for the first time, were the little witch dolls on broomsticks being sold in the Altermarkt (Old Market Place), which I was told were very common and traditional! For such things to have apparently lost their essence and become mere trinkets for the amusement of tourists, was, I thought, a sad state of affairs. We had been warned before embarking on this tour, that the history of NEO's visits (marked clearly by the memoirs of Chris Bell in Chapter 1 – *Kicking the ball off the spot!*) were chequered by encountering spiritual warfare. This glorious new piece expressed the life of four separate nations: Britain, Austria, South America (particularly Argentina) and Israel. It involved players, singers and dancers all working seamlessly together. It was obvious that the leadership of NEO, though thrilled to be taking such a dynamic spectacle at that time, were aware it might literally 'cause a storm'! It did!

Ruth Miller writes in her wonderful 1985 prayer letter report following the tour:

Symphony of the Nations

Somehow the weather was an indication of the spiritual battle that was raging in heavenly places. You will remember that this work was designed to be performed in the open air, and that this summer has been exceptional throughout Europe. During the day on Monday 29th July, while the heavy work of erecting the staging took place, the sun beat down with temperatures in the Kapitelplatz in the 100s. However, as when Jesus was on His way to deliver a man of unclean spirits and a storm tried to prevent Him (Mark 4 v 35 onwards), when we had all arrived in the evening, it began to rain. There was a great determination among the party to perform. We huddled under some archways, sang choruses and prayed until the rain eased.

Lizzie Swinford and Mike Castle as Mary and Jesus

We played a few short pieces (including the Hallelujah Chorus), but the rain returned. By this stage, human excitement was washed away and we were reminded of what the Lord had brought us that morning in our worship time. From Mark 14 vv 1-9 we learned that our talents were not just to be offered to the Lord, but that the box had to be broken in order that the perfume should flow. For many, to play and sing and dance in such conditions involved great sacrifice of gifts and a total act of faith. Stringed instruments particularly can be damaged by rain, music print can run, and the special dance flooring was very slippery when wet. However, we were able to complete the performance since the rain stopped after we had begun.

On the second occasion, on Thursday, 1st August, it all seemed very familiar as the clouds rolled over, but we sensed that the situation was different. Again, we sang praise under the arches and watched the sky but there was no sign of change, and throughout the party there was a sense of peace that we should go home and have an early night! We had originally planned only 2 performances, and by that stage of the tour there had been other strategic moves.

Monday, 5th August

As someone remarked early in the morning, 'a typical Kapitelplatz day', i.e. clear sky and hot sun during the setting up work in the city centre. Many in the party were sunbathing until the last possible moment, but then the dramatic change. As our first group of performers entered

Jedermannbuhne, Domplatz, 1987

the square, the rain began. It quickly became the severe storm which was reported in the British press. We again stood under the arches singing praise songs and watching gales which were destroying trees around the city, and thunder and lightning. Good weather was on the way, but as we watched it coming, the wind blowing the flag on the castle was coming the other way. For half an hour the weather travelled in opposite directions, but a beautiful rainbow assured us that God was in control. Eventually the rain eased, but we had to move quickly. The police had visited the Kapitelplatz twice to insist that we finished when our performing permission expired at 11pm. It was after 9.30pm when we began, so we had to keep 'up tempo'. We were able to complete the work, but as the dancers and singers had just left the stage, the clock struck 11pm ...and the rain began and continued for 36 hours.

We praise God for the way in which we have seen His hand in control of the weather and for the privilege of being able to perform this work in this central place. Despite the weather conditions, many sat through the entire

performances and the reception was enthusiastic, touching the hearts of the Austrians.

Quotations from some of our Austrian friends:

"Austria reckons with you because you keep coming back!"

"You're getting to the roots of our culture, it will be tough."

"You don't know what you've done for our people."

"Whatever you do, don't stop!"

"All of you are exactly where God wants you to be in this spiritual fight. We are thankful that you have experienced this fight, and that God in His mercy made it possible that you could play and dance. It's nothing we've earned, it's His grace. It's Jesus saying 'Stop it!' and the evil spirits had to stop it." (From a letter received since our return).

Jedermannbuhne in the growing dusk

These extracts from Ruth's prayer letter are a testament to the reality of the spiritual battle, which was felt by those Austrians who loved the Lord and were able to recognise both the real source of their trials and the active compassion of the true Author and Finisher of their faith! Often we have been called upon to engage with the powers and principalities Paul speaks of, whether or not the members of our audiences have been aware of it. In other words, we have often battled on their behalf. Here however, there were people who could see only too clearly what our work represented. They felt the force of it and were glad and grateful.

Be counter-culture: work from a place of rest, not rest from a place of work!

Salzburg 1987

This turned out to be an extraordinary visit for NEO, heralding the first time we had ever been allowed to perform on the *Jedermannbuhne* (the stage set up each summer outside the Dom for the famous *Everyman* play) on a truly glorious evening under a beautiful night sky. In Chapter 3 – *Of Mountains...*, I refer to the moment in which we walked into the University Church (on 29th July to be precise) to be met by a ghastly scaffold with body parts hanging from it. Tony Pokorny wrote in his Austrian Bible Mission News Letter:

Several days during that week, a theatre company performed what was to have been a religious play, 'The Book of the Seven Seals', supposed to be based on St John's Revelation. As we got into the church, we found in the centre a huge metal scaffolding, decorated with odd parts of the body and some weird things hanging about. Some of the actors, we were told, and read about in the papers, appeared topless and put on an outrageous show. This aroused popular reaction in the press and on TV news, particularly as it happened in a church, and it resulted that the actors were prevented from performing only the musical part and in a few days it was stopped altogether. Our concert took place just in the middle of all this. However, we had a full church and a wonderful response from the congregation.

Nigel wrote a detailed letter to all participants before this tour, from which I want to extract just these five short 'hints' he gave us for our preparation, which I think, against the backdrop of the above scenario, were very timely!

1. *We can expect to know God's love and power in a wonderful way both as individuals and as a group.*

2. *We shall see great victories and triumphs.*

3. *Things will not always be easy. Our maturity and faith will be tested and sometimes there may be real difficulties and unexpected trials. The enemy hates what we are doing and will oppose it. But we shall learn about being "more than conquerors through Him that loved us."*

4. *It will be helpful to remember that the operation is not a Christian conference or a course. It is an aggressive act. We are part of Christ's army going out to gain ground for Him. It's important to grasp that we are not going to Salzburg for our own benefit or blessing, or even to get ourselves 'sorted out', but to fight for Him.*

5. *It's not a cosy little concert tour. As we go out, there is the usual number of unknowns. From this distance it is not always easy to know how practical the seating/standing/dancing arrangements will be. Sometimes when things are inconvenient we have to remember that we're not there just to enjoy performing, but are part of Christ's much greater purposes.*

Salzburg 1995!

This surely goes down in history as one of the Lord's great conquests for NEO! We had planned to take a spectacular performance to the famous *Jedermann* Stage, situated outside the Dom, and had booked a number of fine dancers to create a danced version of Handel's 'Messiah' (very slightly abridged). This involved not only our own singers' rehearsals, but extra ones for dancers (their costumes having had to be purchased, or hand-made by Nige's wife Caro). It introduced amazing choreography of high quality, created by the dancers themselves, all of whom travelled miles to and from rehearsals, over a period of six months. There was also of course, the cost per head of coming on this tour (paid by each individual) and the efforts of the team of enablers who had to work so hard to set up these large open air events, lay dance floor etc.

The problem had begun when ORF (the national television station) had applied for use of the stage on the same day and time as our booking. The ensuing mix-up left us with no booking for our Dance Messiah performance.

Lizzie Swinford, Sarah Christopher and Liz Cassidy

Living statues

Hiroshi Gunji, Prof János Czifra and Nigel

So we arrived to find this challenge staring us in the face in the form of a huge metal construction housing a large screen which was being used to show film of operas which had been staged in Salzburg in previous years! In short, we were unable to use the stage.

We had for some time been working closely and happily with János, who in his post as Music Director for the Cathedral, which was closely interlinked with the International Music Festival, providing church concerts as part of its programming. We had been invited to share in joint performances and a couple of times we worked with a Japanese choir, whose conductor would be allowed to conduct our orchestra. This in itself was not always an easy situation. I recall the Japanese maestro who came out on this occasion had at times reduced one or two of our female players to tears, either by his rather different approach from Nigel's, or because of the long hours they were expected to

work with him! The choir members were delightful and from the many little gifts and souvenirs they gave us, obviously all 'black belts' in origami! We had all prepared an open-air performance of Mendelssohn's 'Elijah'. Their singers would join with ours, some of our soloists would join theirs, and we would all be accompanied by our orchestra.

Faced however, with this impasse on the *Dance Messiah* front, Nigel and the P & P concluded, with deep regret, that there was no alternative but for Nigel and Roger Beasley, with input from Matt Baynham (the latter both experienced advisors who understood the ins and outs of spiritual contest) to take the stance that if the stage were not released to us as booked, we must cancel our involvement in the 'Elijah' performance. (Meanwhile, at the hostel, rehearsals took a break as all the NEO families gathered to pray!) The Press were going to be informed (it was noted) and in short, this would have caused such an impossible situation that János capitulated and contacted ORF, who reluctantly agreed to withdraw and take down their screen! It was a horrible experience for us all, and one we wished had never had to occur, but we had to deal with it as well and as honourably as we could, bearing in mind the cost to NEO personnel who had given so much to be there for this performance as well as other scheduled events using excerpts from it. The publicity had gone out of course, and our supporters were expecting a spectacular evening.

Coming now to the day itself – our enablers arrived (Pete was one of them and has vivid memories of the occasion) to find the burly technicians working on behalf of ORF to dismantle the large screen. They were 'not happy'! One of them, a large man with attitude, spoke to Pete, who was working with Peter Mortimore, and insisted that there was a huge storm due to blow in that evening and that there was no way we would be able to perform anyway! Pete recalls how Peter Mortimore responded graciously and with faith, stating "No, it will be fine, our God will help us!" So the NEO lorry drove in, the scene was set, we all arrived and 'top and tailed' the performance on stage with the dancers, and the audience began to gather on the tiered wooden seats. We knew we had to end and de-rig as ever, at 11pm.

The performance was exquisite in every sense, and is beautifully captured by Peter Mortimore on video (now DVD) thankfully! (We now have a huge number of lovely visible memories of our work thanks to his efforts and those of other friends, as listed later in *Appendix III* – *Their sound has gone out* and *Caught on camera*). Having watched this very recently, it still brings a lump to the throat in places, as dancers en pointe, or in jazz shoes, displayed their skill in interpreting Scripture to music so wonderfully – the orchestra, singers and soloists all blending seamlessly together under the lights, against the backdrop of the huge cathedral and its gigantic statues. The clouds gathered, a chill breeze blew up, and we continued through to the final glorious 'Amen Chorus' – in the last few bars of which, the first heavy raindrops began to fall, wetting the dance floor, and causing Abigail Butler, one of our young dancers, to briefly slip and fall, and quickly regain her position, to continue dancing in an impressively professional manner! Then it was over – we had completed the performance to a delighted audience and the rain began in earnest as everyone scattered and the NEO team began the de-rig. What could have been utter disaster became the Lord's own triumph over the elements.

Some may find difficulty in regarding all the above occasions as 'spiritual warfare'. Wasn't it just bad luck – the element of human error, plus the type of weather which is a recurrent problem in such a climate? I would have to reply, that in looking back over the years at those events which I have witnessed first-hand, and those I have heard recounted by others, we have encountered this far too often for it to be considered coincidental. From the very clear perspective which hindsight brings, these things have usually occurred in strategic sites, at the point of a significantly powerful event or production, and have usually also resulted in a significant spiritual breakthrough of some kind. I would have to state to the unconvinced – it's difficult to argue with forty years' experience!

The sad part of the above account was that our friendship with János became very strained for some twenty years afterwards, though we were often in contact with him as he was always involved in our applications for permission to hold our *Recreatio* events in the Dom in later years. We ceased working with him, simply because he no longer requested us to, but even that was, I now believe, within the Lord's plan for us, as He thereby led us into greater freedom to plan our own tours. He gave us the venues we prayed for, and we were not beholden to setting aside a large part of each tour to do various joint ventures, often costly to our own endeavours. However, there is a happy outcome to this story – which can be found in Chapter 17 – *The Phenomenon of the Recce*!

The 'Ash Cloud' Tour! Salzburg – April 2010

I can best open this story with the prayer letter I found myself called upon to write immediately before the tour:

Dear Friends,

Please could I ask you to pray for the New English Orchestra team who will be working in Salzburg this week? I and a few others are going ahead today, and the others arrive on Monday evening. For some time now, whenever we have held events in Salzburg, the Christians, of all denominations, and particularly people from the fringes of the church, have told us that our music helps them to see the Lord more clearly and they have often asked us to sing songs about Jesus – because this feeds them. So at last, this is what we are doing – instead of our usual outreach, we are doing 'inreach'! Our mission is to feed the lambs.

We are performing four events from Tuesday to Friday, at 8pm, which will explore the dimensions of the love of God, as described in Ephesians 3. Tuesday will look at the breadth and length, Wednesday will be a concert to welcome any newcomers people have brought along, and then Thursday will look at the depth – and here we'll be tackling some serious issues like suffering and pain. On Friday we shall look at the glorious height of God's love. We shall use music and singing, dramatic presentation, dance and some visual symbolism throughout the church – but the events are interspersed throughout with scripture on these themes, read in both English and German.

We planned this some months ago, and the new Abbot of St Peter's Monastery Church was to be our host and to do the German readings – but just about a month ago, he was suddenly accused of an incident of child abuse which had taken place forty years previously, before he was a priest. He had to resign his post and has now gone, leaving the monastery brothers and also the church in general in Salzburg in a state of shock and horror, especially in the wake of all the international media on this subject in the Catholic Church at the moment. So it's into this situation that we are calling God's people to stand together – Catholics and Protestants alike, from all the denominations in the city, to resist the temptation to slag each other off, and come and study the full extent of the love of God.

We're a very small team. Each person is essential and three of them have been ill this week and are only just about in

recovery now. Please pray for us all but most of all that God will act and will bring healing and restoration to these lovely Austrian people. Many thanks,

Blessings and love,

Julie

To follow, here is Nigel's comment in our subsequent bulletin, followed by my own:

It was an extraordinary time – Salzburg 2010. "When the Lord restored the fortunes of Zion, we were like those who dream." (Psalm 126 v 1). It seemed like a dream to me. On the last night we sang, as a recessional, 'You shall go out with joy' – and I literally felt as though I was walking on air. It was that rare privilege of having seen something before in vision, then watching the reality, yet being unable to spot any differences! The visions were challenging indeed: a red cord (or as it turned out, a foot-wide band of material) had to extend across the width of St. Peter's to illustrate the width of the love of Christ (Ephesians 3 vv 14 ff). It had to be high in the air. Then a long band of the same material had to extend the whole length of the Abbey – at a considerable height, to illustrate the length, the everlasting nature of His love. How could this be achieved? Our dear friend, the artist Michaela Helfer, working with the young monk, Brother Virgil, caused it to happen in a remarkable way. It was discovered that there was an unobtrusive pulley, which when operated electronically, descended from the vast cupola of St Peter's and could be used to cause these wonderful red bands to rise up high in the air. The effect for the audience sitting in the pews was to be able to look up and see, way above their heads, a huge cross made up of the width and length of Christ's love, while underneath we sang, played and spoke holy words and music about redemption, grace, mercy and peace with God. And that was only one of the four nights.

The purpose of the Arts in the Lord's business is to cause, by the power of the Spirit, Gospel information to drop the nine inches from someone's head into their heart, thus causing them to experience the Lord very deeply. These 'Moving Pictures' were in effect, teaching evenings, but it was the teaching of the heart, not just the mind that we were concerned with. They were gifts to the body of Christ in Salzburg; and the Lord's people came to receive in excellent numbers. The Lord blessed His people. The lambs were fed.

These 'Moving Pictures' were a kind of distillation of everything the NEO stands for. The music and musicians were fantastic in all respects – sublime singing and playing, yet we had moved into a realm which was way beyond music. The music was an essential part of something infinitely greater, which it was expressing: the very Word of life.

Julie continues:

Nigel asked me to pop down a few thoughts, and really it's an almost impossible task to choose from the many memories I shall keep of that time. I think Amy Chidley coined the phrase 'other-worldly' to describe how it felt out there – and how difficult it was therefore to adjust to being home afterwards.

As is so often the case, there were folk who struggled bravely with all sorts of issues either back at home or within themselves, including illness, but my abiding memory will be of my simultaneously marvelling at the beauty of the improvisations played by various ones in our company, and being unable to take my eyes from the faces of the people who came to explore with us the huge dimensions of the love of God. We had no idea whether the publicity (sent only by email to be printed off in each church etc.) would work, and anyone would actually come. But on the first evening, there they were – not an absolutely full church, but many faces we recognised, many more we didn't. They were muffled up in their cold weather gear, and sat on those hard and uncomfortable pews throughout the whole presentation – gazing upward in astonishment as the glorious visual aids created by Michaela Helfer appeared, one by one.

That first evening tackled the breadth and length of the love of God. First, they watched as Simon Johnston (one of our Singers) stretched out his arms as the narrator read: "I asked Jesus how much He loved me. He said, 'This much' and stretched out His arms and died." Then Simon completed a slow and 'painful' symbolic walk down the length of the aisle, 'out into the wilderness' carrying a huge burden on his back, as did the goat carry the sins of the people far away to an uninhabited place. The Bible readings were very clear in every sense, and read beautifully by Samuel Lange (so

St. Peter's and the length and breadth of God's love

usefully bilingual!) A band of red fabric was slowly stretched right across the front of the church from balcony to balcony – and then Michaela unrolled from the back of the church a hugely long band which she eventually attached to a small hoist coming down from the cupola and operated by a discreet remote control which lifted it way up high, to form a gigantic cross with the first piece. I had seen it in rehearsal – the congregation had not. It was an effective tool.

It was whilst some of us were sitting in a restaurant having lunch that I recall Thea Hoelscher telephoning to let us know that Pater Benedikt had rung, asking his brothers and sisters in NEO to offer 'ceaseless prayer' as, to our astonishment, the vote was to be taken the next morning (Wednesday) for the new Abbot of St Peter's Monastery. We realised how important it was that our visit had coincided with this vital decision. (This tour had originally been planned for the first week in March, but had been postponed. As you know, there then followed the breaking news of the Abbot's resignation – and now this!)

The Church, as mentioned, was extremely cold. But these members of the body of Christ in Salzburg came back, night after night. The next evening of course was a wonderful, bright concert. My memory of that one will be Hannah Monkhouse playing an astounding cello solo, for which Nigel invited those at the back to come up to the front and sides to get a closer view before she began. In our summing up at the end of the week, Hannah told how a lady had come up to her after the concert to express how moved she was by the playing, and how she had found 'a new relationship with the Lord' as a consequence.

The next evening, which we spent studying the depth of God's love, who could describe? We tackled some extremely moving music, e.g. the 'Preisner Lacrimosa' and the evocative spiritual, 'Lord how come me here?' to name but two pieces. Pater Benedikt, our dear friend, had agreed a while ago to be with us for that evening to preside and do the readings in German, whilst Samuel switched where necessary, to English! That very morning, the result of the vote had been that the post of Abbot had been delayed for three years, and Pater Benedikt himself was appointed as Administrator of the Abbey. We watched as the red fabric fell in two long pieces from the balconies to the ground, and was gathered and put into Benedikt's hands while he read the Scriptures. God's love can be relied upon to reach far deeper than anything we can experience. My personal 'special moment' that evening was hearing again the beautiful 'Lydian Healing Piece' which Nigel wrote years ago as part of the Feast of Trumpets. It was so perfect at this point.

Later in the programme, Benedikt was to address the whole assembled congregation of the Christians of Salzburg, from all denominations and from both Catholic and Protestant confessions – and thank them for their prayers and ask them to continue in prayer for the Monastery as it went forward out of this recent sad experience. He referred to the NEO as God's gift at this time. It was a deeply moving moment. We continue to pray for him and for all the brothers in this ancient place of witness to Christ.

And finally came the evening which celebrated the height of God's love. This time the stunning visual was a bright

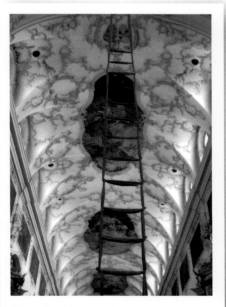

The ladder to heaven!

red, rather huge ladder, which (again attached to the hoist), soared up above just in front of the altar area behind the Singers – as we were singing 'Soon and very soon, we are goin' to see the King'! Again the faces were a sight to see. Pages could be filled on each of these evenings as you can tell, but suffice it to say that I can't remember such a feast of joy as we recessed out of the church singing, 'You shall go out with joy and be led forth with peace'. Every person in the church was on their feet clapping, smiling, laughing, as we virtually danced down the aisle! We ended though, at Benedikt's behest, by singing, 'Be still and know that I am God' at the back, and allowing the Lord space to continue blessing as He wished.

And yes, we'd heard the news early on Thursday morning of the volcano and the closed airports and the fact that we probably couldn't get home – and I would love to spend another few pages telling you the astonishing answers to prayer which brought us all back, most of us with incredible speed and efficiency. At least one couple felt they might have been not only entertaining angels unawares, but driven home by one! How can one give thanks to God for such love? I can only suggest that you read, as we did, Ephesians.3 vv 14 to 19, and yes on to 20 and 21, and marvel, as we did, at just how much He does love us all, and how He can do infinitely more than we ever dare to ask or imagine!

More next week from Matthew Baynham...

With love,

Nigel and Julie

And finally, here is that wonderful contribution from Matthew. Few could describe it better!

Immortal diamond

Icelandic volcanoes do not, on any reading, erupt because twenty Christian musicians are playing for a few hundred people in a cold church in Salzburg. To particularise such an event – to relate its significance to the priorities, however spiritual, of an individual Christian or group of Christians – must surely be some kind of mistake. We all understand this perfectly well in the NEO, and at one level we perfectly well accept it: but we pack our tin hats anyway because it just keeps on happening. So, again with a kind of amused wonder, we note that our new venture in Salzburg was marked by circumstances of difficulty which none of us will ever forget, and which, for some of us, were really tough.

On the evening when Nigel's text in St Peter's church dealt with the depth of God's love, he was strikingly frank about those different aspects of our personalities than which the love of God is deeper: that Christ deals with us at a level beyond even our darkest temptations. So much of what we are taught now misses this: we seem to think that Christ tidies up the insecurities to which our particular kind of personality is prone, rather than creating in us something radically new, which is of deeper, even eternal, significance.

It struck me forcibly through the week that one aspect of personality is how you respond to difficulty. Do you confront it, fight it? Grin and bear it, make a joke of it? Deny it, try to get round it? Or perhaps what strikes one person as a difficulty does not have the same impact on another, whose personality is different. Take, er, me, for example: when details of organisation go wrong, it has very little impact on me at all, because I'm so congenitally disorganised that it's just like normal life. Or perhaps that's just my defence mechanism, or whatever those clever psychological profilers are calling it this week.

In the Salzburg week, I was particularly conscious, for some reason, that I was watching people I have known for thirty years and people I have known for only a few months, dealing with illness, and many other kinds of difficulty, in their own individual ways. They were surrounded by others,

Matt Baynham at play

again in both categories, unobtrusively but effectively supporting them. They all did it – and always have done it – very differently, according to their different personalities, but I found the Lord showing me that in every case, there was something going on beyond the individual personality and its coping strategies, something at a deeper and more precious level, which was directly related to Nigel's teaching, which shone brighter in adversity, and which was often deeply moving.

Ash, and its tendency to harden into glass (when passed through the turmoil of extreme heat), were something of a theme by the end of the week. Perhaps it was this that enabled me to find, in the work of the Catholic poet Gerard Manley Hopkins, a name which seems to fit what it was which was so admirable and so moving in my brothers and sisters...

> *"Flesh fade, and mortal trash fall to the residuary worm. World's wildfire, leave but ash In a flash, at a trumpet clash I am all at once what Christ is, since he was what I am, and this Jack, joke, poor potsherd, patch, matchwood, immortal diamond, Is become immortal diamond."*

Matthew Baynham

Julie continues:

For me, this visit with a smaller grouping of NEO personnel, proved one of the most memorable occasions in Salzburg, because of the intensity of the work itself. The music was both beautiful and powerful, but its effect, under the hand of God, rendered it rather more like a Molotov cocktail to our audiences! The scenario, into which we had walked, was one of turmoil at St Peter's monastery church, and our friend Pater Benedikt was in the midst of it all. As above, he was subsequently called upon to take the position of acting Abbot until the situation was finally resolved some years later, with the appointment of one of the other serving brothers, Pater Korbinian. So we were in on the beginnings of a very unsettled period in this, one of the oldest established churches in Europe. That had indeed been something about which we had been much in prayer before we ever left England.

I wish we had thought to take film of the presentations of the *Moving Pictures* depicting the love of God. It was a huge tribute to Michaela Helfer (a local artist and dancer) who not only devised the practical outworking of Nigel's ideas, but made them so effective by tireless hours of effort, during the span of the events themselves. Few people would have realised that one item, after being used in one presentation, had to be recreated overnight to form the next! Many people in this world are what might be termed 'visual learners' – something of which educationalists are more aware these days – but this definitely applies in the church also. The striking visual aids to the Scriptures were hugely effective and I shall never forget the looks on the faces of the congregation as they viewed the enormous red bands of material being raised to form the cross above their heads, or watched the incredible ladder rising to heaven! As Nigel intimated in his part of the bulletin above, that 'drop' from head to heart could be successfully made, and I doubt anyone who was present on those occasions will ever forget those scenes.

Here again there was sacrifice involved. The incident mentioned of Hannah, who played the cello solo, actually took place just at the point where Hannah felt she had not played her best, and was inwardly in some turmoil – and yet a woman encountered the Lord through her offering. Nigel continually reminds us that, as with the shattered alabaster box of perfume, the fragrance is strongest when it comes through our own brokenness (Mark 14). He also, in this our final year (2016), has exhorted us to remember that it's not ultimately our gifts the Lord wants, though He gave them to us for a purpose, but ultimately it is our whole selves He desires. Sometimes it's not until we are in some way fractured and the ability even to use those gifts is challenged, that we realise this fact more fully.

As mentioned, the timing of this tour had had to be changed for various reasons, landing us there at precisely the correct moment in God's scheme of things – but also landing us in pole position for the eruption of a certain Icelandic volcano at the end of the tour! My personal memory of this is that I was sitting happily at breakfast the morning before our departure for the UK, when our son Luke rang my mobile, asking if we knew that there had been a volcanic eruption which had sent a gigantic cloud of ash into the atmosphere, causing innumerable flights to be cancelled! Of course we had been very busy, and many of us knew nothing, so the news was rather a shock. A few of us had had to be accommodated for the last night at a Gasthof a little further out from Salzburg, and having left the hostel, we had to be kept informed next morning of what was going to happen.

I have to pay tribute here (as in so many other places in the NEO story) to Martin Lowe, who with his usual calm, unflustered, methodical way of dealing with any sudden logistical nightmare, decided on that morning he would take a little band to the airport and try a bit of flawless English negotiation! By persisting with our airlines (and with the undoubted help of the Lord), he found that we were eventually offered coaches to literally drive us all the way back to the UK! (May the person or persons who finally brought this about be forever blessed!) I also recall that this service only applied to some members of our party! Others had to make their own way by one means or another. Nigel and his family ended up having to stay a while elsewhere in Austria and then return much later, after great trial and expense along the way! Rebecca Nicolson, our bassoonist, was in contact with her family by mobile, and decided to take the opportunity of an adventure by train across Europe, as she needed to be back in time for a concert commitment! Another memory of my own, is of being at the Gasthof meanwhile, dealing with these various situations, some people finding themselves tired and quite emotionally upset by everything, and in some cases tearful. Ruth Miller, my dear friend, had herself been going through an extremely difficult time in her life and had been wonderfully upheld during this tour. I have known her to be a 'fighter' over many years, but I recall her dissolving into my arms with tears of relief when I was able to tell her that we were going home – even if it was by coach!

Nathan Laxton had just experienced Salzburg for the first time – a dangerous escapade if ever there was one! We

After the concert at Olten Church Switzerland

Hannah Parker, Andy Phillips, Fiona Ormiston and Andrea Young

Fiona Ormiston (choreography) , Hannah Parker, and Sam Openshaw

Caro, Fr Andrew Headon, Nigel, Monsignor Nicholas Hudson and Julie

Florence Odonga dancing at St Peter's Halliwell, her home church!

John and Lesley Thompson in Rome

March 2006 in Switzerland!

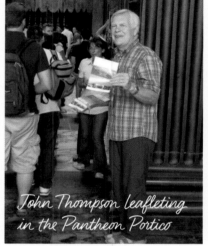
John Thompson leafleting in the Pantheon Portico

Our evening audience in the Domplatz

Our wonderful 'Messiah' dancers!

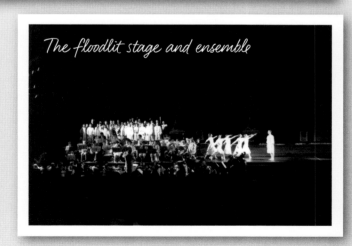
The floodlit stage and ensemble

often found that 'first-timers' were extraordinarily targeted. (Many found their suitcases mysteriously redirected to some far-flung place on the globe! In fact a few of our team experienced this much more recently on Rome flights also – and though they took it well, it was always an irritating nuisance, only ameliorated by the generosity and understanding of their team members.) First of all Nathan was extremely cold for most of the tour, not having brought quite the right gear with him, so hat, gloves etc. were purchased and other things borrowed to keep him alive and functioning! But also, I recall he had bitten into a sandwich and broken a tooth, and spent most of that tour in agony. He was astonishingly dedicated and determined to do all he came to do, but by the end, he was delighted to be going home! Such occurrences were not the last for Nathan!

The Gerrards (Nick, our Marketing Manager and tenor, and Nicola, principal flute) had an astonishing experience, having turned up at the airport to find themselves trying desperately to book a hire car in which they intended to drive all the way home – but of course loads of other people had had the same idea. They found themselves behind a British chap who, it turned out, had just secured the last vehicle permitted to leave Austria, and who apparently lived very close to them! 'Dave', not only insisted on doing all the driving, but on paying for the fuel costs, as his was some kind of business trip! For quite a while the Gerrards wondered whether this paragon was actually an 'angel in disguise'! Thanks to the provision of this wonderful character, Nick and Nicola were able to get home in record time (we kept up an exciting text commentary as I was on the coach) and they managed to arrive later that same day, as requested in prayer, before their young children woke up in the morning!

The coach journey home was otherwise not particularly pleasant, despite our gratitude for it. The drivers were on a tight timetable and we had very few fifteen minute comfort stops during the night and day – and barely time to find something to buy to eat or drink en route. However we were extremely glad to arrive back in Blighty! It had been an unforgettable tour, perhaps one of the most significant?

Our hosts' house in the snow

"Oh look, it's snowing!" Switzerland

Here, throughout the month of March 2006, we took three separate weekend trips to join Brigitta Hofer and some of her players from the NEuO (New European Orchestra) to work in Oberentfelden and various other towns, offering concerts to bless the Swiss! We stayed in people's homes

Oberentfelden 4th March 2006. Nick in the deep, deep snow!

and had a wonderful time together. However the second weekend was rather unforgettable for the fact that it began to snow, gently at first, and then heavily, continuing right through the weekend, day and night, such that reports from the media pronounced it the highest snowfall the area had experienced for thirty-one years! We literally had to dig out the car park at one point before people could park on arrival at a particular concert venue. I recall Matt Baynham being out there in his shirt sleeves in the freezing weather, digging away merrily and not seeming to feel the cold at all! It was a tribute to the nation of Switzerland, always so very efficient, that the public transport was not disrupted – I remember no cancellations, possibly just a train coming a second or so later than usual! How different from the UK, where it would definitely have been hailed as 'the wrong type of snow'!

The snow machine

Other random memories of that weekend include Helen Friday (alto soloist) slipping over and landing fully on her back in the snow laughing her head off, (Photo) and everyone refusing to help her up until she had been suitably captured on camera. Fiona Ormiston (soprano) built the cutest little snowman with twigs for arms, and there was much merriment, as we hadn't seen so much snow for ages! Pete and I were grateful for the lovely home we were invited to share with our kind hosts. I mention all the above, because whilst the weather may have been seen as just an

Helen Friday on her back having hysterics

unusual amount of snow that spring, we did feel that there was a relevance in the fact it arrived when we did, and was so significant statistically for the nation. It didn't mean that we didn't enjoy it, have fun, build memories out of it all – but we did take great care to be vigilant, to pray fervently for each rehearsal and concert, for all travel issues, for everyone to be freely available to get to the venues, both ourselves and our audiences. We didn't moan about it, we worked through it – and were hugely blessed, as were those who came.

Switzerland has an interesting history spiritually, and I recall we had a long and fascinating conversation with our host, who openly admitted that given Swiss church history, he no longer knew quite what to believe! I think several of our NEO personnel had meaningful conversations with their hosts and hostesses – and all were important. Perhaps fewer of those would have taken place if we had not been forced sometimes to stay indoors?

"Daddy, why is there a big hole in the roof?" (overheard in the Pantheon)

In Rome, mentioned elsewhere in its own chapter (Chapter 17 – *To the Saints in Rome...*) again we found ourselves in a fascinating and unique situation – performing in a huge ancient building, a church within a public monument, thereby requiring all sorts of permissions and good relationships to be forged with state, church and city council (not to mention the Carabinieri!). It had the added interest of the 'oculus' – a whacking great hole in its roof! The Pantheon

The Oculus in the Pantheon

was of course famous, among other things, for the fact that if it rained, it caused quite a stir within, giving the officials who worked there a hard time clearing up and adhering to health and safety regulations. The umpteen holes in the marble floor would normally allow the rainwater to drain away, but on the particular occasion I have in mind, the weather was rather unusual even for Rome. Normally, the locals explained, there was a wind which would blow through the city in August, to refresh and cool it, clearing away some of the humidity. But this year (2014) the wind had failed to arrive, and people were melting in the heat on days like the one to which I refer. It felt ominously like Salzburg to me!

We had completed our morning's work, and were returning for our next *Recreatio* only to find that the sky went a rather dull grey outside, a capricious breeze blew in and suddenly rain began pouring down through the oculus. All participants of that tour will never forget the 'Hallelujah chorus' during which an enormous peal of thunder roared out! My memory of the moment is of seeing all the folk who had been, until then, seated on the hundred and fifty or so chairs (arranged behind the usual pews by our faithful enablers) jumping up and running to the sides to get out of the rain – all except one lady, wearing a waterproof cape with a hood, who tucked herself inside it, and ran to actually sit on one of the soaking wet chairs so that she could see us better, smiling away as the rain poured down on her!

Pete met a couple who were celebrating their Golden Wedding anniversary and had been thrilled with the whole event – but the husband was particularly elated, as all his life he had longed to be in the Pantheon when it rained!

There was a definite 'draw' to this spectacle – but several dangers also. We were featuring a rather daring experiment on this particular occasion, in adding a Charleston dance to the already riotous and much loved song, 'The Hallelujah Meeting'. This had been designed to have a spectacular ending, in which Andrea Young (alto and dancer) was raised by the other dancers in a high lift. However, on this occasion she slipped and fell, and we were deeply grateful that the ankle was only bruised and not broken as a result. It was a huge tribute to Ian Pickup and our enablers that the wet areas were wiped dry as soon as possible, and because of their efficiency in taking care of ourselves and the audience throughout, we were able to continue with very little disruption to our plans that day.

Andrea Young – dance lift in Pantheon

A similar instance threatened in 2015, during our last tour to Rome – when we woke to torrential rain. It was so bad that we knew people would get soaked just trying to get into the city, and our P & P meeting that morning had the one big agenda item of how we would face this in terms of logistical layout in this extraordinary building! Martin Lowe, whose supreme gift is, as mentioned, logistics, was already thinking through a few possible ideas, but it was agreed that Nigel, Martin, Ian Pickup and I should go early by taxi to try out a few thoughts and check them with the officials. A problem arose however, in that the reception desk at Villa Maria, where we were staying, was unable to call us a taxi because of the sudden high demand across the city! At that moment I remember seeing Dirk Busse, one of our enablers, outside in his weatherproofs, having just come in from his car – I asked his daughter Angelika to enquire if he could possibly take us into the city and as near as he could to the Pantheon (which we knew would not be very near because of traffic regulations). He did this very willingly and dropped us at a point where we could hail a city centre taxi and go the rest of the way without getting too wet. It was quite a morning! Paul Thompson (husband of Binnie, one our singers) captured the ensuing pow-wow in the Pantheon on camera and posted it on Facebook, as we decided to move our position to one side to avoid instruments becoming spotted by the rain.

Pow-wow in the Pantheon

that by that time, the rain had stopped, the clouds had rolled away and the sun had suddenly come out and was shining brightly down through said hole in roof! At a time like that it would have been so good to have that totally prophetic skill to know that none of it would have been necessary (!) but as ever we dealt with what faced us, and though it meant that we seemed miles away from the folk sitting on the far side of the auditorium, there was one advantage to this new position. Unusually, I recall waking that morning at Villa Maria and being slightly niggled by a question in my mind: there was always a small altar (in front of the high altar in the Pantheon), which in previous visits, we had been allowed to move to one side, as it would otherwise stand between the singers and the orchestra – but as I came to consciousness

Wet weather contingency plans in the Pantheon

We managed all of this in time to squeeze in the singers and have a little rehearsal before the 11am event, only to find

The small altar in the Pantheon

that morning I remember thinking, "I wonder if it will be okay to move that little altar?" Sure enough, we were absolutely forbidden that day to move anything – and even my personal call to Monsignor Micheletti confirmed this. In fact we were actually observed by one of his priests, sent to the Pantheon especially, who watched to see that we didn't put a step out of place! This was unheard of and I still have no idea why it suddenly occurred on this tour. Consequently we had to work incredibly hard with our singing, to ensure we were in time and in tune with the players and also at the correct volume across all parts – tricky! We were not complaining, we still had the enormous privilege of playing in this astonishing venue, surely one of the best platforms in the world for sharing the Gospel in music. In our new position, it was great to have a more cohesive sound among ourselves for the remainder of that day. However, if there was one aspect which was similar to previous encounters with various 'threats' to our performance or performance space, it was the amount of extra work involved; time spent thinking and planning, having to go into the venue extra early, move the positioning, make the extra effort with the sound etc. It was absolutely fine as it turned out, but could so easily have become a distraction that could have spoiled the day. Such things are typical but they need to be well handled!

Gremlins in Cyber–Space!

I cannot tell of our 'away' tours without a mention of this phenomenon! If anyone needed convincing, following NEO's leap into the sphere of computer technology, that there is an enemy who objects strongly to this ministry – they should read and note the following!

I used to keep it on my wall, but it is now hidden in a file somewhere – my little page of 'Procedures' which Nigel set out for me when I first took the dual role of NEO Central Administrator and that of his own Personal Assistant. One of the items mentioned, was the need for me to be kept informed by Nigel and all NEO secretaries, of everything going on around me, and likewise I was in turn to keep all others informed of all information they would need for their own tasks. This process was helped enormously by our P & P meetings of course, but for the rest, like every other

communication barring mobile texts or actual phone calls, this had to be carried out by email.

I can remember a time when contacting János Czifra (Domkapellmeister) if he could not be reached by telephone, involved letter writing (yes, snail mail!) and waiting up to three weeks for a reply! So it was that with the next big rush of technical invention, a fax machine landed on my desk. I was delighted that with a few whirrs and clicks, and a length of thermal paper roll, I could literally receive the answer to my questions from Gertraud, his secretary, the very same day! Then we all hailed the arrival of the hyper-efficiency of email!

The rest is history! The reader will simply have to take it as truth that for years now, since I was given these roles in the NEO, and particularly since centralising the administration for our major trips to Salzburg and Rome, my computer has played up seriously before virtually every single tour! The other computer most prone to this type of behaviour was of course the one belonging to the Artistic Director! The timing was always impeccable. I am not going to spend too long on this as this chapter is meant ultimately to state the facts and bring glory to God for ensuring we overcame all these obstacles. I confess however, that this has been the one issue which has most often driven Nigel and me to utter distraction!

My most debilitating experience involved a serious hacking. I found myself, as is usual in these instances, locked out of my own email account. Normally this procedure is the instant reaction of the email provider, to protect the account, and normally it can be resolved by changing one's password. However, when I contacted BT (whom we use) this hacking had not shown up on their system and they were mystified. I was in the midst of a great deal of admin work, and each time I rang a technician (and was instantly transported to an unknown region in India) he or she began with the same questions and the same routine checks until I felt I could have usefully recorded my part in the conversation on tape for them! Enter the 'institution motif' here (of which I shall tell shortly) in that each technician is only allowed so many minutes for each client. We would get so far, and then they would have to ring off, promising either to ring back next day, or telling me to ring again and speak to another person!

After quite some days of this, I was desperate and prayed that the Lord would break through this impasse. I rang again and this time begged the technician to stay with me until we resolved this. He listened, put me on hold for a while (which turned out to be worth the deafening electronic 'music' which assaulted my ear) and returned to say his manager had given him special permission to extend his time! He remotely accessed my computer, but let me handle the various searches he wanted to make. Together we worked at it for quite some time, exploring all possible avenues, until at last we discovered the problem – an unknown email address sitting there, diverting all my emails to itself! The offender was noted and blocked officially by BT, and then I had to begin trying to contact all those whom I assumed were the most likely to have emailed me during that period.

It could be argued by some that of course it's never convenient for such things to occur – why make a fuss about what can happen to anyone? Again it's the timing that proves the case – somebody does not want you to get this information out – somebody is unhappy about this tour taking place – somebody wants to make your life a misery today. Be alert and ready! Even in the writing of this book there have been multiple issues and both Nigel and I had cause to send our computers away to be 'mended' on more than one occasion!

...and whether or not we're well!

Since working closely with Nigel, I have grown to love, as he does, the writings of J.B. Phillips. I have often searched out old books by him, and purchased them second-hand. One was entitled, 'Through the year with J.B. Phillips', and without actually quoting from it, one of his paragraphs concerned the phenomenon which he noticed, that it is possible for people to go about their daily lives fairly unhindered by any great or particular trial, until the moment they step into the kingdom of God. Then it's as though the enemy's focus is suddenly drawn to them, and they are soon made aware of all that Jesus Himself, and the writers of the New Testament letters, warned us about. However, the Lord is sovereign and able to both protect us and help us to either go through the ordeal aware of His grace, or take steps to stand against or defeat it.

Anthony Thompson

In Chapter 17 – *To the Saints in Rome,* you will read of Anthony Thompson, (principal trumpet) being struck down with severe tonsillitis and unable to play or rehearse until he came to each individual *Recreatio,* when he played perfectly. He went home at the end of the tour still unwell, until the condition healed naturally some weeks later!

As a teenager in the *Come Together* days I had a similar experience. There, we had with us in the audience the entire cast of *Lonesome Stone* from America – another Christian musical featuring some incredible singers and a big impact. So it was with some dismay that I found myself with a very sudden attack of laryngitis, unable to speak properly, let alone sing. I wondered what on earth I was supposed to do that night. In rehearsal, not having had much time to do anything other than whisper to some friends to pray for me, I stepped to the microphone, opened my mouth – and sang! It wasn't brilliant, but it was there. So again during the actual event, I mimed through all the choral parts and then went, with not a little sense of trepidation, to the microphone – and sang. In the section where we went out to greet members of the congregation, one of the American singers came up and said, "Are you struggling, honey?" I nodded, and I think she prayed for me. But I'm not sure she realised that there had been virtually no voice at all, except when I had to sing those solos!

I recall Lesley Thompson, one of our wonderful soprano soloists, coming to Baden Powell House in London to rehearse for a concert we were doing for Tearfund in 1987. It was Valentine's Day, and we were due to do an event in Westminster Central Hall. She had contracted gastric flu and was laid up in bed. She had rung Nigel to explain, and he had informed her that such things were quite common in NEO, and were just the enemy trying to stop her – so she should come anyway! Her doctor (a Christian elder of her church) had, at the start, forbidden her to travel, but a while later, he apparently arrived at her door telling her he had prayed, and she was to go! She encountered a dreadful journey and arrived still very ill and claiming she could not see how she could possibly do what we were expecting of her. A loving group drew around her and told her quite cheerfully, as had Nigel, that this often happened and that the Lord would take it away if we prayed. He did, and she sang beautifully. The Lord was preparing her for the many other then unforeseen and much weightier battles she would fight in her future – with enormous grace and an amazing heart.

Nick and Nicola Gerrard were in exactly the same position in the Bradford Vigil mentioned in Chapter 4 – *Vigil!*, which demanded huge determination from them both as they drove from their home, and then had to literally lie flat out on the floor in the vestry of the cathedral until they were called, Nick to join the singers and Nicola to play her flute. They did it! They never forgot it, but they did it! Daphne and Janet Ryland recall being in another room caring for equally sick children meanwhile!

The same happened again to Nick during our October 2009 trip to Rome to work with the Venerable English College (VEC) to celebrate their chapel refurbishment – and also to Amy Chidley, another of our brave women of God! I cannot relate every time this gifted lady has found herself struggling with health issues, some extremely emotionally upsetting, at exactly the point in time when called upon to make a specific and always significant contribution to NEO's ministry. But despite all she goes through, she comes up

Talented sisters Amy Chidley & Hannah Cawston in the Pantheon!

shining like gold. Nick and she (as two of only nine singers) were terribly ill during this tour – and it was made slightly more complex by the fact that on this occasion, we were staying at the College's 'Palazolla' accommodation, situated some distance from the city centre, and had to go in and out each day by coach through dense traffic.

The NEO ensemble in the Chapel

Refurbished Chapel at Venerable English College

Reviewing this particular Rome trip, to assist the Venerable English College with its celebrations in this memorable chapel, I began with hindsight, to realise its significance. The VEC had an astonishing history. On 27th January 1362, a group of English merchants had bought a house on what is now the Via Monserrato, to serve as a hostel for English and Welsh pilgrims to Rome. In 1579, it became a seminary for training Catholic priests who would return to England to serve. This then, is the oldest English building in Rome.

The walls were covered with frescos, which at first appeared beautiful, until I realised they contained the most vivid depictions of the tortures and various means of death inflicted on the priests during times of Protestant monarchy. One of these showed clearly a gate or archway, with a road leading through to a beautiful, verdant country, which, I believe, symbolised the start of their journey into England. However, they knew that it was very likely their end would be horrific.

Was it not an amazing incident then, that our ecumenical, but in that particular instance, very largely Protestant group, had been specifically invited into that chapel so many centuries later, to effectively lead worship for the college staff, students and all their guests? It was a strategic event in spiritual terms, as we gloried in the Lord together and contemplated, in our three *Recreatio* events that day, aspects of the priestly function, seen in the mysterious Melchizedek, the appointed Levite tribe, and of course ultimately in Christ, our eternal High Priest. No wonder then that there was a sense of something having been disturbed in the 'heavenlies'. Such matters as restoration and reconciliation (particularly from long historical divisions) understanding and harmony, appear to irritate the enemy intensely.

Institutions!

As mentioned at the start of this chapter, Nigel often refers to principalities and powers as 'systems of thought', and nowhere do we see this more clearly than when suddenly faced with one of the institutional bodies common in our society. As to their characteristics, they appear as rather amorphous groupings with a definite agenda to their corporate thinking. It's often difficult however, to find out

At the end of this tour, the weather also started up – we had the most terrific storm which raged through our last night, with wind howling through the corridors and setting doors banging. We had had troubles right from the start of the week, with some folk having to arrive late due to travel issues – but at this end of the tour, the situation became quite severe, with loud thunder and considerable lightning. The electric lights were taken out, such that when we rose early in the morning to prepare to leave, we had to do all literally by candlelight, treading very carefully down the long hallways and down winding stone steps to wait for our coaches. It was a memorable time, but a wonderful few days' work, reaching out to the many who came to join us to hear such pieces as the glorious 'Non vos relinquam' by Byrd – 'I will not leave you as orphans', spoken by Jesus in John's Gospel (chapter 14 v 18) which I recall being particularly beautiful in that acoustic.

where the real movers and shakers are hidden. One meets only representatives. They tend in general, I find, to deal not in grace but in law – and that, usually in minute detail.

These institutions for us in NEO, have appeared as anything from the established church (either Anglican or Catholic) to the Carabinieri in Rome, but the one with which we found ourselves intensively involved for several years, was the BBC. (See Chapter 11 – *The Media Decade,* for more of these stories).

Yes, it was a huge and worthwhile privilege placing ourselves at the disposal of a company which could reach audiences of millions instead of hundreds, but there were some drawbacks, not only for ourselves, but also sometimes for the producers who were also believers.

In July/August 1996, Nigel was invited to accompany a Christian radio producer to Africa to create an Arts programme for Radio 2. It featured the local handmade ethnic instruments and their unique sounds. I recall the whole trip was a massive experience for Nigel – such that he could hardly tell me anything about it afterwards – it had left such a deep impression on him. The programme was subsequently broadcast on October 19th of that year, between 11pm and midnight! It was beautiful, and very moving, and must have been well received by the public, as it was actually nominated for an award for Racial Equality and won the second prize. Nigel and I were away on one of our many recces when the awards ceremony took place, but the producer himself went along. He told Nigel later on however, that the 'powers that be' had subsequently told him quite clearly that he was *'…never to book Nigel Swinford for anything ever again.'* Such a comment seemed quite incredible.

Eventually a little light was cast on this, as Nigel had occasion to speak to another Christian producer and good friend, asking her why it was that when we had so many wonderful ideas and the ability to deliver them, they were never taken up? She replied quite honestly, explaining that he had in fact just stated the reason – they were NEO ideas, not BBC ones! I personally felt this situation was very sad, in view of the following, which can be found on the BBC website,

featuring the new London BBC building, now replete with modern works of art and with newer modes of expression alongside this original one:

Above the Sower statue is the gilded inscription placed there on the opening of the building in 1932. It reads:

This temple of the arts and muses is dedicated to Almighty God by the first Governors in the year of our Lord 1931, John Reith being Director-General. And they pray that good seed sown may bring forth good harvest, and that all things foul or hostile to peace may be banished thence, and that the people inclining their ear to whatsoever things are lovely and honest, whatsoever things are of good report, may tread the path of virtue and wisdom.

The stream had had a pure source, how had it become so trammelled? Nigel's view, shared on many occasions when teaching groups of NEO members on tour, is that the enemy tends to like to view 'institutional bodies' as his own personal territory. Readers may smile to read my comments in Chapter 11 – *The Media Decade,* about feeling that we were left swimming in the 'sprat tank', but we truly did feel that it was as though there were an invisible barrier placed – not actually around *us*, but around the BBC itself – which would only come down at very specific times, when it was felt safe to welcome in a particular project. Strange that the reason given for such action was all said to be down to the 'ratings' i.e. what *Joe Public* wanted. Strange, because it was almost embarrassing that so often when NEO had exposure via the media, the resultant mail, either to the BBC or to me or Nigel, were hugely positive. Somehow, some kind of 'fear' seemed to have been injected into the whole system. Thankfully there are still very good Christian programmes appearing on radio and television today nevertheless, but if I were to look back at our own involvement with the BBC, I would have to say my view is somewhat wistful – so much more could have been done with the wonderfully versatile outfit we were able to offer. Being involved in any institution trying to cope with 'what the public demands' is a challenge indeed, but we certainly had been attempting to assist people to 'incline their ear to whatsoever things are lovely and honest' and 'of good report'!

This institutional problem was also the cause of much of the hard graft Nigel and I had to put in when preparing for tours in the months beforehand. More of this can be found in Chapter 17 – *The Phenomenon of the Recce*. But perhaps it may be helpful at this point to clarify a few of the things we have learned over the years as a result of our experiences of spiritual warfare.

Powerful Principles – here are five helpful ones we have seen in action in NEO

1. The Power of Prayer

I recall reading a short while ago, how Charles Price, an American evangelist with a notable healing ministry, once commented to a friend in the aftermath of the Pearl Harbour incident during World War II, that contrary to popular belief, such a ministry as his was not all it might appear. He accentuated the need to understand that it was, topically at the time, like being 'on the front line' which of course is where people get hurt or even destroyed. He also made the point however, that he would often receive adulation for his ministry, but that this was of no importance to him – what truly thrilled him was when people let him know they were committed to *praying* for him!

One of our regular habits in the P & P, as directed by Nigel, was to hold days of prayer and fasting before any major event or tour. We normally held these on Thursdays. We observed them as each felt able, in their varying circumstances (most members having full time day jobs) and then came together in the evening, in Birmingham or wherever, for our regular fortnightly meeting, to share what each felt the Lord had given. These were precious times. Occasionally it was a matter of spending the meeting covering every detail together in prayer – but there were evenings when it seemed the contributions came in rapid fire from around the room, as each person was brimful of what they had heard or seen or felt during the day, or read in their daily readings. Such days, plus the regular prayer we put into those meetings for years and the prayers of our supporters generated by our bulletins, proved to be the powerhouse of the NEO ministry, as God answered, often very specifically.

We needed also to protect one another, as we were often sharing on a quite intimate level, because NEO for most of us, was a life calling – a major priority. As when a railroad is built, which forges through everything ahead in the landscape all things end up having to take it into consideration. As mentioned elsewhere, we often used to joke about the need to ensure all births, deaths and marriages were arranged around the NEO schedule, but in reality, this was often the case! No one can satisfactorily divorce that type of commitment from everything else that happens to them – their personal walk with God, their family life, their occupation, their health etc. This was a prime reason of course for the type of attack we often encountered, which didn't just affect the work itself, but our homes, our goods, our cars, our families.

All needs were shared with the team and with the Lord. The same applied of course to our intercession for all those in the ministry, in whatever role they played. We would hold issues confidential when required, but we could still name a loved one needing prayer. We never neglected such obvious matters as weather, travel, or the family members left behind, for example, when someone was going to be on tour. We prayed too, of course, for those whom the Lord would draw to our events, and often 'saw' some exciting possibilities as we prayed. It never failed to impress me that time and again I would be about to pray for a particular subject and someone else would pray for exactly that, and I know that was the experience of others too. By the appointed time we had covered everything that we could think of!

Sometimes vision was shared and there would be almost a corporate sigh of agreement around the room – at other times something might be suggested and everyone would have a different point of view – so we would need to apply one of Nigel's tried and tested methods: "Let's look at it from this angle, then run down to the other end of the corridor and look at it from there!" There was no hocus-pocus, we always knew this ministry had to walk on human legs and be intensely practical, even though the Lord would inevitably add to it His own unfathomable depths.

Why do I add all this into a chapter which is intrinsically about spiritual warfare? Well, I think because we learned that working together by these means – running NEO like a family which knew the Lord as its Head – kept us in a very strong position. We took great care never to become an institution ourselves – or even purely a business venture, (though latterly we had to become a charitable company which had to make its way in the world according to the law of the land). We did however, carefully consider such issues as finance, modus operandi (down to the last detail), and especially motive: why were we contemplating this? Why was this church or group of people asking us to do this? What does the Lord think about it? Does it fit what we have already been told? Will it detract from our aims or distract from other work in hand? All these deliberations not only helped us to make right choices, but gave us useful methods of testing everything. I have found them very applicable to many other situations in my life over the years, as have others, I'm sure.

Nevertheless, when all else has been attempted, there is no way we can adequately express our thanks to all those who have come alongside this ministry over the years, and interceded for us! It is to them that we owe so much. We have been astonished at the commitment of many of our praying supporters, who have remained faithful even though it may have been years since they were able to hear us in concert! Why does someone in Scotland or Wales continue praying for a music ministry which rarely visits their neck of the woods? Because they believe the Lord is in the midst of it, and as mentioned elsewhere, it has integrity – it's whole and complete, the genuine article. We have found that people either 'see' it or they don't. Mercifully, a great many saw it very clearly and we are so thankful for them.

Nigel, as the founder, the one to whom the Lord gave the vision and the one who has faithfully followed His leading, has very often been called upon to face physical illness and indeed some occasions when only God's enabling and his own courage have allowed him to do what has been required of him. I thought of him immediately I read the comments of Charles Price mentioned above. I will not, for Nigel's sake, elaborate too much here (there are specifics elsewhere as I have felt them to be relevant) but I do remember him saying to me once: "I find that if you can try

to be where you are supposed to be, to do what the Lord wants, He will usually help you to do it."

This is why on one occasion he chose to literally crawl on his hands and knees onto the platform of the Victoria Hall, Bolton to conduct, while smitten with a bout of labyrinthitis – an ear condition which made him incredibly dizzy and nauseous. It was a successful televised *Sankey Songs of Praise*, in which Nigel's own arrangements presented each item as though it had been selected from its historical treasure chest and presented with a fresh musical sparkle. The piano accompaniment was particularly wonderful. Nigel conducted it brilliantly and we felt God's grace. Afterwards we were told this programme drew a mailbag of six hundred letters of appreciative comment to the BBC!

Our power of choice is so important. God respects it I believe. Of course there are times when it is very obvious that we cannot take part in something, and we will usually recognise those times. At others, if we decide we just can't face it, He will probably accept that, but we may have to accept too that others may or may not be able to cover for our lack in that moment – changes may have to be made to 'what would have happened'. The NEO ministry has been designed in such a way that every person is important and would be missed. Another time though, when we choose to 'go for it' against all the apparent odds, the Lord will delight that we have grown in our determination, and we may discover more about His startling provision and His amazing grace. He may do great things with even our first small gesture of faithfulness and trust. That experience is the positive and indeed glorious side of the 'battle' and every inch worth the fight! Practice in the smaller instances, can only make us better equipped when faced with the huge ones. In fact it's often the smaller, but apparently incessant onslaughts that trouble us the most! A dear Cornish friend of mine once put it this way: "Dear," she would say, "it's not the great boulders in the road ahead that trip us up, we can see those and find our way around them – it's the little stones that fly in the wind... and my, how they sting!"

2. Humour!

I should add here that the camaraderie of NEO is an excellent foil to many situations. I stress I do not refer here

Cotswold Farm, our beautiful rehearsal venue

to flippancy – we always need to take any type of conflict seriously – but rather to the joy we have in Christ which produces 'good humour' even in the midst of our trials. As you read from Matthew in the 'ash cloud' account above, times of extreme difficulty can throw the worst at people and bring the best out of them, it seems. Those few important days in Rome, working at the VEC, had been prepared as we stayed for a weekend in the beautiful Costwold home of a dear friend of NEO – Iona Birchall. She had been marvellously helpful in sending me a detailed room plan so I could fit us all in as appropriately as possible. Somewhere in my stash of old memorabilia, I have that room plan, written out for a lark, in the manner of a 'whodunnit' – with each member of the NEO team being placed as though in a Cluedo game: "Mr or Miss so and so, in the ...room with a... usually their instrument). We had a wonderful time rehearsing in Iona's glorious library (well of course there *had* to be a library in the plot!). There was much special closeness of fellowship and prayerful conversation, teaching from Nigel and deepening of friendships in our shared rooms, before we left for this particular Rome adventure. Such is the grace of God and the provision of His people to help us en route with each project. We could never have anticipated how important that preparation would be. It was good to mingle the intensity with lightness and laughter.

Sometimes it's possible to encounter a real 'heaviness' in an audience, and it seems that no matter what you perform, the impact is not what was hoped for. Thankfully that hasn't happened often, but it can be quite a difficult thing to be faced with. One senses there is a contest over that particular group of people.

I often think of the times that Nigel has chosen to deliberately place what he calls 'a few *lollipops*' in a concert hall programme, which leaves the entire audience laughing. People suddenly lose the reserve which at the start of the evening barely allowed them to look at the person sitting in the next seat, and are now seen to be smiling and nodding knowingly to their neighbours! There is an overwhelming atmosphere of cheerful refreshment which sweeps through the auditorium, dispensing with inhibitions, breaking down barriers. However, the next item, coming in perhaps with a deeply vital spiritual message, then has a forceful impact, free to soar with unerring aim and implode in the hearts and minds of the hearers. I loved those moments especially! The enemy *detests* good clean fun!

Dimples

Blessed are the cracked, for they shall let in the light

3. Time spent waiting on God

As a P & P we would often agree upon a time of 'sabbatical' from public events, whilst we sought the Lord both together and individually, for the next step, if for any reason that was not clear. Those times were so important. Nigel would also keep a pastoral eye on us all, and note if we were going through a particularly challenging time in our personal lives. In such cases, he would suggest a personal sabbatical – a complete break from service for maybe six months or a year. Such times usually fulfilled their purpose and sent that particular team member back refreshed and able to continue in their role. The cessation of public events was particularly challenging for Nick, as Marketing Manager, as of course though this practice was recognisable to our Christian supporters and prayer partners, it was more difficult to express to the general concert going public we aimed to reach in our concerts! However, good communications were again the way forward. We never regretted for a moment the time spent in waiting and in prayer – it usually led to a particularly blessed renewal of vision, or an amendment to our modus operandi, and often a hefty and exciting workload!

4. Praise!

There is always the Biblical injunction to praise the Lord at all times – but times of warfare are particularly apt – and I do remember those times referred to in Ruth's prayer letter of 1985 (and once in 1987) when we gathered under the archways in Salzburg to sing praise songs to the Lord as the rain poured down. We had no idea then whether or not we would be allowed to perform, but the Lord was still worthy to be praised! We did not spend the time moaning about the weather or filling one another with miserable doubt! Just as in the Old Testament when the singers and musicians led the army into battle, praise is powerful!

5. Fellowship – and the 'Open Palm Principle'

Nigel has often said that many of life's problems can be solved by means of good fellowship. Over the years of this ministry, that has definitely been so. It was particularly the case in the special year of dedication in 2000 mentioned elsewhere in Chapter 10 – *Jubilee! Into the new Millennium*. It behoves us to keep fellowship healthy then, both at home in our church gatherings and within any ministry we undertake. I think it's probably in this context that we most need that vital principle which Nigel taught us from the very beginning of NEO – to hold everything on an 'open palm' – hence the title of this book.

Here is Philippians 2 vv 5-7, in which Paul expresses this about Christ Himself. I've quoted this from the Revised Standard Version as the wording is particularly apt:

*Have this mind among yourselves, which you have in Christ Jesus, who, though He was in the form of God, did not count equality with God a thing to be **grasped**, but emptied Himself, taking the form of a servant, being born in the likeness of men.*

Nigel always encouraged us to keep our involvement, not just in the work of NEO but in all our service for the Lord,

on an open hand, so that He is free to take it from us for a while, or even permanently, if He needs to. It's when we begin to *grasp* things, or to put it another way, to 'dig our heels in', that problems begin. Once we take on a role, either in a para-church organisation like NEO, or in our local congregation, and it becomes so much our own property that no one can take it from us without a fight, we have ceased to truly live in obedience and submission to the Lord. We also, to put it bluntly, can become a pain in the neck to our brothers and sisters!

It's a good principle for keeping a grip on our emotions too – it won't stop us feeling them, but it may help to keep them under control at those critical moments – say perhaps if we are not one of the ones chosen for a particular team or task. In NEO, it was vital that Nigel felt he had the freedom to use his own discretion in any given situation, the right of a conductor in a musical issue, or the casting vote in a vital trustee decision – rather like a football manager employing the 'squad system'.

In life, when we concede all rights to the Lord, then ultimately we will find ourselves where He wants us to be.

At the top of the next page is a photograph which captures a very poignant moment when all the string instruments had been left on the altar in one of the early Austrian venues! I think that says it all really!

Instruments laid on the altar

Giving all the praise to Jesus

Spotlit stage

Salzburg Dom and the stage in the Kapitelplatz 1985

Symphony of the Nations 1987

6
Acts '86 and Gothenburg '90
From Birmingham to Sweden

Acts 86 National Exhibition Centre

NEO was privileged to be invited to perform the *Symphony of the Nations* (mentioned in Chapter 3 – *Of Mountains...*) each evening, at a huge conference to be held in the National Exhibition Centre, West Midlands, in the summer of 1986. The speakers were to be Michael Green from the UK and John Wimber of the USA, Rev Canon David MacInnes (as he now is), and such familiar names to us as Rev Tom Walker (vicar of St John's Harborne at the time), Michael

Harper, Clive Calver, plus many others from around the world, including Jean Darnell, who had been instrumental in bringing the Owens' musicals to Birmingham all those years ago. (Chapter 2 – *Earliest Beginnings*). We very nearly had her billeted in our home!

This was a very exciting venture for us all and our input went down very well. So we were even more thrilled when we found that this conference (including the installation of its enormous stage backdrop, on what I believe may have been a large piece of canvas) was to be repeated four years later, in Gothenburg, Sweden, including the same main speakers, and the NEO! We were able to contribute our performances of concert items, together with movements from the symphony, and benefit from conference speakers as much as we were able, in return.

Nigel put much thought and prayer into this opportunity, and decided to write an extra movement for the nation of Sweden, to add on to the four nations already within the *Symphony*. He set about creating a hugely memorable piece about purity – using verses from Hosea – the prophet whom God called to address the issue of its antithesis among the children of Israel, by marrying a prostitute, and thus 'living out' the pain the Lord felt at the behaviour of His people as they indulged in idolatry instead of remaining faithful to Him.

Like the remainder of the symphony, this was a full scale dance production involving orchestra, singers, many excellent dancers and in this case, a number of young children, including our Lucy, aged eight at the time, the children of John and Jane Kane (two of our NEO string players), and the daughter of one of our dancers, Linda Wells. For Lucy, Nigel devised the role of the young and innocent 'Sweden', dancing and playing in the driven snow with her friends. Then, Lizzie Swinford takes the part of the now grown up 'Sweden', joining her in a danced duet, whilst the singers sing the verses adapted from Hosea 1 v 11: "When Israel (Sweden) was young, I loved her..."etc., after which they part, with a theatrical wave, and the mature Sweden bids farewell to her younger self.

Having rejoiced in her freedom in the Lord and the delight of all things provided for her in life, Sweden becomes distracted by the sound of modern music, coloured lights appear behind her on stage, and gradually the audience sees a group of people dressed like models, being served cocktails on trays by smart waiters, and beginning to dance to the music. Sweden joins in, finding herself gradually intoxicated by this new and unknown lifestyle. The music grows more strident, more demanding, almost robotic, and as the dancers lose control and seem to be possessed by the rhythm, making them jerk around in a hideous fashion.

Lucy dancing in Manchester Free Trade Hall

Lizzie joins Lucy

Then in a very dramatic flourish, appears the Scarlet Woman we meet in Revelation 17 – drunk with the blood of the saints and of the martyrs! The dancers, now in thrall to her, lift 'Sweden' and thrust her before the woman, who takes 'blood' from her chalice and spreads it across the front of 'Sweden's' dress. There is then complete darkness, a desperate scream, and suddenly 'Sweden' is left alone, centre-stage, writhing in agony, attempting to rid herself of the red stain and becoming exhausted with grief.

At length, a group of dancers appears, each dressed in flowing robes and carrying white veils, as they gather around 'Sweden', gradually encouraging her to join them, until at last she feels able to dance with them – there is then a 'transformation scene' in which two of the 'bridesmaids' take away 'Sweden's' stained dress and replace it with a bridal gown and her very own veil. There follows a wedding scene, as the children reappear, also dressed for a wedding, sprinkling 'Sweden' with silver confetti. Eventually, the whole scene ends with a two-minute theatrical snowfall, as the singers improvise softly in the background and the dancers twirl around, with arms raised to the falling snow.

The wedding scene, Lizzie, Lucy, Stephanie and Andrew Miller

Two minute snowfall scene to close Swedish movement

Dramatic is hardly an adequate description! The unforgettable memory I have of our first (and the subsequent performances) of this in Sweden, at the enormous Scandinavium Arena hired for this conference, was the sound of the flip-seats banging as thousands of people jumped to their feet for a standing ovation at the end! It was pretty overwhelming. They knew what this piece was speaking about to their nation.

Lucy, Andrew and Stephanie, Manchester Free Trade Hall

The background to this whole production was fascinating. Nigel shared the concept with us in our singers' rehearsals, and we went through the book of Hosea together as he explained what he was trying to depict. I recall the day Nigel came to our home to ask if he could use our children for the piece, and whilst I didn't think it was quite Luke's thing – Lucy, I knew, would want any opportunity to dance, as she had been going to ballet lessons from a very young age. We had wonderful rehearsals with Julia Myles in which the steps were taught to her, and with a lot of Smarties from Nigel, she learned it well enough for a 'try out' in front of a live audience in Birmingham Cathedral before we went on tour. Lucy remembers managing the choreography well on the first public attempt, but back-to-front, so she ended up dancing away from the audience instead of towards them! It didn't matter at all – that's what 'try outs' are for – but she often laughs about it. Sweden was her first 'away' tour with just me rather than the whole family, and we and the dancers and orchestra left early on Monday 2nd July, to get settled and begin rehearsals, while the singers joined us on the 4th, the day the conference actually opened.

The Scarlet Woman, I have to say, turned out to be a major spectacle! For the Sweden tour we had devised what I think

The Scarlet Woman

was a large octagonal (or however many sides it had!) piece of wood mounted on wheels, and Nigel's rather gruesome idea was that a number of ladies from the singers would provide the 'legs' which would propel this structure around the stage – just the lower part of the leg from the knee to the foot being visible to the audience, as we were to be draped in the huge scarlet satin skirt of the woman's dress. The 'woman' herself was Gwen Davies (now Elliott), a singer who also had valuable acting experience, and with her very dark hair, made a stunning figure. Her dress fitted to her waist and was then wound around her and spun out across the rest of us. Beneath the skirt, we (yes I was one of the unlucky ones whose legs were deemed suitable for this extraordinary palaver!) had to lie with our heads towards the centre of the platform where Gwen stood, with us holding onto her own legs to keep her stable, as we manipulated this massive object around with our feet. We did actually have some stage problems with the casters on which it was mounted, such that some of the men, from both enablers and singers, had to push us almost into position before we could start our 'crab-like' foot movements. It must have been a direful sight! Beneath the skirt we were all in agony, not only trying to imagine where on earth we were heading on stage, but also trying to hold Gwen safely, keep ourselves well covered, do our moves effectively, and at all costs, not burst out laughing! It was also pretty airless in there (of all the mental escapades of Mr N. Swinford, this had to be the worst in my opinion!) – and so I hit on the idea of somebody bringing with them a small battery operated

fan, just to keep some kind of life giving air flow! The effect, however, was awesome! People couldn't stop talking about it, including the family Lucy and I, and Jane Kane and her family stayed with. It was a very horrifying picture.

Lizzie would recall no doubt that this was a rather heart stopping performance for her wherever it occurred – not only involving a huge amount of athletic dance, and a 'hidden' transformation scene, but on one occasion, the mixture of theatrical blood and washing up liquid (which did not forever ruin her dress as the bodice held a secret waterproof lining!) actually splashed into one of her eyes! She gave a particularly bona fide performance of agony that night!

Paul Myles came again to the rescue in setting up the theatrical snowfall and the snow itself, a small bag of which we still have here, treasured to this day by Lucy. It was wonderfully effective and we have some precious film of both this Swedish visit and other performances in halls in the UK, when we took it around on a Christmas tour a few years later. A new group of small children for Lucy's snow-friends, in those later performances, involved her little sister Stephanie (aged four or five) and Ruth Miller's son, Andrew. It made very adorable viewing, but very powerful too as one could not help but remember Christ's words in Matthew 6 v 18: (J. B. Phillips)

> But if anyone leads astray one of these little children who believe in me, he would be better off thrown into the depths of the sea with a mill-stone hung round his neck! Alas for the world with its pitfalls! In the nature of things there must be pitfalls. Yet alas for the man who is responsible for them!

How true this is today all across the world!

For the UK performances we abandoned the 'crab' and our 'scarlet Gwen' came up through a trapdoor in the floor, with equal drama! I do remember someone complaining when we went to Manchester with this production however. I guess having paid a ticket price to see a musical concert, one was not anticipating manic disco-dancers, blood and gore and screams in the dark, no matter how beautiful the final wedding scene beneath the snowfall may have been! Happily, I seem to recall the hall manager taking the stance that, taken altogether, the chap had been given a 'really good concert' and leaving it at that! This sort of reaction didn't happen often, but we certainly did write to anyone who had any problems with anything we had done – either refunding their ticket, or in one case, Nigel befriending them over coffee and finding a mutual joy and friendship in cricket!

Whilst in Sweden, we were accommodated in beautiful homes and enjoyed fellowship with Swedish Christian families – experiencing the foods and exploring all sorts of things in conversation. One of our humorous joint memories of the Scandinavium was the packed lunches, which were sometimes blessed with smoked salmon, but *always* seemed to contain potato salad! The only deviation from this was when beetroot was added, in which case we had *pink* potato salad! We were hugely grateful for Valborg Bystedt-Melberg, who acted as our link organiser to this major event. She was wonderfully dedicated and must have worked incredibly hard on our behalf.

There were other blessings, as recorded by Nigel in the Prayer diary after our return:

> *One little personal cameo I shall never forget; at the end of one of the performances, I was confronted by a huge, tall, strongly built young man, obviously Jewish, looking down at me. He said, "Will you do this at the Feast in Jerusalem?" Then he embraced me and as he held me he began to weep with great loud sobs, then he withdrew and looked at me again and said – "You see, this is our story."*

Another deeply moving memory was the presence at this conference, of a group of believers from Estonia – the first occasion I believe, that they had been able to leave their country to join such a gathering. A couple of them came up to Nigel after one of our performances and presented him with a book of Estonian songs, two of which we later performed, after a huge effort learning to pronounce the language. Our dear friend Aileen Mitchell came to rehearsals to teach us how, as it was quite akin to Finnish in its pronunciation, which she knew well from living and working in Finland for some time. The songs were astounding in their spiritual depth and beauty. Quite a few 'crib sheets' (extremely rare in NEO) were apparent in performances nevertheless – it was a tough call remembering it all by heart!

We were also privileged to have on stage Peter Sandwall and Lars Morlid (who once sang with the incredible Swedish choir Choralerna, beloved of so many of us in our teen years!). We performed one or two of their songs with them both, and have film of Roger Beasley being somewhat crushed in Peter's arm as he sang alongside him sharing a microphone! It was a great moment – 'I want to be more like Jesus' was the song I recall! (We often used to place their 'Footprints of Jesus' into our NEO programmes, with Catherine Swinford-White doing the solo which melted everyone's hearts!) They wrote some great songs! The evening in which this occurred, was a wonderful time and had a great review in the Gothenburg Post.

These instances, over all the years of our NEO work, were probably the only big 'Christian conferences' oddly enough, to which we were ever invited – though our players were often involved, and still may be, in some of the current ones. All the more reason therefore to have made them unforgettable!

7

Solemn feasts and laughter in the heavenlies

The Feast of Trumpets

Experimental fun reconstructing Biblical Orchestrations using a modern orchestra and Singers

Nigel's own précis, as sent to John Forrest, then a BBC producer

1. *At Mount Sinai, (Exodus 19 v 19ff) "And when the voice of the trumpet sounded long, and waxed louder and louder, Moses spake and God answered him by a voice". For the startling effect of this very long note emanating from the mountain see The Feast of Trumpets, Movement 1.*

2. *The Old Testament Orchestra (2 Chronicles) – 288 musicians including a proliferation of harps, cymbals, trumpets and singers – The Feast of Trumpets, Movement 1*

3. *The idea of a whole Jewish feast day devoted to the blowing of trumpets, all improvised presumably, is fascinating for a modern composer. The Feast of Trumpets was the precursor to the Day of Atonement in the festive year.*

4. *Trumpets moving in a circle, i.e. round the walls of Jericho.*

5. *Gideon – surrounding the Midianites with percussive effects from the breaking of pitchers, lights, encircling trumpets and shouts.*

6. *The orchestra of Psalm 150*

7. *Pipes, harps, psalteries and tabrets coming down the hill with the prophets (1 Samuel 10 v 5). A delicious combination of sounds, all descending at the same time!*

8. i) *Singing. It's a Pythagorean idea that each planet emits a certain note – the Music of the Spheres. But this idea is mentioned in the oldest known book of the Bible (Job Chapter 38). God says, "Where wast thou.... when the morning stars sang together and all the sons of God shouted for joy?" Gustav Holst experimented with such imagined sounds in the last piece of The Planet Suite – Neptune the Mystic – i.e. women singing very high with very long notes.*

   ii) *The idea of the 'Shout' which occurs constantly in the Old Testament. It's as if the whole army is shouting. See The Feast of Trumpets for various experiments with improvised shouts and singing.*

   iii) *Processional singing in time of war: Jehoshaphat (2 Chronicles) – sends the choir into battle in front of the army. What might such a procession have sounded like?*

9. *"And he breathed on them, and said, 'Receive ye the Holy Ghost'"– see track 7 of Feast of Trumpets for breathing effects in a piece of music.*

****

Oh my! What a production this was! I can truly say that in all the years I have worked with NEO, this was the one that involved the most extraordinary and diverse number of tasks for the entire ensemble, and for me personally too!

I've always found Nigel's teaching refreshing, and am alarmed as I write now, at how few sermons I have heard on events of the Old Testament over recent years – I trust that is not the case universally! Nigel had among his God-given gifts, an ability to bring both ancient music, and events from the Old Testament accounts, right up to the minute;

shining, poignant, relevant, commanding – and even huge fun! I remember my own vicar saying of Nigel, after he had watched one of our concerts: "Nigel has a light touch!" He is so right.

This was not an entirely 'light touch' however – it involved lots of loud noise from the brass section, heavily augmented by extra brass which we called in for the occasion. Wonderfully, when performed in Salzburg on the famous *Jedermann* stage in front of the Cathedral (Dom), this included members of the Vienna Philharmonic, who just happened to have a day off!

Players – play as many notes as you can!

It entailed lots of audience participation – shaking of keys or anything that would make a noise, and waving torches, as we re-lived Joshua and his trumpeters walking around the city walls, and breaking their vessels to reveal lights inside, conquering the city of Jericho!

It starred a dear friend of ours who wondrously combined a career as a farmer, with singing bass at Covent Garden Opera House! Dressed in his full regalia as a priest, complete with beard, and being a tall and commanding figure with a voice like the last trumpet, he was a sight to behold!

It included also...a series of shop mannequins, each performance requiring one male and one female (more anon) and for each singer, a full length white robe! We also recruited the indefatigable efforts of Paul Myles (mentioned quite often among these pages) who worked at the BBC and was capable of producing just about any kind of prop! On this occasion, for the 'Horns of the Altar' movement, we needed some kind of contraption which would allow four sets of three very long strands of red satin ribbon to be slowly unwound, representing the love of Christ going out to the four corners of the world, unravelled by four 'dancers' – of whom I became one for the first and last time in my NEO career! I also remember taking down the required measurements we would need and going off to market, to

order the largest amount of ribbon I have ever purchased!

As can be seen in Nigel's précis at the start of this chapter, this extravaganza combined a number of vital feasts and special events of the Old Testament, in a vibrant and imaginative, musical and theatrical way. As a group of singers, we suddenly found we had to learn to lose all our inhibitions – this would involve walking onto stage, initially singing a repetitive 'Alleluia' (sung after a jazz duet by two harps, would you believe?). We had to appear confident and worshipful, despite often having to make this entrance by walking down several steps in the relevant concert hall, in long white robes!

Secondly we had to learn to be theatrical – to sing loudly when required, using our own improvisations or 'singing in the Spirit' – learning to keep those sounds both in tune and in key – and to shout out verses of Scripture, learned by heart, praising God in many different languages across the group as a whole. We had to be trained in all these arts, and it was for some, quite a gruelling and unusually demanding process! We were grateful to Dave Isgrove, (see Chapter 2 – *Earliest Beginnings*) himself an accomplished performer, who came along to knock us into shape! Well, most were grateful, and certainly all benefited!

Some people's improvising is speculative!

However, to backtrack several paces, there was a long period of planning, while Nigel was actually composing the stunning music for this performance. We discussed the whole business in our Prayer and Planning group, and it emerged that a number of props, e.g. the aforesaid ribbon machines, a large cross (capable of being carried by a man and fixed into place amid said ribbon machines) goodness knows how many white robes (!), costumes for the dancers, the priest and for a little group of people who would finally act out the nailing of Christ to the cross – and not only a large number of mannequins (as their fate was actually to be destroyed in each performance) but all the clothing needed to drape them in, including ladies' heeled shoes, and men's smart lace-ups..........would all be needed! *Where to begin??*

In a moment, you will find below, an article I wrote at the time, with a few addendums as I look back, but first let me explain how the white robes came about! My mother-in-law had always wanted to experience the famous *Oberammergau Passion Play*. At last she managed it (it only comes around every ten years or so I believe) and she brought back a beautiful book full of photographs. Among these, I noticed there were some effective, flowing, white gowns worn by many of the actors and actresses, which looked very much as though they could easily be adapted to various sizes, but were absolutely 'unisex' in design. So when Nigel began hankering after a cast dressed in white – I showed him the book and this type of design became our aim! Of course we had to find people who could create a simplified version of it (and also make them) and we had to track down an enormous amount of white fabric which would not crease easily, would wash and dry quickly if necessary and would look wonderful!

My Salzburg lady – in my husband's arms!

Julie & Pete in Residenz Palace concert gear

Enter Yvonne Mitchell from Nigel's church, St Peter's, Halliwell, and Ann Fasham from St John's, Harborne and their respective teams. They were quite magnificent, and did a marvellous job! The material could be purchased from a mill Yvonne knew in the north, and well before the time that they were needed for dress rehearsals,

these garments arrived, and were distributed according to the basic measurements of each singer! It was quite a procedure. They did look good though! There was much hilarity, most of which was at the expense of Matt Baynham, whose gown turned out rather like a bell tent! Now for the mannequins, who became the stars of the section of the production, where the priest took on the role of Gideon, dramatically cleansing the nation of Israel of its idols – and the article I promised.

Idol Talk

'The Feast of Trumpets' which was featured by NEO a few years ago, must still rank as one of the most spectacular pieces we have ever performed. It included wonderful music and dance, stunning improvisation both vocal and instrumental, offstage brass ringing round the auditorium, and even the Singers appearing in costume! And who better to provide the resounding bass solos than Paul Hodges, who manages to combine being a husband and father, with being a farmer and a Covent Garden opera singer! Paul took two roles during the 'Feast', the most memorable for me being Gideon, making his gigantic statement against idolatry as in the Old Testament account.

You see Nigel had this wonderful idea of depicting here the 'ideal man' and the 'ideal woman'. You know, the ones we see in the advertisements on TV every day of our lives – who insidiously tempt our subconscious minds to emulate the latest 'hip and cool' images in society. So I suppose it was natural for him to decide that the most expedient way to portray this was by means of fashionably dressed mannequins, posing in the spotlights on stage. What I can't recall is actually having volunteered to find some...but I think I must have done!

My earliest memory of my unlooked for relationship with these creatures was of fingering the business columns of the telephone directory, and seeing a certain men's outfitters leap out of the page and demand to be contacted immediately. Having done so, I was told that yes, they had lots of spare mannequins (all male of course). In fact, funny I should have rung then, but they were just planning to replace all their stock and if I cared to visit their store, I could take my pick. How much? Oh, around £17.50 per head, which I thought was pretty steep, as I went along ready to roll up the sleeves and do a little bartering! It was only later than I was to discover that a brand new, fully painted-up model with wig and glass stand can cost around £300.00!

(Julie: and this was in the 1990s!)

So there we were, Doug Gallaher and I, travelling home with the car boot full of bodies, which were subsequently dumped unceremoniously all over the study floor. An assortment of very realistic bare legs and feet protruded out into the hall. It was unfortunate that I was out when my husband came home that afternoon....I often wonder whether it was the momentary shock of thinking that his family had been done away with, that first started his hair turning grey!

Then, of course, I had the job of finding some 'ladies' to accompany the 'men' as well as something to dress them all in. In fact, a wide selection of costumes had to be found, because, as the whole point of the evening was to allow Paul to smash these objects to smithereens, it stood to reason that most of the clothes would be ruined by having bits of jagged fibreglass ripped through them! I found this out only after having dressed the first of my 'men' in one of Pete's new summer shirts, ready for the rehearsal at which Paul was to try out his first 'throw'! (There is still a little row of stitches just discernible on one sleeve...)

The first thing to grasp about these mannequins you understand, is that they stand up by means of a base of plate glass on which is secured a steel rod, which in turn is meant to fit snugly into a deep hole set at an angle up the middle of one of their feet! (I bet you didn't know that!) Well of course, it's all very well going off with a rough idea of their foot-size

and having a spree around the charity shops looking for ladies' black patent leather high heels and smart black lace-up shoes for men, but then you see you couldn't just slip their shoes on, you had to first talk your husband (the one who was already going prematurely grey and wore stitched shirtsleeves) into spending a good hour drilling through the steel plates which we found occur between the sole and the heel of ladies' shoes. (I bet you didn't know that either!) (Julie: As a result of all the recces I have done over the years, which involve having to go through scanners at airports, I now realize this is why they often make you take off your shoes!)

I eventually came across a wonderful man in the wilds of Staffordshire who not only made these mannequins but who also restored old ones! (What a fascinating way to spend one's life!) You wouldn't believe what a trade goes on in these things – and how much is charged round and about for a good right hand or a left leg with a bend in just the right place....! We struck up a friendship this chap and I, and it was he who provided me with my first lady ('Gladys', I called her) along with all the others who later followed in her dubious wake. It was a most profitable relationship this, because whenever Paul had done his bit on stage, I ended up with a box of highly saleable 'body parts' which could be returned to my friend in exchange for a newish looking 'lady'.

I soon learned to mix my stock of acrylic paints for retouching faces, into good matches for skin colour and lipstick – and to this day (Julie: Yes – just checked, and it's still there even after all these years!) I have in a tiny box in my desk drawer, a few pairs of false eyelashes which were meticulously peeled from numerous bodiless heads at the end of performances, and carefully stored ready to stick onto the next pair of beautifully made up eyes! Soon it was common knowledge that the Fry household had a host of these 'people' living in its cellar – a tale told by many a wide-eyed child!

The dressing process of course was a mischief in itself. I never counted the bruises I acquired from my earliest attempts at quick-changing these inflexible characters. Believe me, those arms and legs can give quite a clout, and sometimes I would be in less than friendly mood by the time I had finally wangled my arm into the most unbelievable position up a shirt front, and managed to secure a shoulder bolt into its appropriate socket.

Mannequins in Festival dress!

the glass porch of the hostel alongside the larger instruments and other paraphernalia – and I soon noticed that various pieces kept disappearing from day to day – subsequently turning up in someone's bed in one of the dormitories! Many a nasty shock was received by a tired player at the end of a long day it seems! (Mind you, I was particularly delighted with our mannequins in their Salzburg Festival dress – it was worth the hours of hunting round the Oxfam shops for a second-hand dinner suit, and fielding comments such as, "What size is the gentleman, madam?" "Ah well, well, you see, it's like this...")

To cap it all, I cannot but admit that one of our most respected viola players (well it would be, wouldn't it?) discreetly requested of me the loan of a particularly good 'hand' he had observed, which I recall was later to be found at the end of his sleeve, causing riotous behaviour in the string section! (He's never played so well!) And as for the wigs (all lengths and colours), it would take an even longer article than this to tell the stories in which those featured!

The limb had to be already inside the shirt and jacket sleeve you see, before being joined to the body. It was a while before I learned that too!

But if nothing else, these mannequins had good entertainment value. They caused chaos wherever they went on tour with us, together with their attendant boxes of 'gear'. My sister Val (once a professional window dresser) came to the first concert with me, to show me how to swathe copious amounts of midnight blue satin very professionally around Gladys, while I was busy taking the curlers out of her wig. (Gladys' wig, not my sister's!) Later, our efforts complete, Val stood on the empty stage, waiting for me to join her after tidying up, and happened to be standing so still, that when at last she did move, she nearly gave a heart attack to Peter Mortimore, who had come into the hall and taken her for one of my 'ladies'!

Then there was the big tour of Salzburg that year. I have a picture of our Roger Knott (Julie: See Appendix I – *The Unforgettables*), offering my Salzburg lady a rosy red apple. This is typical of the affection in which my mannequins were held by the NEO at large. At the hostel my 'bodies' were kept in

Paul Hodges practising his moves aided by Roger Beasley

Julie dealing with wreckage at the Residenz!

It has to be said that the Salzburg tour took the biscuit however, for it was there, in the most beautiful Residenz Palace Grosser Saal, that Paul Hodges gave his most sensational performance as a demolisher of idols! I think it was Roger Beasley who came up with the idea of strapping the mannequins' stands with gaffer tape to the high marble balustrade above the rest of the 'stage' area, from which elevated position Paul was to do his stuff. I believe I mentioned that Paul is a farmer among other things, and not short of a muscle or two – so it was, that when a mannequin refused to come off its stand at the crucial moment (Julie: having forgotten to tug it at the correct angle) he just gave a great heave and ripped the entire thing, plate glass stand included, off its perch, and smashed the lot on the marble floor! You have never seen such a stunned audience in the history of NEO. You could have heard an eyelash peeling off in the ensuing silence!

So much more could be told – but suffice to say that my mannequins served their purpose well, and it was quite nostalgic to discover a long black wig, and remnants of tattered

garments here a few months ago in an old suitcase. Otherwise, not even a finger-end remains! But let us hope we may learn the lessons taught us, as the writer of that good old hymn put it, "The dearest idol I possess, whate'er that idol be, help me to tear it from Thy throne, and worship only Thee."

Well, that article was written in humorous vein of course, as it was to appear in our Friends' Magazine (Opus 5) of Autumn 1996. We always tried to keep our NEO Friends smiling!

This, however, was no party entertainment! The message of this piece was utterly sincere, in fact grave at times, and it was composed in a mode which even now appears completely timeless – and not perhaps in the same bracket in which Nigel would describe much of his other music, which he calls 'Gebrauchmusik' i.e. music 'for a specific purpose'. I would have loved to have seen this performed, had it been possible, in the Grosser Festspielhaus in Salzburg! It would not have been at all out of place in terms of its avant-garde and spectacular style, only perhaps in its exceptional holiness.

The music itself was a mixture of the bold and dramatic, and the breathtakingly beautiful. I remember holding back the tears in one of our earliest attempts to sing what was to be the off-stage 'How long?' which represented the martyrs beneath the altar in the book of Revelation, enquiring of the Lord how long it would be until their deaths would be avenged? Looking at world events today – how desperately relevant this is, and so, very sadly, it may continue to be.

The jazz duet of the two harps thrilled me, and even now when I hear it, it brings back that heart-thumping sensation of getting ready to walk out singing the 'Alleluia' which built up into a great crescendo of praise. Later on in the piece came more moments of praise with dancing, as the priest swayed with arms uplifted, calling us all to rejoice in the Lord, and none of us could stand still.

After all, who knows how many beats there are in a bar?

Horns of the Altar movement on Jedermannbuhne

The 'Horns of the Altar' movement was played literally by four horns, calling from the cross to the four corners of the world, after a number of singers in modern day costumes, representing unrequited love, materialism, the mania for fitness and other up-to-the minute issues in society, had succeeded in nailing Christ to the cross, in their determination to do away with Him. Then the horns would sound and the ribbons, red for the blood of Christ, would be unwound by us four girls (only two of which were real dancers – Lizzie Swinford and Julia Myles – the other two were myself and Ruth Miller – we found this a moving and memorable experience!) and were gradually stretched out and lifted high, until the piece ended. Our arms may have ached, but I can still remember the huge sense of privilege and the many thoughts that went through my mind in those moments. The audience would be completely hushed, watching every move and entranced by the music – and then from each 'corner of the world' would come the answer of the trumpets – it was spine-tingling and ended

in what may be a hackneyed phrase, but is so completely apt – a 'paean of praise'!

Strange the silly things one remembers – but Nigel was keen to have a small group of children singing the old Sunday school song: 'Jesus died for all the children', during the walk of Christ carrying his cross. They were helped by Alison Hawcutt (one of our sopranos and a former NEO Administrator) and had to be trained against the backdrop of Nigel bashing discords out on the piano, because the orchestra would be playing some pretty scary music while they would be singing this! They became accustomed to their starting note during this training. Sometime later, Pete and I took our kids to Bolton, where we were to stay in Nigel and Carolyn's home while they were on holiday, to enjoy some rambles in their local woods. We arrived at Bolton station, loaded with suitcases and a buggy, and pressed the button for the lift. When it arrived, it let out a 'ping', on exactly the correct note and straight off, the two children began singing 'Jesus died for all the children....'!

Perhaps the most unusual and unexpected part of the 'Feast' was the time of public testimony which Nigel wove into this production. He asked one or two of our number, who had gone through particularly harrowing times in their lives, to share their stories briefly over the microphone, against the backdrop of gentle music. These included such matters as; the terror of living through the regime of Idi Amin in Uganda; the heartbreak of childlessness, fulfilled at last by adoption, but not until after having suffered the shock of miscarriage; the sudden knowledge that one's baby was to be born with Down's Syndrome, and that on top of having had to cope with the father's battle with cancer. People listened attentively, but it wasn't until the last movement, as we all, with our husbands or wives and families (if they were with us) came onto the stage in our robes, depicting that final coming together in heaven, and singing the old hymn, – 'What a gathering' – that people realised all those stories were true!

There stood Florence Odonga (who had to eventually flee from Uganda), alongside Lesley and John, their elder daughter Celia, and the younger Sarah-Joy, the object of that last testimony, smiling and looking happily around at everyone. As I write, all these years later, Lesley, (the singer I mention in Chapter 5 – 'Whatever the weather' as encountering her first lesson with NEO about God's provision of healing), has astonished us all with her courage and determination to praise the Lord. Sarah-Joy went through difficulties, illnesses and serious operations and yet is now married and living with her beloved husband Daniel, in Lesley and John's home. John battled, I think three times in all with cancer, and now, as I write, has not only been diagnosed with Alzheimer's, but with Motor Neurone Disease. These trials are unfathomable – and yet for as long as John was able, he would sit at the piano and play hymns to the Lord, beautifully. These dear friends are a tribute to the amazing grace of God and have been, and still are, an incredible example to us all.

As for Roger and Dawn, founder members of NEO, who courageously shared their brokenness with everyone – their elder daughter is now our much-loved daughter-in-law and her sister now has a family of her own – how could we have known the future blessings in store for us all alongside the trials and tribulations. Such is the family of God – and such was the tribe of Israel, depicted in such startling reality in this veritable 'Feast'.

'What a Gathering' – The Feast of Trumpets

Nut the audience with your voice!

I could not hope to describe adequately the effect that this production had on its audiences. I do recall that some time after its first performance in Symphony Hall Birmingham, Julia Myles received a call from a lady who had had a significant encounter it seems, with the Lord. She had bought her ticket, not realising she was to be seated at the very top of the auditorium, which is pretty high in this magnificent hall. Unfortunately, she was also seated in the middle of a row, and was shaken because she was subject to vertigo and panic attacks. However, her story was quite something: after the orchestra had played the first chords of the piece, she recounted that she felt a complete calm descend on her, and she was able to stay seated, right the way through the performance. My memory of her account is that she had said she had not encountered any further attacks since the concert – and though I am uncertain as to when the news came through exactly, I often wonder whether she was totally healed.

In Salzburg, as mentioned, we had an incredibly capable set of 'extra offstage brass' that night from the Vienna Phil', and the atmosphere on the stage before the great Dom, with brass being stationed on the high buildings around the square wherever possible, was completely overwhelming. I shall never forget the sound of both instruments and singers as we 'let rip' with the various pieces into the night air!

This was my first tour with not only our older children, Luke and Lucy, but now little Stephanie, who was just around eighteen months. There seemed to be so much to do, so much to think about every day for all those of us with families – not just the older children's needs, but for us, a toddler's too, and the 'interesting' nature of hostel life, as much as we loved the experience of all being together, made this a challenge indeed with this particular performance. We had begun the tour feeling tired, after a twenty-seven hour coach journey. There were odd moments 'off' though, and

Paul, our wonderful operatic bass and farmer!

photos capture one which depicted myself and Ruth Miller lying on our backs in the 'family corridor' with our legs up the wall, trying to rest our tired muscles – and another, a friendly chat with others (little Steph looking on) whilst I curled and combed the wig on its stand!

Rest for Julie & Ruth in the families' corridor!

Julie combing wig watched by Rachel, Ruth and little Stephanie

For me, one of the most beautiful pieces was the song, 'Jesu joy of our hearts', led by Carole Corpe and sung with her usual clarity and feeling. I found the words and music the other day, handwritten by Nigel, (and hitherto unpublished, as so much of his music is). For me that puts another meaning to the phrase, 'treasure in jars of clay'! So much more could be told of this piece, but it must be recounted by others.

Nigel told me once that when he was little, his mother told him to "Stop banging the piano!" – little did she know then, how very important it was, that he did not!

—————— **Dimples** ——————

I'd defend it to the death if I was in the right mood!

8
To Russia, with love and spare violin strings

THIS was one of those once in a lifetime opportunities that came along for NEO to contribute in the aftermath of a political coup in the life of another nation. We had all been glued to either our televisions or radios as news broke of what was occurring in Russia, whereby the major city which throughout the Communist regime had been re-named Leningrad, was now to return to its former title of St. Petersburg. These developments seemed almost incredible, and yet they happened. What followed was quite wonderful, in that the Mayor of the city decided he needed to bring in some wholesome input at the beginning of this new society, and – as you will read in a moment – he hit on a truly innovative way of doing so!

The team flew out on Thursday 2nd January 1992, for a tour which would prove an extremely memorable one for the entire party. We had been told by the organisers that for security reasons, the incoming participants of this Festival would need to be accommodated in a five star hotel. This of course was not going to sit easily with those involved, at a time when the majority of the people of St. Petersburg were standing for hours in queues even to buy their bread! It also meant, however, that we needed to find quite a lot of money to launch this exercise. Gifts did come in, for which we were hugely grateful, but we needed around another five thousand pounds and the Lord put it on my heart at the time to try and find it. In a nutshell, I committed this need to prayer, asking the Lord to help me find this money quickly, even though I hadn't the faintest idea how. As I prayed I clearly saw the face of our good friend Clare MacInnes (from our *Youthquake* and Jesus Centre days) and I felt the Lord was indicating I should phone her. I hadn't had any contact with Clare or David for ages, so this necessitated a bit of explanation, but she immediately caught onto the urgency, and told me of someone she felt I should contact. I had never heard of him, but she assured me he was the

man for this task, and not only so, but that he and his wife were on the international board of 'Youth With A Mission' (YWAM), which was of course the organisation behind this Russia project! I duly wrote, and received a prompt and positive letter back, which not only supplied the funding, but forged a long, ongoing friendship which was a huge encouragement to both NEO and our family in ways too numerous to include here.

I had been involved together with Lucy our daughter, in the Swedish visit in 1990, having left Pete, Luke and little Stephanie to the kind care of Ruth Miller and her family. With the prospect of our forthcoming Spanish tour in the summer of 1992, which would also involve leaving two children behind, I didn't feel I could take part in this visit. So we looked after Nigel and Carolyn's home and dog and had a little break for a few days, enjoying the view of the New Year firework display across the hills from their windows, and covering the NEO team in prayer.

This is one of the occasions therefore when I have enlisted the contributions of others who took part, and here is a fantastic memoir of the tour from Roger Beasley:

> My overwhelming memory of this trip was of a series of traveller's tales of the train journey from Moscow to St. Petersburg and the unique experience of flying Aeroflot between those two great cities in the middle of a Russian winter. These stories along with eating bad food have probably been etched into our corporate memory for those participating in this particular tour.
>
> I could tell you about the dead rat I found back stage that was still warm, having recently been despatched by the resident cat of The Palace of Culture, but thought it wise not to share this news with the rest of the group because they were just starting a time of prayer; or of Robin sitting next to me on our Aeroflot return flight to Moscow who had no safety belt,

Roger Beasley

because it was completely missing, as was the safety briefing, the safety card and life jackets. I could even reminisce about spending a happy fifteen minutes chewing a single mouthful of Russian steak. All of these stories are true but might lead you to believe that this was all that happened.

We were invited by the director of the Academy of Christian Art, Cambridge, Canada to be part of the First St. Petersburg Festival in 1991. The timing of this invitation in October 1991, three years after the fall of the Berlin Wall, seemed to be an opportunity too good to miss. We would be able to take spiritual music banned under USSR and proclaim it to an audience who had never had the opportunity to hear it before. Imagine this: we were able to deliver great portions of Scripture as we performed sections from Handel's 'Messiah', and to sing simple worship choruses in the Byelozyerskii Palace, formerly the headquarters of the Communist Party and now the home of the St. Petersburg State Chamber Orchestra. Praising and worshipping Jesus in this place and at this time I believe, meant we were bringing redemption to not only the people but to the very buildings as well.

Our final hours were spent in the International Airport in Moscow. Six of us sat at a table, all of us had a drink and four of us ordered food. The total cost of the meal was a mere $2. I ordered spring chicken. If this was a spring chicken it must have been the spring of 1917. This bird had been beaten to death by a club. Every bone in its body had been broken and this bird had been trained for the Olympics. The meat was so tough that even with my teeth the meat would not leave the bone.

I would not like to think that I am obsessed with food but as you can see food did play an important part of our time in the new Russia.

In the beautiful setting of the Pantheon in Rome, and some twenty-one years after our visit to Russia, at the end of one of the NEO Recreatios, Dawn and I found ourselves in conversation with two young Russians, Artem and Dasha, who were taking a holiday in Rome. Like thousands of others they had wondered into the Pantheon and on this occasion we were playing. Being moved by our performance, they decided to stay and listen. They came on both the Wednesday and Thursday and on our second encounter they simply wanted to talk about `our religion' as they put it. They understood religion as something dark and heavy but what they had been experiencing with us was nothing like this. We were able to explain how knowing Jesus personally changes everything as we are no longer following some religious code but experiencing a real relationship with Jesus, who died and rose again to take away our sin. We explained that the life they could see in us was the life that Jesus had given us as we had received His forgiveness for the things we had done wrong and had decided to follow Him. They got it, they understood it and when I asked them if they would allow me to pray with them, there was no hesitation in their saying, "Yes". After praying with them we exchanged names and numbers and we said if ever they should come to England to look us up. The final piece of this story is that over twelve months later Dawn and I received them as guests in our home when they visited the UK. What a privilege it is to be in the place the Lord has put us and on this occasion to both sow and reap the harvest.

Dawn & Roger Beasley

Wonderful! Our NEO report on this tour fills in more of the story:

Praises ring in former Communist Party HQ

In early autumn 1991, the Byelozyerskii Palace, recently vacated by the Communist Party in Russia's second largest city (six million inhabitants) became the home of the St. Petersburg State Chamber Orchestra and a centre of very 'high-brow' classical music.

At about the same time, the Mayor, Anatoli Sobchak, seeking the best moral foundation for the new free society, contacted YWAM in Canada and asked them to organise a Christian East/West Arts Festival. In three months Christians from Peru, Hawaii, North America, Britain, Samoa and Korea arranged to attend, all at their own expense.

So on 3rd and 5th January, the New English Orchestra, involving fifty musicians, singers, dancers and enablers, including two players from Norway, became the first foreign orchestra since the Revolution to play in the magnificent six hundred and fifty-seat concert hall. Because of problems over publicity, only about a hundred were there on the first evening. Word spread rapidly and the second concert was a 'sell-out'. As happens in many of the NEO concerts in the Salzburg Festival, musicians and singers moved out among the audience and led them in worship.

Concert with NEO in the Byelozyerskii Palace, St. Petersburg

Part of the second concert was given by the resident orchestra. Afterwards their musicians were overwhelming in their comments on the high professional standard of the NEO. A Russian Professor of Philosophy commented on the strange quality of the music which, "made it better than he had ever heard". His mind wouldn't allow him to accept the explanation given. Nigel Swinford, the conductor of the NEO, has been invited to conduct the St. Petersburg Orchestra whenever possible and to train their choir and to present the 'Messiah' (previously 'not loved in Russia' for obvious reasons) and other great Christian oratorios with the two orchestras and choirs. A Russian composer of modern music made contact; he is organising a Festival in May/June to consider the philosophy of music. As so much modern music is inspired by New Age and Zen Buddhism, what an opportunity for Christians to get involved! The City Council want a second Festival, with the NEO, next year. Praise the Lord for these strategic opportunities and for ways of encouraging the churches and giving practical help to individual Russians.

The offerings for the orphanages in St. Petersburg taken at the presentations of the Feast of Trumpets in this country, totalled £5,800, to which £1,000 of donations from churches and individuals has been added. A Trust is being set up by Russian and Western Christians to avoid the danger of monies being siphoned off by officialdom.

Nigel Swinford is currently composing some of the parables of Jesus interpreted in Jazz Dance. These will be included in the concert at the Free Trade Hall on Saturday 5th December, with Christian dancers from the Birmingham Royal Ballet.

I remember being thrilled that our audiences warmed to this project and gave so generously so that we could help the city's orphanages, it was a wonderful outcome.

Nigel actually referred to this trip in the souvenir programme of NEO's last public concert in Birmingham Town Hall, on January 16th 2016. It contains mention of another rather lovely blessing for the Russian orchestra:

...What didn't get written up though was the 'conflab' that happened after the concert between the NEO string players and those of the St. Petersburg State Chamber Orchestra. You see, in the Communist regime, new violin strings were

phenomenally expensive and also scarce. So these poor players were playing on grossly worn out strings, which did not even match. We had the privilege of being able to give them, as a token of our Christian love, our spare sets of new high quality western violin strings. So I suppose that the sound of the St. Petersburg State Chamber Orchestra may well have changed overnight! But of course no one would ever guess why...

In perusing the memorabilia of this astonishing visit however, I found letters like this one, written in the autumn of the previous year, so moving. They gave an insight into what life was really like there at this critical period in the history of the city:

I'm sure there would be innumerable stories available from folk who went on this tour! Not all of them were humorous either. One of our singers, Jo Garbutt, was unfortunate enough to contract the infamous giardia disease, and was ill for quite a while after her return as I recall. Susan Mole, meanwhile, reminded me that everyone had been asked to take a few basic items with them as gifts when they flew out, like soap and toiletries which were hard to come by out there. She told me that she had decided to travel out wearing a fur coat that she didn't feel she could any longer wear here in the UK, with the intention of giving it away when she arrived, which she duly did. She had a warm fluffy jumper and someone gave her a large rain mackintosh to wear over the top, so she felt quite warm enough. However, she told me that she was very tired at the airport awaiting the return flight, and so she curled up on a bench and went to sleep, wrapped in this mackintosh, with the hood over her face. A few minutes later she was awoken by a compassionate NEO member offering her a bar of soap! Much laughter ensued!

We were unable to follow up any of the invitations given to Nigel and the NEO in Russia, as the Lord, it seemed, had other plans for us – as He often does – even in the face of what seems humanly a very good thing to do. (Hence our need, elsewhere mentioned, to stay close to Him for our directions.) I was given the gift of a set of Russian dolls after this tour, which our grandchildren now enjoy, and whenever I look at them I remember the stories, both humorous and heart-rending, that came out of this amazing window of opportunity.

I read only this very morning of how times are changing again in Russia, and draconian measures being seriously contemplated, in the name of terrorism prevention, to clamp down on all forms of religious expression. It has been reported that it's likely it could soon be impossible to invite someone to church or have a conversation about Christianity with a person who is not a church member, without the permission of the state. We pray on.

Gerry Hopkin looking happy!

Always smiling — Kathryn Coleman, soon to be Masters!

Georg Hoelscher

Hannah Gerrard, Fiona Ormiston and Hannah Parker in Scottish reel

Enthusiasm!

Katie LeFeuvre and Gill Sutton, smiling viola players!

Binnie Thompson, Judith Pickup, Kristen Rigby & Ruth Miller

9

Expo '92 in Seville – the NEO in Spain

Report by Keith Buckler: *The European Christian Mission (ECM) had been working in Cordoba Province for fifteen years. It was one of the hardest areas of Spain and 1992 had proved a year in which there had been a tremendous effort to reach out in evangelism. In this year the New English Orchestra was invited to perform concerts in four of the towns of the southern area of Cordoba province.*

1992 was a special year for Spain, the five hundredth anniversary of Columbus sailing across the Atlantic to discover the New World, the twenty-fifth Olympic Games being held in Barcelona, Madrid the Capital of Culture for 1992 and the Expo Exhibition for six months of the year at Seville. In Spain in 1992 opportunities existed which were probably unique. New roads had been built and in Montilla, where the NEO team were based, a special sports complex had been barely finished, which proved ideal for rehearsals, particularly for the dancers. At Puente Genil, the auditorium seats were only installed the previous week and had never been used until the NEO concert on the Tuesday evening. At the Expo Exhibition (which lasts for 176 days) August 13th, the day on which the NEO visited, was in fact the one day when the Pavilion of Promise (the Christian exhibition tent) received international television coverage in El Palenque Stadium. Cordoba Province is in fact a crucial area. Cordoba is recognised by many Muslims to be the second most important religious centre in the Islamic world and the area where we were holding these events was a special frontier between Christianity and the Muslim empire of the past.

The stage at Puente Genil

Another view of the stage

On the Tuesday we visited Puente Genil, where the concert was held in a special outdoor auditorium some distance from the centre of town. The orchestra and singers were on a raised stage and the dancers on a floor below it, which was easily viewed from the banked seating. On the Tuesday morning, arrangements had been made for the Puente Genil authorities to provide a dance floor and staging, but at 12.30pm, just at the beginning of siesta time, Ron Anderson was told that

they were unable to do this. Miraculously, he was able to find sheets of hardboard of an adequate size and texture (I think at Lucena) purchase them and transport them across to Puente Genil and actually build a stage suitable for the dancers and for the dance floor to be laid on top. This stage and dance flooring, which was in fact taken up and rebuilt at each of the other sites apart from Expo, proved very satisfactory to the dancers!

Paul Myles setting lights in Spain

of Promise had been greatly used and we were impressed to learn that by the time we visited it, over one hundred and twenty thousand people had heard the Gospel in a multimedia

Tap rehearsals on El Palenque Stadium Expo 92

Jesus was uplifted and all who attended rejoiced at this wonderful concert. The singing of 'Jesus is the Answer' proved to be a key part of the evening and it was difficult to get away, so we were not in bed until 2.30am back in Montilla, as this was one of the longer trips that we made.

On Wednesday at Lucena, the venue had a feeling of fiesta, with coloured bunting and lights and the audience proved very attentive and received the concert with great joy. Some leading local and in fact national dance figures were present and once again it proved an opportunity to rejoice in the glory of the Gospel. We arrived back as speedily as possible as we had to leave at 5.45am to travel on the Thursday to Expo.

The journey to Seville went very smoothly and a buffet breakfast was provided in the coach. The facilities at El Palenque were exceptionally good, with a very large removable stage, over an acre under canvas, with lights and speakers. The initial opening ceremony between 11am and 12noon, proved a great occasion, with the NEO contributing 'Resucito' and 'Boliviana'. The dancers performed a tap rendition of 'David danced before the Lord' by Duke Ellington, plus 'Psalm 63' in closing. The Pavilion

presentation, of whom forty thousand had enrolled for Bible instruction and fourteen thousand had already prayed a prayer of commitment of their lives to the Lord Jesus Christ. The evening proved most enjoyable, allowing further visits to the exhibition and also an excellent meal, provided by our hosts from the Pavilion of Promise. We left at 10pm and most were very tired by the time we arrived back in Montilla at midnight.

Caro, Nigel and the dancers with a new friend

The Spain Team!

On Friday, we had less distance to travel to Aguilar de la Frontera, which was a somewhat more rural town than some of the others. We had a good time of fellowship in the afternoon and the concert was held in what appeared to be the local cattle market! Seating had to be conveyed from neighbouring towns, as this was in fact a fiesta time, their particularly important date being the Assumption of Mary into heaven. The concert proved a time of great rejoicing and celebration of the glory of God. There were four encores to the 'Eight-fold Alleluia' and the audience joined in the celebrations of dancing and singing with those who came down from the stage. There had been much prayerful protection of the dancers, particularly on a stage such as this, where the flooring had to be rolled up at the edges and there was little room, and there were also solid metal pillars at the side of the stage. It was during the alfresco dancing celebration outside, that one of the dancers sprained her ankle extremely badly. It was thought initially to be broken but as hands were laid upon the ankle and prayer made, the swelling subsided and the pain disappeared. The presence of Operation Mobilisation (OM) workers and the ECM team who had come from other areas proved, as at Lucena, most apposite as there were several people present who wished to give their heart to the

Lord and receive eternal life through the blood of Jesus. At Lucena, where ECM had been working for fourteen years, there was only one committed Christian living in the town until the time of these concerts, when fruit was gathered for eternal harvest.

On the final Saturday, the concert was held in a local square at Montilla. As the evening progressed there was once more a time of great celebration and rejoicing, and again it was good to see many people involved in serious conversation, discussion and commitment of their lives to the Lord with the welcome leading of OM workers and ECM team members.

The journey back the following morning proved peaceful and uncomplicated. On this occasion it was the Manchester team that left first whilst the Birmingham and London parties were able to enjoy a day on the beach before travelling back late at night!

ECM saw the NEO visit as part of their ongoing ministry in Cordoba Province. Whilst it was a great joy and privilege to be involved in wonderful concerts and times of fellowship, this tour was part of an ongoing plan in which not only the ECM team and OM visitors, but also many resident Christians were involved.

As a very privileged member of this tour, I recall it as a time which contained particularly happy memories. I spoke a little of the language, having acquired an A level some years previously and I loved all things Spanish. In fact, in recent years we have discovered, rather coincidentally, that both Pete and I may each have some Spanish blood! Pete had been able to learn to play the charango, which is a wonderful instrument, albeit (rather gruesomely) originally made from

Musicians in rehearsal

the shells of armadillos! He came along to both sing and help play the glorious South American music we performed. Paul Sheppard, Nick Lacey and Pete Desmond showed great prowess with genuine South American sampoñas (huge panpipes) which shared the melody between them, note for note and were wonderful to watch in action! Nick played a wooden flute, the 'quena' and as ever, produced an unimaginably beautiful sound. Though we had heard these instruments back in the UK, somehow they were transported to new heights in a Spanish environment.

Discussions with South American experts

Another reason for my joy was that our eldest daughter, Lucy, who had become a young contributor to the NEO

dance team in Sweden a couple of years previously (Gothenburg '90) when she was nearly eight years old, was asked to come and take the part of the child in the South American movement of 'Symphony of the Nations'. This had been played by both Maria Beasley (now Maria Fry) and also by a very young Mary Burton in previous years!

Somewhere, to this day, I have an old cassette recording of the mock up of the Jazz Parable, 'The Wise and Foolish Virgins'. Nigel and I had travelled down to London, where Nick Lacey and Pete Desmond had set up equipment to record the piece for the benefit of dance rehearsals. Nigel asked me to sing 'Marriage at Sunrise' (Day/Swinford, now lovingly known as 'The Bridegroom song' and sung beautifully in more recent years by Catherine Swinford-White). On the way home, I recall Nigel decided to stop on the motorway for coffee and during our break he asked me to consider becoming the Central Administrator of the NEO, now that the role was becoming increasingly necessary. Up until that time, I had served on the P & P as Singers' Secretary, with occasional other administrative tasks when called for and so this was a further step for me. As ever, even in the midst of preparations for a major tour, the functioning of the core of the NEO's administration was being thoughtfully and prayerfully considered by Nigel. This has been a lifelong aspect of his work, never taken for granted or overlooked.

Despite a few 'takes' – the tape was created successfully, thanks to the exemplary patience of Nigel, Nick and Pete,

Sunset rehearsals

and by the end of the day, we had a product we could give to the dancers, and I found myself with a significant role change which would last until the NEO ended in 2016!

We took an exciting repertoire to Spain, including Duke Ellington numbers, a jazz band style 'Hallelujah chorus', some lovely Christian songs translated into Spanish, the glorious 'Resucito' and the above mentioned South American movement of 'Symphony of the Nations', plus two fantastic salsa pieces. The visual extravaganza added by the dance

Wise & Foolish Virgins, Jazz Parable

group was a real crowd-puller. Nigel's new jazz dance version of the 'Parable of the Wise and Foolish Virgins' went down really well, being simultaneously very funny and incredibly

Gillian Mackrill and Julian Adkins in 'Marriage at Sunrise'

moving. Julian (mentioned above) also danced the beautiful pas de deux with Jillian Mackrill (also of Birmingham Royal Ballet), which took place in the middle of a dream scene in the parable, which Jillian had choreographed and which captivated all onlookers whenever it was performed. The audience watched transfixed. The amazing ballet lifts were particularly stunning! Alison Holden gave a lovely rendition of the song 'Marriage at Sunrise' during that particular moment in this tour.

Julie narrates 'Wise & Foolish Virgins' Jazz Parable

My active part in the parable however, was the narration. I remember being a little surprised (having been taught Madrid Spanish, lisp and all) when it was suggested I use the softer, South American Spanish for this. It was assumed that this was used in Cordoba Province and would be more easily understood. I was very relieved when people told me after our performances that they *had* understood all I read perfectly, but the confusion arose when one man asked me why I was speaking it with a South American accent. That wasn't my only linguistic problem! As we travelled around the various areas during this tour, I encountered ever more confusion, because always people came up to speak to me, assuming I was fluent in Spanish because of the narration (which I most certainly was not!) but in every single place they sounded completely different. I struggled hugely in one town to understand what the chap who was happily chattering to me was actually saying – until he dropped a giant clue when he happened to mention 'Epana' (Spain) and I at last realised that in fact he was leaving the 's' out of every word! Once I made up for this deviation from the norm, I began to be able to respond to him! By far my best memory of trying to work with this beautiful language was the privilege of standing beside Ron and hearing him explain the Gospel to some of the young teenagers we encountered, and then leading them in a prayer of commitment. In one town, we prayed together over a lad with a malformed arm, who wanted to ask for healing. He was not visibly healed at that time, but it was wonderful to hear how gently and sensitively Ron prayed with him.

As someone who was somewhat pulled hither and yon during this tour, with singers' rehearsals in one place, and then having to suddenly join dance rehearsals elsewhere with Lucy, some memories are, I confess, a bit higgledy-piggledy. I do recall being so glad that we were eventually rescued during our coach journey, after the hydraulics had broken down. We seemed to wait for hours and were very tired. All thanks were due to Raul D'Oliveira who, being Portuguese, was able to converse fairly easily with the Spanish driver and then explain to the rest of us what on earth was going on. One of my oddest recollections of that seemingly interminable night was stopping at a garage, to find umpteen cages of particularly cross-looking pigeons outside it! Another recollection was of the camaraderie on board our coach! After we had been stationary for longer than we could have imagined, someone shouted, "Never mind, we'll look back at this one day and laugh!" Pete yelled in reply, "Yeah, from three yards down the road!" But my abiding memory is of dear Keith and Janet's care of us throughout the tour, hurriedly preparing buns when we had to set out in the early hours, spread either with Nutella or some other delight. They even gave us a *choice* which we could order beforehand! They were first up in the morning all through the week in fact, getting the tea urn on and breakfast ready. True enablers!

Most of our concerts were actually in the late evening, hence our gratitude for afternoon siesta! It felt a little odd at first to get used to this routine, but it was fantastic to see how the villages came alive at the traditional time of the 'promenade',

when the local people would don their bright clothes and venture into the gloriously warm night to enjoy being with their friends and come excitedly to our concerts. There were lots of children and young people, as well as Ron and Brenda's own children, who were great company for Lucy.

A not so pleasant memory of this tour was the number of us Brits' who had nosebleeds! Lucy and I were also among the ones who experienced this – and Ginny Cornish, our lovely blonde saxophonist who also happened to be a GP – would help us with cotton wool plugs and advice about keeping a damp (and therefore cool) cloth handy to apply to the forehead in the dry heat which was causing this phenomenon. She would patiently haul us out of rehearsal or prayer meeting and minister to us in another room whenever this occurred to anyone.

In true NEO style, the party was soon in the swing of fun-filled fellowship and I recall one evening, after we had been given generous helpings of watermelon for our dessert after the evening meal, some bright spark initiated a game of flicking the black seeds at each other across the tables! (I hope we cleared up after ourselves!) Our chef made a special effort for us one evening, appearing with a big grin on his face and an enormous dish of paella, in which 'NEO' was written in anchovies on the top, in his arms!

As ever, there had been suffering and sacrifice involved. Caro Swinford's father had just passed away, immediately before this tour. She bravely came, doing all required of her with God's grace. The funeral was arranged for after her return.

The food was good and the college where we were able to stay, comfortable, and having gone expecting no free time, we had quite a number of nice surprises; a trip to a swimming pool and a visit to a local vineyard in Montilla, with time to taste a little of its famous sherry (some folk bringing back a small souvenir barrel!). Perhaps the loveliest thing for the group however, was the way the Lord touched so many in our party, enriching lives, refreshing and encouraging. The fellowship was very sweet indeed and there was the usual unique humour which hallmarks the NEO throughout.

For me, this was a lovely pairing of ministries, as we brought our particular expertise in music, song and dance, to the ongoing work of this faithful missionary organisation.

It blessed both, and we all came away the richer for it. Surely the opportunities we had in *Expo '92* were very rare privileges, and I shall never forget performing in the heat on the huge stage (El Palenque Stadium) which was surrounded on three sides by fountains, which were timed to sporadically leap skyward at different levels, to cool and refresh the air. The crowds were wonderfully 'Spanish' in their response, none of the British reserve! It was a delight to receive their visible and audible enthusiasm! The 'South American Movement' was always a favourite of mine from the first moment of arriving in what had become the New English Orchestra Singers. The music was so joyous and vibrant and the beautiful dances were so wonderful. Having done a floristry course early on in our married life, I had enjoyed making hair combs of silk flowers for all the girls in the singers to wear. I can still recall sitting cross-legged on the floor during a rehearsal at City Road Methodist Church parlour, with baby Stephanie beside me, as I made more of these for newcomers who would take part in this tour. The last jubilant chords of the finale consisted of sheer outrageous celebration, including party poppers, as Christ came to right all wrongs, free the oppressed and join in the dancing! Don't we long for that day?

Lucy Fry, still dancing whenever she can

Nige & Caro with a small barrel of Montilla sherry

10
Jubilee!
Into the new millennium

To begin, these notes comprise my diary entry for 'YK2', which I actually wrote retrospectively, using brief notes taken throughout the year in my 'handbag diary'. The year itself was too full to keep very detailed records intact on a daily basis! It had the following note attached: *To be read in conjunction with the Bible study notes of the times we spent together in NEO led by Nigel,* and these appear at the end. For clarity, I have added some bracketed comments in hindsight.

I don't mind if I have to go through this year with three sopranos and a dog!

This special year with NEO did hold a number of unpleasant experiences for some of us, but if I were to single out the most positive memory of our times together, it would be the sweetness of the fellowship between us all.

The year contained a huge amount of work for those of us concerned – the spring saw eight venues booked for the 'Jubilee – A Litany of Thanksgiving' events in cathedrals around the country, then a summer trip to Salzburg, followed by an autumn cabaret-style event called 'Fascinatin' Rhythm' in hotels and one vineyard (at which venues the audience sat at tables enjoying cheese and wine) and eventually culminated in a Christmas tour.

As members of the body of Christ we often feel pressure to be seen as positive and cheerful, and if we meet one another only sporadically, such an attitude is often possible to achieve. However, meeting with the same party of people so often throughout a twelve-month period, in all seasons and through the inevitable scenes of life; house moves, job changes, health and sickness, death and bereavement, the threat or the reality of cancer, the joyful news of a new baby, a wedding, a birthday, or simply the grim 'hanging on' from day to day, week to week in a tough situation, then one sees one's friends much more clearly! Then we can truly 'rejoice with those who rejoice and weep with those who weep'. NEO has often been like this for the singers, who meet more regularly, and of course for the Prayer and Planning group who attempt to meet fortnightly, but among this group of people who had committed themselves to the entire year, it was quite remarkable.

It's impossible to ignore the fact that one of your company has just left the rehearsal room in tears, or that another has a migraine coming on just before a performance, or indeed by contrast, that the loud squeals of delight outside during lunch at a hostel in Austria, are the result of a telephone call announcing the arrival of a first grandchild! These are all family matters, and though inevitably the bitter is mingled in at times, yes the fellowship is sweet. It has a special savour, of which, having once tasted it, one would not wish to lose the memory.

I particularly noticed how comments came in from our audiences, (very noticeably after the intimacy of 'Fascinatin' Rhythm') about the quality of our friendships in NEO. There is always a great camaraderie in performing together on stage, but this had obviously gone deeper. People hadn't been idly amused but genuinely impressed by what they had seen. They believed it. It wasn't just part of the show. Our fellowship on and offstage had the integrity of the presence of Jesus.

I've often remembered how my Dad used to say that it takes a deal of courage to lay a plan for a whole year and then stick to it! How right he was. And we had enough potential to cause some to feel like pulling out – but they didn't. I don't think we felt we had all shone with a consistent brightness, but we did find that through God's grace, when one burned low, there came alongside those who burned more strongly who could quicken the flame. Surely this is what it's all about, what the Lord always intended for us. The effect to the audiences of course was in fact a consistent light shining through that part of the body of Christ, and did we not begin the year with exhortations to 'remember the body of Christ'? (See Bible study notes following.)

The events themselves were new and experimental. The autumn tour included a 'Disputation' – a staged discussion, brilliantly executed by NEO members, Prof Robin Mason, Dr Chrissie Cairns and Paul Sheppard. I have to admit the only doubts on this new departure which I heard, were actually from highly intelligent Christians who felt we should stick to music-making! But we can't move freely in this work if we are tied to the 'way we used to do it' or the way our audiences would like us to do it! The endless repetition of a formula can spell death to a creative soul. NEO however, has always been ready to follow the Shepherd all over the crags, and that inevitably led to some precarious moments! God forbid that we ever end up being nothing more than an entertainment agency!

-------------------- Dimples --------------------
I just wanted to hear you judder like that!

Nigel told us that we shouldn't expect to get from one end to the other of a year dedicated to God, with no surprises. Sometimes we are called to follow, and sometimes just to stand our ground – and we've done both this year. So this twelve- month period was an experiment, partly to see whether people would be prepared to carve an entire year out of their lives to focus on God through the ministry of NEO and partly to see how God would speak and move through such a group and the events He inspired.

(Julie: Here follow the written memories indelibly fixed in my own mind. These accounts may serve to show how NEO members often found that during significant NEO activity, life could become hugely challenging for them personally also. A life- calling becomes a major priority which cannot be divorced from everything else which affects us. God however remains sovereign throughout, and if I had to live my life again, I would hope that I would be more ready to accept the hard times as part of my learning the availability of God's grace, rather than often feeling distressed that something was going badly wrong!)

January 1st 2000

My mother died at four o'clock in the afternoon after a horrible time lasting several months (though things had been very challenging for several years). My sister had to deal with some extremely difficult situations during that time. Single, and living in the family home, she had borne the brunt of Mum's care for a long time, with only very intermittent relief from me (with the family to care for and the NEO work). Mum never learned that she had in fact developed an unknown primary cancer which had formed metasteses in both lungs and brain. We just thought she had dementia.

In the middle of all this, someone suddenly and quite unexpectedly gave us a gift with which we were able to buy a much needed new carpet for our front room – a precious encouragement.

Our mother, we found, had left no will, so there was a big hassle, lots of legal wrangles – also a late funeral. Pete had to be away taking part in a school trip in Cornwall for the whole of the week in which the cremation occurred – coming home just for the service, but then having to return – leaving me alone with the children after the funeral and utterly miserable. My sister's suffering was intense and I needed to be strong for her but felt I couldn't achieve it.

Throughout this period, there was music to learn and rehearsals to attend. When we first met together after Christmas and New Year, we found that one of our alto singers, Kate Harrod-Wild (née Ansell) had lost her father also with cancer, during the Christmas holidays and another of our altos, Christina Thomson, had to tell us that her mother had suffered a fatal car accident whilst out to buy the turkey on Christmas Eve. We began the year sharing each other's grief.

The music itself however, was wonderful. We worked on Nigel's vision for 'Jubilee – A Litany of Thanksgiving', an event filled with different kinds of music which began with a mingling of plainsong 'Veni sancte spiritus' and a modern song 'Let us give thanks' – a glorious combination of old and new, flowing together and exalting the Lord who is the same yesterday, today and forever. It continued with hymns, spiritual songs and pieces especially composed by Nigel. I remember singing with real joy one minute and struggling through tears the next as we worshipped the Lord.

Pete blessed me one evening through those early months; he'd been sharing a reading about Moses' experience when he encountered the bitter waters of 'Marah'. God's instruction to him was to throw a log into the waters to make them sweet. The commentary noted that the tree of wood of course represented the cross of Christ, and again we were reminded that when we hit the depths, things that leave a bitter taste in our mouths, the remedy is the crucified and risen Christ. Only in looking at one who suffered so much more than ourselves, do we find our perspectives fully restored.

While embarked on one tour, we had to continue organising the remaining ones for the year. There was much to do. One of the Autumn cabaret performances we were planning ('Fascinatin' Rhythm') was going to be in Bristol, and so Nigel decided to take me with him and Caro that afternoon so we could visit the hotel venue, stay overnight and have our meeting next day with the relevant staff member. That morning, Pete noticed a chap trying to rob the back of a workman's van full of tools over the road, and leaned out of the front room window to warn him that he was being watched and should stop. He hadn't realised an unseen accomplice was on the lookout nearby and the result, a few minutes later after Pete had come into the lounge, was that said accomplice had picked up a paving stone from our front garden and lobbed it through the front room bay window, shattering the glass and narrowly missing our daughter Lucy's head! It was accompanied by abusive language and the threat of our house being torched. It took me all the rest of the time between that incident and Nigel's arrival, to clear away the shards of broken glass which were absolutely everywhere and we were thankful that an emergency glazier could come to repair and secure the window.

We had instigated a 'Watch Service' at the end of the Jubilee performances, masterminded by Nick and Nicola Gerrard, allowing a moment in time for people to either make a decision for Christ or rededicate themselves. Some did indeed come forward and take that glorious opportunity. These were very

'active' times spiritually. Each evening was so precious, many were deeply blessed.

The next incident at home early one morning, was a fire in the washing machine which burned some of Luke's and Pete's clothes which had been in the wash, but which occurred, mercifully, before Luke left the house, as I was still in bed. We were hugely thankful we didn't have a major house fire – just no washing machine! Pete ended up with a pair of shorts full of holes where the fire had penetrated the drum! I remember holding them up in the midst of the chaotic mess and roaring with laughter – had he worn them he would have looked like a chap peppered with shot by a gamekeeper, having incurred a nasty bout of 'Poacher's Bottom'! Not for the first time did we find humour helping us along!

March saw a big issue flare up about our hopes to make a CD out of DAT tape recordings of the Jubilee performances. Having genuinely thought I had dealt with it, I realised I had forgotten to ask permission of Worcester Cathedral to make such a recording and had thereby caused a major mess up! I did write, but to no avail. We desperately needed fifteen minutes of that particular venue's recording to complete our 'Jubilee' CD. This, I have to admit, reduced me to a bag of misery and I could hardly explain to Nigel on the telephone what had occurred. I believe I had to ring off for a while to collect myself! (Julie: As ever, he was wonderful about it, and later wrote himself in such terms as won the day, and the CD!)

March 3rd

In the midst of all this 'busyness' Nigel's daughter Catherine was married to Pete White. The wedding was a lovely occasion, and I was privileged to read a poem they had chosen during the service. They had to take their honeymoon in sections between NEO events! They suddenly arrived together for a rehearsal, and Caro introduced them as 'Mr and Mrs White' so we all clapped them in!

Back home we were plagued in our local community by drugs-based prostitution and the crime that accompanied it. Pete was horrendously busy in his role as Neighbourhood Watch Coordinator, in which he grew so involved in linking various agencies in the community together, that he became a member of the Ladywood Advisory Board and was eventually able to do something about it all. We didn't get much sleep however during this period! Tiredness was a plague in a year as busy as this – we were beginning to feel the exertions of someone who didn't want these NEO experiments to be a success.

However, we were given a new washing machine by Catherine when she left her flat in Scarborough and moved into her new home! How astonishing are the workings of God's big family! Nige and Caro lovingly delivered it by car to our home.

April

There was major police activity following a big all night prayer meeting at our church, with local houses raided and many arrests made. Remarkably though, half way through the actual prayer meeting, two policemen came into the church. They had been sitting outside in their car that night, and were mystified as to why everything was so quiet. They hadn't received a single emergency call of any kind, which was extremely unusual. When they knew there was a prayer meeting going on which included praying for the local police and focusing on what had been an intensive increase in crime, they were astonished. "Well that explains it!" was their comment. They went away with something to think about. A couple of days later, while hauling over a car for dangerous driving, a local police officer found himself staring down the barrel of a revolver wielded by the driver. Mercifully, though the trigger was pulled, the gun jammed, and his life was saved. We heard about this afterwards and attributed that also to the covering of prayer and God's grace at that difficult time.

We also learned that Pete's school might have to close and his job might be on the line. Local 'working girls' had become very unpleasant. One of their pimps tried to kick our front door down. We had to look for a secondary school for Stephanie for the following year, not an easy decision in Birmingham at that time.

May

I read some poetry at an early NEO micro-orchestra event at a church in Parbold (see Chapter 15 – 'To the Saints in Rome...'). We made friendships there with the organiser, Margaret Atherton, a friend of Lesley and John Thompson, who attended the same church at one time. (Julie: This event was to have good repercussions!)

We also found that our cooker had broken, but again someone very dear to us bought us a new one. I recall having to go to my sister's home and sort out Mum's belongings – an emotional time. The next day, I had the entire Poffley family to stay the weekend. (Julie: In those days there were six – now there are seven!) Glorious fun! (I was so glad of that cooker!)

In NEO we were debating on the future of the work in Europe, particularly with Brigitta Hofer's players. More big decisions had to be made. I had to write a major document for Nigel on this in the summertime, which was quite sensitive. This was the first time we had been led to contemplate whether or not this ministry was actually in any way 'transferable' (e.g. rather like the cloak of Elijah upon Elisha). (Julie: The conclusion, after the passage of much time, debate and attempts to action such a trial, was that it was not. Looking back on this comment from 2016 after the last public event of NEO and during the year of its closure – it still is not – for all the same reasons!)

I had loads to sort out admin-wise and we also had an important visit to Salzburg that summer, too much to record in detail. Lucy sang with the Singers for the first time.

September

Stephanie started at her new school, a place we felt was on an upward path. She was happy, praise God.

I took Lucy to a conference in Ridley Hall, Cambridge entitled 'Sounding the Depths', which would assist her A level Art assignments, one of which was based around the etched glass 'Millennium Window' designed by Mark Cazalet, now in place in Worcester Cathedral. We spent some time talking to one of Nigel's friends, who lectured there, Jeremy Begbie (Julie: now in a professorial role in America). That proved a fascinating weekend, in which we noted the art installations of the artist who designed the question mark motif for the Holy Trinity Brompton Alpha course, Charlie Mackesy. It consisted of two half torsos, with heads and chests made of boxes whose interiors were painted black. One of them, representing someone who has the life of Christ in them, simply had a lit light bulb in place of the heart! How simple is that?

Catherine Swinford-White sings Let the Bright Seraphim with Pete Desmond on trumpet

Lizzie Swinford, Sarah Christopher and Christopher Poffley

Lizzie Swinford and Sarah Christopher in site specific dance

Sarah and Lizzie looking thoughtful!

Dr. Christine Joynes (AKA 'Chrissy Cairns)

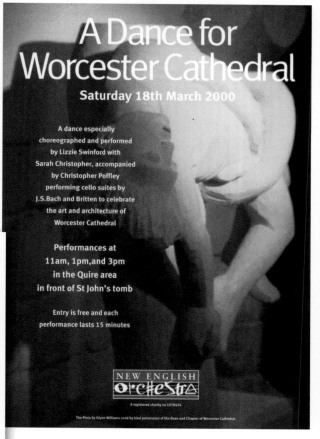

A Dance for Worcester Cathedral

Saturday 18th March 2000

A dance especially choreographed and performed by Lizzie Swinford with Sarah Christopher, accompanied by Christopher Poffley performing cello suites by J.S.Bach and Britten to celebrate the art and architecture of Worcester Cathedral

Performances at 11am, 1pm, and 3pm in the Quire area in front of St John's tomb

Entry is free and each performance lasts 15 minutes

NEW ENGLISH ORCHESTRA

A registered charity no 1078426

The Pieta by Glynn Williams used by kind permission of the Dean and Chapter of Worcester Cathedral.

Poster for Site Specific dance at Worcester Cathedral, 2000

Lots of NEO rehearsals

I vividly remember Nigel and I having a telephone conversation in which we both, rather unusually, had hysterics and laughed until we cried. For various reasons I will not give the purport of the amusement here. It was that night however, that Nigel first had chest pains and was taken to hospital, where they discovered over the next day or two, that X-rays displayed a large shadow on his lungs. They started predicting advanced lung cancer and planning further tests. We couldn't believe that this man, who had recently been tanking up and down mountains in Austria, could possibly have this disease! At the time I thought he'd just laughed too much that day and made his ribs ache! How wrong I was!

Tests eventually showed he had a thymoma, a tumour on the thymus gland. Surgery had to be scheduled. None of us had ever heard of such a condition. Carolyn mentioned that the growth was the size of a doughnut – and in another of those absurd moments when humour breaks through even the darkest clouds, she suggested the X-ray had probably just shown up a large tea bag!

Before the final diagnosis was made however, we had a Gaines Conference Centre weekend for rehearsals with Singers and Orchestra to get through. I had to explain to everyone what was happening to Nigel (and Carolyn) back in Bolton. Catherine, Pete, Lizzie and Robin were present with us. It was a tender time. I'd taken a final phone call from Nigel in the lane outside the Centre on my mobile, while walking with Ruth Miller. I spent a little time outside letting the tears flow, before going in to have the evening meal and then attempting to make all the difficult announcements and chivvy everyone up to make a great weekend of it all! We certainly managed that, under the expert direction of Pete Desmond and Martin Lowe.

My next 'Bolton day' (days I spent from time to time working with Nigel in his own home office) involved catching the bus from the Swinford home to Bolton Hospital and sitting taking instructions from Nige's bedside, where he was remarkably cheerful. I had to lead P & P meetings in his absence and much, much prayer went up from our ranks through that time.

October

Luke passed his driving test and soon bought his first car!

We entered 'Fascinatin' Rhythm' the hotel tour, with a 'Disputation' in the middle. Nigel made it to a couple of performances as a member of the audience! No one would believe the complexities we went through over dress code for this event! But in the end (as photographs still show) we all turned out rather well!

Nigel's operation took place on November 9th, 2000 at around 8.30am (Julie: Many things of a very mixed nature have seemed to occur since then in the lives of NEO members on that particular date.) *It was a long and complex affair involving sawing through the breastbone and wiring it back together again – but it was successful!*

Julia Myles (once head of NEO dancers) had her third child by caesarean section, and was extremely ill. Again the 'family' was much in prayer for her.

Nigel's tumour was benign, but radiotherapy would have to be applied for around three weeks when he had recovered from surgery, to prevent any re-growth. That was an awful time for him. Caro made him loads of wonderful soups for his very sore throat.

Preparations began for the Christmas Tour

One of the venues was St Paul's Hammersmith, London, and I travelled with Janet Fox in her car. En route, a stone flew up from the motorway and smashed the window right next to me, which meant a whole episode of stopping to have it repaired and arriving late to the concert. This was part of Janet's initiation into spiritual warfare situations while in active NEO ministry – and particularly those involving transporting any members of the Fry family!

(Julie: Throughout her many kindnesses in giving lifts to myself and my family to various events over the years, Janet encountered such matters as Luke being suddenly, and for no reason, bitten by a large Dalmatian dog, who just happened to be walking past our home as Luke came down the path to get into the car! We had to spend time visiting the hospital first, for a check-up and a tetanus injection. On a journey to Manchester for a Vigil in the Cathedral, we had to leave Pete behind, about to go to hospital with severe chest pains and a suspected heart problem, whilst in fact it was nothing more than indigestion! That was an awful moment, but he had absolutely insisted on my going! The timings were astonishing.)

A big street party was held in Link Road, to encourage a whole group of Iranian and Iraqi Asylum Seekers who had been moved into houses on the other side of our road.

Christmas

Nigel was still up and down

I was still up and down

Pete was still up and down

New Year 2001

Everybody seemed up and down!

Nigel began finding himself suddenly subject to panic attacks and entered a whole year of mental suffering, through which he was enormously brave but very unwell with what we found was anxiety syndrome in official terms – nothing short of horrific in practical terms. I recall Brenda Lowe explaining that she had heard how this after- effect of invasive surgery had apparently become common during the Kosovo conflict during the late nineties, in men requiring it after incurring chest injuries. Our 'Bolton days' through this period consisted (happily for me) of long, detailed talks as we got into the car and drove equally long distances – perhaps over the moors, or to the Lake District to see Keith and Janet for an hour or so over soup and coffee. Driving helped his mind to relax, so we could discuss ongoing issues in NEO. It was a coping procedure for Nigel which I admit I enjoyed hugely, though I longed for him to be well. Mercifully Nigel has never been one to keep asking the 'whys' of times of suffering like this – so we just got on with it.

Pete was stressed. His school situation was very serious and the area around our home still extremely difficult. The Christmas tour had to be conducted by Pete Desmond and Martin Lowe in Nigel's continuing absence. I had loads of work and concern in whichever direction I turned!

I'm reminded of a quote from 'Anne of Green Gables'. When someone asked how Anne was, she replied: "Well in body, but considerably rumpled in spirit thank you." Pretty good summary of the turn of the year I think!

During this last year then, I've asked more questions which have no ready answers; I've learned about unwillingness in me to suffer, and about weaknesses in my character. I've risen to heights of great joy and sunk to depths of near despair. Between times there have been places of huge encouragement and times of rest and enjoyment, with some good laughs. Generally though, there were very few plateaux and very little plain, easy walking for any great distance. Have I read more of the Bible? No, less – but I've read certain bits of it over and over and over again!

Have I prayed more? Not always in words. I've wept a lot and prayed in tongues more than I usually do – probably because it was so much easier and less problematic than trying to put things into English! Sometimes we need His 'groans too deep for words' in the times when we can say nothing at all.

I've read huge amounts of glorious CS Lewis and spent a lot of time talking 'at' rather than 'to' God, just telling him how I felt. I've felt less obedient, more tempted, angrier, more inadequate, less Christian, less lovable and much, much more aware of God's holiness. Someone once told me of a nun she knew, who used to say that the more she was aware of the Lord's radiance, the filthier she felt. So perhaps all I've been experiencing is in fact all part of coming close to God. I hope so.

I think more these days about where I want to go and what I want to eventually leave behind and how the great 'marriage' between Christ and his miraculously purified Bride, will one day more than make up for 'soiled clothes en route to the wedding, and muddy footprints right up to the door'. (Thoughts of CS Lewis.)

Brigitte Furze (in her inimitable Swiss frankness) said in one of her telephone calls: "Don't you feel we've seen the worst of each other this year?" I know she hasn't found it easy either, but I think she was expressing what I was trying to say earlier: we've loved each other warts and all! For that and for all His amazing and enabling grace, may God be praised!

Deliver us, Lord, from making it sound like a beach mission!

Nigel's Input during the year 2000

Throughout the life of the family of the New English Orchestra, one of the hallmarks of its growth in the Lord has been the constant, fresh, bubbling spring of teaching which Nigel (with occasional contributions from others) has provided. This is, in fact, one element which some of our folk most dreaded losing when the news broke that we were to close in 2016. From the earliest beginnings, I can recall Nigel opening his Bible and simply sharing from his personal devotions which had been going on in the background, or which he had studied with a view to whatever situation we were tackling at the time. His viewpoint was usually fresh, unusual, inspirational – sometimes controversial perhaps, until one realised what he was in fact leading up to. Some of the most serious topics would be threaded through with asides which would bring a burst of hilarity from the floor, and a moment of recovery might be necessary before we could continue in a 'quiet and refined' manner!

I don't think Nigel ever set out to be a Bible teacher or even a preacher, though he apparently had a very good training ground as he grew to manhood in the congregations of the Plymouth Brethren. He tells me that there was opportunity given for anyone to stand and deliver a word, and that he took that opportunity again and again (embarrassingly often, he recalls!) but that his elders allowed him to speak and would address anything they felt needed a slight amendment or further comment, in a loving and mature manner.

Various golden threads (to change the metaphor) which we have enjoyed over the years have come, we understand via Nigel, from the inspiration of commentaries written by the Plymouth Brethren theologians. Some of these teachings have found their way onto our NEO website, though sadly only one major series, (in our 'Insights' section) which Nigel entitled 'The Gospel in Art'. This covered all matters to do with one of Nigel's most beloved topics, namely the Tabernacle, as described in the Old Testament Pentateuch. This subject was very important also to Derek Prince, who wrote a brilliant book entitled 'Entering the Presence of God' on this subject and covered many of the same issues. As both Nigel and Prince make clear, the layout and makeup of the Tabernacle and all its implements both large and small, are in themselves a fundamental picture of the 'process' whereby we come into the presence of and are enabled to worship our Holy God. It is truly an inspirational topic and should (in my humble opinion) be studied by every Christian. The subject also gives clarity on the difference, sometimes confusingly mingled these days, between justification and sanctification – huge subjects which need to be clearly understood.

Looking miserable is our default position!
(Thankfully not for long with Nigel around!)

Another topic which frequently had to be taught by Nigel, is that of spiritual warfare. As no doubt the accounts in this collection will bear witness, (e.g. Chapter 5 – *Whatever the weather*). NEO has long been acquainted with the reality of this. I remember that when we were on tour in 2014, Nigel taught us about the effect that events involving spiritual conflict can have on the cosmos itself – and reminded us of the many, many occasions over the years (some again mentioned in these pages) when the weather itself seemed to be caught up in the turmoil. To the humanist, these things would be utter nonsense. The humanist is, as ever, entitled to his own opinion. We simply retain the right to log the actual experience we have witnessed and draw our own conclusions.

8th January 2000 Preparation for the Litany of Thanksgiving (to take place in eight venues during the spring)

(Julie: The quote which occurs under the main title of this chapter, indicates that Nigel had set out to go through this year dedicated to the Lord, with anyone who wanted to join him – whether that provided the right balance of voices and instruments or not!)

Our first Saturday Singers' rehearsal from 12 noon to 5pm

Nigel read Luke 6 – the Beatitudes (from the Authorised Version) and talked to us of 'leaping for joy'!

The watchword (or phrase) for this year is surely to be, 'Draw near to God and He will draw near to you.' Only God knows what we need for this year, which is all about meeting with Him in a new way.

Nigel shared a prayer he prays each day if he can: 'Make my mind a palace fit for the King.' He also shared a useful mental picture of God in working clothes, with His sleeves rolled up, and working around inside our minds – a very loving and strong figure. We should pray that God should rule day and night in our minds, gripping the various rooms that need dealing with, moving our 'furniture' around – opening cupboards we perhaps don't want Him to open, but He needs to deal with their contents; some may contain terror, fears, shame – the things we would never speak of.

If our minds are renewed, our thinking will change – if our thinking changes, everything changes.

In the Litanies we shall direct our thinking towards Christianity and its impact on our lives; starting with Gregorian chant ('Fill us with your Spirit' is its message), we go on to give thanks, not that devils flee in His name, but that our names are written in Heaven – in the Book of Life, and inscribed upon His palms. NB The concept of Heaven has been driven out of society's thinking – it is controversial – assumes a presumptuous attitude.

Luke 10 vv 17-21 about the seventy apostles returning after Christ had sent them out. We should not rejoice in our ministry, our successes, our gifts, but that we are going to heaven.

Nigel described this coming year rather humorously as a 'Year of poise' in which somehow we needed to 'leap for joy'! So the

first notion here is – we are going to heaven! The second notion in this coming year is that of the body of Christ. God's whole aim and objective is to create a bride for His Son.

Ref. Ephesians 5: 'Husbands love your wives....' The bride of Christ is to be holy and without blemish. This isn't about individual Christians, but a body, a bride.

Ref. Ephesians 4 vv 7-8 & 11 – this tells us that the perfecting of all the saints for the work of ministry is for the 'edifying of the Body of Christ'.

Nigel shared how he has never been able to imagine NEO being permanent. It will disperse one day and break into little pieces, all of them going on to build up the Body of Christ.

(Julie: Well Nige, here we are, undergoing that process as I write, sixteen years on!)

So: Rejoice in heaven

Remember the body of Christ.

Nigel then shared the story of a man named Fred Little, whom he remembers from childhood. Nige recalled that as a lad between the ages of five and thirteen, he often used to cycle home from school and would see Fred at the side of the street with his cart, sweeping the gutter clean. He would stop and chat to Fred, who had a round face with very bright eyes and the air of someone so full of the Holy Spirit that he might burst at any moment! Fred loved being a dustman – he chose that job because it gave him so much time to meditate on the Lord. He was a very good speaker with a wonderful voice – a convention speaker. He might have been criticised for not aiming at a 'higher' career, but his son became a well-known Oxford Don, Dr Philip Little, and his daughter took a profession. He was a man who had given himself entirely to Christ and the developing of Christ's body. Forty years on he is so memorable for just being the way he was – and that in part is responsible for Nigel being as he is today also. (Julie: I recall a dear friend of mine, Colin Bourne, recounting the tale of a humble motor mechanic he knew in a village in Cornwall years ago, who was obviously of the same ilk as Fred. He was the one to whom all the locals came for prayer with the laying on of hands for healing! How wonderful! (Presumably God's economy involved such people returning home not only healed, but driving home in a fully-functional vehicle also!)

This year is about FOCUS – not commitment. Nigel reminded us of the parable of the man who found treasure in a field and so went and sold all he had to buy that field. *That's 'focus'. The modern man however, would be more likely to take a mortgage out so that he could keep all he had and have the field – but with it would come many COMMITMENTS! Beware!*

So:

Rejoice in heaven – leap for joy in a year of poise!

Remember the body of Christ – to be His bride is the most prestigious aim and objective.

Look for focus on God, not commitments (even commitments for the sake of Christian things). What is the one thing needful? To sit at Jesus' feet, to listen to Him. That takes time!

We then sang through practically all the new programme for the Litanies.

First weekend away at The Gaines – 21st–23rd January 2000

Fellowship meeting, at 9.30am

Jeremiah 33 vv 2-3 'Thus saith the Lord....'

'Call unto me and I will answer thee'

Is there cynicism of the new when ageing? Tiredness when one hears that 'the Lord is doing a new thing'?

'I'm going to show you something you don't know!'

1 Corinthians 1 v 30

(Wisdom, righteousness, salvation and sanctification)

This year will be about the renewal of our minds – the centrality of Christ – all we need is in Him. He is more important than any of those items. "Christian thinking is like a tightrope – one topples from side to side."

The Disputation Team (Julie: these prepared discussions between three of our NEO members for public presentation, formed a part of the Litany of Thanksgiving) *is considering morality/absolutes. Where are these latter, even in music?*

As one can see from all the above, we were dealing with some deep and broad topics throughout that year, and looking honestly at our ministry and at the word of God. It was a rich time.

Special Memories, looking back now from the present day 2016

In case one is left thinking that I've only described the entire year in negative terms, let me redress that! This was a year of the most incredible privilege, fantastic outbreaks of joy and the delivery of some powerful musical ministry to a great number of people both in various parts of the UK and away in Salzburg.

The year definitely had an extraordinary blessing from the Lord upon it. As has already been mentioned, I do recall Nigel saying that he would go through that year with anyone who was prepared to join him in it, but we actually had a most wonderful team of people, and a wonderful and 'genuine' sound! The sufferings previously mentioned, only served to hone the various sufferers and make them more aware of the Lord's grace over their lives. I hope in retrospect they would agree with me on that.

16th February

We met as a group of four Trustees of the new charity for the first time at Nick and Nicola Gerrard's home on this particular evening. For me it all felt very new, never having been a director or a company secretary before. There was lots to learn and it all felt rather 'official' but we pledged ourselves to get on with the job and try to do it well, and with as little bother to the P & P and the NEO proper as possible. Looking back over the years, I think we achieved it too!

Litany of Thanksgiving – Memories from the music itself

We used to open the *Litany of Thanksgiving* (as mentioned above in my diary account) with a rather neat mingling of a Gregorian chant with 'Let us give thanks' – which whenever I listen to it on our 'Jubilee' recording, takes me right from echoing cloisters down the centuries, sweeping suddenly into the memory of the Fisherfolk, (mentioned in Chapter 2 – *Earliest beginnings*) who were so very instrumental (literally) in impressing Scripture into my mind when I was a teenager. They gave the first rendition I had ever heard of this piece and I loved it. Yes, we should rejoice that we can know, having put our trust in Jesus, that our names are *written in the Book of Life* and *inscribed upon His palms.* Today, amidst the huge variety of Christian thinking from those who constantly find themselves on the 'cutting edge' of spiritual warfare – casting out demons and delivering the oppressed on the one hand, being vessels of God's amazing healing power on the other – it still remains the case that the greatest miracle of all, is that of being transferred from the dominion of darkness into God's kingdom of glorious light! We have often since reminded one another, both in NEO and at my home church, that one of the few times the Lord used the phrase, *You must...* was when His sentence ended, *...be born again.*

'The Touching Piece'

This was one of the many pieces Nigel composed especially for this remarkable year's work. It was very delicate, unusual and striking in the way that it portrayed in music, the sense of Christ reaching out to minister to specific needs.

The Timpani solo

Val Dalton, at one point in the proceedings, had to give a spine-chilling solo which spoke of the sufferings of Christ on the cross, which never failed to give me goose bumps and call all sorts of images to mind each time she played it.

The final gathering we all enjoyed in a room in Rochester Cathedral

On 1st April, at the end of our Litany of Thanksgiving tour, Brigitte Furze shared about a visit she and Richard had made to Canada in the famous 'Fall' and how she had been so impressed by the glorious colours of the leaves we hear so much about. She related that she had decided to collect a few to take home, but as she stooped and took up leaf after leaf, she found herself rejecting each one, either because of a hole in it or some other disfigurement,

or because it turned out not to be an entire leaf after all, etc. In the end she was content to just look at them all, magnificently beautiful just as they lay. I never forgot her comment that this must be just how it is as the Lord looks at us, knowing our individual imperfections, but together, gloriously colourful, beautiful, precious and beloved! What a wonderful thought! Thanks Briggie for sharing that all those years ago!

Salzburg

What a full year this was – it's impossible to record everything here, but this tour was particularly memorable for the fact that we assisted Brigitta Hofer and the New European Orchestra (NEuO) to record a CD entitled 'Stimpt an die Seiten' ('Awake harp!' Psalm 57 v 8) which contained a variety of beautiful orchestral pieces, and also a good deal of singing! We recorded this with a professional company, in a church in the town of Hallein (famous for its salt mines and rather wonderful ice cream parlour – a necessary perk for our troops, as it turned out, after what proved to be a slightly harrowing experience!). As with many recordings we have made, we expected that we would have to repeat things a few times to get them sounding as one would wish – but to say the least, the recording crew were rather *particular* in this respect. I think this experience was only topped by a later occasion in the UK (which you will spot elsewhere among these pages). The experience was pretty exhausting, but we made a very lovely, and memorable, CD!

Fascinatin' Rhythm

The Grand Hotel Birmingham 7th October

We stood to deliver *Fascinatin' Rhythm*, with ladies wearing either black and silver blouses, with black skirts/trousers or joining the men in white shirts with the 'Y2000' black and silver waistcoats, with black trousers, in all cases looking very polished. We responded well to Pete Desmond's encouraging conducting of some of the pieces he had particularly arranged for the event, one of which involved claps and hand percussion, which were a new venture for the singers! The room in which we performed was in those days a large, beautiful hall with generous round tables,

Prof. Robin Mason of the Disputation Team

'Chrissy' Cairns — Disputation Team

where our audience members were seated comfortably, their spread of cheese and wine before them to enjoy, as we played and sang to them 'cabaret style'. I was delighted to see, at one table near the door, my own GP, whom I knew to be a Christian, sitting with a group of friends or family. That particularly thrilled me – we had never talked about our faith, but it was lovely to see her there, though we didn't get to speak to one another that evening. Pete's headmistress was also there – she was a believer too. Luke, our son, who was a photographer at the time, took a great photo of that whole scene and it brings back so many memories each time I see it at Nigel's.

Denbies Wine Estate 28th October

This was the last venue for *Fascinatin' Rhythm*, and was rather special! We enjoyed it hugely, and I was particularly happy that our good friends, Michael and Gillie Warren, were able to be present with us. Several of our party took the opportunity to purchase the odd bottle of wine from the shop there. (I wasn't entirely sure what I thought of English

wine I confess!) I thought it rather fitting, knowing Nigel as I do, that despite all he was going through, he managed to come to this venue as well as the Manchester one! These events took place just immediately before his operation in early November, so he was very much in our thoughts and prayers. Apart from that slight cloud over the proceedings, this had been a happy tour, and remarkable for the incredible display of talent, particularly that contributed by the 'Disputation' team. I think we left people with plenty to think about, but within a happy and congenial setting in each venue. Again, one could see not only the 'light touch' of Nigel, but sense the presence of the Holy Spirit. This last venue was a good one for contemplating the wine of the Kingdom! As with the miraculous wine of Cana though, I have no doubt there will be nothing whatsoever to criticise in the taste of that one!

The final concert tour of the year 1st–8th December

Looking Forward to Christmas: conducted by Pete Desmond and Martin Lowe in Nigel's absence. We all knew it would feel strange to go through the later events of the year without the Boss, but it had been super to see him at our Manchester cabaret event and of course, Denbies! I seem to recall, funnily enough, that it was in this tour that we first openly declared ourselves in our publicity, to be a Christian ensemble. Not that this had ever been hidden as such by any means, but Nigel had always wanted NEO to be viewed primarily as a bona fide Arts project, valuable in its own right, and able to perform anywhere it may be called to on the planet – whether the Christian faith was known to be welcome there or not. We lost nothing by the revelation, but rather gained from that point on I feel, though I remember wondering if we had done the right thing in this exposure at the time. Strange the things one remembers!

Martin and Pete did a wonderful job in the rehearsal and conducting of these concerts. It was a tribute, not only to their skill in music (and in Martin's case his astonishing gift for logistics also) but to their own God-given personalities and long- term commitment to the NEO family (which made them beloved of us all) that they were able to carry everyone through fairly seamlessly, despite the absence of Nigel.

Stand up comedy from Paul Sheppard at the Grand Hotel, Birmingham

It was a great tour – but it was on the journey to the final venue, St Paul's Hammersmith, that the incident recalled in my diary above occurred. Janet and I were rather put out by the window suddenly smashing on a very cold and breezy December afternoon on the motorway, with the sudden realisation that we would have absolutely no alternative but to stop off and have it replaced, which would make us late for this event.

So ended the year 2000, and with it, the whole experience of learning how to 'leap for joy' in 'a year of poise' and to explore the privilege of being part of the bride of Christ. Personally, and despite all that was so difficult for many within that period of time, I think it was a totally *brilliant* way to start a new millennium!

Vicky Perham's Art Exhibition during our Fascinatin' Rhythm tour

In the Grand Hotel, Birmingham — photo by Luke Fry

Stephanie Fry (now Sidery) and Almut Jungmann Kallenberg

Doug Gallaher holds forth!

Our very own 'Flying Dutchman' during the solo which ends 'Ride on King Jesus'!

Howard Masters in action

Smiling cellists – Renata Busse and Hannah Cawston, with Heidi Wenger behind on viola

Janet Fox, Kristine Mole and Suzanne Fisher

Rehearsing in the basement at Villa Maria

Wonderful duo, Anthony Thompson and Peter Koetsveld

11
The media decade
(or, 'life in the sprat tank')

Nigel was working one day at Salford Technical College (now Salford University), when he had a telephone call from a BBC Radio producer named Norman Winter. Norman worked with Noel Vincent, who was one of the Songs of Praise producers, who had a programme to do in a church in Cheadle Hulme in which he thought the NEO might like to take part. Noel also produced Daily Services on radio.

Our first Songs of Praise experience was broadcast on 14th April 1991 and featured some of our NEO children. It was a special event to celebrate a hymn-writing competition and was a happy time for all! Soon after that, Nigel was invited to become one of the music directors for the Daily Service on Radio 4, and later he also became a regular presenter.

Prior to the above, on July 13th 1990, we had helped with a radio programme featuring the Choir Girl of the Year Competition, presented by Don Maclean as we recall, and after these first occasions we found that BBC work became a fairly regular occurrence in the nineties. Of course, we accepted such invitations if we could because of the wonderful opportunity of reaching the huge audiences possible either by radio or TV broadcasting, i.e. millions rather than hundreds! I cannot say these were always wonderful experiences, but certainly they were memorable! A little further down the road, Nigel and I often used to share our hopes, not to say longings, that one day we would be allowed to indulge in a broadcast of our own design – without the firmly drawn lines which should not be crossed, the fascination with having celebrities pop up etc., and the rigorous budget. We wondered whether one day this might happen, almost on the Biblical principle that if you are faithful in the little things you may come to be trusted with much. I remember being rather amused when Nigel once referred in this context, to the old saying about 'using a sprat to catch a whale' (I am told the original was 'to catch a mackerel', but Nigel was never one to skimp!) but as the years went by and we continued doing as we were asked, with as good a will as

we could muster (and producing, I might add, some excellent programmes which were very much enjoyed by the public) I began to refer to our relationship with the 'Beeb' as being 'stuck in the sprat tank'!

However, not wishing to draw a bleak sketch, I hope the next few paragraphs will allow a glimpse into one or two of the most interesting invitations we received, and how we (and the general public) felt about them.

Daily Service

As mentioned above, certainly by the time I had become Nigel's Personal Assistant, he was discovered to be, among other things, a valuable music director and presenter for the regular BBC Daily Service of worship. This involved a very early departure from his bed, and any number of interesting journeys on motorways in order to arrive at Didsbury, Manchester, for the live broadcast, with time for a quick rehearsal with the musicians and singers and a run through beforehand as directed by the producer.

My own part in this was to wait until Nigel had received the inspiration and formulated the particular angle he would take from the Bible verses or theme given to him on each occasion, at which point I would receive the awaited telephone call. We would post these potential dates in our diaries as priorities, no matter what was happening in our lives at the time – and it sometimes involved my dashing back home – or Nigel needing to dictate in the early morning or late evening, if he likewise was due somewhere else pronto. I would don my headphones (neatly attached to a fax phone which I still have) and I would type as he dictated – times which were occasionally peppered with the odd laugh from myself, or a silent nod of appreciation, or frankly (when he was at his best) holding back a tear or two as I tapped away. I used to prepare these scripts ahead of time on screen with the date of the programme, the heading 'Daily

Service Talk' and Nigel's name – and I would ensure all was set in double-line spacing (so the producer could mess around with it if wished – and frequently did!) and then I would always put in the words 'Good morning!', and await the rest. Each script usually ended with 'Blessing – from the card' – which Nigel often referred to as "sweets from the trolley"! Thankfully, I was wise to these habits! (Incidentally, that phrase of his was to recur in a slightly different spelling later on, see Chapter 15 – To the Saints in Rome...)

Afterwards, I would email a copy to Nigel for checking, and await any further comment or amendment, and then would send it along to the producer in question. We then went through the very slightly tense period of two or three days or more, while we both waited to see whether it would 'go through', with or without amends. There would often be a few trials at this point – but we bore them bravely most of the time. I have to admit that Nigel is one of the most equably tempered people I have ever met. For example, at times when I have witnessed from the passenger seat of his car, someone doing something dangerously ridiculous right in front of him on the motorway – his reaction has been, "Why did you do that?" in a perfectly calm and well modulated voice. If someone was obviously wishing to overtake or in some other way interfere with his progress, he would usually give way with a gentle, "Come on then darling!"

I think in the history of the DS (as it was abbreviated in my diaries – in fact DS-MD for when he was directing the music or DS-P when he was presenting) there was only one occasion when Nige admitted he had had what he described as 'a blazing row with the producer' – they are both good friends incidentally! So by my reckoning that's probably an excellent record taken over all the possibilities involved in something as potentially stressful as this!

However, it was the subsequent 'mailbags' that interested me. I still have on file umpteen letters and cards, some in my own memorabilia, some in Nigel's, written and sent by post from people all over the country, who appreciated what Nigel had shared – or the special quality of the music. There were some who, perhaps turning on the radio a few seconds late, had recognised either the music itself as Nigel's, or his inimitable voice. Emails would come in asking for a copy of the script etc., or a particular song. There was very often quite an impact.

This then was very much a part of the NEO ministry in Nigel's eyes, even though it was actually for me more of a 'PA' job than an NEO Central Administration one. The purpose in all was the same – to share the riches of Christ at every opportunity. Over the years, there were fewer and fewer amendments, and he tells me of a rich sense of fellowship among the Daily Service Singers and various producers whenever he is involved these days. Longevity has many blessings.

Songs of Praise

Nigel began working with the Songs of Praise (SoP) team as mentioned above, in 1991. He would sometimes be required to act as a researcher and go to churches to listen to their choirs or worship groups, and generally comment on whether the venue and congregation would be suitable. On one memorable occasion, he commented rather amusingly of a particular worship group, "The PA was pitched at just such a level that it didn't matter whether the congregation was singing or not!" Happily there were many good discoveries and lovely programmes. Nigel would be appointed as the Music Director, and would conduct everyone during the recording, having arranged the music beforehand – or he would be asked to bring along an ensemble from NEO to head up the music, and the same would apply. They were fascinating times. On our present list of DVDs, we have so many broadcasts that it's impossible to mention them all, but one of the most memorable occasions was of the Thirty-fifth Anniversary of Songs of Praise which took place in Symphony Hall, Birmingham in 1996. That was an amazing evening, with congratulations sent in throughout the programme by various celebrities, including the Archbishops of Canterbury and York, a host of TV presenters and Cliff Richard.

——————————— Dimples ———————————

In the words of the Psalmist: O that they might feel the beat!

Nigel and BBC member sharing a mad moment!

The Ravenscraig Steelworks

The team in Scotland

People on the Way

This was a Lent series in 1993, which ran for six consecutive weekends, up to and including Easter. It was produced by Andrew Barr (BBC Scotland), and I rather felt he should have been highly commended for it. Looking back, I would personally class it as the one of the most overtly Christian programmes ever produced. It consisted of two visits each to sites of significance in Wales, Scotland and Northern Ireland, to explore the testimonies/stories of triumph in adversity, as presented by one or two folk local to each area. Throughout there was music, Bible reading and prayers, and then once the week's story had been told, members of the public were invited to write in with their own accounts on that or a similar theme, or with their prayer needs, and there would be prayers spoken on air each week for those who had asked for them. They were remarkable times. The subjects dealt with were many and varied over the weeks, comprising for example, coping with the death of a loved one during the IRA troubles in Ireland, the closure of the Ravenscraig steelworks in Scotland, the death of a much-loved son from cancer, recovery from alcoholism, and the terrible Lockerbie air disaster.

For these programmes we used a very small group which varied according to the needs of the music and the availability of NEO personnel. Nigel had many pieces to arrange or compose (e.g. bridge pieces between items), all of which were very beautiful and featured a variety of instruments, e.g. violin, Celtic harp, guitar, cor anglais, flute (either played by Nick Lacey, whose interesting parking habits, along with those of Nick Gerrard, led to the series forever since being dubbed 'People in the way') or Simeon Wood, who I remember played a wonderful version which Nigel arranged for panpipes of 'Drop, drop slow tears'. We would receive our music each week on the Wednesday and have to learn it off by heart in time for a rehearsal on Friday evening, somewhere en route to wherever we had to travel to by road,

People on the Way – Lockerbie

rail or air. Then we would normally arrive at our destination early on the Saturday morning, and would rehearse all day, with the BBC crew simultaneously rehearsing their sound and shots with us and giving us our instructions. Then on Sunday morning it would be a live broadcast, with intermittent recorded clips as necessary. This entire process continued for six weeks. I was greatly indebted to Nigel for sending a tape recording with my own music pack each week as I am not a good music reader, and thankfully I learned quickly – but it was a 'push' for everyone involved. However, these were hugely worthwhile programmes and I'm sure blessed a lot more people than we would ever realise.

In Appendix I – The Unforgettables, this series is mentioned in my tribute to John Trow-Poole, who was responsible for ensuring the harp and any other necessary instruments or paraphernalia arrived by van at the appropriate time and destination! I enjoy watching the DVDs of this series and seeing him featured wearing his favourite Austrian hat, complete with 'shaving brush' as he used to call it! (See Appendix I – The Unforgettables)

Apart from the spiritual value of these times, there were other enjoyments to be had – for example in those days we seemed to be right royally entertained by the BBC roving canteen! We had creamy porridge in Scotland I recall (served by a chef with a glorious accent!) marvellous cooked lunches and dinners at various hotels, and frankly the only negative, as I look back, is that I reckon that period as the time when I personally began to notice I was putting on a little weight! The fellowship with one another was superb of course, as it has always been in NEO, and the sense of pressure, which is inevitably part of being involved in live broadcasting, galvanised us as a team in a memorable way. It stays in my memory as a time when we laughed and sometimes cried together – the jokes being hilarious, the personal stories of the folk who shared each week, often being heart-breaking. As a Lent exercise, I count it the best ever.

The ensuing video (now DVD) of this first programme, presented beautifully, as they all were, by Linda Mary Evans, is often held up as an example of the NEO at its best in the worst circumstances – and whenever we show it (as we did on our first Legacy Day in March 2016), it results in hoots of laughter! On top of the grassy sward of the cliff, with the backdrop of the waves crashing in, stood a row of basses and tenors, somehow managing to hold their voices steady to sing 'Create in me a clean heart O God' by Jim Strathdee. The camera then panned across the whole team and showed that in fact they were shielding us, (sopranos and altos) as we stood in front of them, from the ferocity of the wind. Even so, with our hoods and scarves hilariously in evidence, and hands thrust in pockets, the wind still wooshed any exposed hair back and forth. It took us all our effort not to rock back and forth ourselves! Meanwhile, Linda Mary eventually came into shot to be seen sitting perched on the grass a little distance away, looking a picture of composed but windswept calm, despite her hair flying about her head in a frenzied manner!

Of repetitive strain and hernia!

Well that's enough of the happy times – now for a few home truths! Let me take you to the south of England for a brief moment (oh that it had been!) at a place which shall not be named, but wherein we found ourselves embarked on what one might have thought a simple task – recording the little song, 'Give me oil in my lamp, keep me burning', which was to be included in a TV broadcast, which again shall not be herein named.

Our group of NEO Singers turned up, smartly presented in our coloured silk shirting and black trousers (or skirts for ladies if wished), and we had a little rehearsal and began recording. The rest is consigned to a blur in my own memory – as we were for various reasons, made to repeat, repeat and repeat again this 'little song' for what I think we counted as roughly forty times! Nigel had produced, as ever, a very pleasing arrangement of it – we had learned it well and I cannot recall what on earth the problem was – but there we were, incarcerated in this place for hour upon hour, standing until we couldn't feel our feet and somehow managing to produce those radiant smiles of joy, over and over and over again!

Our hearts went out during this period of repetitious torture, to our dear friend and excellent tenor, Matthew Baynham, who was having long term problems with a hernia at that time, so it was with great angst, but little surprise, that we heard that having left the building in the late evening, he had ended up in hospital at 4am, the situation having become acute!

Andrew Barr, Producer. Great cake, wrong year!

John Trow-Poole and Keith Buckler, partners in crime!

BBC studios Sankey Hymns rehearsal

Cor anglais played by Gillian Callow née Woodrow

Christmas Day live service St. Peter's Halliwell Bolton

Ensemble at Carfin Grotto

Live Christmas Day service at St. Peter's Halliwell, Bolton 2002

Getting a nice shot of the candles!

Simeon Wood and his wonderful panpipes

Simeon Wood and Nick Lacey duet

People on the Way – Benburb

The sequel to this unhappy episode however, was that when the programme was actually put on air, we discovered to our horror and disbelief, that this piece had been abridged! I think a whole verse had been taken out, so that the piece fitted better into the timing of the programme as a whole. It remains only for me to confess that from that point on, my inner self has always slightly modified the title of this particular song from 'Give me oil' to 'Give me strength'!

Other events were happier of course, though we ever longed for that time when we could put some of our own ideas into practice. Nigel had so many good ones, and of course we had the ability and the resources to deliver them – but most of the proposals remained proposals only.

One or two more difficult experiences occurred (see Chapter 5 – Whatever the weather) but some of the opportunities were outstanding. A producer named Jonathan Fulford, for example, invited us to take part in a televised service for Good Friday. The DVD brings the memories flooding back. This was the one occasion when a small group of us were able to sing Allegri's beautiful 'Miserere' on television. Nigel's daughter Catherine was at that time sporting her 'no. 2' level haircut (in hair-trimmer terms), which was popular at the time. She remains a devotee of fashion! However, it served not only to accentuate the exquisite beauty of her face, but to put a 'cutting edge' as it were, onto the famously incredible top C soprano solo which occurs in the quartet sections. Her voice is very pure and the sound was unspeakably beautiful, clear and accurate, and cannot have failed to provide good television, coming as it did from one of such youthful and up-to-the-minute appearance. It brought an ancient piece of music soaring through the centuries into the present day with some force. We all felt it a great privilege to have been able to present this programme and particularly so, as Jonathan is himself a believer, and had put forth his skill in the planning of it. As to the God-given gifts of Catherine herself, a book could probably be written about those also, but this was definitely one of her innumerable special 'moments' for Jesus!

Another very happy programme, which in fact was celebrated in DVD clips at our farewell concert in Nigel's own congregation – took place at his church, St Peter's Halliwell, Bolton, in this final year of NEO. It was broadcast live on Christmas morning 2002, entitled No Room at the Inn. Rev Roger Oldfield was the vicar at that time, and preached a marvellous sermon. There were clips of missionary work contributed from that congregation in Israel, and a great sense of camaraderie among us all on such a festive occasion. We looked back and smiled at the shots of some of our young adults in NEO, who were children then! We were able, this year, to thank the church for nurturing them in so many ways and for supporting us over the years in NEO so faithfully. The programme provided quite a marker buoy, I think, in the church's history.

There are many more instances I could mention, but space does not allow – though in all those experiences, suffice it to say that we could never have imagined that the biggest physical audience (80,000) and the largest international audience, in broadcasting terms, that we had ever encountered, was to occur in September 2010, when we found ourselves providing the core music for Pope Benedict XVI's Vigil for Young People in Hyde Park, London. This came entirely as the result of the work in Rome, and was nothing to do with the links we already had with the BBC. Such are the mysterious ways of God. (More anon in Chapter 15 – To the Saints in Rome...)

Dimples

We'll do it from the top without the diddly-doo bits!

Looking Forward to Christmas, Symphony Hall Christmas concert in the year 2000, conducted by Pete Desmond and Martin Lowe, in Nigel's absence

Catherine Swinford White & Liz Davidson (Llewellyn) Flower Duet

Sankey stage set with armchairs & aspidistra!

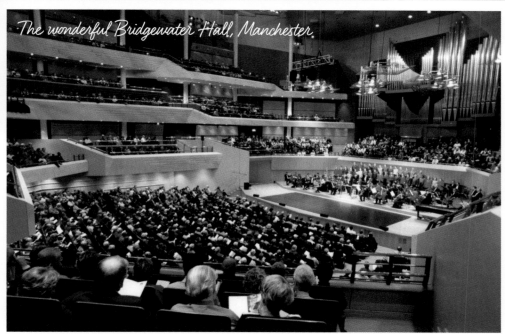

The wonderful Bridgewater Hall, Manchester

12
The Recreatio is born

This genre became so vital a part of our outreach to tourists in both Salzburg and Rome, that I think it merits some explanation.

The whole idea sprang originally from conversations held between Nigel and Brigitta Hofer, our good friend from Switzerland. Brigitta, a very creative person and an immensely sincere Christian, was always ready to explore ways of worshipping and serving the Lord in her beloved country of Switzerland, but found great liberty in working with Nigel and the NEO whenever and wherever possible. Though for many years she had her own initiative in the 'sister' ensemble, New European Orchestra (NEuO), with which Nigel assisted whenever he could, she was also able to share NEO's vision and contributed much over the years in so many ways, not least in introducing us to many wonderful European players and singers.

At this point in time, Brigitta had been evolving an idea of playing in literally empty churches, simply for the praise and worship of God Himself. In time, this idea moved forward in discussion with Nigel, and formulated itself into that of setting up in a large cathedral or church building, devising a short forty-five minute programme and delivering it for the benefit of those who were present in the building at the time. Of course, the whole aspect of the music would be centred on worshipping the Lord, but there would be a strong sense of presenting the Gospel to those present.

Finally the picture became clearer: a series of events in which music, both church music and modern spiritual songs, Bible readings and perhaps times of extempore playing from a soloist, would all combine – all it needed was a title. Brigitta provided this also, in the word *Recreatio* which seemed more familiar in Europe than it would perhaps be in the UK. Here is what it means according to the Oxford Latin Dictionary, 1982 (OLD):

Noun

- *declension: 3rd declension*
- *gender: feminine*

Definitions:

1. *recovery/convalescence (L+S)*
2. *refreshment, diversion/entertainment*
3. *restoration*

- *Age: In use throughout the ages/unknown*
- *Area: All or none*
- *Geography: All or none*
- *Frequency: 2 or 3 citations*

Well I hope that satisfies any Latin scholars reading this!

All in all, the idea of recovery, refreshment, diversion, entertainment, and particularly restoration, seemed perfectly matched to the perceived need of manic twenty-first century humanity! So the concept of taking this particular experiment into, for example, the Dom in Salzburg, began to look like a wonderful opportunity to reach out to the tourists, who flocked to the city for the Music Festival every summer.

July/August 2004 happened to be the first opportunity for this and so Nigel called out a small group of singers and players to take the idea forward for its first airing. I remember this very well indeed, as I was to be one of those singers engaging in this first experiment, but things took a little turn in our family life and I had to relinquish my post to Myrtle Lawrence, who graciously came in at the last moment, learned everything and did a wonderful job!

Pete's mother had been very ill and we were growing more and more concerned, until at last we were told that she was critical and we should not expect her to live much longer. This was the point at which I knew I should not leave Pete in charge of our family as well as this burden, and so I pulled out, and I recall being in a hospital waiting room speaking to Thea Hoelscher, a fellow soprano who lived in Salzburg, on the day that the team was flying out. As close friends, we were sorry to miss each other on this occasion and there were promises of mutual prayer. Ironically, as it transpired, my mum-in-law recovered on that occasion and went on to live for another twelve months or so! But it was good to keep in touch with the team, mainly by means of Luke telephoning me in his role as head of technical enablers for that tour, and to hear his enthusiastic reports of how the Lord was wonderfully providing for them all.

It was a decisive experiment – even with this minimal NEO ensemble, the large audience in the Dom had been effectively won over with this new genre – and St Peter's Stiftskirche also had been blessed. It seemed that all those taking part learned a huge amount from the experience – and probably one of the biggest changes to our past modus operandi, in Salzburg particularly, was the ability to dispense with our previous routine of setting up and performing in the hot open-air Altermarkt to flag up the evening events! Here, the team simply turned up at the Dom ahead of the appointed time (permission having been given of course!) set up their small ensemble and played – and the usually considerable crowd of people who just happened to be in the building at the time, would sit wherever they could, and listen. We also discovered that this lessened the need for massive pre-advertisement before a tour. The midday *Recreatio* events in the Dom would adequately win people to whatever was due to happen in the evening. Leaflets were produced as ever, but we took to producing printed banners (of which Luke had experience, in his role as a professional photographer in those days). These would stand in front of whichever building was in use, and would attract interested tourists, giving them all the information they required. Enablers could position themselves beside the banner to hand out leaflets and answer any questions.

We had no idea that this genre would come to be the main thrust of our work in Rome in the later phase of NEO's history. It was incredibly effective and hugely popular, probably reaching the largest numbers of people ever, across Salzburg and Rome. There was scope for a great variety of music and of course the many spatial effects which Nigel employed to keep every part of the crowd focused. However, one of the greatest advantages of the *Recreatio* was in the interspersing of readings of Scripture, very often from the J.B. Phillips version of the New Testament, and a variety of versions of the Old Testament – all with great effect. It was an unforgettable experience to see folk come in, hot and weary, to find a seat and remain, entranced by the music and readings, to encounter the presence of Jesus and enjoy the shade of His rest.

13

Faith and hope we knew about, now for charity

September 25th 1999

This was a historic morning – I spent it with Romaine Thompson of Anthony Collins Solicitors in Birmingham, discussing the whole question of charitable status for NEO. Complete with copious notes and having prayed I would leave out nothing vital, I had to present all this information to the P & P that evening. We opened the meeting, I remember, by spending time in the Lord's presence, meditating on the cross together and sharing bread and wine. There was a great sense of peace, gratitude and togetherness among us. We knew the Lord would lead us forward.

I found it a little daunting to contemplate taking this step – after all, we had worked together on so many events since 1976, technically without actually 'existing' other than as a growing and developing family of friends. I can remember speaking one evening, at a meeting at St John's, Harborne (one of our two main supporting churches), and explaining this phenomenon in terms of what St Paul once said:

1 Corinthians 1 v 27 ff:

For God chose the foolish things of the world to shame the wise; God chose the weak things of the world to shame the strong. God chose the lowly things of this world and the despised things – and the things that are not – to nullify the things that are, so that no one may boast before Him.

It could be said that NEO, for many years, could have been classed as one of the things that 'were not'. Yet so much blessing had been lavished not only on us as its members, but on so many others who might fall into that category over the years, by the Good Shepherd's relentless love and determination to reach his lambs, by every possible means!

So now, because of our need to adopt best practice in the world's eyes, within every area of our work, and with tax laws changing and the high turnover we often had when performing Christmas tours in expensive halls, we were required to take the step of becoming a company limited by guarantee and a charity registered in England and Wales!

As ever, Nigel's wisdom came to the fore, and he decreed that we should ensure at all costs that the whole business should change neither the fundamental ethos of NEO, nor the outworking and fellowship of the Prayer and Planning group, which had always been at the core of its machinery. So we opted to have only four directors/trustees, who would meet as such only at times of specific need. In all other respects, the P & P would continue in the same way it always had. Nigel (Chairman), myself (Company Secretary), Nick Gerrard (Trustee and of course our Marketing Manager) and Catherine Taylor (Finance Secretary) initially became those four. Catherine had stepped in to help us after the passing of Roger Knott and we were immensely grateful to her for doing so. She brought many updates and improvements to the system and kept an eye on us. Otherwise, Nick was the only one of us who had had any previous experience of charity matters and he guided us through those very early weeks. I took up my duties in taking minutes of the meetings and fashioning them in such a way as to record mainly the decisions which carried a financial tab or a significant event. As time went on, Catherine moved on and was replaced by David Harvey. I can recall vividly the point at which Nigel asked me if I had any idea whatsoever who might come and fill this post for us – and my replying that David (our church treasurer at St John's, Harborne at the time) was the only person I could think of.

To cut to the chase, Nigel and I visited him at the family home one evening. David and his wife Edwina (Edi, whom Pete and I had known since *Come Together* days) had recently purchased a large and beautiful house, which was still under refurbishment at the time, but which was destined to become a meeting place for small rehearsals and a regular P & P venue in future years. We began explaining the situation to David as he sat in his armchair patiently listening, and then we asked the all important question. I thought it was possible he might just agree to the work itself, but my doubts concerned the huge commitment to fortnightly Prayer and Planning meetings! However, when Nigel plucked up the courage to enquire, David responded that he would 'love to do it' – 'it', meaning the entirety of the job, (and a good deal more in years to come could he have foreseen it!). So we went home rejoicing, leaving David to sort the finer points, e.g. bestowing a night out to Edi to make up for each evening he had to be out with us! (I wonder how long Edi was able to hold him to that?)

More recently, Janet Ryland agreed to join us as a fifth trustee and give us the benefit of her own very practical wisdom, coming from years of experience both in her career in the Civil Service and her church work at St John's, Harborne.

We had two main aims and objectives: firstly, that of promoting the Christian faith, and secondly that of education. The former needs no explanation, as the sharing of the Gospel in music and the whole matter of living our lives together in this ministry for the glory of God, had been there from the conception of the NEO. We were thankful, in more recent years, that this remained open to us as a charitable objective!

However, the latter objective was to spark wonderful blessing, as the Lord spoke to Nigel and to us as a P & P at a certain point, about 'new wineskins' for new wine! (See Chapter 14 – *Good News is for sharing* for more on this).

Charitable status also meant of course, that we could more easily receive gifts and donations from other charities and individuals, and I can honestly say that we have never needed to bite our fingernails on that score. The faithful provision of finances for the work the Lord led us to do was constant throughout the years.

We are hugely indebted to the groups who supported us, either as and when they were able, or on an ongoing basis, and to the innumerable individuals who gave donations to NEO (from the precious widow's mite to large one-off gifts) as well as the various sponsorships we were privileged to have for specific events or tours over the years. I am also deeply grateful to the indefatigable David Harvey who took on all matters legal and financial, which were most certainly not in my personal gift! Like Roger Knott and Catherine Taylor, he also had the ability to be a responsible and careful manager, but take a risk when necessary!

Being a company also brought with it the run-of-the-mill minutiae that came with what many of the nationally disgruntled would call our *Nanny State!* We were brought, kicking and struggling, into the realm of health and safety issues, child protection policies, hygiene regulations and the growing need to assess every single person's dietary needs, in case we accidentally debilitated them. We found to our amusement, even when faced with regulations about technical matters when trying to publish a DVD, we simply couldn't tick any of the standard boxes – even after attempting to comply withal, we were still it seemed...utterly unique!

14

Good News is for sharing
The arrival of the NEO 'Invitation Concert'

Sometimes it's actually possible, even in a wonderful family like the NEO, for there to be a need to refresh the ministry and make radical changes.

Also, we had become a charity in 1999, and this (see Chapter 13 – *Faith and Hope...*) brought a whole new experience of having two essential aims and objectives – to promote the Christian faith through our music, and to address education. So as a result we began to pray that the Lord would show us a way through.

_____ **Dimples** _____

For this repertoire I took the Christmas one and slotted in Easter!

In the year 2000 Nigel was of course, subjected to major surgery for a thymoma, and from then on for him, nothing would ever be quite as it was. By the grace of God, despite an incredibly difficult year following his surgery, he woke up one morning in 2001 feeling instantly back to normal, as though, in his own words, the Lord had, "...put his SIM card back in!" This was to have a lasting significance however, for the whole of the NEO family, because Nigel was able at this point, to see quite clearly where adjustments needed to be made, and it was obvious that he needed to refresh the system and find those who felt genuinely that this particular music ministry was, as far as possible, their first priority.

Nigel began actively seeking young talent from the music colleges and holding meetings with these young believers who showed that inimitable blend of fantastic musical ability, exciting potential, and the all-important ingredient, vibrant faith in Christ. From the first moment I met Nigel back in the mid-seventies, it was obvious not only from his

work as a music teacher, but in the way he gently led us in our teens and twenties (*tweenties?*) that he had a huge gift for encouraging the young. Many of the original NEO founder members, who have had a lifetime calling to this ministry, have seen their own children grow up and become the next generation of singers/players/dancers/enablers. It happened organically and most of our kids who joined the singers, did so around an average age of twelve or thirteen – little budding dancers were often younger, much younger (my daughters were seven and three respectively and I think my daughter-in-law Maria was almost five!) But this was a very specific moment in our history, when the Lord directed us to make a special effort to bring in fresh talent. To skim the surface here, we found that this initiative blended beautifully with the beginnings of our *Invitation Concert* genre.

The whole process of welcoming young, even secondary school age 'green shoots' (to change the metaphor) into NEO, continued of course throughout our work and so provided the most glorious opportunities for these folk, which perhaps some may not have otherwise enjoyed until quite a few years later. I recall being blown away by seeing some of our highly experienced section leaders stepping back to allow young 'upcoming' talents to take over the section, while they themselves remained available should they require advice or guidance from that wealth of experience behind them! It was heart-warming and a wonderful process to watch. Even for that final public event on our 40th birthday, we had players with us for the very first time, and one youngster (third generation daughter of one of our lovely long term NEO families) sang beside me – and very competently too!

This as ever, can only be a précis, but suffice it to say that by a few years later, we had been told by the Lord very specifically as a P & P (interestingly enough that word came at the same time to both Nicola Gerrard and myself) to 'seek new wine skins for new wine', and we had begun to find the most wonderful young players (very fitting for our education aims) who were a total inspiration to us, and for whom NEO was to be an inspiration for them and also a springboard for their future careers, not to mention their Christian experience.

Dimples

Be serene – like a swan without bird flu!

The other issue, of which we were becoming acutely aware even at this time in the early twenty-first century, was that classical concert halls were not as well filled as they used to be. The costs involved in hiring them and their staff, plus the percentages added onto just about everything that passed from hand to hand, made it quite a risky enterprise. After much thoughtful discussion and prayer, we came up with a new genre of event called the *Invitation Concert*, and we found that the above instruction from the Lord found a perfect fit in this genre.

Here, we threw out a welcome to churches or local Christian groups, to hire a very small NEO ensemble (e.g. a handful of players and as many singers as would fit into their venue's 'performance space' or, even more economical, a 'micro-ensemble' consisting of around three or four players and the singers). This brought a new opportunity for local congregations to host a top-quality evening concert, which could be a focus of their outreach to their area, and brought the costs within their reach if they could charge a fairly nominal ticket price. I remember writing up the document which gave this offer, under the heading, 'Good News is for sharing'. The hosting church would provide, for their part, refreshments and a lunch for players, who rehearsed from around 10am, and a supper for the whole party (singers would join at some point in the afternoon) together with any necessary overnight accommodation. They would create their own publicity and perhaps name the event themselves if they wished, and of course make

their Performing Rights Society submission. The big 'win' for them however, was that there is no easier way to do local outreach than to invite people to a concert!

It took off, and for many years we had a marvellous time visiting local churches, the first of which was a small church in Lindfield, West Sussex in 2006. I recall Nigel and I would initially make the site visits for these events (before later handing on this responsibility to Martin Lowe along with project management of this genre). On this first occasion, we stayed overnight with Michael and Gillie Warren, who had become great NEO friends. The concert evening was a very happy one and we felt we were on track for this new approach.

Many of these times not only featured some pretty astounding virtuoso playing, but were also memorable long after, for the reactions of the audience. More than once we encountered a long silence in the room after the last note of 'Be still and know that I am God' had died away – as people wanted the moment to linger and be savoured for as long as possible – others could not have spoken if they had tried, they were too full of tears.

Other students of the Royal Northern College of Music, such as Cathy Studman (one of the first of them to join us, along with her sister Hannah Smith and close friend, Becca Dinning, née Eves) went on to become regular leaders of the NEO, beloved of us all, not just for their style of leadership and their virtuosity as players, but also for their faith and their wonderful personalities. Becca also endeared herself to younger members of NEO in Rome, some of whom were very new to NEO tours, by meeting with them for Bible study on a number of occasions, which was very much valued and enjoyed. This had been a wise suggestion of Nigel's and she grasped it well and thoroughly, and so the *new wine* of the kingdom flowed on into and out of these glorious new wineskins!

Over time, (see NEO Timeline at the back of this book) we found ourselves being invited to many churches up and down the country, our final two venues (in 2016) being Rawtenstall in Lancashire, and Allithwaite in Cumbria. Those two were particularly memorable for the astounding grace of God and the courage of Nigel, who was suffering

This photo of Christ Church Tettenhall reminds me how faithful and expectant a congregation they were — they really caught the vision and invited us back several times!

(unbeknown to him and Carolyn at the time) from what was rapidly becoming a totally non-functional thyroid gland when we were at Rawtenstall, and by the time we reached Allithwaite, he was (unknown to him) in need of hospitalisation, and finding difficulty even speaking normally, let alone keeping warm and awake. I recall sitting and praying under my breath through most of these two concerts and being completely in awe of the fact that he managed not only to conduct, but to play through so many pieces, including Jeffes' 'Perpetuum Mobile' and to share a joke with the audience!

Dimples

I'd like you to do it like this just because it's wrong!

Another spin-off from these events was that they were often able to provide vehicles for us to launch a new piece of repertoire, which would also be used in whatever away tour we were planning for later in the year. Sarah Stuart (a brilliant and very versatile percussionist) joined us, and was found to have the added gift of fiddle-playing for Scottish

reels! She brought new, vibrant and very useful additions to our repertoire. Now married to David Hatch, she also brought us, for too short a time, an excellent clarinettist too!

In God's economy, this genre was a wonderful blessing within the fabric of NEO as well as in our outreach. So yes, 'Good news is for sharing' – and we've certainly enjoyed doing so!

A typical Invitation Concert programme.

Invitation Concert
St. Peter's Church Harold Wood, Saturday 1st March 2014
Programme

In Te Domine speravi (In you O Lord have I trusted, let me never be confounded) (Charpentier) - – soloists, Helen Friday, Matthew Baynham, Martin Lowe

Spiritual song – **Living words** (soloists: Roger Beasley, Catherine Swinford White)

Gloria - from Missa Brevis (Swinford)

Andrea Falconieri – **Ciaccona** (soloists, Rebecca Eves and Caroline Sharp)

Pachelbel Canon

Diego Ortiz – **Ricercata Segunda**

And with His stripes we are healed
Surely He hath borne our griefs (Handel – Messiah)

Spiritual Song: **Jesus He died**

Bagatelles for clarinet and strings (Finzi) (Soloist – Lucy Downer)

Worthy is the Lamb (Handel - Messiah)

I N T E R V A L

Lift up your heads (Handel – Messiah)

Trumpet concerto in D by Torelli - soloist Nathan Richards

Gospel: **I'd rather have Jesus** (Jimmy Wyatt) (soloist - Sam Openshaw)

Spiritual: **My God is so high**

Syrinx - for Flute (Debussy) (soloist Nicola Gerrard)

Spiritual – **Somebody's knocking at your door**

Spiritual song – **I heard the voice of Jesus say** (Horatius Bonar)

Hallelujah Chorus - (Handel - Messiah)

15
To the saints in Rome...

The City of Rome

Extraordinary coincidences!

The roots of this story grew at a time when Nigel and his family began travelling onward from NEO Salzburg tours, chasing the sunshine as they drove south to Italy for a much needed holiday. There they would visit places like Florence, Assissi, San Giminiano, Siena, with its astonishing cathedral, or Pisa, with its famous leaning tower and stunning architecture.

Nigel was impressed by the large crowds of people who flocked to see not only the buildings, but their glorious paintings and statues. Many of these of course, form part of our Christian heritage and are inspired by events or characters from the Bible, some depicting aspects of the Gospel, if only you *understood* the picture and the truth it was portraying! Nigel longed to find a way to show the hundreds of 'sheep without a shepherd' who were to be encountered in these venues, what lay behind all they were seeing.

Back in the year 2000, Nigel had tried a couple of experiments with really tiny ensembles, to see how that would feel, and what impact they would have. Two *micro-orchestra* events occurred in the spring of that year, one at Nigel's own home church (St Peter's, Halliwell) and one towards the end of May, which came as the result of an invitation from a lady named Margaret Atherton. Margaret was a good friend of one of our soloists, Lesley Thompson (who with her family had been members of the same church in Parbold, to which we had been invited). Margaret wanted to raise funds for the National Children's Home, and Nigel put together a tiny team which included his daughter, Catherine, and her husband Pete (married just two months earlier), and one or two string players, with himself on keyboard. He also invited me along to give a fifteen-minute presentation of poetry and readings on the subject of heaven. It was a happy evening and went off very well to the enjoyment of all concerned, but somehow (and I can't quite remember how) I discovered either then or soon afterwards, that Margaret had contacts in Italy. I logged that fact.

So when a few years later in 2006, Nigel again began wondering about reaching out to the tourists in Italy, and how to make contacts in such places as those mentioned above, I promised to look up Margaret's details, which I knew I had somewhere in the filing system. I soon realised this

Arch of Constantine

would involve retrieving heavy boxes buried in the loft and would take a little longer! However, it was either that same day or a couple of days later, that the telephone rang, and who should it be, but Margaret! She had phoned out of the blue (as it were) with a query on behalf of a contact of hers, and when we had completed that topic, I confessed I had been searching high and low for her details – and why! It's worthy of note here that we genuinely hadn't been in touch for years! At this point she became quite animated, and insisted that none of the aforesaid places originally envisaged were to be considered – no, we should go straight to the capital – Rome!

She went on to tell me exactly where we should stay and faxed me contact numbers of friends in the hotel she recommended, friends in the Vatican and friends in local churches in the city who could help us to find a place to try out our *Recreatio* events 'Italian style'! From that point on my file was nicknamed *The Italian Job* and I duly reported all findings back to the boss!

Meanwhile, in February of that year, Nigel and I had made one of our memorable recces to Salzburg, where we met with our dear friend, Pater Benedikt, of St Peter's Monastery Church, arriving (to my delight!) to find deep snow! We discovered from him that of all things, he had been asked to go to Rome later on in May, to deliver a lecture on the Rule of St Benedict (in English) for young novices on a Formation Course. As we prayed with him and talked through our hopes for Salzburg, it became clear that this might also be a very significant move towards a Rome venture! As ever,

The Fontana di Trevi

2007 Ambassador to the Holy See, Francis Campbell, with Catherine Swinford-White, Nigel Swinford and members of the NEO ensemble outside Chiesa di SS Anastasio e Vincenzo

Andrew Durban and Andrew Simm

David MacDonald, cellist, alias '00David'!

Christopher Poffley in pensive mood

Enthusiastic audience in the Pantheon

Family Gerrard

Jamie Dalton, Matt Lowe (to whom we owe many wonderful later photos of Rome herein) and Rick Masters in the Pantheon!

Holly and Sam Openshaw

Ian Pickup doing leaflet duty in Rome

Julie, Stephanie and Pete

Pete White, classical guitar

that recce turned out to be significant for the future in a number of respects!

Nigel, during a visit to Rome at Easter (by which time Pater Benedikt had also arrived in the city) had been astonished at the huge crowds which were drawn, by day or night, to the Trevi Fountain. Just opposite the fountain was a little church at the top of a flight of steps, with metal rails around and a gate which stood open whenever the church itself was open. He and Carolyn had agreed to meet Benedikt by the fountain, but the tourists were so sardine-like at that time of year, that they hadn't a hope of finding him, until they looked up and saw him very sensibly stationed at the top of the steps, waving enthusiastically! Nigel felt drawn to this church as a potential base for a first 'strike' by NEO – perhaps with a smallish group, but wondered how to go about finding the right person for permission to do so.

By May, we engaged in a very short (Saturday to Wednesday) recce to coincide with Benedikt's continuing visit during the Formation Course. This was to be my own first visit to Rome, and I was fairly excited, but a little wary also. I was used to Salzburg, and knew my way around, and enjoyed listening to Nige's inimitable German when the need arose, but neither of us had any Italian, and I hadn't a clue how I would get on with this city, despite its international acclaim and historical importance!

We stayed (I think only for the first night) at a hotel in the San Silvestro district where Nigel had stayed on previous occasions when on holiday. Everything in Rome seemed noisy, dusty, bustling, hot and confusing to my eyes and ears. My room at the top of the hotel was blisteringly hot and airless, and I confess that for a brief moment, despite all the vast privileges of my situation, I rather rudely wondered what on earth I'd come to! As I looked through my window, I remembered Nigel telling me that here there was no sophisticated and pristine elegance, as in Salzburg! I did recall however, from a trip with Pete, Nige and Caro to Florence in the late nineties, how right he was when he said it nevertheless had a way of 'biting you' and in the end you loved it. So I hung on and was prepared to wait for that process to kick in! We began to find our way around the bewildering streets. Nigel took me for a refreshing ice cream

at a café in the square outside the impressive Pantheon, and afterwards we went in to see it. Now this was the place for a *Recreatio* I thought, and said as much. I hadn't realised it was actually a church as well as a city monument, and as I looked at it and at the massive crowds milling about, I was more convinced than ever that this was the sort of place we should be aiming for. Nigel agreed of course but was a little sceptical! How on earth could it be achieved? However, we eventually came out, and were in the portico of the Pantheon, when Nige's mobile rang – it was Benedikt, laughing his head off! He had made friends with a monk on his course (an Eritrean man named Negusse) and had discovered that he was based at the church by the Trevi Fountain! We were to meet together that night anyway for a meal, so Negusse was invited to come along as well.

Nigel, I must relate, had arrived sporting a spanking new pair of designer sunglasses (they suited both him and the country we were in rather well I thought) which had involved a substantial price tag as they included his optical prescription. On arrival back from St Peter's Square by taxi, he groaned as he realised, just as the taxi was driving away, that he had left them on the back seat! I could still see our taxi just up the road and gave chase! I drew almost level with the car at the traffic lights where it had to stop for a few seconds, and was just about to reach over to bang on the window, when the lights changed and it sped off, in the habit of most Rome taxis, like a bullet from a gun! I wandered back feeling rather disconsolate, and we subsequently tried by all means possible to retrieve those sunglasses (including enlisting the help of the hotel manager at San Silvestro and even Negusse's kind attempts to make phone calls for us) but all failed, and the lovely sun specs had to be replaced on insurance later on! The new ones still look good however! I mention this crazy incident only because it seemed so fitting to have a pair of designer sunglasses and a car chase featured in anything to do with Italy and its capital! It was getting more like 'The Italian Job' every minute!

I have to admit my first memory of seeing the 'church by the Trevi' (Chiesa dei Santi Vincenzo e Anastasio) which had captivated Nige's vision, was that it was puny in size and pretty small beer for a *Recreatio*! My mental pictures were based on the Dom in Salzburg, which could be filled with hundreds and hundreds of people, but this was tiny, dark, fusty and candlelit (with electric candles) and was home to members of an order I knew nothing about. It looked very old and rather unkempt, with chapels in niches along the walls, bedecked with plastic flowers and lots of Latin inscriptions I couldn't understand. I commented merely that I thought it was too small, but Nige calmly replied that he felt it would be good for 'making a start'. Knowing he was usually right in these visionary matters, I held my peace. It was when we turned to come out, and I saw the doorway, bright with the blinding sunshine from outside, and glimpsed the hundreds of people milling about right outside its doors, that I could see exactly what he meant, and 'caught' the vision. Yes, it could work at that! It was easy to imagine people hearing the strains of music coming from the open doorway and venturing in, maybe to sit and stay awhile in the shade and the coolness. I was won over! From then on we needed to bend all our efforts to finding the 'way in'. This was always the point I loved about recces, and which I often describe as 'the thrill of the chase'!

Benedikt met us, again atop the steps of the church, waving two red roses he had bought for us from a street-seller, and looking thoroughly 'demob happy', having delivered his English lecture and found it had gone well! He was so relieved, and we rejoiced with him. To leap ahead, Negusse had managed to arrange a meeting for us with Father Paciolla, priest of the church in question. We were staying a couple of nights at the Lancelot Hotel before returning to the UK, and at that point, I recall telephoning one of the contacts we had been given, who was the priest at the church of San Clemente, just around the corner from the hotel. He advised me that the first thing we must do to be assured of success, was to take our potential programme to the Head of Liturgy for Rome, at the headquarters which were on the site of the huge Basilica of San Giovanni in Laterano (St John Lateran) – again a short walk from our hotel. So it was, that within the first hour after breakfast that day, we found ourselves within those marble corridors (which reminded me of others we had had to brave in Salzburg from time to time) meeting Monsignor Frisina – Head of Liturgy for the city of Rome. San Giovanni in Laterano was itself a highly strategic place, being officially regarded as the Pope's own church in his dual role as Bishop of Rome.

Suffice it to say, that after discussions with Msgr Frisina, and his careful perusal of our proposed *Recreatio* scripts, he pronounced it "a beautiful programme", and gave us carte blanche to use it wherever we found a priest happy to host us!

Father Paciolla turned out to be a quiet and thoughtful man, who listened to all we had to say, and agreed it was indeed, "a beautiful programme". He was happy for us to go ahead and we placed some dates in the diary for the following September. Not for the first time, we felt as though we were simply treading in Someone's pre-trodden footprints! It was very exciting.

We put everything in place with the hotel for our proposed visit in September, which we had been advised was a really good time to come out to Rome, and we were able to sit and draft a personnel list, comprising the smallish group of instrumentalists and vocalists Nigel felt he would need for this first venture into Rome!

I realised I would have to translate all I had learned from our years of planning Salzburg tours, into the new Rome scenario. I was so thrilled that all the staff at the Lancelot spoke such good English, and that we were able to discover the relevant bus routes, and plot our journey into and out of town and along the main Via del Corso where we would need to alight and disappear down an alley (lined with market stalls selling jewellery, religious paraphernalia, calendars and handbags), weave through innumerable motorbikes, bypass an inviting Gelateria and finally enter the packed and bustling Piazza di Trevi!

It now becomes necessary to leap ahead to our first Rome Tour of September 2007, which we approached with huge excitement! Here is the letter Nigel wrote to the newly appointed Rome team!

Dear Friends,

This is to wish you a hearty welcome to the Rome excursion! I greatly look forward to sitting down with you on Sunday just a few hundred yards from the Colosseum and the Forum in the nice little hostelry that Julie has hopefully booked for us. It should be a hugely joyful coming together.

As you know this is a completely new departure for the NEO. It is a small group affair and should be thought of as a kind of Commando Raid! The scriptures we've been reading are: Numbers 13 and Joshua 2, in which spies are sent out into the Promised Land and into Jericho to see what happened, what it looked like, felt like and to hear what God had to say. Obviously we in the NEO are talking about the spiritual territory of men and women's hearts, not physical territory. Perhaps we could see this as a spiritual incision into our western culture, presenting the Gospel of our Lord and Saviour Jesus Christ to many who have long ago dismissed Christianity, yet who have come to Rome, perhaps to get in touch with their roots – certainly to see many of the sights associated with the foundations of our civilisation. We shall see them with their guide books and maps, perhaps showing openness and curiosity which they don't reveal under the pressures of everyday life at home. Our venue is a priceless one from the point of view of 'passing trade'. Thus we must pray that it remains open for us and that we make happy relations with Father Paciolla and the Eritrean monks who administer the building. Everything possible has already been done to ensure this (four visits, plus copious faxes).

But Salzburg has shown us that when you have a venue where all the people actually **are**, spiritual battle sometimes ensues.

Like any posse of commandos, we have to look after each other, use our ingenuity and imagination. One of the first issues to confront us will be where on earth we can meet to pray. There will also be no rehearsal facility, nowhere for teaching and fellowship, no easy way of communicating with the group after we have gone to our rooms. All such things we have to find out and receive when we arrive, and as God gives. Each person has to take responsibility like 'a good soldier of Jesus Christ' (2 Timothy, chapter 2 v 3). There are no red carpets (except perhaps in the hotel!), and no welcoming committees. Having said that, the Recreatio at 2pm on Tuesday will be attended by the British Ambassador to the Holy See (i.e. the Vatican), Mr Francis Campbell. Afterwards we are all invited to meet him and to pose for press photographs. Word does get around!

Let's pray for each other's health, each other's joy and each other's witness. And let's pray above all that the name of Jesus is truly honoured and glorified.

Yours with much love,

Nigel

As Nigel had indicated, word had indeed got around, and Peter Jennings, (1947-2013), our indefatigable Catholic journalist friend of many years, had been preparing the ground. I had first met Peter when I was still a teenager, at *Youthquake* (see Chapter 2 – *Earliest Beginnings*) in Birmingham Cathedral, and much of his life's work had been rather a mystery to me until this point in time. It seemed that the Lord had ordained that this was Peter's moment to come and fulfil a long-held desire of his to introduce the NEO to Rome using his contacts and experience from working there. This was to coincide with a most fruitful time of ministry for the NEO. Here is an extract from his report on the tour:

REFRESHING MUSICAL MOMENTS AT THE TREVI FOUNTAIN

By Peter Jennings in Rome

Chiesa di SS Vincenzo e Anastasio

The New English Orchestra and Singers gave a series of nine memorable Recreatios (literally meaning times of rest and refreshment) in the church of SS Vincenzo e Anastasio, situated opposite the Trevi Fountain, one of the most popular tourist spots in Rome, Monday 24 to Wednesday 26 September.

The Recreatios, reflective meditations in music, linked by words from the Bible, were performed by a versatile group of six professional musicians from Britain and Europe, plus 14 singers.

Mr Swinford explained that the Recreatios, comprising a varied and hugely popular short musical format were based on three themes: 'Living Water', 'Praise', and 'God's Calling'. The programme varied with each performance but included music by Bach, Handel, Telemann, Vaughan Williams, Duke Ellington, Spirituals and Gospel Music.

The NEO was put in contact with Fr Sebastiano Paciolla, a Cistercian monk and rector of SS Vincenzo e Anastasio, by the Prior of the Benedictine church of St Peter, in Salzburg. Fr Paciolla, a distinguished Canon Lawyer, who lectures at the Angelicum and Gregoriana, met Mr Swinford earlier this year. He willingly agreed that the spectacular baroque church of medieval origin could be used by the NEO for the Recreatios, admission free.

The sound of a trumpet from the portico called the tourists into the church before each of the performances at 11.00am, 2.20pm and 4.00pm. The small church was soon packed to capacity with people standing at the back and down the side aisles for each of the forty-minute Recreatios.

At the final performance of the series on 26 September, the bright afternoon sunshine streamed in through the windows high above the sanctuary. Six lighted candles on the high altar burned brightly throughout as the sound of joyful praise engulfed the beautiful interior of the church.

Congregations don't normally give a standing ovation at the end of a service in a Catholic church, but that's what happened at the end of a rousing rendition of the popular Gospel song, 'O Happy Day'!

The Recreatio ended with the beautiful Christian song, 'Be Still and Know that I am God', during which Nigel Swinford led the singers and musicians slowly out of the church onto the portico with its panoramic view of the Trevi Fountain. For a few precious moments the cacophony of noise from the square was replaced by something far more profound.

All the Recreatios evoked a response from members of the congregation. As the church fell silent, a lady tourist in the pew behind me wiped away the tears rolling gently down her face.

Francis Campbell, British Ambassador to the Holy See, said: "A wonderful performance and great cultural ambassadors for Britain." Philippa Hitchen, a reporter in the English Section of the Vatican for the past twenty years, added: "What an uplifting experience."

Earlier last year, Nigel Swinford met Mgr Marco Frisina, a distinguished composer and choirmaster of the Pope's Cathedral, St John Lateran, to explain the project. Mgr Frisina would not sanction a concert by the NEO in a Catholic church in Rome but was happy for the series of reflective meditations in words and music to take place...

So... from all the above, you will glean that I had obviously thought rather too little and too rudely, back on our recce, of what to others was a "spectacular baroque church of medieval origin" with a "beautiful interior". As ever, the NEO was teaching me to acquire new appreciations at a considerable rate of knots – a learning curve which also comprised the realisation that we were moving through new vistas here in the Italian capital, and meeting some very strategic people – all part of the mysterious ways of God. I made a mental note during this tour to watch carefully and keep what Nigel and I often call our 'spiritual antennae' well alert!

The tour was a wonderful one, needless to say. I remember sharing a room at the Lancelot with Lesley Thompson and Mary Burton and finding that Margaret Atherton had decided to join us all on tour as well, to see what happened on this first essay into Rome and her favourite hotel! She came ready to help out in whatever way presented itself, and our first meeting took place when we were settling into our room. A knock at the door revealed Margaret, laden with a tray of steaming tea and four cups! It was wonderful to see her! Later, she took us out to a tiny place just around the corner for lunch. There was much catching up to do, and she was a marvellous help in showing us speedy routes to and from town and filling in background on various things (not least the best ice cream parlours!). She was part of the furniture at the Lancelot, that was easy to see, and she provided another wholesome link between NEO and the wonderful family, headed by Helen Khan, who owned the hotel. Over the years, even when NEO moved to other accommodation for its tours, Nigel and I always stayed at the Lancelot on recces, at all times of the year, and we will always think of Helen and her family as the very kind and helpful friends who encouraged us in our work in Rome.

I don't think I shall ever forget the feel of that first *Recreatio* event in this appointed venue. Not only was it, as it ever is, totally glorious to actually be singing the much- rehearsed repertoire for real, with the attendant atmosphere, but it was the experience of seeing dreams come to life! I remember telling various folk that as I looked out from our position in front of the altar steps, through the doorway into the bright

Kristen Rigby and Beth Winter (née Howells)

Robin Dalton and Nick Evans-Pughe, and Georg and Thea Hoelscher behind

Kristine and Jonathan Mole

Sarah Hatch (née Stuart) Percussionist during 'Somebody's knocking at your door' in the Pantheon!

Nicholas and Andrea Young – Rome 2015

Nige and Caro – Rome 2015

Roger and Dawn Beasley Rome 2015

Scottish Reel in the Pantheon!

The Oculus Glow!

Peter Koetsveld

Sisters! Hannah Smith and Cathy Studman (née 'The Bessant Girls'!)

The two Masters!

Two Rylands and Two Beasleys!

glare of the sun, and saw yet more people coming into the building as they became aware of the sound of our music – it took me back to that 'recce' moment when I first believed it could happen here! Yes, it was a small church (compared to the Pantheon or San Giovanni in Laterano) and perhaps it was never entirely full at any one time, but the experiment had worked – and we so loved seeing experiments work in NEO! This was to be our training ground for bigger things yet to come yes, but it was not a dummy run – these were real people whose lives were being touched by the real Saviour – it was thrilling.

It was not without humour either! For a start, we were using a hired keyboard and when Nigel came to play the exciting introduction for the Duke Ellington version of Psalm 150, his fingers fled across the keys and accidentally pressed the 'off' button at the end of the instrument, at which point, realising the keyboard had died completely, he threw up his arms in despair for a moment. It was soon remedied, and having logged this new knowledge, he began again and all went very well! The whole tour was a great success, and taught us many useful things. We had all been used to the Salzburg work, but now we were learning how to tackle a new and very different city.

Our fellowship was quite remarkable. Writing these memoirs is quite a new experience for me obviously, but not least because it's so difficult puzzling out where and how to relate some of the things that happened, as they could definitely appear in more than one chapter. This next incident is one such.

Our dear friend and superb principal trumpet, Anthony Thompson, had come out to Rome with us to play a very important role, not just in the events themselves, but in playing on the steps outside beforehand, to call to people in! So it was with some consternation that we found he had arrived to this first tour feeling very ill. I believe it was some form of severe tonsillitis, but it had actually begun during our tour to Salzburg earlier that summer, and really had a hold of him, such that he had been unable to rehearse at all. He explained to us that he didn't know what would happen when he took up the instrument – for a trumpeter it didn't just mean that the lip was not ready, but the diaphragm wasn't prepared either – both essential to a trumpet player. But the Lord was about to show us one of His special provisions, in that on every occasion during that tour when Anthony had to play, he played flawlessly. He was as amazed as we were! Nevertheless, between times, he still felt awful, and at the end of the tour he went home and remained ill for some weeks until the problem eased and eventually disappeared naturally.

Dimples

Nigel in Rome – when bothered by somebody in Italian: "Nein Danke!"

As mentioned above, the challenge of memoirs, is that of knowing *where* to put *what* – and the extraordinary tale of how we actually managed to acquire one of most famous buildings in Rome, the Pantheon, therefore takes place in Chapter 17 – *The Phenomenon of the Recce!* But for now, let's just go on to that next amazing tour and see what it was really like to be there!

NEO Rome visit – 21st – 26th September 2008

Sunday 21st

The NEO evening gathering: we filed into the new basement conference room of the hotel, which we were allowed to use for free for this tour. (So the puzzle of where to rehearse was solved!) It was long and narrow with rather nice cream leather chairs. Nigel opened by introducing us to what we would be studying together whenever time allowed – Romans (of course!) and how the entire Gospel is centred in God's Son. He read the opening verses of Romans 1 (from the J.B. Phillips version, again, of course!) and spoke briefly about how Paul was:

1. A servant.

2. A messenger of the Gospel

He explained how it might technically be possible to talk about God, the Holy Spirit, spiritual experience, refreshment, guidance etc., but all that still might not be the Gospel. The Gospel is *always* centred on God's Son. The Cross, the Lamb, the Throne are always in the CENTRE.

This is what the New Testament tells us – particularly in Romans – Paul was not ashamed of the Gospel (see Chapter 1 v 16) – it is God's plan for making men right! This is a process begun and continued in faith. (v 17)

The new plan is explained carefully in the first five chapters of Romans – it is quite revolutionary! God's plan is that we should have peace with God, *irrespective of our performance.* Other religions depend on performance. We however, are justified by Christ. It is as though He says to us: "I'm thrilled with you! Come into the light!"

(Chapter 5 v 3) *We can be full of joy here and now even in our trials and troubles*

(Chapter 5 v 2) *Through Him we have confidently entered into the new relationship of grace, and here we take our stand, in happy certainty of the glorious things he has for us in the future.*

We are (in NEO) offering all this treasure to others – we also need to drink it in ourselves, though our flesh militates against it at times!

In the context of NEO, Nigel took time to explain how, right from the beginning, he looked for people who were primarily servants of the Lord (and musicians second!) and who were, out of that servant heart, called to be God's messengers. This was a fundamental building-block of NEO.

Monday 22nd

A day of rehearsals!

The day began with (first, a wonderful breakfast!) a little warm-up for singers in the patio garden and then we moved back to the basement conference room for serious rehearsal of the three *Recreatios*, in order of performance.

These went well, though we battled with a rather difficult acoustic in this long narrow room. (This made excellent preparation for the Pantheon however, which was set to be possibly our biggest acoustic challenge yet.)

The ensemble, however, sounded delicious. At lunchtime, Martin and Nigel set off to go and see the room where we

Patio of Lancelot Hotel

were set to perform on Wednesday evening at the Ambassador's Residence – to check out the exact amount of performance space. That all went very successfully. (I was excused from this jaunt and so took my room mates Helen Friday and Janet Fox, together with Lesley Thompson, out to a favourite little haunt, discovered by Nigel and me during our recces, for a nice lunch of bruschetta or pizza and a singularly pleasant red wine! We sat on a roof terrace directly opposite the Colosseum, with an extremely busy and noisy dual carriageway in between – all rather incongruous, but very invigorating!)

Back to rehearse *Recreatio* 3, which again was hard work, but it went well. We had to move various singers around for the different pieces, as the group was so small that position mattered in terms of the blend of voices and parts.

Later, Martin and I set off by bus in the early evening, to meet Nigel and the enablers by taxi with the keyboard and instruments, ready to lodge them at the Pantheon for 6.30pm with (hopefully) Davide, the priest's assistant. When we arrived however, Davide was nowhere to be seen, the door to the vestry was closed and no amount of knocking or buzzing brought anyone to us, despite my having seen someone go in a few minutes earlier. I tried ringing the priest's number at his other church and ended up involved in a brief conversation with someone who insisted on speaking French to me – and I had just tried to explain, likewise in (rather deficient) French, what was occurring, when Davide suddenly appeared like a benison and let us in. We unloaded everything into the vestry area and proceeded to try and go over the details of all our arrangements for the next day – at which point Davide realised that *no one* in our party spoke Italian. He then disappeared into the labyrinth of corridors which seems to run around the outside of the great Pantheon building and came back a few minutes later, having successfully tracked down a colleague who spoke English. We then proceeded very well and eventually secured all we needed. This included agreement that none of the audience area would be roped off, though for reasons too complex to explain, this meant giving up any idea of having extra chairs put out. We were told that we could not use the one toilet available there: it would be pleading with local café owners for us (and an interesting time we had of it!). I did manage, however, to secure it for Catherine, Nige's daughter, in the special circumstances of

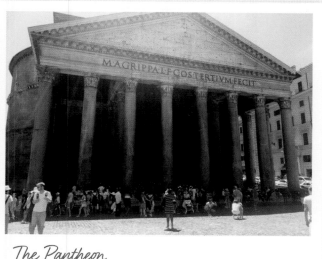

The Pantheon

her first pregnancy and her needing to rest, rather than walk around piazzas between events! We also learned the happy news that in the morning Davide would have another colleague, a girl named Serena, who also spoke English (and who in the end turned out to be as calming as her name) to look after our every need!

Nigel, Martin and I returned to the hotel by taxi, with both Nigel and myself feeling that familiar sensation of having spent an hour beating one's head against a wall, a mental tiredness that sometimes comes at such points in this ministry, even when everything has been fairly okay and has come to a happy conclusion. Happily Martin seemed quite untouched by such ravages! The (again wonderful) evening meal and fellowship revived us!

Tuesday 23rd

(Rather disturbed night, not least because my alarm clock played up and went off at 2.55am, at which point Helen and I were amused to see Janet shoot out of bed and get ready to shower, thankfully just double-checking her watch before she went any further! Needless to say, my alarm clock setting skills were the butt of some enthusiastic *goss'* among the party that day!)

The big day had come at last! One I had hoped for since I first went into the Pantheon, but had wondered if we would ever see! We were due to meet up there at 8.30am, with the hope of getting in some rehearsal before too many tourists began flowing through. A group of us, including Martin, set off again on the bus, arriving rather too early, and found cleaners in operation

Stephanie Fry (now Sidery), Fiona Ormiston and Janet Fox

who asked us to return at 8.30am proper. So I took my little party off to see the Chiesa di Santa Maria sopra Minerva, just a minute or two's walk away, and we had a pleasant 'recce' of this beautiful venue, which hid many of its glories in a cloak of near darkness, even in the morning sunshine which glimmered through its rose windows. Martin gave it the 'once over' with an experienced eye, and loved the performance area. The tomb of the famous Catherine of Siena, a patron saint of Italy, glowed up at the high altar level, lit by golden light and topped by several gold candlesticks. (I was to comment later in the week when we had finished our day in that venue that people had come in to pay homage to the tomb of a dead saint, but had unexpectedly encountered a very much alive Saviour – in the inimitable words of my dear friend Helen Friday, '*Mahvellous!*'

On our return, we found everyone else had arrived, gathered under the huge portico made up of several sixty-foot high pillars (literally cut out of the granite quarry in Egypt, owned by the Emperor Hadrian, and transported by ship to Rome, only to find they were around ten feet too short for the original design! This is why there is rather an odd view to be had of the front of the building from any height. The roof had to be built below the original roof-line which can be clearly seen above it!). We went in, to begin our set up.

The enormous and beautiful marble-clad interior is quite awesome, and the eye is drawn up into the great dome (the largest self-supporting one of its kind in Europe), in the centre of which is the oculus, some twenty-two feet across, through which sunlight comes to rest on some part or other of the dome wall at different points during the

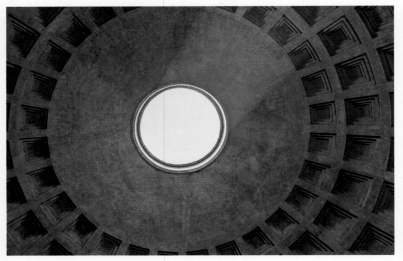

The Oculus in the Pantheon

day. The effect is stunning. On this early morning, however, it was all rather grey, and the 'fresh air' effect, which was also intended by the creation of the oculus, and which acts like a natural air-conditioning system, meant that we were greeted by a freezing cold breeze which ruffled everyone's music (pegs were needed on music stands) and left many of the troop wishing they'd brought something warmer to wear over their summer shirting!

In this somewhat shivering state, occasionally blowing and rubbing fingers, we took up our positions and tried out the acoustic. The trumpeters, Anthony (mentioned above) and Tom (Osborne) played a fanfare in the portico and then came

into the building, separating at the doorway and moving to each side, playing the well-known Catholic 'Alleluia' Nigel had arranged for us, to open the first and second *Recreatios*. The sound was incredible! Miraculously, despite the vast space between them, they were able to keep in perfect time with one another as they took up their central positions at either side of the enormous round auditorium.

We were astonished at how well we were able to blend and to hear each other (always a gift if it can be achieved!) and we found it was a high-note favouring acoustic, so a lot of work had to be put in by the lower parts and all of us of course needed terrific attention to diction in view of the sound reverberating around the great chamber.

Tourists soon flowed in – many of them transfixed even by the rehearsal! The cameras and camcorders were already out, and the odd enthusiast clapped when we finished an item. We broke for coffee in wonderfully warming sunshine in the piazza cafés outside, and gratefully soaked up the reviving rays, chatting together in our little groups as we watched the tourists swarming around the central fountain and pouring in and out of the Pantheon itself. It was lovely to find Brian, Ruth and Andrew Miller and have fellowship with them. They had come on holiday to pray and support us. Wonderful commitment!

Recreatio 1

I was asked to light a candle, which had been provided by Davide, at one side of the platform. We stood ready on the steps in front of the altar (praise the Lord, we were actually allowed to do this!) with the players on the lower platform in front of us. We heard the trumpeters playing their wonderful fanfare in the portico, with Nick Gerrard shouting to the crowds, and then Anthony and Tom opened the 'Alleluia' as planned (to great effect) and we joined in the final chorus. Then Nigel went straight into his keyboard introduction to 'Psalm 150' (Duke Ellington) which Catherine sang superbly, with the instrumentalists' entries equally exciting. The final high note soared up and around the dome and the audience (now building up but very noisy!) showed their appreciation. Then Msgr Micheletti (our beloved *Pantheon Man*), dressed extremely casually in a large T-shirt, read

Cameras of every kind!

the first reading in Italian: *Ascribe to the Lord, O families of nations, ascribe to the Lord, glory and strength!* The trumpets converged on the performance space and the musicians struck up the 'Hallelujah chorus' from Handel's 'Messiah'! There was a terrific wall of sound and our voices seemed to reach up into the dome and out towards the huge iron doorway, lit by the bright sun and showing silhouettes of people pouring in. We had great liberty and it was wonderful for once, to be able to sing God's praises literally at full pelt!

Canon Roger Oldfield declaimed from his microphone, "Come all you who are thirsty, come to the waters, and you who have no money, come buy and eat! Come buy wine and milk without money and without cost!" This was followed by other readings and then the haunting melody of 'There is a longing in our hearts O Lord' (by Anne Quigley) at which people were already visibly moved in the auditorium, and some who had been standing watching quizzically, decided to sit down in any spare seats on the benches provided. Pure worship and joy followed, interspersed by more wonderful Bible verses.

The flute improvisations were delicate, each in turn coming from various points around the hall, and floating mysteriously up and around the dome, causing people to search for the source. Following the last of these, Nigel began to beat the thrilling call of the djembe and the singers let fly with 'We are marching in the light of God', bringing warm smiles and infectious enthusiasm from the watchers.

After the blessing came the final triumphant 'Sing the Lord!' (Haydn's 'Creation') and a very warm response ensued from

around the auditorium. Then after the blessing, soft notes were played to the singers for 'Be still and know', and as we began to descend from either side of the platform to meet in the central aisle and walk through the audience, we saw the now familiar looks of total surprise and bewilderment, giving way to all kinds of heartfelt responses, of the kind indicated by the tiniest sensations as one looks into someone else's eyes for a lingering moment. We began to see tears, and people (many of them grown men, as we have often found) becoming unable to control their facial features. We knew the Lord was responding in His own inimitable way, inhabiting the praises of His people, ministering His love to endless needs unknown to us. Sharing the 'treasure' is such a privilege!

Lunchtime followed, with everyone dispersing to find their favourite eating place, or discover a new one, or just browse the shops, and in no time we were back for *Recreatio* 2. Whilst we were out, apparently, Msgr Micheletti had called Nigel and Roger Oldfield into the vestry and presented them with medallions, the last of a batch made five years ago to commemorate a centenary celebration of the Pantheon. He had also invited us all back next year!

Recreatio 2

We took our positions and I lit the candle once again. This time, Msgr Micheletti was nowhere to be seen, having left Davide, his assistant, to do the readings in Italian for the next two events of the day, and arranged that Roger would give the blessings.

It was more of the same, though a little more 'intense' in terms of spiritual action I thought. The responses in people's faces seemed more ready and open and one felt that some folk had perhaps come a second time. There were lots of cameras and video film being taken. There seemed to be a bigger crowd. Sometimes it was extremely noisy, and sometimes more hushed. As some (I think Roger and Nick) later commented, it was like being in a market place but inside a building, the ideal situation then for the Gospel! Speaking of the Gospel, 'Oh Happy Day' went down incredibly well, with cheering, clapping and great enthusiasm from the onlookers. There were one or two

The crowd in the Pantheon

faces split by laughter at that moment, which I inwardly felt had probably not laughed like that for a while: it was a 'clean', innocent and joyful laughter somehow, the sort that dispelled a lot of negatives.

By the time we walked down the aisle again, singing 'Be still and know that I am God', we had found that a pause right beneath the oculus was a great idea, as it was completely central to the hall and a definite hush fell all around, which we were later told by several people, was because at that point, we reached the optimum acoustic. Every single word could be clearly heard, right around the building. Fantastic! A young woman to my right was in floods of tears and buried her face in her hands. Mary Burton (soprano) threw an arm around her and embraced her, still singing gently, until the sobs subsided. (She was an American Christian living in Rome for four months with her husband, who was on a placement lecturing in architecture and she later became quite a friend. Ruth had met her earlier and found her to be just setting out as a writer of poetry, with so far one poem published – so she introduced

Walking out to sing to the audience!

her to me for a chat and she asked me to send her a copy of my own little poetry book. Later in the week, Mary went to lunch at her apartment and had a great time. These unexpected friendships were always such a blessing!)

A smaller gap of time then occurs on these occasions, between *Recreatios* 2 and 3 –time enough however, for a refreshing lemon sorbet from the nearest 'Gelateria'! The owner did a roaring trade from the NEO family that afternoon! Later we went back through the vestry door into the corridor area which had been allotted to us, and Roger Oldfield told us all about the presentation from Msgr Micheletti, and showed us the heavy medallion in a presentation case. Roger was a huge help to us throughout the day and a special atmosphere occurred whenever he gave the blessing. He was keen to tell us how privileged he felt and how excited he was to be able to read the word of God in the Pantheon in particular. It was a place where people from all over the world gathered, again, ideal for the Gospel, and he is definitely a messenger of the Gospel!

Recreatio 3

This one was designed to begin with Vaughan Williams' 'O taste and see', heralded by the trumpet as Anthony walked in from the doorway. It was a powerful moment. Catherine's voice soared as beautifully as ever and captivated people's hearts.

I had to ask Matt Baynham to light the candle this time, as the wick was gradually disappearing down the funnel inside the candle and I was no longer tall enough to find and light it, even on tiptoe! Things of all sorts were going deeper! The first thing that we noticed as we stood in readiness was the huge number of people. There were hundreds and hundreds of them now. An entire row of (noticeably) young folk had seated themselves on the floor in front of the first arc of bench-pews, despite the fact that sitting on the floor is one of the many things forbidden by the tall notice boards of the Pantheon! Davide however, did nothing to dissuade them.

Generally this third compilation of readings and music has become known as the 'quiet one', as there are one or two very poignant pieces like 'O taste', together with 'The Apple Tree', 'As we are gathered,' 'Give yourself to Jesus', and the beautiful Bach 'Concerto for Two Violins'. Despite the brighter and vivacious pieces ('The Heavens are Telling', from Haydn's 'The Creation', 'My God is so High', Vivaldi 'Double Trumpet Concerto', and finally the stunning 'Resucito' sung in South American Spanish – which we later heard Davide had been seen singing with us, with eyes sparkling, apparently knowing every single word!) there is a deeper mood to this *Recreatio*. Certainly, by the time we came to the recessional with 'Be still', there was a most unbelievable atmosphere, and as we gathered under the oculus, Nigel later told us that there was a really terrific press of people all around us, desperately trying to get near – hundreds of cameras (films will go back all over the globe!), and so, so many people, deeply moved, visibly sobbing, tears everywhere – hence Anthony's quip about the need for a health and safety sign, *Wet floor!* We were very much aware of the Lord's presence and would have loved to know more of what He was doing and saying to those folk that afternoon. Some, of course, were able to give an inkling of what was in their hearts, as we learned in the feedback sessions later on. It made someone comment that they realised that this is how people must have looked at Jesus, and Nigel made the point that we are told on occasion, 'Jesus was unable to do anything because of the press'(and not, he pointed out, the paparazzi!). We began to understand how that might feel.

At the close, when we returned to the vestry, word was put about that Davide and Serena wanted to meet us in the small chapel, to show us the original icon given to the Pantheon years before, reputedly painted by St Luke! It was shortly to be coming to the British Museum apparently. As we gathered there and he made all his explanations, he told us, via Serena's interpretation, that we had 'done something for the church', and to do something for the church, meant to do something for Christ. He said a lot which I can't recall, though others no doubt will, but he was very warm and thankful and obviously had 'seen' what NEO is all about!

This then, was the culmination of our first day in the Pantheon! The interior was bathed in late afternoon light by

Rev. Canon Roger Oldfield, Davide, Serena & Nigel

the time we packed up and left the building, and needless to say, we felt similarly 'aglow'. I remember a heartfelt 'thank you' welling up in me as I walked out.

Back at the hotel, we had agreed to give a little impromptu concert in the hotel lounge for the guests and staff who were there on duty that evening. It was rather cramped, but great fun and very much appreciated! Someone among the guests also had a birthday I recall, and there was a special moment when Faris (the chef) took a musical box playing the traditional 'Happy birthday to you' to the table, and encouraged us all to sing to this delighted guest. This was followed by the lights being dimmed and a parade of waiters carrying individual Baked Alaska desserts to their table, each with a live indoor firework in the centre, shooting sparks about a foot high! It was quite spectacular! We found, to our delight, that Faris had obviously made several larger versions of this delectable pud, and we all had a great slice delivered to our plate (meringue over a meltingly delicious layer of ice cream and exotic fruits, on a bed of sponge cake). A memorable and happy family occasion, typical of this hotel! Free champagne also followed and an air of celebration prevailed!

Wednesday 24th

We gathered for a meeting before rehearsals began, to hear Nige's next instalment of Romans, headed "Come and see!" (So headed, because that really is all we can ask people to do, as we ourselves don't know what God will do anyway!)

He talked about how, in our own attempt to live the Christian life, we often develop our own 'model', which can sometimes be quite harsh, but how wonderful it is that we have real *peace with God* through our Lord Jesus Christ.

He made a brief comparison between NEO and *Songs of Praise*, which he described as sometimes seeming like a camp fire sing-song! He made the point that we in NEO are not on a 'jolly'. We have something truly wonderful to proclaim. Our griefs and difficulties, though real, are passing, transitory. We can have joy even in our trials and troubles. We have security for the future. We really are going to heaven. Through Christ, we have an 'unclouded relationship' with the Lord. (I thought of those words several times and quoted them to Helen and Janet whenever we were smiled on by totally clear, blue skies in Rome.)

(Chapter 5 v 5) Our difficulties are given us so that *taken in the right spirit*, says J.B. Phillips, they will lead to *patient endurance; this in turn will develop a mature character, and a character of this sort produces a steady hope, a hope that will never disappoint us.* When we start out as Christians, we're often really 'up and down' but maturity helps us to learn how to manage our trials. We are full of hope.

Music can often be a prophetic instrument. If we want to be really used by God, he prepares us *internally*. The prophets often had to *feel* the prophecy, e.g. Hosea, who learned about God's love of the unfaithful (repeatedly unfaithful at that) by being sent to marry a prostitute – no doubt a beautiful and attractive woman – but incapable of being constant. Nigel made the point: "You can't talk about what you don't know."

(V 5 – v 11) God's grace: It was *while we were yet sinners* that Christ died for the ungodly. (J.B. Phillips puts it*: It was while we were powerless to help ourselves that Christ died for sinful men*.). Nigel remarked that none of us can repent anyway until we have heard Christ calling, but it is in our *worst possible state* that God moves in grace to us. This is still the case and more so, now we are His!

If we are not now under a 'rule model', then how do we live? (We are no longer under the law). How do we deal with the internal things, cope with our personalities etc. These matters are all dealt with superbly by Paul in chapters 6

and 7, and then at last we are brought into the wonders of chapter 8!

J.B. Phillips: *No condemnation now hangs over the head of those who are 'in' Christ Jesus. For the new spiritual principle of life 'in' Christ Jesus lifts me out of the old vicious circle of sin and death.* We are out of the vicious circle!

When the model is removed then, God's Spirit replaces it and we find ourselves doing what God requires. God can even affect our mortal bodies (and here Nigel reminded us of the incredible experience, already mentioned, of Anthony Thompson last year in Rome, who though arriving in a state of illness and weakness, was miraculously upheld). We could only assume that the Lord, by this means, made it clear that this was a special blessing for Ant and for all of us, simply for the four days of that tour. Instances like those must always be a reminder to us never to stop interceding for the *obvious* practicalities, like one another's health on these tours!

Nigel then opened a time of sharing and feedback, and this was the point at which he told us what he had seen at the end of the last *Recreatio* in the Pantheon, the huge crowd pressing around us, seeing and hearing what they wanted and needed.

Comments from the floor

Daphne Ryland: Heads were bowed right across the hall when Roger said we would pray for the blessing at the end.

Briggie Furze: Amazing responses from people: hand-shaking, thanks etc.

Matt Baynham: Met some self-confessed atheists, members of a male voice choir who had come to Rome to sing, but had had two concerts cancelled because their repertoire had included the 'Chorus of the Hebrew Slaves' (reputedly because Catholics don't like this reference to the Jews). They claimed not to be believers, but were in tears.

Andrea Young: Found an American lady who was astonished and relieved to find that there were, after all, Christians in England! (This was not the first time we heard this said during the tour by Americans – rather sobering!)

Ruth Oldfield: Commented on the honouring of the Lord in the work done beforehand in meeting Davide at the Pantheon (on previous recce). It was she who told us how his eyes had sparkled and Ant had seen him singing all of 'Resucito'.

Nick Gerrard: The Pantheon was like the 'Altermarkt' of Salzburg, but inside a building. He had found 'The Apple Tree' particularly powerful (I agree! Throughout the tour in both *Recreatio* 3 performances, this piece was amazingly used). 'Be still' was very precious. Nick went on to describe his own personal battles as he tried to speak out for the Lord more evangelistically in his appeals to the public to get them inside beforehand. But each time he had managed it, more people had come in.

Various others mentioned particular people they had spoken to and situations they had encountered, including a female tour guide who was really angry with NEO, but in the end Ant managed to make her laugh! (How unusual!)

I mentioned the spiritual influences lingering in Rome from its long past history of the gods of Rome, now 'cloaked' as it were, with all the trappings of modern day religiosity generally, but still active in a sense. Thea Hoelscher had particularly felt this and we had spent some time in her room earlier chatting it through over a cup of tea. It was in just this situation however, that the powerful love of Christ, the 'treasure' we had been talking about, came with such forceful reality, making a huge impact. The warming, melting reaction of Davide reminded me so much of the similar reaction we had with Brother Virgil in a previous Salzburg tour, when he had taken us all into the private chapel of St Peter's Stiftskirche, where the monks prayed, to show us the statue of Jesus and stand directly beneath it, to see the eyes, which were in fact open, and looking down. Also, last year in Rome, of Brother Mahari, whose face lit up when he had spent a whole *Recreatio* with us and finally understood why we were there, and had ended by giving an eloquent blessing. Their hearts had been touched by the love of Christ and they wanted to give us something in return. The 'afterglow' was there! This too is what we encountered in so many of the people who came along to our events.

We then had to tear ourselves away from all this reminiscing, and do some serious rehearsal of the extra pieces for the evening concert.

After that, the girls (Helen, Janet and Lesley) and I went down to a little local restaurant around the corner to have a decent lunch, as we didn't know what the reception fare would comprise in the evening. Janet had been struggling with a three-day headache, and needed to return for rest and I later joined her and we enjoyed a quiet pot of tea on our terrace and some sharing time together, while the others browsed around a little. Such times were precious.

We changed for the evening, donning our 'NEO red and black', and I had arranged to take the girls and Keith by taxi to the Ambassador's residence in the middle of Rome. We waited outside for quite a while, being greeted by Peter and Stella Jennings (who were staying with the Ambassador, Francis Campbell, in his flat there) until Martin and the others all arrived. There was a tiny, two-person lift (good for the keyboard and for the singers, who were told to come in last of all. For the remainder of us, (Martin, myself, the rest of the enablers and all the players) we took the stairs, five flights of concrete steps! We gathered for a moment at the top to regain our breath and our composure, before announcing our arrival at the apartment door and being summoned up by Pat Corby (Diplomatic Events Manager) to see the really beautiful dining room where we were to perform. Then everyone was asked to go to the roof terrace for drinks, whilst all was made ready below and so I stayed down at the doorway to direct singers accordingly. We had time for a brief rehearsal and to try out Nigel's plan for a graded entry, so that by the end of the third item, all performers were present! It worked wonderfully, as the performance space was quite small, and we managed by this means, not to overwhelm everyone all at once!

The guests were summoned and took their places. (To our joy we were able to bring in ALL our personnel, including enablers, and they were able to sit towards the back and enjoy the whole evening). Nigel, together with Christopher Poffley, opened the evening gloriously with 'The Swan' by Saint-Saëns, and then Catherine and Anthony and most of the other players entered and gave a much appreciated version of 'Let the Bright Seraphim' (we were meanwhile gathered on the narrow staircase outside, from where we could hear the ripples of laughter and the enthusiastic applause!) Next, Matt joined Catherine for 'Arise my love'

Concert at the residence of the Ambassador to the Holy See — 2008

and after Matt's now famous verse about 'the turtle dove' we quietly sang the refrain at the appropriate moment from our offstage position! For the final chorus, we quietly filed in singing (led by Tom Osborne (trumpet) and Rebecca Coward (bassoon) simply carrying their instruments and silently taking their positions for later items in the programme), and we all managed to be in place by the time the song ended. The audience looked about as close to both impressed and in bliss as is humanly possible! We had to admit it was another of Nigel's triumphs of imagination!

From there, Nigel took over and described how we were going to take our guests all around the world! He produced out of the hat pieces as diverse as 'We are Marching' (Africa) and 'Great and Wonderful' (Israeli style), 'Resucito' (South America) and 'Jesus your light' (Taizé, France). We ended with Monteverdi's 'Laetatus Sum' which went down incredibly well, and finally the Mascagni 'Easter Hymn', which almost, but not quite, blew the ancient beamed roof off! All was wonderfully well received, and followed by a lovely speech by Francis Campbell, showing enormous appreciation and again mentioning what great ambassadors we were for Britain and what a wonderful contribution this work made to culture in Rome, but with the added element of faith! We were invited to return again, we later heard, and he hoped to find a larger venue next time!

Peter Jennings responded with a short speech, and in the line of Embassy business, a much honoured female secretary, who was leaving her post, was thanked and given a farewell amid much applause, and then we were all summoned again to the upstairs roof terrace, now embellished with a glorious pink sunset over the rooftops of Rome, to enjoy some rather nice food and drinks. The most interesting part of this (apart from some excellent conversations) was the little towers of sandwiches which had been prepared for us, made of pannetone, cut into four quarters but re-fitted into a perfect round, with the lid put back on the top to look just like the Pantheon! They were unsurprisingly short-lived.

There were many guests, including several people whom we were later told had important positions at the Vatican. Philippa Hitchen was there, and we were so glad to be able to greet her. I had seen her fleetingly at the middle *Recreatio* of the day, taking a recording, and she afterwards made an excellent programme of it for Vatican Radio, which we were able to hear via the internet. The Archbishop of Canterbury's representative to the Vatican was there; several nuns, Monsignor Philip Whitmore, (responsible for coaching Pope Benedict in English pronunciation at that time) and interestingly enough, both the Principal and the Vice Chancellor of the English College (where our British Catholic priests are trained). They were so impressed, they invited Nigel to bring NEO next mid-October to the opening of their (hopefully by then), refurbished College chapel.

Having ordered a taxi for one or two tired or ailing members of the party to return to the hotel, I went back upstairs and Nigel and I were taken out by Peter and Stella Jennings, into the fascinating old streets of Trastevere, (lit with strings of sparkling lights) for drinks and time to chat, after giving necessary accurate detail for Peter's forthcoming article to the Catholic press.

Thursday 25th

The last 'big push'– our day in Chiesa di Santa Maria sopra Minerva! At breakfast, the girls and I sat at one of the famous 'round tables' of the Lancelot Hotel, and chatted to a couple we had met (husband Australian and wife Canadian) from Vancouver. They were interested to know about the NEO, and I gave them detailed instructions of how to find the above church and they promised to come along with some Italian friends they were due to meet that afternoon.

I then registered my intention of popping down to the local florist for a bunch of something pretty for Nicoletta, the English-speaking secretary who had helped make this particular day's adventure possible. I would then meet the group at the bus stop. This I did, red roses in hand, and we arrived at the church, where I had promised to take Martin straight round to Nicoletta's office to introduce him and get the ball rolling for our set up.

At our call, she opened the automatic door latch and we ascended, to find her smiling and welcoming us (her boss was out!), but looking rather puzzled for a second, "Ah, Julie!" We greeted each other with the familiar kiss on each cheek, but then she put her head on one side and asked, "Is it today?" "Yes!" I replied, with a niggling feeling in the pit of my stomach, "Is Father Ballicu here?" "He had to go away," she replied, "He is in *Sardeenia*!" She has a delightful English accent and spoke those words with such childlike innocence. (For a split second I fought the desire to roll my eyes and exclaim, "Well how typical is that?!") However, I inwardly re-grouped my thoughts and replied, "Well is it alright if we go ahead and get set up in the church?" She had no objection whatsoever! As far as she was concerned, it was in the diary and all was well. Phew!

"But who do we speak to if we have a problem?" (I knew she had said she couldn't come down with us, and she would only be there in any case until lunchtime, when she had to run off to her second job!) "Francesco." she replied, "He speaks a little Eenglish, he will help you!" She was wonderful!

We toddled off down the stairs, relieved that we could get on with things, and I suggested Martin press on with the layout for the orchestra, while I encouraged enablers/singers et al to put out the chairs that were stacked at the rear of the church, and which we had been given permission to use.

Martin came after a while, to say he really needed the lights put on (remember my mentioning this was quite a dark church) and I had also ascertained that the vestry area was gated and locked. Whispering a prayer that somehow I would find this Father Francesco, (as I assumed him to be one of the English-speaking monks I had encountered on a previous recce) I looked around, and suddenly saw a dark-haired young man in a corner with a mop. I asked if he spoke English, to which he nodded his head and smiled, and when I asked if he could direct me to Father Francesco, he replied delightfully, "Not Father! I am he!" I began to tell him we were the New English Orchestra, booked for three events during the day at – and he filled in the times for me! He obviously knew all! From then on we got on famously. He asked for a second or two to finish his mopping and then came along and opened the vestry gates, showed me that the toilets (no less than two!) were situated within this area (oh bliss!) and then shot a switch somewhere which brought the whole area around the altar alive with colour. Suddenly the high vaulted roof of the church (coloured a deep blue with patterns which looked like stars and some glorious paintings) came into view, and at last the place looked awake! I was tempted to whisper 'Now we're cooking with gas!' and scampered off to direct waiting singers and players to the vestry area and encourage them that relief was at hand for any struggling bladders!

Not long after that, I remember being (as I so often am) thankful for Lesley Thompson! On the plane out, we had been reading our respective Italian phrase books, and I had mentioned to her how badly I needed, on this trip, to find out the word for an extension lead. It didn't occur in my book, but she found it in hers, and announced loudly and with great enthusiasm to our entire section of the aeroplane: "La prolunga!" I had logged this securely in the noggin and so was ready when Ernie Dalton popped up, holding a wire with an odd-looking plug on the end and told me he needed an extra cable with the proper fitting, and could I ask Francesco where the nearest shop was? However, I did see Italian-only speaking Father Mario, whom I knew to be an official verger, coming down the church, and I managed to catch him and try out my new word on him, saying also that it was for the 'trastere', which I miraculously recalled was the word for a keyboard! He smiled, and took me to a large door, which he opened with a massive bunch of keys and then, leaning into a sort of large pigeon-hole area filled with electrical stuff, he brought out a suitably lengthy 'prolunga', and all was well with the world! In fact, as I looked around there was a veritable nest of about thirty prolungas hidden away in there!

After that preamble, we were eventually able to gather in the performance area before the lower altar, and gaze down the length of this huge church. We tried a few pieces and enjoyed the acoustic, which was totally glorious. It was again top- favouring and we had to take care and keep listening and attending to diction, but it did sound and feel wonderful! Faris, the chef from our hotel, had brought a friend with a very professional looking camera and tripod, obviously all set to film the whole proceedings. Faris' brother Sheqib, who helps manage the hotel, was there with his own camcorder, and seemed to pop up all over the place during the event, but always smiling!

(Wonderfully, even though the Oldfields had come, ready at any time to do all the readings in English together, a young monk appeared on the scene, sent by Nicoletta to do the readings in Italian on behalf of Father Ballicu. He turned out to be appointed by God we think, probably mainly for his own blessing. Though looking rather terrified throughout, he enjoyed himself immensely, had some good conversations with Roger, and I heard later at home from Nicoletta via email, that he had told her how absolutely beautiful it all was and how privileged he was to take part. Roger found out he was about to take his vows the following week! Surely this was a loving touch from his heavenly Father.)

We had requested that the huge double doors at the entrance to the church, which usually stood firmly closed, be opened – and so they were! We heard the trumpets, and Nick's cries, and enjoyed the 'Alleluia' as Ant and Tom walked in down the aisle.

For the first *Recreatio*, the church was by no means full, but it was obvious that there was already a work of the Holy Spirit going on in those who were there. We were again blessed by the facial responses to each item, and it was wonderful to watch expressions changing, from vacant to interested, to warmed and enlightened, to moved or amused. By the time we came to 'Be still' there were again many tears, and we were once again bowled over by the almost palpable presence of the Holy Spirit. I hope one day in heaven we

hear some of what was going on during these occasions! Again, there was wonderful liberty, and increasing blessing, I think, to us all as we communicated with individuals with our eyes while we sang.

This *Recreatio* had been altered slightly from last year, to include the Mascagni 'Easter Hymn', which was magnificent as ever, (but really set my right temple banging with the reverb from the high last notes) and was very well received by the Italian contingent! Despite feeling unwell from time to time in the early stages of her pregnancy, Catherine did so well all throughout the tour and all her solos were as glorious as ever.

By the end, the intensity was growing, both in terms of audience reaction (tears everywhere) and people getting straight onto their mobiles (a phenomenon I had noticed at the end of the first *Recreatio)*. The enablers reported that people kept coming back and bringing friends with them! Thank God that good news can travel every bit as fast as bad sometimes!

Recreatio 3 was truly wonderful! The church was full! I don't think there were any free seats at all, and people were standing at the sides. The enablers had moved some more of the chairs from the back and put a row up inside the aisle. The Australian chap we had met at breakfast was over on the right behind a pillar, with his camcorder on a tripod and a big grin on his face. A lovely couple, Wally Huckle and his wife and a friend, who are 'Friends of NEO', had deliberately been in touch with me for information earlier in the year, so they could coincide their holiday in Rome with our visit and, as usual, they were in their seats, smiling happily up at us.

The 'quiet' one went so deep that day! Again, the Lord's presence was almost palpable, the music seemed especially beautiful and people responded amazingly. There was a lot of symbolism apparent in this tour. One of the most beautiful and memorable moments was of Nicola having crept quietly into a very ornate balcony, ready to do her improvisation on the flute, just as a bird was seen to swoop down from the ceiling towards the back of the church and fly out of the door into the sunshine. She stood to play, and some beautiful shafts of sunlight streamed down on her from the rose window opposite, like a smile from the

Lord. She played some beautiful fluid notes like bird calls, which I recall she did the previous year in Rome and which particularly blessed me.

It's hard to describe what happened as we concluded that final event with the last great chorus of 'Resucito', sung so loudly and clearly and in proclamatory fashion – "He rose!" (Though I admit it nearly did for me with the pain in my head which was now a migraine, doubtless started by our standing so long in the day, facing the open door where incoming people were mere silhouettes against the fierce brightness of the sun!) Every single person in the church stood up clapping. I know it's happened often before in NEO events, but there was something for me personally about this moment that dissolved me into tears, and it was all I could do to keep my own facial expression under control! It was a standing ovation with a difference somehow!

Then of course the final 'Be still' procession – and here we really saw the Lord at work mightily, so many people were moved. Mary Burton will tell (as she did at a final feedback session) of one Dutch man who was moved with anger – no one can tell it better than Mary – he had sat with his arms folded and a grim expression throughout, but he said to her, "You do this to people!" and removing his glasses, there were tears streaming down his face. People handle emotion in different ways...

The singing was particularly anointed as we walked down the aisle, and there were many openly sobbing; one woman in particular, with whom one or two of us spent a second or two, just to touch a shoulder as we walked by. (We learned later that she was a Catholic, like one or two others our folk met, who told us that only here had she felt the reality of the Lord Jesus, and wondered why she had not seen Him this way before!) One or two reached out hands to us, some of them looked into our eyes with the most indescribable expressions, searching, finding, perhaps beginning to understand, but so many weeping. It was extraordinarily powerful, and for me, only a need to keep going and to continue doing the job to the end, actually kept me upright, it was almost too strong for me that time and not just because of the migraine!

I walked back up the aisle afterwards as we greeted folk, or said farewells to those leaving, and the Australian chap came up and shook my hand and said how completely beautiful it was and how delighted he was to have been there. But then his wife came down the aisle, having already hugged Janet and Helen, and she fell into my arms in floods of tears, constantly wiping her eyes and trying to find the words to tell me what she was feeling. It really was overwhelming! Wonderful conversations ensued, and we left the building feeling a huge sense of having been gathered into something great which the Lord had planned for that day and accomplished beautifully, though of course we could only glimpse tiny cameos through some of the conversations, of what He was actually achieving.

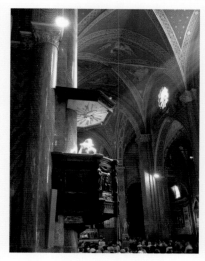

Church of Santa Maria sopra Minerva and Nicola's balcony

We gathered our belongings from the vestry and walked down to leave the church, at which point I looked up at 'Nicola's balcony' and noticed for the first time, in the centre of its small wooden ceiling, a lovely carving of the white dove of the Holy Spirit, with bright gold rays spreading out from it...

Back at the hotel, we gathered in the basement for a final feedback meeting before dinner. Others must tell of the various points that were shared at that time, which I largely missed, and couldn't concentrate on the remainder because of the migraine.

The evening was pretty wonderful for our party, with a happy evening meal and more free champagne from Faris, ordered in honour of NEO. I believe Janet brought my meal up to our room, as I had to lie down in the dark. I was grateful to Janet and Helen and to Matt Baynham who cared for me on the flight home, with Matt procuring a wheelchair to push me to the car at Birmingham Airport, still in a painful state. That

Suites from the Trolley!
Christopher Poffley in tow!

particular migraine lasted in total, five days. These things have a tendency to occur we know, when on 'active service' but on a more positive note, a little enforced rest after such an exciting tour was admittedly welcome!

————————— Dimples —————————

This song is the budget version of Lift up your heads

Sweets from the trolley?

Our trips to Rome and exciting *Recreatio* events in the Pantheon became the stuff of NEO legend. Nigel would constantly be inventing ways of keeping the enormous crowd quiet and focused on what we were doing. So, for example, the idea of a small group of players and a team of men processing from the door to the front, playing and singing, 'There's new life in Jesus, lift up your hearts', or of

placing a couple of players for a duet on risers in front of the rest of the orchestra, or even of having singers suddenly turn into dancers and dance a Charleston in the middle of one song, became 'normal'! However, during the process of getting our instruments to Rome, usually via Salzburg, where they were first hired from a contact of Thea and Georg Hoelscher, and then transported by van, through the remarkable dedication of Howard Masters and Georg, all the way to Rome – we did have a slight 'incident' one year. One of the hired timpani suffered a little damage through being jostled in transport. After having it repaired, Georg set to work creating a special wooden 'case' for it, together with a trolley to move it, once they arrived, from the van to the rear of the Pantheon! This latter piece of kit was to become the latest inspiration for another of Nigel's innovative ideas!

Procession of instrumentalists
in the Pantheon

In his mind's eye, he could see a solo cellist – let's call him Christopher Poffley (a fantastic Baroque expert) – seated upon this trolley and being wheeled by two willing assistants (the chosen two were Corrie Gerrard and Angelika Busse) from the great doors of the Pantheon to the altar, from which position he would literally play Bach 'suites from the trolley'! It was a huge success. One member of the audience found it utterly spine-tingling, when the glorious sound of the cello gradually increased as Christopher drew nearer, giving a superb rendering of Bach's 'Prelude for unaccompanied cello', from 'Suite no. 1 in G major'! Eventually he was 'parked' at the front centre of the orchestra, to continue his piece until the end. Georg even managed to adapt his trolley so that it would securely hold a music stand for Chris's music! It could only happen in NEO!

We'll do verses 1 and 2, and then carry on with the ladies!

The Hyde Park Vigil – September 18th 2010

So that's how the Rome adventure all began. We had no idea we would visit so many times, nor did we guess how significant a surprise the Lord had lined up for us! It is quite fascinating how He can bring someone across your path, you enjoy meeting them and hearing all about their work – only to discover very soon that you have just met the person who is going to be responsible for leading you into the next phase of the Lord's plan for your *own* work!

In Chapter 5 – *Whatever the weather…*, I mention the exciting day we spent celebrating the newly refurbished chapel of the Venerable English College (VEC). We had returned to Rome in September 2009, and then a small group of us flew out again for this visit in October. Father Andrew Headon had invited us to join him for this project, after having been with us during one of the Santa Maria sopra Minerva *Recreatios* mentioned in the account above, where he had felt deeply touched by the Lord.

After the success of the VEC project therefore, we began to hear rumours that Andrew was to leave his post at the VEC, and return to parish work in England. It was soon confirmed however, that he had been asked to co-ordinate Pope Benedict XVI's *Vigil for Young People* in Hyde Park! Nigel had been advised privately, (by Francis Campbell, Ambassador to the Holy See) not to go to Rome in September 2010, just in case we were needed in the UK at that time!

So it came about that one sunny spring afternoon, as I sat on a bench, alternately reading and sketching at the Birmingham Botanical Gardens, I received a call on my mobile from Nigel, to say it had happened! The call had come through from Andrew Headon, asking if NEO would indeed provide the core music for the *Hyde Park Vigil*! Not only so, but Nigel had been asked to be part of the Standing Committee which would organise it – and the first date would clash with an important hospital appointment of his, so would I go instead? Andrew was happy for me to be part of the committee too!

That was the start of many fascinating visits to Eccleston Square, London, where stand the offices of the Catholic Bishops' Conference of England and Wales. We were to meet some wonderful people, and do an awful lot of pen-pushing, paper- shifting and fact-absorbing over the next few months. I have an enormous file still in my cabinet, of all the administration leading up to this huge event – easily the biggest NEO had ever been involved in. Andrew had to guide us through each stage, not only involving the preparation of the event itself, with all the many participants, the construction of the actual service, the music it would require etc., but at various times introducing us to those involved in the wider field for matters of Police Security (Nationwide Command at both Silver and Gold levels) and leaders of all the organisational teams for health and safety, technical support, not to mention the press etc. It was a simply mammoth operation! As we drew nearer to the point at which more NEO input was required, Martin Lowe was drafted in and it was wonderful, as ever, to have him there. Initially, even the staging itself had been a challenge for Father Andrew, as a stage he had hoped to use, which was already in place for another event, proved out of the question for various reasons, and a new company had to be drafted in and a new stage design employed, right in the middle of all this! He was astoundingly calm and efficient throughout all, though only the Lord knows how he must have felt inwardly!

When all was prepared however, it was a beautiful event, and we were quite blown away to come up at last onto the stage for real, after all rehearsals were over, and see the vast crowd of 80,000 people in the park before us! I think we ended up performing the 'Messiah' set we had prepared, two or three times in its entirety by the time the Papal buggy came into view, amid roars and cheers from the crowd.

I have so many random memories of the day; for example, Nigel directing the process of 'melding' with the enlarged choir which joined us for some items; the little group of us who had practised 'backing' the famous trio, 'The Priests' in their own items, (which they sang beautifully); listening to the offerings of the other groups who each took part; a few of our younger sopranos sporting false eyelashes for the occasion, just for fun (!). For the main presentation, *The Heart of the Church*, we were actually off-stage and attempting to find our way around the huge campus to find food, drinks, toilets, our own allotted changing tents etc. We could hear other folk rehearsing their numbers prior to going onstage and everywhere there was a hubbub of activity. The queues for portaloos were rather long!

The compere for the event was of course the TV presenter, Carol Vorderman. She had joined us for some of our Standing Committee meetings, and was charming.

I have only two less fond memories, one of Janet Fox having to contact Helen and myself during the rehearsal, to say that her stepmother had passed away, after a long battle with cancer. Janet had had to miss the whole event through nursing her and caring for her father through this long illness.

The second occurred at the most holy moment during the Eucharist, when we were about to sing, after a time of silence, the beautiful Taizé song, 'Jesus your light'. There were many tiny insects flying around in the night air under the stage lights, and I suddenly and inadvertently inhaled one! My eyes began to water, my throat was choking and tickling and I had no idea how to prevent myself from a noisy fit of coughing, except to keep watching Nigel and somehow force myself to continue singing. I kept thinking, with every repeat, 'This will be the last, then I can have a quiet cough into my handkerchief' – but no, round we went again! At last it ended, by which time my eyes were streaming with tears and I have no idea how I was still breathing! We never had much indication of when the cameras might be upon us, so I hoped profoundly that if any of that had been captured,

I might simply have appeared to have been 'deeply moved'!

Andrew had arranged for several of our number to meet Pope Benedict and shake his hand, including Sophy Cartledge, our NEO 'Archangel,' who has been our principal harpist for many years. Nigel and I had also been invited to meet the Pope, but we had realised we would still be on stage at that point and it would be impossible. From something Andrew mentioned to me however, it seemed he had an idea up his sleeve. Nigel therefore suddenly found himself approached by two burly security guards, who took him by the arm and led him away from his podium. All was soon revealed however; the Pope was coming across to him, where he shook Nigel's hand warmly and they spoke a few words together. The moment is captured on a beautiful photograph we were able to order when next in Rome, along with others of and for our friends who also enjoyed this experience.

It was quite wonderful to meet with one another that night for an Italian meal, having walked back through the park as all the crowds dispersed, feeling a wonderful sense of privilege, and the relief that comes at the end of a 'job well done' after months of work for us all. Seeing ourselves on screen later as news broadcasts covered the whole Papal visit, was great fun, as were the enthusiastic reports of friends and neighbours who had spotted us! After all those years of NEO working in buildings in Europe owned by the Catholic church, here we were, an 'ecumenical missionary orchestra' – providing the core music for the largest number of Catholics I had ever seen, with film going out across the world via television and radio, here in a London park – and all because the Lord spoke one afternoon to one of His sons as he sat in a pew at a Rome *Recreatio*!

Dimples

That needs a musical epilator! (When individual voices were standing out!)

Pope Benedict XVI comes to greet and thank Nigel

Audience of 80,000 in Hyde Park 2010

16
Commissions to contemporary British composers

'Squeak and grunt' music?

I remember being fascinated by the whole concept Nigel devised, of commissioning British composers who specialised in 'modern' music, which was sometimes 'atonal' or employed 'microtones', and belonged to that cutting-edge of the music world which was popular with some, but not with others! I remember laughing the first time Nigel referred to it, as was apparently sometimes the case, by the above term!

This was, however, a serious business, as we invited some of the known names in this style of music, to sit down and read the New Testament, choose for themselves an event from the life of Christ, and compose a piece of music of around eight minutes or so in length, which we would then premier in our ongoing tours. When I say 'ongoing tours', we had just begun (at the time I took over from Ruth Miller as Singers' Secretary for NEO) the process of regular Christmas tours to large concert halls, in Birmingham, Manchester, Nottingham and Northampton, possibly a venue in London, and Bristol. I remember Nigel being inspired around that time, by the account of Joshua and his troops walking round and round the city of Jericho, playing and shouting and making a huge noise, before the walls finally fell on the seventh circuit, on the seventh day! What we actually achieved over the decade or so of these tours, was a wonderful rapport with the believers in those cities, who took up the opportunity to bring their own contacts, friends, colleagues, family members, along to our concerts – often with profound and lasting results!

We were not quite sure how this genre of music would go down amid the usually wide variety of repertoire (anything from Christmas Carols to well known classics, spiritual songs or Big Band jazz) but in order to fulfil the promise of giving these pieces a good airing, we were committed to making this experiment!

The 1990 Christmas tour NEO poster

'Transfiguration – A Meditation'

The first commission was accepted by David Bedford in 1988, and its world premier was performed at the Derngate Centre, Northampton that November. He chose for his piece the Transfiguration (Matthew 17). David had received many commissions from major orchestras and also been involved in working for the BBC and in composing film music for such films as 'The Killing Fields', 'Absolute Beginners' and 'The Mission'.

He described the piece as not intended to depict the events of the Transfiguration, but... *a meditation on its meaning and its effects on the disciples who witnessed it.*

Our concert notes in the programme for *Look Forward to Christmas, with the New English Orchestra Singers and Dancers* stated the following:

...the mood of the piece is predominantly quiet and meditative. Musically, the work divides into three sections; in the first, the trumpet announces the theme on which all of the music of the piece is derived. This is followed by an intense adagio second section which builds to a central climax. During the build-up, Bedford treats all of the stringed instruments soloistically, creating a texture of twelve solo-string lines. As he points out in the score's preface, these lines are independent but nonetheless related, 'rather as though the disciples are pondering on the significance of the event both for themselves individually and for them as a group.' After the climax, the music begins to subside as it enters the third section. Here, the three percussionists emphasise the 'other-worldly' nature of the Transfiguration by producing an ethereal chord from six wine glasses filled with differing amounts of water. Against this shimmering haze of sound, the oboe quietly recalls the opening trumpet theme as the piece gently fades into silence.

I honestly do not recall what the majority of our NEO members felt about this work, but I know we were glad we had embarked on this commissioning project. It was truly riveting to hear this piece played for the first time in rehearsal. Nigel recalls that the percussionists found that the wine glasses gave a much better sound when they used wine instead of water – we will not ask what happened to the wine after the piece! For someone like me, this type of music was an eye (or ear) opener! At first it was difficult to make headway with it, as the brain naturally tried to treat it as music would normally be treated by the brain I suppose. But here I found the power of repetition so valuable – by the end of the tour I was really looking forward to hearing it all again! It had become part of my memory and I knew

my way around the piece, so I could pick out passages that I really loved. How fantastic to take someone of this ilk and hear what comes forth when they have studied an event from the life of Jesus!

We had embarked on this tour incidentally, after working on a pretty spectacular event in October of that year, called *Cry Africa*! This comprised African music, worship and testimony to 'stimulate prayerful concern and missionary calling'! Following this, came a promotional concert for the Shaftesbury Society, at Wembley Hall in November. So as ever, NEO was working on an incredible diversity of events, not to say musical genres!

'Eph-phatha'

By the following spring, 1989, we had, rather unusually, arranged a Spring Tour, beginning once again at the Derngate Centre Northampton, on 2nd May, and continuing with four events on consecutive days in other cities until 6th May, ending at the Free Trade Hall Manchester on 13th of that month. Michael Finnissy's piece entitled 'Eph-phatha' was therefore able to have its world premier in Northampton and then feature throughout the rest of this tour.

Michael had a very interesting career, having studied composition with Bernard Stevens and Humphrey Searle, piano with Edwin Benbow and Ian Lake at the Royal College of Music, and in Italy with Roman Vlad. He had created the music department of the London School of Contemporary Dance and been associated with other dance companies including London Contemporary Dance Theatre, Ballet Rambert, Strider, and Second Stride. His work was widely performed and broadcast around the world and had attracted many compositions written for him as a pianist. Our programme for that evening stated:

The title of the piece comes from the account in the Gospel of St Mark of the healing of a deaf mute. Jesus is confronted by a deaf man with a speech impediment. His reaction is to take the man on one side, and touching his ears and spitting on his tongue, he commands in Aramaic 'Eph'phatha', meaning 'Be opened'. Finnissy's piece is scored for: eight wind and brass, strings, piano, harp and percussion. It starts with high writing in upper wind and strings, where the emphasis is not so much on harmonic or melodic considerations, but on shifting tone colour. Each instrumental line is characterised by small intervals including microtones, which produce the effect of meandering around a pivotal note. The use of lower pitched instruments is reserved until about a third of the way through, and is marked by the entry of the piano. An unusual feature of the work is the fact that the piccolo, horn and one of the three cellos are used exclusively offstage. The first entry of this offstage trio comes at the central climax. The full onstage orchestra is completely arrested in full flow to allow the offstage trio to be heard. There is a cleanness of line about the offstage writing that contrasts sharply with the textures that precede it onstage. The effect can quite easily be seen as a musical representation of deaf ears being unstopped. The clean lines correspond to the new world of sensation that must have been opened up in an instant to a formerly deaf man. Equally, the use of a trio of instruments has a clear Trinitarian symbolism, which although present in other parts of the work, is perhaps most apparent here. Although the main orchestra re-enters, it is left to the offstage trio with its almost diatonic writing to close the piece.

For me this was a most unusual tour – not just because of the time of year in which it was placed, but because I was (for once) in the audience and not on stage. I was actually heavily pregnant with Stephanie our youngest, who had decided to arrive a little later than planned – and my hope in attending this concert, and perhaps particularly experiencing this vibrant piece, was that labour might be set in motion!

It was not – that came another five days later – it was, however, a wonderful concert, also featuring the Ibert 'Divertissement', the beautiful 'Fantasia on Greensleeves' by R. Vaughan Williams, music from the Baroque era, from Russia and from South America (Nigel always liked to take his audiences on a world tour!) and the Finale from Haydn's 'The Creation'. Interestingly there was one song which Nigel had composed, using lyrics by Colin Day (see Chapter 2 – *Earliest Beginnings*) which was featured in this programme and which I don't remember ever being performed again after this point – it was called 'Your Way'. Astonishing what one remembers.

'Eph-phatha' was amazing! I sat in my seat wondering how I would cope with the microtones we had been learning about (well those of us who knew nothing about them already!) and the sound was quite incredible. It wasn't an easy piece to listen to, and unfortunately for me of course, there was no chance of the repetition I had enjoyed the previous year, as I was not part of this performance team – but the experience of that piece, and indeed the whole evening, was a great blessing, not least of course, because it gave me the priceless opportunity to watch my friends and be able to enjoy every moment of their facial expressions, their sound, and the enigma which is NEO fellowship on stage!

_____ Dimples _____

I'm sure he borrows a chord from Mars!

'Gethsemane Fragment'

The final piece in our trio of commissions, came the following December in 1990. Here we had approached Michael Berkeley, and he had chosen the experience of Jesus in the Garden of Gethsemane as his inspiration. Michael, we noted in our programme, was the eldest son of Sir Lennox Berkeley, and had begun serious composition whilst studying in his late twenties with Richard Rodney Bennett. His writing had apparently undergone a significant change during the previous decade, in which he explored 'a more demanding musical language' consolidated in his then more recent works 'For the Savage Messiah' and 'Songs of Awakening Love.' Our programme notes continued:

"I chose this passage", says Michael Berkeley, "because it seems to me that at Gethsemane we see Christ at his most human, revealing a moment of weakness. I find this very moving. Combined with his human fears are his visionary fears about what he knows the outcome will be. Thus the night at Gethsemane was laden with drama as well as trauma. My piece attempts to capture a moment of the gnawing and nagging thoughts going through Christ's mind."

At the end of the piece the mood moves upwards towards the heavenly dimension as Christ lets the decision be taken from his hands. The nagging chord in the bass representing the earlier mood remains to the end however, beneath the high ethereal harmonics in the upper voices.

What an evening this was! Berkeley's piece took place between music from Vaughan Williams, Handel, Grainger, Rutter, Britten, Strauss, Bach and Elgar! It was obvious from the first that these contemporary commissions were going to be very different from the remainder of the programme – but that was the whole point! It placed them in a setting for maximum impact – far more dynamic I believe than had they been performed within a set of pieces of a similar idiom. For their part, the composers themselves were pleased and appreciative, not only that our orchestral players had made a good fist of their writing, but also for the exposure, which such pieces frankly struggled at the time to achieve. They had exposure certainly, but to smaller audiences of those with a specialist interest. Here, we exposed several thousands of people up and down the country to these extraordinary compositions and they listened spellbound – whatever they finally thought of the music itself – because they knew that they had been inspired by Biblical events familiar to many of them. It was quite an achievement.

The next year 1991, was of course going to set the scene for some pretty 'modern' exploratory music of Nigel's own composing, as we headed towards the tremendously exciting 'Feast of Trumpets' (see Chapter 7 – *Solemn Feasts and laughter in the heavenlies*). Little did our audiences know during this tour, that our next would involve finding brass players out in the auditorium with them, suddenly blasting forth with a shockingly outrageous sequence of 'Mexican waves' of extempore playing which would bounce around the walls leaving everyone completely stunned!

NEO concerts were completely unpredictable, musically speaking (on occasion even to those of us actually taking part!) but always a wonderful opportunity for the Lord of all creation to say 'hello' through the huge variety of styles and the incredible imagination of His people. I expect He enjoyed the microtones – after all it was His idea, didn't He give such to the 'birds of the air'?

_____ **Dimples** _____
Sing as if you're in a rugby scrum!

On an open palm

17

The phenomenon of the 'Recce'

Nigel: The prophetic ministry can be described as, 'Nothing is known until God shows you.' NEO has always been like that.

Nigel was so right in saying this! I learned from him however, that if we are prepared to put some effort into the process of exploration, the Lord very often responds with delight in 'showing us'! In fact – I now know that seeking the Lord is not always a still, silent, meditative business. It can be a highly active, exciting, adrenaline-surging trip – a 'white-knuckle ride' at times redolent of a roller coaster, as one tempting prospect seems to emerge, only to fall at the last moment, before the one the Lord means to give you finally arises before your eyes!

From the very beginning of NEO's history, the practice of flying out (initially to Salzburg) to 'spy out the land', meet the relevant people, book venues etc., became essential preparation for any away tour. I believe Nigel made his first visit in the company of David MacInnes all those years ago – later it fell to Chris Bell to make an occasional trip, and later still to Roger Knott to accompany Nigel, which he did for probably around a decade. My own turn came in the autumn of 1995, when (as mentioned in Chapter 3 – *Of Mountains...*) I first accompanied Nigel and Caro on holiday to Yvonne Pokorny's home, but we made a few important visits to Salzburg during the week, so that I could begin to learn the ropes!

The main one of these, about which we were much in prayer, was a visit to János Czifra, following the regrettable events of 1995, when we almost lost the *Jedermannbuhne* for our 'Dance Messiah' production. We felt compelled to talk this through with János – he had been our friend and colleague for so long. It was a difficult meeting, where we also had to use an interpreter, which can at best give such times an unduly 'formal' feel. He was convinced we had taken the problem "to the wrong address" and was of course upset – the whole business had caused him nervous stress, and it was apparent at that time that though the situation itself had been saved and the Lord had quite miraculously allowed us to perform, there was a rift here that would take some healing. As I write, my mind is soaring through the years from that time to just one year ago, when we were on a wonderful recce to Salzburg, where this incident was to receive that healing and resolution from the hands of the Master!

Nigel and János – a happy coffee time at Tomasellis!

The happy ending!

We met János accidentally in the city one day as we went about our business, and he invited us to coffee, where we sat at his behest, and he explained that he had realised that it had been seven years since we had really worked together. He told us he felt awful that our friendship had been

Georg and Nigel at Tomaselli's

Nigel, Julie, Thea and Georg Hoelscher on the roof terrace of the Dom

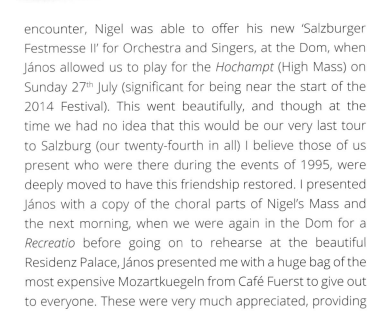

Thea at Tomaselli's

A shot for the grandchildren — Nigel makes friends with a plastic crow!

damaged. We told him we felt the same, and over the next half hour or so, we chatted much as we might have done in previous times.

A few years later, on our final recce in March 2014, we again encountered János – he was always involved in the process of booking the Dom for our more recent *Recreatio* events, and we were often represented by Georg Hoelscher, as János struggled a little with English. But on this occasion, Georg reported back that János wanted to meet with us personally, and on our next recce, we did so, arriving at his offices at the appointed time, only to find him double-booked with a student. He was hugely busy and had forgotten. He spent a few precious minutes with us and was eager to express friendship, so invited Nigel, Thea, Georg and myself to Tomaselli's (a famous cafe in the Altermarkt) for coffee the next morning, where we had the most delightful reunion together over coffee and cakes, to which he insisted on treating us. I photographed the occasion, and we went over old ground, thinking only of the happy times. He even gave us a guided tour of the newly refurbished gallery in the Dom, leading out onto the rooftop, where we gazed out over the city. János had in fact always loved our orchestra, and in July of 1991 had come to London, to St John's Smith Square, and conducted our players for a couple of concerts, which he was delighted to be able to do. He always made the same comment, that they played 'mit Geist!' (with Spirit!) and he would put his hand over his heart as he said it. He understood, I'm sure, where the priorities of this orchestra lay.

encounter, Nigel was able to offer his new 'Salzburger Festmesse II' for Orchestra and Singers, at the Dom, when János allowed us to play for the *Hochampt* (High Mass) on Sunday 27th July (significant for being near the start of the 2014 Festival). This went beautifully, and though at the time we had no idea that this would be our very last tour to Salzburg (our twenty-fourth in all) I believe those of us present who were there during the events of 1995, were deeply moved to have this friendship restored. I presented János with a copy of the choral parts of Nigel's Mass and the next morning, when we were again in the Dom for a *Recreatio* before going on to rehearse at the beautiful Residenz Palace, János presented me with a huge bag of the most expensive Mozartkuegeln from Café Fuerst to give out to everyone. These were very much appreciated, providing extra energy and plenty of smiles! It was literally as though the events of 1995 had been erased from memory.

Such is the grace of the Lord, that even when the worst seems to occur to a relationship, He can turn it around completely and present it whole and unblemished, where the parties are truly willing. The best restorations however, do often take a long time, but they are incredibly precious to all concerned and give enormous hope for the future as we go through the ups and downs of life.

'Offended'!

So, now to return from our brief flight into 2014, back to April 1996, and my first 'proper' recce! Linda Cooper, soprano and also then a travel agent, booked our flights and hotel (the 'Turnewirt,' I recall on this occasion). I remember sporting a smart pink suit I'd bought for some occasion or other – because Nigel had warned me we would be going to try and achieve a meeting with one Dr Helga Rabl-Stadler – no less than the President of the Salzburg Festival. I have to point out that at this time I knew nothing whatsoever about her.

She is however, quite something, a lady with an illustrious career! From 1983-1990, her biography tells me, she was a member of the Austrian National Council for the party Oesterreichische Volkspartei, making innovations to retail law, then from 1985 to 1988 she became the first female Vice President of the Salzburg Chamber of Commerce. Her family owned the business of 'Modehaus Resmann' with stores in Salzburg and Linz. She soon took up the post of Festival President, laying down all her other roles to concentrate on this.

And so on this particular (slightly snowy) April morning, Nigel led me into her Salzburg store, where we asked if we might have an appointment and we were duly ushered to a room which looked remarkably like a lounge, with changing rooms around it. When she appeared, she offered us a glass of champagne! Having explained who we were however, she laughed and commented that she had thought we were prospective buyers! (We felt suitably smart!) So we began a conversation with this astonishing woman, who to this day remains in post at the Festival, and has been responsible

during her presidency it seems, for sponsorship deals with the likes of Nestlé, Audi, Siemens and Rolex, Roche, JTI and Swarovski, and no doubt has myriad other achievements to her name. We however, had gone to simply tell her that we were *miffed*!

We were miffed because we had almost lost our stage and our expensive production in 1995 – and equably tempered though we were – we needed to express that we had been 'offended'. We had the temerity to ask whether, having endured this rough-handling from the Festival, we could be allowed the use of the Festival Hall, or the Riding School, as a compensatory venture. We were already planning our twenty-first birthday event which would be celebrated during the tour of 1997. The word 'offended' was one which obviously hit home, as after this interview, Dr Rabl-Stadler diplomatically arranged for us to meet with Prof Dr Hans Landesmann, a figure of international repute. A Daily Telegraph article dated September 2013, recording his death, explains that he had been of great importance to the Festival:

Hans Landesmann, who has died aged 81, was the Austrian impresario who helped to steady the Salzburg Festival after the death of Herbert von Karajan; he also introduced large-scale thematic programming to the Barbican and co-founded the Gustav Mahler Youth Orchestra with Claudio Abbado.

Landesmann joined the Salzburg board in January 1989 but within months von Karajan – who had earlier dismissed Landesmann's proposals for avant-garde theatre and contemporary music as the "soap bubbles [of a] dilettante" – was dead. Quietly taking on the dual roles of business director and concert director, Landesmann transformed the festival's finances, ridding it of a reputation for corruption, while musically he introduced the work of living composers.

This meeting duly took place, and I vividly recall Dr Landesmann being astonished that we funded our own trips to Salzburg in order to present our concerts free to the people of the city! Here is the brief paragraph Nigel wrote in the prayer diary of June-August 1996 in the 'Quick Notes from Nige' section:

We had a meeting with the President of the Salzburg Festival and with Dr Hans Landesmann – a member of the Directorium of the Festival. This was a wonderful development in itself – we have never come near anyone like that in recent times. After what happened in the summer, you may be interested to know that the President said: "The Salzburg Festival has two special friends: the Soli Di Venetti and the New English Orchestra. We will do everything we can to help you and to accommodate your wishes." They were both extremely nice to us, having already done their homework and felt that it was important for them politically to be on good terms with the NEO. Dr Landesmann even looked in the diary to investigate possibilities for us to have the Festspielhaus for a 21st birthday concert! Please would you pray about this possibility? There are certain genuine difficulties regarding this from the Festival's point of view, but we shall be contacting them again about the time that you receive this letter. It's good to reflect on the ways of God, n'est-ce-pas?

NEO's Happy 21st!

In the final analysis, we were unable to be given any part of the Festspielhaus, though I still think it amazing that it was actually considered! But by our next recce, from 5th-10th May 1997, it seemed that we were to be allowed the Mozarteum Grosser Saal. We found ourselves once again seated in an office, but this time at the desk of a young man named Stephan Gehmacher. We only ever met him once, though I believe I spoke to him on the telephone afterwards

Francis, alias Frannie Cummings

once or twice. He listened to our request and saw fit to allow us use of this wonderful hall – the only caveat, that we pay for the duty staff that day/evening. He gave us advice on how to sell tickets (though Roger Knott had already researched this in detail, and we eventually acquired the services of the Sparkasse Bank to assist us in this process). This paragon had no secretary, so sat humbly at another desk to type up the documentation we would require. At length, the interview complete, we shook his hand and left the room.

Outside in the blazing sunshine, we decided in rather a dazed way, to head for a restaurant known as 'K & K' – where we sat outside and felt there was nothing better we could order than bread and wine! This would be the first of many occasions when 'moments with bread and wine' were to occur on these trips, as the rollercoaster ride which had begun in the summer of the previous year, finally deposited us in a wonderful place, for which we gave thanks to God.

The concert itself (Monday 4th August 1997) was a glorious occasion. At home, we recall an amusing memory of Pete being sent to the hall ahead of the event day, to query something (having a little German) and he climbed up a staircase and approached someone who seemed to be part of an orchestra rehearsing there at the time. He began to introduce himself in German, at which point the chap said, "Well, how English!" Then just beside him Pete saw Frannie Cummings, one of our regular players. He was there with the orchestra he worked with! Laughter all round! Such things occurred from time to time, as players who worked

The NEO's Happy 21st!

with NEO would find themselves in Salzburg in their 'day job' taking part in the Festival programme during our tour!

I remember we ordered a large gateau so that we could celebrate with invited guests at a reception afterwards. (I also recall my pal John Trow-Poole, looking slightly squiffy at one point, leading me to ensure someone gently took him aside before he began practising his German! See Appendix I – *The Unforgettables*). Kate Ansell wrote an excellent article about this special evening in our Friends' *Opus 7* of the following autumn. The tour had included a *Spirituals Gala with Dance* on the *Jedermannbuhne*, which featured Mozart's 'Eine Kleine Nachtmusik', especially choreographed by our dancers, and extracts (also with dance) of Bizet's 'L'Arlesienne'. Julia Myles also wrote a wonderful article in the same *Opus* entitled *Salzburg 1997 – A Dancer's Perspective*. Another wondrous, unforgettable tour!

_____ **Dimples** _____

In Salzburg, after a long day's work: "Okay Jules, relaxieren!"

Modus Operandi!

Thus began the regular pattern of exploration of the outworking of vision brought to Nigel over the following years – it had always been that way, and now I was beginning to learn his methods and was privileged to share the sense of vision, being surprised that sometimes the Lord would speak to *both* of us while on these recces. I have as a result, innumerable notebooks in my memorabilia, as well as journal entries, which cover these special weeks – far too many to make the choice of what to cover here an easy one! They were all vital. I guess looking back however these trips fell into roughly three categories:

1. The 'breathing of the air' as Nigel would call it, to sense what the Lord was saying next, and if He would show us something specific. We would not necessarily have any appointments fixed, but we would visit friends and significant places, and have conversations. Some of these weeks had startling results and led to very

formative tours. These would be wonderful at times when Nigel perhaps had the seed of an idea but was not sure – or when we had all been engaged in a time of waiting on God for the next move.

2. The 'business trip' recce – where perhaps inroads had already been made for us but we needed to have meetings to firm up plans, ensure that dates were in the relevant diaries, work on the programme, stage-notes etc. There was much to achieve in a short space of time. Of course by the time Rome came on the scene, this type of recce was quite hard work for us, as apart from the help of the friends the Lord brought to us, like Nicoletta Vanuccini of the Chiesa di Santa Maria sopra Minerva, or Barbara Donovan of the Venerable English College (or Peter Jennings from the UK) we often had to rely on the Holy Spirit and our own wits to guide us through in those early days! I remember being grateful for a good pair of reading specs to see the tiny print on the Rome maps as we finally found out where on earth we were each time we ventured forth into the packed streets!

3. The follow up! This was often an essential part of the work – to go out again once the event was over, and assess what the Lord had done, or said – how our input had affected the place where we had worked, what our friends thought of it, and whether it was right to go back. We never assumed, we explored and we made certain. These away tours were quite a commitment for all our NEO members. We needed to be certain for many reasons.

And so to Roma...

I don't often quote Shakespeare, but just this once, let me refer you to this famous speech from his play *Julius Caesar* (Act Four, scene three):

Nige and Julie on Rome Recce – photo courtesy of Peter Jennings

Brutus

There is a tide in the affairs of men.
Which, taken at the flood, leads on to fortune:
Omitted, all the voyage of their life
Is bound in shallows and in miseries.
On such a full sea are we now afloat
And we must take the current when it serves,
Or lose our ventures.

On occasion, depending on what the Lord had been saying to Nigel, or the things we seemed to be seeing happening in the ministry, we would find Nige inserting a new phrase into all his expressions – and in this case it was 'the rising tide'. The whole story of how we were directed to this great city of Rome is found in Chapter 15 – *To the Saints in Rome...*, where I described the events leading up to performing our first *Recreatio* events in a tiny church by the Trevi Fountain. Nigel wanted to return there the following year, but there were some unknowns, e.g. the priest we had worked with had just left! So reconnoitering we had to go – and in this instance, I thought you might like to join us, to see what it was like on a day to day basis, at this interesting point in our work! If you have ever been on a paper-chase, you may see a similarity...

Report on Rome Recce 18th – 25th January 2008

We had begun our adventures with a wonderful extended P & P meeting on Thursday evening (17th January). After praising the Lord and sharing our hopes and dreams for a continuing 'rising tide' following the amazing tours of Salzburg and Rome 2007, we had listed together the numerous 'unknowns' which needed to be investigated in this recce; what would the new priest at the church by the Trevi Fountain be like? Would we be allowed to return and take up where we left off? What would await us at the British Embassy to the Holy See? What about the Baptist pastor who wanted to meet up, and indeed the other protestant Christians in the city who would love us to do something with them?

Saturday 19th January

To cut a longish story short, we knew the answer to the first two questions by the end of our first Saturday! We had woken to a beautiful sunny, 'blue sky' day and had walked to the Trevi to see if the doors were open at the church – which they were not. In going round the back and ringing the bell, we found there was no reply. We went to a café for a while and waited until after 4pm, and then returned to try again. Traditionally, the church had always been opened at 4pm each day, but not now. All was closed and silent. We went for a walk, intending to return after 5pm, in the hope that the priest would arrive for the usual evening Mass which takes place on Saturdays, and at last there was a little activity. A small cluster of people waited by the back door and we found that one girl spoke some English, so we began chatting. From her, we learned that the new priest was her spiritual guide and mentor (the hotel staff later looked on the internet and were able to tell us that he ran some kind of prayer group) but the girl explained that he specialised in the teachings of the previous Pope. She seemed to revere him highly. At last he arrived and there was some bustle to take in armfuls of flowers and florist's foam, apparently to decorate the church in due course for the priest's induction service later in the week.

In the hubbub, the priest realised we were not with the party and the girl had to introduce us and explain what we wanted, which brought a fairly swift and decisive reaction. The priest rattled away in Italian, hardly giving the poor girl a chance to properly translate, but, as he viewed our literature and programmes, the summary was that what we had done in the church the previous September was quite illegal and never should have been allowed by Father Paciolla; that these were *concerts* not services and that despite the music being, doubtless, beautiful there was a great difference between church liturgy and secular music; that permission was needed from him as the priest, from the liturgical office (i.e. Msgr Frisina) and from the State! On top of all this he didn't know what would be happening in the church come September anyway (and he was obviously busy now) but he took our paperwork and said he would get in touch, and in the meantime we should speak to Msgr Frisina, which we said we certainly would.

We left, feeling as though the door had been well and truly slammed in our faces. We retired to a small café for a quick coffee, a prayer, and time to ring Margaret Atherton to see if her friend in Assisi (a nun who sometimes translated for us) could do anything to make the situation clearer to this man, but the nun was heading off to India next morning, so it was pointless to enquire.

We did return and attend the Mass. We left unobtrusively during communion itself, as we could not partake. We returned to our hotel and popped down the road for a meal, spending the evening in earnest discussion. We planned to visit Msgr Frisina first thing on Monday morning.

Sunday 20th January

After breakfast, we had to taxi to Chiesa di Nuovo, where we had agreed to meet Peter Jennings and then go on to attend morning Mass at the English College, after which we chatted to several student priests from various dioceses in the UK. Peter then insisted we accompany him to St Peter's Square in time for the Papal Audience at 12noon. This was obviously going to be a big occasion. There had been a 'contretemps' the previous week, when Pope Benedict had been invited to visit Rome University. A student protest march had ensued, in which the students stated that they didn't want him, and so the visit had been duly cancelled. Subsequent to this, Peter informed us, there had been a missive to the Church of Rome, asking its faithful adherents to be at St Peter's Square on time, to show their solidarity for the Pope! Needless to say, they turned up in their thousands, with banners, balloons and encouraging slogans! Peter acquired a copy of the Papal speech, with greetings fit for the Week of Prayer for Christian Unity, in five languages, and we watched the spectacle with interest. After this, we headed for lunch together, and explained to Peter all that had occurred at the Trevi.

We had plans to see Philippa Hitchin (Vatican Radio – who had made a very good programme of our first day at the

Trevi Church the previous year) next morning if possible, and Peter felt she would be a good ally. Peter also told us that he had had a good meeting earlier in the week with the British Ambassador to the Holy See (Francis Campbell) and that we should have all arrangements sewn up quite well during our own meeting on Wednesday morning. We returned to the hotel for a break. We had received encouraging texts from both Janet Fox and Nick Gerrard. We felt peace that the Lord knew what he was doing, even if we couldn't see it yet.

Monday 21st January

We set off to Msgr Frisina's offices to find he was not there, but we did meet one Adelindo Giuliani, a colleague of Frisina's, who spoke English and turned out to be God's man for the moment! We sat and explained the whole situation, and he not only suggested we look for another venue, but set about ringing various people to help us find one. (At this point I remember having a curious déjà vu image of that day which found us sitting opposite Stephan Gehmacher in Salzburg!) At Nigel's request, he even investigated the Pantheon for us (Church of St Mary and Martyrs) and carefully wrote down the name of the present incumbent, whom he told us was newly appointed, adding his address and telephone number. Then he suggested perhaps we might use Frisina's own church in Piazza del Popolo. Lastly he rang Msgr Frisina himself, and made an appointment for us next morning at 10.30am. We found refuge in a small café (again!) and discussed what had just occurred, and then rang Philippa to find that she couldn't see us that day but could meet at 12noon the following day (Tuesday). Somehow we sensed the timing of that would be better.

We returned to the hotel to make plans, and Mrs Khan's son in law helped us with bus routes, to find our way to see Jane Paone of the Salvation Army (a contact of Anthony Thompson's) that afternoon at 2pm as planned. Jane was to prove a great friend to us in many ways in future tours.

First however, we rode by bus into town and had a good look at the Pantheon! Exciting and challenging were the two obvious descriptions! We had a light lunch in town and bought a bouquet of flowers, as a thank you to Jane, and set off to meet her at the Salvation Army headquarters on the other side of town. That was a very happy meeting. We also met her husband Massimo, and some of her colleagues. We learned that she had become the president of Rome 'Churches Together', that the Baptist pastor had been away (hence radio silence) but that he did want to meet us sometime during our stay. After leaving Jane, we travelled into town again and went to look at the churches in Piazza del Popolo, and finally found out which was Frisina's – the one which was all closed up and looked quite unused! We were not desperately thrilled with the piazza itself, or the venues, though one of the churches might have worked, but nothing 'clicked'. Caro phoned at this point, with a lovely message from Keith Buckler (Appendix 1 – *The Unforgettables...*) confirming what we had felt already, that this setback with the Trevi church was probably going to be a *springboard to something greater* in the Lord's scheme of things.

We had a pleasant evening, some of which was spent talking to Faris, Mrs Khan's son. All the family members were intent on helping us as much as possible and we had to skirt round the suggestions for many possible church venues several times!

Tuesday 22nd January

We set off to see Msgr Frisina for 10.30am. We found him accompanied by a young priest who spoke some English – obviously on this occasion he felt the need of an interpreter.

We had a very pleasant interview with Msgr Frisina, (via the good offices of his young colleague) during which our *Recreatio* programmes from last September were perused and proclaimed perfectly acceptable. He explained however that he had no power to request anything of the priest on our behalf, as the latter really did have the right to say yea or nay to our using his church. It transpired that we could not use Msgr Frisina's own church either, because he felt it would leave him open to having to agree to all the other musical ensembles who applied to him. (We just took that as a 'no' from the Lord.) Msgr Frisina then had to leave for another appointment and the young colleague took the priest's card from me when we asked again what we could

do about this 'impasse'. He took it to someone else in the office and returned a moment later. We did learn, however, that the priest did some work at Vatican Radio! This was an astonishing piece of news as we were just about to go there!

We left and kept our appointment at Vatican Radio with Philippa Hitchin, who was delightful and very interested in our plight. She treated us to coffee and pastries and we explained all. She took the priest's card and promised to try and phone him and speak to him on our behalf, perhaps once his Induction service was over. We knew she was busy, as the Archbishop of York, John Sentamu, was in Rome for the week of Christian Unity, and she had to interview him on the Thursday, which would be a big day, with special services etc. She encouraged us in the meantime to follow up the Pantheon idea and to ensure that we had some kind of obvious approval of our programmes from Frisina (e.g. stamped documentation etc.).

We walked back around St Peter's Square and tried phoning Father Hank (a friend of Margaret Atherton's) who sounded rather nonplussed, but said he would put his thinking cap on for us and let us know, if we would ring later, whether he had any useful ideas as to venues. Straight after that, Philippa rang us again and told us she'd remembered the church of Santa Agnese in Agone, which was in the huge Piazza Navona, and which was owned by a noble Italian family (Doria-Pamphili) the present generation of which was half-English. Also, the church was backed by a Centre for Unity (Ecumenical Centre). She gave us a contact number for the priest she thought could best help us and left us to try.

Later at the hotel, we sent an email to the praying troops of the extended P & P! Then Nigel began making a whole stream of telephone calls using the contacts we had been given. He couldn't reach the priest for the Pantheon (Msgr Daniele Micheletti) so tried Father Jim Pugliese (Philippa's contact) who was connected with the Ecumenical Centre. Nigel ended up speaking to all sorts of people in the space of a few minutes, including an English woman (if not *the* English woman from the noble family above) who gave him the number for a Father Don Gianni whom we learned was priest of the church of St Agnes. There was no success however, so we set off to the Piazza Navona and found the church, which *looked* enormous. The door was blocked by builder's paraphernalia but we squeezed through and were told by a builder (once we had eventually realised what he meant) that we needed to return at 4pm, when the church opened. Meanwhile, we found the Centre for Unity and learned from a secretary with a bad cough (who kept disappearing into the collar of her pullover) that the priest would be there around 4.30pm.

We retreated to a favourite café of Nigel's opposite the church, to be entertained, fed and watered by 'Tony of Rome' and wait until we could go back. (Yes, I read your thoughts! The café culture of Europe was always much in evidence in these trips, and we were so grateful for that on so many occasions as we pounded the streets in the heat or even the cold and wet!) We had sent, I recall, a message to the troops back home to say that 'the ministry in Rome hung by a thread' – it looked so bleak at times!

_____ **Dimples** _____

When paying a café bill, and impressively throwing across the table the contents of a pocket – a handful of coins of several nations, the odd bus ticket and his favourite brand of felt pen:

"There, Jules! Let 'em sort it all out!"

Eventually we did meet the priest inside the church (which is beautiful, circular in design beneath the church dome, and actually surprisingly *small*!). He spoke no English, but I was able to recruit a passer-by in the church, able to interpret for us sufficiently to make the priest understand who we were and what we wanted. ('Recce-ing' even teaches you to be bold enough to grab complete strangers and talk them into using their skills on your behalf! I was becoming a changed woman!) Father Don Gianni then gave us the telephone number of his own secretary, who, he told us, spoke some English, and suggested we ring her. Not for the first time did we whisper praise for the word 'ecumenical'!

We then left and went to the Pantheon and talked to a security guard there, who told us that Msgr Micheletti could be found at a church on the Via Nazionale. Nigel decided, once outside the Pantheon, to try again to ring this man. He succeeded, and though this priest spoke no English either, he laughed loudly down the telephone (we know not why) and managed to convey that if we went there for 5.30 pm, there would be a colleague there who spoke some English! Laughter is so refreshing, we had an instant feeling that we might be able to work with this man!

I should state at this point that this was a cloudy, drab and wet day, the only one of its kind really that we encountered during that week. We set off in the gathering dusk, to walk the length of Via Nazionale in search of this church which was said to be at number 194b. By this point, as you can imagine, we both felt as though the entire day had been somewhat of the paper-chase, or treasure hunt, with clue after clue coming to lead us onward in pursuit! We mistook one building for the right address and disturbed a man in a suit who came out to wave a hand in the direction of the street ahead where we would find the church.

We walked on, first seeing something which looked like a huge edifice with impressive steps leading up to it, which turned out to be a theatre or some such. We strode on, seeing nothing else ahead that looked remotely like a church, though the numbers indicated that we were virtually on top of it. Then suddenly the wall on our left came to an abrupt end and there opened a deep and wide stair of marble, rather wet by now, leading down and down into the darkness. Studying the building in front of us (or should I say below us!) we realised this was probably it! We actually *were* almost on top of it! We began to go down what later proved to be thirty-four steps, rather carefully to avoid slipping, at which point I was distinctly reminded of that part of the creed which states, *'He descended into hell...'* whereupon I completely lost it and had a fit of hysterical laughter, which didn't really help the descent itself at all. Nige was similarly affected by the atmosphere of the moment (!), it was undoubtedly a release of tension, but we pulled ourselves together, tried to stop laughing, and found a door to push open.

It was a quite large, but dimly lit church interior, decorated with frescos and apart from lights near the altar, there was just one lit window into a room to the left of the altar, at the far end of the church. We walked softly to this point and pushed through into some kind of robing room, but there was no one there. Then we saw another door (with a glass panel in it) leading into a side vestry, where it sounded as though someone was speaking on the telephone.

Eventually we became aware of two men, one of whom eventually beckoned us into the vestry and there we beheld the gentleman who will now forever live in our memory as *Pantheon Man*! He had a great sense of humour, was delightfully jolly, and was of substantial girth, wedged tightly into his chair in the space between the filing cabinets behind him and the desk in front. Nigel reflected afterwards that there was no empirical evidence to establish that he had legs! He remained wedged into his chair throughout the entire interview! I swallowed down another deep desire to laugh out loud.

However, all rude comments (however innocently made) aside, he turned out to be a real star! Via his English-speaking assistant (one of the men) he listened to all we had to say (once again the theme of an 'ecumenical missionary orchestra ministering to English speaking tourists' won through). He looked at our programme and approved it almost instantly. He thought carefully and consulted his colleagues, once he had understood all we were asking, and studied our projected tour dates. After realising we wanted to perform three *Recreatios* in one day, he agreed to the 23rd September, 2008, and made a great show of explaining how we would have to write to him, he would write to Frisina, then everything would have to go to the Department of Social Communications and then they would get back to him, and he would get back to us! Nigel cut in pretty efficiently here by suggesting that as we needed a quick answer, it would be more desirable to use email! He took this on board immediately and set about carefully inscribing his email address on a paper, which was then expertly but unnecessarily re-written by his helpful colleague. Msgr Micheletti also then told us that in 2009, there would be great celebrations to mark the fourteen-hundredth anniversary of the Pantheon being consecrated as a church, and maybe our programme would be good for that too! We eventually left the building in a sort of happy daze! If we were not mistaken, and if all the permits went through, the Lord might just have given us a *whole day* in the Pantheon!

We had a pleasant evening going over the events of the whole day and wondering what on earth would happen during the rest of our stay. We were, in any event, so glad we had booked a whole week, it seemed it was going to be necessary! This was another of those moments we deliberately set aside to sit and eat bread rolls and drink wine together. It seemed very appropriate.

Wednesday 23rd January

After breakfast, discussions and prayer, we asked Lubna (Mrs Khan's daughter at the Lancelot Hotel) to translate into Italian our official application for the Pantheon, and we mailed it to Msgr Micheletti. We then left by taxi for the British Embassy to the Holy See, and had a happy half hour or so with Simona Prete (secretary to the Ambassador) and Pat Corby. We had very productive discussions and fixed arrangements for a thirty-minute performance at the Ambassador's Residence, (in a room which appeared to be an attic) to be followed by cocktails and a finger buffet, with the opportunity of meeting the other Ambassadors and hopefully of inviting some of the contacts we had just made.

Later on, back at the hotel, Nigel tried ringing the secretary of Father Don Gianni of St Agnes Church, and found himself speaking to a German lady (Ursula Siebigs) who was actually based at the German Embassy. We had to use her mobile number because her children were sick and she was at home caring for them. Her English was not brilliant, but enough to get by. We were not content that this would be sufficient however, so Nigel rang our friend Adelindo Giuliani at the Liturgical Office of the Vicariato, and asked if we could go and speak to him to ask his advice. When we arrived at the appointed time of 4pm, he wasn't there, and the secretary was quite embarrassed. We checked his office, and it was closed, but with a key in the door on the outside.

The new terrace atop the Dom

San Giovanni in Laterano

Basilica of San Giovanni in Laterano

Interior of the Dom from the rear gallery

We waited until almost 4.30pm, but were secretly joyful that he was late, as we hoped to ask him to ring Father Don Gianni on our behalf, and we knew that the nearer to 4.30pm we came, the more likely it was that Father Don Gianni would have arrived at St Agnes! Sure enough this is what happened. Right on cue he arrived, and was perfectly amiable and helpful, and when he rang, the priest answered. The result of this conversation was that Adelindo took upon himself the job of putting this application through on our behalf, and asked me to email him all the details of the official request. He promised to try and let us know within a week. The date requested would be either Monday 22nd, or Thursday 25th September. (In all things, as we often remind ourselves, *My (our) times are in His hands*! Psalm 31 v 15, NIV)

We left feeling well blessed in this unlooked for friendship! We sent another report home for prayer. I think it was at this point that I received a sudden call on my mobile from the Baptist pastor who had attended our *Recreatios* last year. He wanted to meet up and show us his church, and was obviously keen to host us for an event. We agreed to meet next afternoon, but were not sure what the outcome would be.

Thursday 24th January

By this time of course, we potentially had two venues for September, though nothing actually secure. So we had to discuss and make the decision whether or not to go ahead with our hotel booking. We had secured rooms a long time ago, but needed to ratify this and pay a deposit. Also, the hope of the Pantheon had led us to feel that we might need a little more power in the party both vocally and physically, and we discussed inviting one or two more people.

At great length, (often after breakfast, with our third cup of coffee on the sofa just beyond the breakfast/dining hall) we worked out a rooming plan and an exact booking, and managed to secure all this at the hotel desk that morning and eventually pay the deposit, based on the fact that if all came to naught in the end, we could reclaim the deposit anyway.

We went to meet Dave Hogdon, the Baptist pastor, at 2.30pm in the Piazza San Laurenzia in Lucina, which was very pleasant. It was quite a small, plain church in which a Bible study was in progress, so he took us next door for a cup of tea at the local café. In brief this turned out to be just a very happy and pleasant time of fellowship with himself and his wife, and when we had explained that we didn't think we would have time in the schedule nor whether it would be right to do anything in his church, he was fine, and simply offered to do anything possible to help us (with publicity or whatever) – a gracious man. From all he told us, the Lord had done something very special for him when he had attended our events the previous September.

After this, we revisited the Pantheon and spent a long time looking round and imagining what we might need, especially in terms of staging blocks to raise certain instruments, as the acoustic is far from easy. (I found one which looked hopeful, but no, that belonged to the Monarchy Society, who regularly sent costumed delegates to stand guard in front of the tomb of the King Vittorio Emannuele!) We walked to the Anglican Church of All Saints, where Rev Jonathan Boardman is the vicar (a friend of Jane Paone's and much involved in 'Churches Together') but he too was away involved with Archbishop Sentamu's visit. It is a lovely church but we were unable to ask our questions (i.e. did they have any staging blocks and maybe even a good quality keyboard?). Later at the hotel, I texted Philippa Hitchin to ask for her email address so I could update her on everything, but had no reply. We spent a happy evening going over everything and being grateful to the Lord for progress so far.

Friday 25th January

We worked at the hotel in the morning, sending a catch up email to Father Don Gianni's secretary, just to keep her in the loop, and also I sent an official request for St Agnes Church to Adelindo Giuliani as agreed. We could only wait and pray that both these applications would go through without hitch. If you will forgive me, I will end this particular trail here, since we decided in the end the building was too small and besides, better things lay ahead!

We were still wondering if anything could be done about the Trevi situation, when Philippa rang, and confirmed that she had in fact spoken to the priest. She told me that once she recognised who he was, she realised she knew him quite well and often saw him 'swishing around the corridors at Vatican Radio' to coin her phrase. She had made sure he understood everything about us, but he was still unwilling to bend, and had said that because of the dilapidations of the building it was likely the church would have to close during renovations in any case, so he genuinely couldn't promise anything for September. This did in fact prove to be what transpired. So for that moment we had to accept that situation as from the Lord, unless he chose to reopen it by some miraculous method!

Apart from a delayed flight, which landed us both back in Birmingham not much before 2am, and a rather indifferent journey back to David Harvey's home for Nigel, in a taxi driven by someone who didn't appear to know where Kings Norton was on the map, all was well. A quite astonishing recce!

Rome Recce 14th–17th March 2008

To recap, Philippa Hitchin of Vatican Radio had been helping me to try and make some sense of those applications by phone, as apart from initial replies from Adelindo and Msgr Micheletti there had been no further news whatsoever.

In the meantime Nigel had visited John Broadley in the UK (ex British Ambassador to the Holy See) and John had put him in touch with Fr Raniero Cantalamessa (preacher to the Papal household) in case he might become a useful ally in some way, and had also obtained a letter from Cardinal Cormac Murphy O'Connor (Archbishop Emeritus of Westminster) addressed to the priest of his titular church (Santa Maria sopra Minerva) situated behind the Pantheon, recommending us for *Recreatio* events there also (hopefully on the Thursday of our schedule). Nigel subsequently received a nice email from Fr Cantalamessa stating when he would be in Rome and so fixed the recce for that weekend.

During the week before the recce, there had been total radio silence from Rome, even from Philippa Hitchin. The latter was very efficient, and I suspected that either she'd been away on an assignment, or she was ill. Meanwhile, I had been

trying, without success, to acquire the name of the priest of Santa Maria sopra Minerva, so we could make arrangements to see him at the weekend. We had an email and phone number but no name. Nigel was also now having difficulties getting any kind of a response out of Cantalamessa to finally fix the time and day for our meeting. He had to contact John Broadley, who contacted head of music Philip Whitmore, at the English College in Rome, asking him to contact Cantalamessa, and all was frustration. This happened a lot over the years! The diary saga picks up again therefore on:

Thursday 16th March

I received a call on my mobile from Philippa in Rome in the morning, to say she had indeed been very ill and away from her desk. She appeared to have returned that day to heaps of work, but still picked up our agenda as soon as she found my emails, and started phoning around for us. She had raised Msgr Micheletti from the depths of his lair and he had confirmed he still definitely wanted us to come. She had also at last, extracted from Adelindo the name of the priest of Santa Maria sopra Minerva. I consulted Nigel and subsequently sent an email to the priest (enter one Father Ballicu) and then we took the decision to mail all the Rome team and tell them to book flights – which were unfortunately, by this time, beginning to rise in price.

I emailed Father Ballicu, and later in the day received a perfectly charming reply in equally perfect English, stating we could meet him at his office behind the church at 4.30pm, on the Saturday of our visit! I breathed a sigh of relief.

Friday 14th March

Nigel and I had both been having a busy time on the run-up to this trip, but before Nigel left, he decided to send one last email to Cantalamessa's address, to say we'd meet him at 9am next morning (Saturday) and left my mobile number as our contact point. He then travelled to Birmingham to collect me. We had a quick lunch and a cuppa before setting off, and at that point my mobile rang and Rome was calling again, this time in the shape of Father Raniero Cantalamessa, who spoke wonderful English and was really friendly, but very concerned because he had at last found Nigel's mail and was actually now leaving Rome for the weekend! However he would be back in time for Monday morning, so I was able to fix for us to see him at 9am, which was the last possible time we could have set, as our plane home would leave at 12.50pm and it takes around three quarters of an hour to get to the airport. The Lord's timing is perfect. Apparently it was Msgr Philip Whitmore (of the Venerable English College) who had kindly completed the communication circle for us.

We left the car at David Harvey's, took a taxi to the airport and en route, Rome called again, and this time it was Philippa. She had spoken to Ursula Siebigs, who casually mentioned that she received around two hundred applications per day for people wanting to perform concerts in that venue! However, the call had focused her mind, and she was going to look again at our application. She had apparently been horrified that we had been in contact with the Vicariato (liturgical office) – she had no time for them, they slowed everything down – better to deal direct with the churches! That was an interesting 'inside' perspective!

We flew off and arrived safely with no delays, and revisited our friendly waiters at the *Naumachie* Restaurant for sustenance, before turning in. At this point, I should say we had been accompanied on the flight by several large but rather 'immature' kilted Scots football supporters coming in for the big match versus Italy.

Saturday 15th March

After breakfast and prayer, we walked up to the liturgical offices, but as we suspected, they were closed. We sat in the beautiful church of San Giovanni in Laterano and meditated for a while, not least on what a fantastic venue that very church would make for an end of tour *Recreatio* day at some future point! (It did too!) I took the odd photo. We then went to the Pantheon where I attempted, among the huge crowds, to take further pictures. The city was really humming – not only because of the footie match, but next day would be Palm Sunday, and also the huge Rome Marathon around the city centre! (What a weekend to be in Roma!)

We then went up to find the church of Santa Maria sopra Minerva and were really pleased with it. It's a beautiful building. Nigel bought the guide book in English. 'St Mary over Minerva', it informed us, used to be the general site of three pagan temples/shrines to Minerva, Sapis and Isis (692 AD), then a tiny church appeared in the 8th century, Santa Maria in Minerva, and it was given to a group of nuns of the order of St Basil. History relates it passed next to Benedictine nuns and on at last to the Dominican order (1275) which still cares for the present day Basilica which eventually evolved there. Father Ballicu is of this order.

We wandered around, making mental notes of everything and then went to find the office at the back where our appointment was scheduled. Later that day we rang the bell at the appointed time of 4.30pm, and were a little disappointed to find no answer from that or any of the other bells available!

We went back into the church through a side door where we saw a little elderly priest taking a Lent Meditation in the Dominican chapel there (and appearing to find it difficult not to fall asleep in the periods of silence between readings etc.) and our thoughts that this might be our man were confirmed when Nigel spoke to a verger who passed us. So there was nothing for it but to sit it out and wait until it was over. An hour later…, we caught Fr Ballicu as he was about to leave the chapel, and found to our horror that he spoke no English at all. We followed him doggedly into the vestry at the rear and thankfully it wasn't long until he began to be joined by other monks, including an elderly, diminutive Indian brother, who was instructed to come and translate for us as he spoke some English! I produced the hard copy of my email which set out all the dates, times etc., of the request and which had that lovely English reply at the top! The little monk got very frustrated and stood rather crossly trying to read the mail out loud to the priest, but in English instead of Italian! He yapped every time any of us tried to intervene, but at length he let me explain slowly line by line what we wanted, and after he had relayed this to Fr Ballicu. He translated the response, which was that we would have to put our request in writing, stating the dates, times, etc.! At this point I grabbed the email and gently pointed out that this was exactly what we had done and we had received this reply, we had come to the appointed meeting and the rest was history!

By the grace of God, two further monks arrived who spoke English, and we began to make slightly better progress. In the end, while Nigel continued trying to get through to the priest, one of these monks, (around sixty I guess, with very good English and an air of integrity) allowed me to take him on one side and slowly explain the whole business of who we were (ecumenical missionary orchestra etc.,); what we wanted to do; what a *Recreatio* was; what happened when we did them in Salzburg Dom and what had happened at the Trevi last year; that they were not concerts but services; that the priest came along and read the Bible readings; that people responded to God etc., (In the depths of my mind were subconscious thoughts like, *Wouldn't it be wonderful if you could just plug a memory stick full of information into someone's ear on these occasions and they would suddenly understand everything, and then you could press their nose or something and they would say, 'Yes of course you can do that – we'd be delighted!')*

To cut the rest of the story short, all was conveyed to the priest and the answer came back, three times in all, from the chaps doing the translation, "There are no problems, the church will be open, you can do what you like!" I went over the date and times, Mario repeated them to Father Ballicu, and they all went off smiling and quite content with life, but leaving us with no assurance that any such thing would be put in the church diary, or that any of them would indeed remember the fact or even the conversation!

Nigel (who was standing with a look of disbelieving horror on his face at this point) and I were left standing alone in the vestry, feeling as though we'd been doing battle with a smiling foe in a large vat of treacle for about an hour. We tried to contact Philippa but couldn't reach her. Our only hope would be (back home) to try and find the person who had written the English email, and discover what lay behind the fact that the priest appeared to know nothing about us coming. Of course, we had produced our best credentials, the letter from Cardinal Cormac Murphy O'Connor (now Archbishop) but that only brought the response, later translated to us, 'Send him my best wishes', with a smile which could have meant anything.

We trundled home by bus, to eat, drink and plan! After sharing a famous Lancelot 'round table' dinner with an American family, I set off to check emails. Nothing much to report home yet either! In the end we had rather a late night after much discussion etc., followed by very little sleep. The hotel was noisy with late-arriving guests. By this time the city was criss-crossed with disappointed wearers of kilts, and probably the police were glad it was all over! I also couldn't understand why there seemed to be what sounded like refuse-lorries clanking around at between 3 and 5am!

Sunday 16th March – Palm Sunday and the Rome Marathon!

We woke to the sound of ever-circling helicopter surveillance, and after a leisurely breakfast and the usual plan making, we set off to find that the whole city was alive with people and the roads had been cut off by large wire-grid fences (obviously having been delivered and set up all through the night) marking out the course for the runners, to the effect that we, and all other pedestrians, had to spend the whole day finding alternative routes and getting rather leg-weary! We had a long day ahead of us!

We did, however, manage to revisit the Pantheon during the Palm Sunday Mass (they use olive branches there instead of palms, which everyone was carrying) and we stood at the barrier outside the door, peering in and listening (we were pleasantly surprised at what one could hear of the singing and speaking with the use of several microphones that were obviously available). No sign of Msgr Micheletti though, as he wasn't presiding today. He was no doubt back in his underground depths in Via Nazionale!

We also checked out the end of the mass at Santa Maria sopra Minerva, before returning for a well earned dinner and an early night, to be ready for Fr Cantalamessa in the morning!

Monday 17th March

Nigel had sensibly arranged with the wonderful Lancelot taxi driver Giovanni, to fetch us at 8.30am and deliver us to the monastery where we were to meet our host, and then on to the airport, possibly via the Liturgical offices. We were deeply impressed with Fr Raniero! He was delighted to welcome us. A humble man with the heart of an evangelist, he belongs to the Franciscan (Cappucin) order and treated us as though we were doing him an honour by visiting him! His heart is for Christians to work together and he explained that today we should not be concentrating on the differences between the confessions/denominations, but rather the challenge of those who do not know Christ at all. (It is this man incidentally, who worked with Nicky Gumbel of Holy Trinity Brompton in London, to create the Catholic Alpha Course.) So he appreciated our work and said he would love to come to one of our events. He explained that he was appointed to preach annually to the Papal Household once a week, throughout Lent and Advent. That coming Good Friday would be the only day that the Pope would not deliver the main sermon in St Peter's Basilica, because Raniero would have the privilege of doing it instead. He gave us each a copy of one of his many books – in this instance about the Transfiguration. We talked of the Alpha course at Holy Trinity, Brompton, London, of his friendship and admiration for Nicky, of his own preaching work abroad and his writing, and we found he also had a television programme. Quite a man! He must have been nearing his seventies and had been in this Papal appointment for twenty-eight years. We could not, at that point, see where he figured in the whole scheme of things, but we definitely felt it was worth the meeting, and that we had an ally in the cause. We decided to try to request him an invitation to the Ambassador's reception in September. The Lord knew all and we didn't need to!

The ever-obliging Giovanni sped us to the Liturgical offices, keeping up a constant tour guide commentary from his astonishingly retentive memory. "You see dis piece of wall here? Ees seeeex thousand years old!" Yes, we did apparently pass bits of original Roman wall dating from six centuries before Christ, before being bombarded with facts about the debauched life of Emperor Nero, as we drove by the spot where his 'Golden House' used to be! Giovanni left us at Fiumicino Airport feeling as though we'd just had a whistle-stop tour of the last few thousand years! We

enjoyed a good flight home, with the only kilted men on the plane being now subdued and rather morose, except for one lively one, who was now sporting a large 'Guinness' hat, having decided to celebrate St Patrick's Day! Having flown home in bright sunshine, we were greeted by a freezing March wind in Birmingham. I never did relish the return journeys to the UK in winter!

During the day, I had opted in our discussions, for immediately asking Philippa's help, but also simultaneously emailing back to the address for Fr Ballicu in the hope of drawing an identity out of the person who had written the English reply, and late that night at home I did manage to send this off, suitably worded, with a mail also to Philippa giving her the whole saga in brief.

Monday 18th March in the UK

My diary notes record: *Perfectly charming English reply on email from one Nicoletta Vanuccini, secretary to the church at Santa Maria sopra Minerva! She confirmed that the date and the times were now in the church diary.*

Santa Maria Sopra Minerva

I replied, and went on to send several emails (after phoning Nigel) and found problems with my broadband connection, which kept cutting off! I wrote a report to the Rome team and again couldn't send this or any other mails – eventually later in the afternoon they went through, but several times!

– I think each person had about three! It's so utterly fascinating how the PC always plays up at the most critical moments in NEO communications!

My report finally ended thus: *The final outcome is that we think we have a 'yes' on our venues, praise Him .... And that, dear friends, is a glimpse of the 'Italian Job' NEO style! If it all feels rather ridiculous, just remember back to the great things the Lord did in meeting with those hundreds of ordinary people, each with their own needs, as we sang and played last year, and pray that these platforms for ministry will be kept for us – protected by Him so that all the holidaymakers who come into those amazing buildings just to enjoy a few minutes of shade from the sun, some amazing architecture and the surprise of some beautiful music for free, might suddenly find they've been given a personal appointment with the God who loves them!*

A Treasure Chest of Memories!

Over all the years of these recces with Nigel, we experienced so many wonderful things that it's easy to forget the tough times we encountered together. There was one occasion when I was unwell and Nigel had to take me to a doctor, and one when he found that one of the fish he had eaten for supper was 'off', landing him in bed for most of the next day! There were even two recces when on separate occasions in different years, Nigel had a chest operation and I had a leg op', but we both found ourselves out in Rome barely the advised six weeks after our surgery, being rattled around painfully in Roman buses over the cobbled streets! At least we both knew how the other felt!

We would pray together – anywhere – in a café in sunshine, or half way up a mountain, sitting at a table in a Gasthof looking out at a snow storm, and talk ceaselessly, dreaming visionary dreams as we asked the Lord to let us think His thoughts after Him. I can remember one morning in Salzburg at the dear old Gasthof Rechenwirt, when Nigel began telling me about his morning reading and we found I had been reading from the exact same passage. There would be memorable meals, mind-boggling views, times of sharing all sorts of things from church life, to events in the world news etc., from the Stein Terrasse in Salzburg, to the rooftop of the Hotel Rafael in Rome, we would continue deliberating on what the Lord might be saying as we looked down on the cities the Lord had called us to (with something at hand to eat and drink of course! Nigel's modus operandi was most particular in that respect!).

Sister Ann Morgan of Villa Maria showing us Rome from the rooftop

We were provided for in every way by the Lord. One example of this is when I rang Pat Corby, (at the Embassy to the Holy See) when we desperately needed large accommodation in Rome, as we decided to take the leap from September tours, to late August, when the streets teemed with people of all ages, including students! Nigel wanted to reach young people! We needed somewhere with a rehearsal capability much larger than that at the Hotel Lancelot, with safe outdoor space for children, air conditioning etc. I had trawled the net for hours unsuccessfully. Pat consulted an elderly priest (Father Charlie Barns, God bless him!) who frequented the Embassy, and came back with the wondrous words "Try Villa Maria!" It was perfect in every way! This is how we came to meet the wonderful Sister Ann Morgan, with her twinkling eyes, Irish accent and deep love of God. She became a dear friend to us, along with Sister Pia, the director. We couldn't believe how tailor- made this lovely villa was, and we were even able to recce the shops and restaurants to ensure people had everything on hand, and organise pizza deliveries from the local Deli owner for our rehearsal day!

We met some extraordinarily important people too, like Archbishop Arthur Roche, Head of Divine Worship for the Worldwide Catholic Church, to whom we showed our wonderful Rome DVD, created by Paul and Julia Myles. He subsequently helped us to create a Rome tour (unusually in June, just prior to the end of the Papal Year) to explore what might happen if we gave a special opportunity at the end of each *Recreatio* for people to commit their lives to the Lord. The new Ambassador to the Holy See, Nigel Baker, kindly assisted me in finding a place for us all to stay on that occasion, as Villa Maria was already booked up. Congregatio Jesu, and more friendly sisters who cared for our every need, were there to make us welcome. It was a worthwhile experiment. Sadly, Archbishop Roche was unwell and unable to be with us himself for that tour, but he sent priests from the Department of Evangelisation, to assist us, one or two for each event, representing other European nations and therefore useful in the 'international conversations' we ended up having! Though we produced prayer cards with a prayer of confession for this tour, we found the old method worked best after all – the Lord seemed to speak most powerfully through our music. Catherine stood on a small stool, with our harpist by her side, and sang a simple, traditional hymn of 'calling', and people flocked to stand around and listen and respond as and how they wished. I remember more than one of the priests who joined us however, being bowled over by the experience of sheer joy! We had decided on one of our Rome tours incidentally, to count the nations represented by the people we encountered in conversation. The total came to eighty-seven! We may never know what the Lord said and did with these thousands of folk over the years, until or unless we are allowed to be told in heaven!

Prayer of commitment

Father God, today I feel I have heard you speaking to me, and I want to respond.

I see that I need your help to live my life in the right way, and I ask your forgiveness for the sin I know is in me.

I understand that you gave your son Jesus to die for all people, including me.

Thank you for raising Him from the dead so that I may also rise from death.

Thank you for the promise of everlasting life with you for those who put their trust in you.

Now I want to hand over my life to you Father, Son and Holy Spirit – please come in and turn my thinking around so that I can walk in your ways.

Cleanse me and fill me, and give me a fresh start.

Be my Guide and Helper all my life.

In the name of Jesus,
Amen.

18
The prophetic ministry

At a singers' rehearsal one day in November 2010, Nigel taught us about aspects of prophetic ministry – I include this because I believe these thoughts count as what Nigel would term 'trade secrets' of the NEO!

Ezekiel Chapter 3

Ezekiel was told to eat the scroll – which was initially sweet in his mouth like honey. He then had to go to the house of Israel, but she would not listen. Having eaten the word of God, Ezekiel's brow was *hardened*, he had a hard forehead and a stubborn *heart,* just like Israel. The word of God becomes a part of us, and can even make physical changes in us. It can change our faces! So, even Ezekiel's body had become a prophetic symbol. Ezekiel had to *receive in [his] heart* and speak to them, whether or not they would hear.

(Verses 22-27) The hand of the Lord was on him and he was summoned to a valley where he saw God's glory. The effect was so great that he fell down, but the Spirit entered him and he was able to stand on his feet again. Then God said, *Go, shut yourself within your house.* Cords were to be bound around him so that he was unable even to speak at all. But when God spoke, then Ezekiel was told he would be able to speak again. We can only move when God tells us to.

Nigel commented that the inspiration of Scripture is similar – it is easy to be naive about the nature of inspired writing, and imagine it to have been dictated, but in fact there is probably an interlinking with God and His word – *the person becomes involved and is then able to speak. He has 'eaten' the word.*

God is Three and yet One, inseparable. So many mighty things of God are like that – who wrote Ezekiel, himself or God? (2 Peter 1 v 20) '*For no prophecy was ever produced by the will of man, but men spoke as they were carried along by the Holy Spirit'* (J.B. Phillips version).

Suffering needs to be seen (Nigel mentioned that there was much suffering in NEO at that time, which indeed there was) *in the context of prophetic ministry.* Hosea the prophet was made to marry a prostitute – he was involved in a practical process – she was unfaithful, and he had to *feel* in his heart what God felt about His unfaithful people Israel. This is one way of viewing what is happening to us. *We have to handle these things 'in the moment' – it can be very tough. However, when we sing and play, it will come through the music. God makes the listeners know what is within us.*

Why does not God give us a plan? Well, because in our human state we would then pack things all around it, all our free dates would be filled. God demands space around the edges so we are free when He speaks. There are many levels of prophetic ministry also. God spoke and creation came into being. *When He acts, He can speak through us into situations and they can be changed.*

Being 'shut away' is important. Ezekiel had to be quiet for ages. This has also happened to Nigel at the most significant points in NEO ministry e.g. the year 2000, when he was first ill and had his major operation. After that the NEO changed completely. *It's no good asking for an agenda, because for a long time there appears to be silence, and perhaps deep suffering.* Nigel at that time couldn't actually think at all. He used to say he felt like a mobile phone with the SIM card taken out! Being 'laid aside' always seems longer than is reasonable. But once he was well again, the changes he knew had to be made to NEO were radical.

Here Nigel shared the news about the night seizure he had experienced a fortnight before on Sunday night around midnight. He was unaware of it, but Caro was terrified and had to call an ambulance, thinking he was dying. His breathing was like a train and he was violently flailing about. He came round half an hour later being put into an ambulance and wondering what on earth was happening.

Nigel strongly felt that if there was a future for NEO, then things would be different again. Earlier in the same week at this rehearsal, Nigel had been invited by Peter Jennings to go as his guest to Rome in December 2010. Peter was to present to Pope Benedict XVI the official record of his State Visit to UK, which he had edited and written for the Catholic Church. NEO had led worship at the Hyde Park Vigil during the Papal visit.

While he was in Rome with Peter, Nigel wanted to take the opportunity to go and try and meet a Cardinal who, during that Vigil had asked to put us forward for the World Youth Day in Madrid, Spain, the following year. This would help our thinking, as if there were a definite possibility of doing that we would know something of God's plans for us. If nothing at all presented itself, it might be time to gradually wind down. Nigel said at that time, *"In the Spirit, one brings something to an end whilst it is still full of life, not when it is dying."*

Doug Gallaher, he told us, had commented of NEO, that it was 'all green' – no dead bits at all!

Julie: As you can see, this was written quite a while ago, but Nigel was, even then, just picking up first hints from the Lord as to the fact that there would be an 'end' to the NEO ministry, and that it would be best carried out, while it was still 'green'. However, to continue the story of the recce, Nigel wanted to visit the Cardinal from Ghana who had approached him on stage at the Hyde Park Vigil. There had been an idea in this man's mind that he could perhaps put us forward for a huge youth gathering in Spain.

On Monday 13th December, we attended a reception at the residence of Ambassador Francis Campbell, to mark the publication of the Official Record of the State Visit. Peter and Stella Jennings and Nigel and I were present, and this took place two days before the general audience on Wednesday 16th, when Peter presented the book.

I distinctly remember wondering how we would fare together, as Nigel was definitely not himself and it has since become apparent that at least for a while, these night seizures (of which he had two more much later on

Nigel at the piano

and another just recently) do seem to somehow affect the memory immediately afterwards for a while. So it was that we arrived in Rome and Nigel literally could not remember the names of the churches we knew so well, or some of the streets, or the cost of a Rome bus ticket. I say that, in no way with the intention of embarrassing Nigel, but to show that in this prophetic ministry we have been led courageously by a man who sees no obstacle to the Lord's work, and has no greater goal in life than to find out what His will is, and to do it, no matter how he is feeling. I was concerned for him, but glad I was there to 'fill in the gaps' and make sure we did all he wanted us to do if we could. We did indeed meet the cardinal in question, who was utterly charming, but nothing had come of his suggestion, we found. We very much enjoyed accompanying Peter and Stella Jennings, watching the presentation to Pope Benedict of Peter's beautiful book. We felt therefore that despite not having found that the original purpose of our visit had led anywhere, we had been privileged to be part of a very significant occasion.

19

The mature tree and the new green shoots

Nigel: I heard the Lord say, 'It's time to let them go'...

And so we came at last to the conversation which first addressed the possible closure of NEO. In November/ December 2014, after two superb tours to both Salzburg and Rome, Nigel had begun to think carefully about our future. It was that season in which he would be seeking the Lord earnestly for the next move. We had enjoyed one or two conversations about the fact that we were approaching the milestone of our fortieth birthday in January 2016, and I think some of us on the P & P had been wondering whether, as on other occasions, this might be celebrated in Salzburg? Nigel felt that it should definitely be marked somehow, but how better than in the venue where it had all begun, Birmingham Town Hall, and as near the original date as possible? In short, I investigated this and found that the 16th January was to be the date. However, Nigel felt that with that in place at the start of 2016, we might feel confident in moving into 2015 as ever we would – i.e. accepting one or two *Invitation Concerts* already in prospect for the spring and autumn of the year, and then having a Rome tour in August, to continue the good work of sharing the love of God with all those tourists from around the globe.

Nigel had been unwell around the turn of 2014/15, and realised it would not be wise for him to attempt to come to that first Prayer and Planning group, scheduled for January 8th of the next year. We had a long talk together therefore, in which he outlined his thoughts to me, which were that after the *40th Birthday Concert*, he would wait a little longer to see what transpired from the Rome tour we had planned for Holy Week 2016, in which we hoped to perform the 'Horns of the Altar' movement of 'The Feast of Trumpets' in the Pantheon on Good Friday! After that, he would, depending on whatever guidance he sensed, make his decision about whether or when to cease the ministry of the NEO. If closure was deemed the way forward, it would then be a matter of taking our time, at least eighteen months to two years, to enable special times of fellowship and consideration of all that the ministry had meant to us (Legacy Days) and all we had learned, and giving people time to share, grieve where necessary, and be built up for whatever the Lord led them into next. We would also gradually wind up the charitable company over that period.

I duly brought this whole matter before the P & P members, and shared Nigel's thoughts. Some members were of course shocked, but in their customary wisdom and maturity, were able to put their own emotions to one side as we looked at the whole scenario before us. The most important issue would be confidentiality, as Nigel's greatest wish was that the ministry itself would not be disrupted in any way, but enabled to continue 'firing on all cylinders' until the very last concert – so it was far better that these plans were kept under wraps until everything was certain and the time was right to break the news to everyone.

Dimples

When being secretive, "Tell it not in Gath..."

We also felt we would like to do some kind of tour which would touch the cities where we had worked so regularly in past times – simply to bless them. We thought that perhaps their cathedrals would be the ideal venues, but when I researched this, we were astounded to see how charges had risen astronomically since the last time we had played in these great public buildings – and we were aware we would also have to work around their normal timetables for evensong, choir practice etc. So at length, we hit on the idea of opening conversations with our main supporting church in Birmingham, St John's Harborne, and as we had already had an approach from St Germain's, we contacted them also. Between us we created a 'hybrid' event which was arranged by ourselves, but ticketed and administrated by the churches. These proved wonderful occasions, each with a different repertoire, and giving us the opportunity to bless those who had stood with us for the long years of our existence. Our dear friends at Christ Church, Tettenhall Wood, led the procession of 2015 events by once again inviting us to return on April 18th. We followed with the events at St John's (May 16th) and St Germain's (June 6th).

The last 'recce'!

Also during June (Monday 15th to Friday 18th) 2015, Nigel and I had embarked on what we had no idea would be our last ever 'recce' together! We visited Rome, intending to conclude arrangements both with our beloved Villa Maria, where we were usually accommodated, and also with Msgr Micheletti of the Pantheon, for our proposed visit in Holy Week 2016. There was much to discuss, even though the essential permission had already been given to work with him at that special time, when of all others, Rome teemed with people.

Unfortunately by this stage, Nigel was very unwell again, but with some severe symptoms which were potentially serious. The other big problem we encountered was that Barbara Donovan, for the only time I can recall, was totally unable to be with us for our meeting at the now familiar Chiesa di San Vitale, with Msgr Micheletti. We had complex matters to discuss, and no hope of making ourselves understood. However, our planned schedule took a little turn when we were asked to go to Villa Maria *prior* to that meeting, rather than after it. Here, we learned that (despite the fact we would need extra accommodation for all the personnel required for the 'Horns of the Altar' movement – brass players, children, dancers etc.) they had in fact already released some of the rooms at the Villa in accordance with the requirements of the Tourist Board, to folk booking independently via online booking sites!

It began to seem extremely doubtful that we were going to be able to find enough beds in the right places at the right times. The whole tour was suddenly looking highly questionable. We also had to continue of course, making plans for that year's own tour, and I do recall that one of our jobs was to purchase everyone's bus tickets. The Lancelot Hotel would order them for us from the local Tabac shop and we would collect. We duly turned up and were asked for the final total of €1,395.00 – only to find when Nigel put his hand into his pocket, that this was the exact amount of money he was carrying! Out on the sunny street, under a bright blue sky, we laughed, as we have done so often, at the Lord's provision, so precise, so timely, so like a father smiling to watch his children discovering his pre-planned surprises!

Nigel's condition became so bad that he rang my room in the early morning to see if I could send him home, while I continued on. I studied the net, but was unable to find a suitable flight that day which would take him straight back into Manchester Airport with no stops elsewhere and long delays which he could not have tolerated in his weakened state. Instead I booked the flight we were due to depart on, but a day earlier (Thursday).

So we ended up having a serious chat over lunch, in which he realised that the increasing debilitation he had been experiencing, in fact since the previous November's Rome recce, was proving unsettling to the ministry, and causing uncertainty among members of the P & P as to how to go forward. By the next day, we had met with Msgr Micheletti and had to leave things very vague, as we simply could not have made him understand the complexity of what was facing us. He tried so hard to ask us in English what we were to do for Easter together – Nigel could only put his hands together and say, 'We must pray'. We left it that we would see him during the planned summer tour of 2015.

With Nigel's condition worsening, I rang down to reception that night and booked the computer at around 1am, to see whether I could actually travel with him, but there were no seats left. I had intended to complete the last appointment of the week, with the Abbot and Arch Priest of St Paul's Outside the Walls, which was another planned venue for

Anthony Thompson in rehearsal

Becca Nicolson
- principal basoon

'Eagles Wings' Legacy Day 10 Sept 2016 courtesy of the King-Smiths

Cathy Studman

Becca Dinning

'Party Benedikt' with Rick Masters, Fiona Ormiston and Miriam Furze

Goodbye concert at St Peter's Halliwell

Nige conducting at BTH concert

NEO's final concert in Birmingham Town Hall

Giving our all at our 40th Birthday Concert in Birmingham Town Hall 16.01.16

the 'Horns of the Altar' in our proposed Holy Week tour – but by this time we realised the tour simply could not take place. I therefore decided to telephone and explain, and cancel the appointment, as Nigel was feeling so unwell that my priority was to accompany him to the airport.

Not even this last task was easy, as Fiumicino Airport had suffered a fire a few weeks before our arrival, which had ripped through most of one terminal, and there was huge disruption to flights. Nigel's, we found, had been rearranged to take off from the small Ciampino Airport some miles away. I was allowed to accompany him on the coach they laid on, and by this time, Caro had made arrangements to meet him at Manchester and take him straight to A & E. I spent some time the next morning with Sister Ann, our dear friend and ally at Villa Maria, and explained that it looked as though the Rome tour that summer would be our last. She promised to 'be there' for our folk however they would be feeling. I remember visiting a café I particularly loved, and sitting over my lunch, alternately sipping coffee and coming to terms with the fact that our last ever recce had ended in such a sadly unexpected way.

Suffice it to say that the results of Nige's tests were fairly inconclusive, and though subsequent treatment took away many of the symptoms, he continued to be unwell in varying degrees throughout that summer, including the actual Rome tour, and indeed the autumn *Invitation Concerts*. We had of course formulated contingency plans for all events, but never needed to employ any of them, as the Lord allowed Nigel to both be present, and to do all that was required of him, even though he felt dire at times, and at one point had even been told, the day before the event, that he may have throat cancer! The final diagnosis was in the end however, a totally non-functional thyroid gland – a long story, with few answers as to why it was not found earlier – but a tribute to the courage and determination of Nigel and the enabling power of the Lord. This condition however, was also curable!

The decision was ratified then, that in view of there being no Rome tour in prospect at Eastertide 2016 our *40th Birthday Concert* would become our final public event. We chose a rehearsal as the best time to break this news to the singers, and first Nigel addressed them, followed later by myself, expressing the desire to remain as buoyant as possible and give ourselves one hundred percent to the task until we crossed the finishing tape. I remember getting up from my seat, turning towards the singers and finding myself faced by rows of tearful faces. It was a difficult day. But they understood of course, and rose to the challenge magnificently. We all pledged to keep the news to ourselves until such time as the P & P reached the point of sending out the mailing referred to below, and releasing the news to everyone on our database.

Please, please get me a ticket!

Wonderfully, by the time we came to Christmas, Nigel was feeling stronger, and the rehearsals in January for the final *40th Birthday Concert,* went extremely well. The event itself deserves more detail than I can write here. It was a brilliant occasion, for which Nick Gerrard had laboured for weeks on a souvenir programme, including photographs from all four decades of NEO history, and which received some very helpful sponsorship from the company of solicitors which had been first formed by our dear friend and my first 'boss', Anthony Collins, now in retirement. We had felt we must write out to the entire database (this was our final mailshot at the home of the Laxton family) not only to advertise the concert, sending publicity, but to inform them of the closure of NEO. Perhaps then we should have seen it coming – but the main auditorium of the Birmingham Town Hall sold out virtually within two weeks of the tickets being released for sale! We then set about selling the choir seats, and in due course all of those were sold also! There was a much to-ing and fro-ing as the great day drew near, and some folk were desolate because they had no tickets, others were equally so, because at the last minute something else had cropped up which meant they couldn't come. Ruth Miller came to the rescue, along with others of us, acting as a clearing house for tickets to ensure that everyone was able to dispose of those they could not now use, to people who desperately wanted them! It was quite incredible!

A few of us from the P & P helped Janet and Daphne Ryland and David and Edi Harvey with all the meal arrangements for the orchestral rehearsals, and enjoyed some priceless fellowship into the bargain. The programme Nigel had devised contained some glorious music: Charpentier 'Te Deum' (sung so often in the Pantheon), Mendelssohn's 'Italian Symphony' (No. 4 in A Major), pieces from Handel's 'Messiah', one of our much beloved Scottish Reels, 'Miss Johnston', two delights which harked back to our Altermarkt days in Salzburg, Strauss's 'Radetsky March' and the 'Thunder and Lightning Polka'. Then the beautiful Danish Folk Tune, 'Five Sheep, Four Goats' (solo flugelhorn, Pete Desmond) and Nigel's own beautiful pieces written only the previous year: 'Sentences from the Song of Loves', with wonderful solo bassoon by Rebecca Nicolson and soprano by Catherine Swinford-White, 'Conversations for Trumpet, (Anthony Thompson), Orchestra (solo violin Amy Chidley) and Narrators', (Sam Baynham and Sam Openshaw) and the 'Christe' from 'Salzburger Festmesse II', sung again by Catherine, with Suzanne Fisher. The final encore was one of my own favourites, which never failed to have a great effect whenever we had sung it at the Pantheon. 'I heard the voice of Jesus say' to the traditional 'Kingsfold' tune. Catherine would open the first verse as a solo, but then, to the astonishment of the audience, the entire orchestra would stand with the singers to sing (with slightly modified words):

> I heard the voice of Jesus say,
> 'I am this dark world's light –
> Look up to me, your morn shall rise
> And all your day be bright.'
> I looked to Jesus, and I found
> In Him my star, my sun,
> And in that light of life I'll walk,
> Till travelling days are done.

This was our joint testimony, the lifeblood of NEO – as Nigel has been quoted elsewhere, "We share what we know – we can do nothing else." It was always an amazing moment and that night was no exception.

Cathy Studman (one of our very first 'new wineskins') led that final concert, with Hannah (Smith) her sister, sitting not far away in the strings, and many others were with us as a tribute to the freshness of talent we were privileged to have welcomed into NEO, alongside those who had faithfully

Julia Myles and Su Castle

served for years – while yet others who had been a major part of our work in earlier times came back especially for this event, either to play, or to support us in the audience.

For me, that evening held only half its delights in the actual performance – it was the time backstage afterwards that blew me apart! I don't think I shall ever forget seeing Becca (Rebecca Dinning, née Eves) having been totally composed and having played wonderfully throughout that concert, breaking into floods of pent up tears the minute she came offstage! It had been an emotional few weeks for her anyway, having broken part of her foot in a fall at home – thereby having to do the entire concert wearing a cumbersome 'boot', and to stand virtually on one leg whenever performing! But she had become, like so many others, such a part of the heart of NEO it was very difficult for her to begin dealing with the fact that this was its last public performance – as it was for us all of course.

It was the sudden sense of the flight of years, and yet a glorious continuity – much as I believe heaven must be, as I came down into the bowels of the Town Hall to be greeted by so many faces I hadn't seen for so long. Sue and Mike

Castle were there – I photographed Sue sharing an embrace with Julia Myles – so many wonderful memories were encapsulated in that single shot! Pete Desmond and Celia his wife were in a corner when I went up to greet them. Pete had for years been our Principal Trumpet. His wonderful playing of the flugelhorn solo in the midst of the Danish Folk Tune had essentially shocked the entire hall into a state of bliss for the too short time it lasted! Orchestra members I hadn't seen for probably twenty years were there, in one case, having just enjoyed their son's playing with us on stage!

As I have stated before, longevity has many blessings – this was never just an Arts project, a music ministry, it was a family which had grown over time, strong, well supported, branching out in all directions and full of the sap of the Holy Spirit – the tree was mature now. It was very much alive and had produced many beautiful green shoots. Wherever I looked I saw abundance, exuberance, love and life and laughter! Memories were shared and tears were shed, to be replaced a moment later with hoots of merriment. This was an act of God, with Jesus in its midst, revelling with us as He shared in our conversations and memories.

And so there followed all the various comments, photographs, film clips etc. on Facebook, to be gathered and enjoyed, and plans made for the first of the Legacy Days, which would take place on March 12th, (followed by a special meeting for players, who were so busy on Saturdays, kindly hosted by Nicholas and Andrea Young at their Farnborough home on 2nd May) then June 11th, September 10th and November 12th, all housed at St John's Harborne and looking at fabulous DVD clips from our enormous archive and studying various themes which have been vital in NEO over the years, and which would prove to be excellent 'trade secrets', as people were called onward into their own new beginnings.

Just one more time!

We were also quite surprised to find that Nigel's own church, St Peter's Halliwell, wanted to 'give us a good send off', and so arranged one further concert in the spring, mainly for the members of their group of four churches, but anyone could buy a ticket. They gave us a wonderful evening, dressing the church with flowers and balloons, including a large '40' balloon which gently bobbed at the front of the church! Some time was spent watching DVD clips of events at that church or in the Bolton area, and the lovely BBC TV footage of Lizzie Swinford (Mason) dancing to 'I know that my Redeemer liveth', in a programme with Joss Ackland, as she sat watching with her children, Iris and Dulcie – her husband Robin had been playing with us that night in the ensemble. The celebrations and thanks to God continued next morning in the service, as one or two of our folk stayed to join the many who actually worship at that church. As I have mentioned elsewhere in the book, there was opportunity to bless those who had blessed us, including Joyce Harper, who had organised the St Peter's dance group, and Yvonne Mitchell, who worked on the northern contingent of white robes for *The Feast of Trumpets* back in 1991. Becca Nicolson (bassoon), who had played in 'Sentences from the Song of Loves' was also a child of St Peter's, as her family had worshipped there – and her story had begun by being inspired by its worship group, and deciding she wanted to become a musician when she grew up!

Incidentally, it was also on that final Rome recce, that Nigel and I had discussed for the first time the possibility of a book of memoirs, and it was only afterwards it dawned on me that I had agreed to be 'commissioned' to attempt to write it!

And so out of the darkness had come that bright and living tree, which suddenly began to produce fruit, and around which a circle of people appeared, picking it and each in turn handing it back to the growing number of concentric circles of people, on and on.........

I can only echo Nigel's chosen title for his article in our final souvenir programme:

40 Years? Surely Not!

—————— **Dimples** ——————

I was foolish enough to ask if the Legacy Days which were to be held in order to gently close our precious ministry together, were going to include the same content each time.

Answer: "No Jules – I don't do repeats!"

Amy Chidley

Post-script

I felt this to be the most appropriate place to include this beautiful piece of writing by Amy Chidley. It gives a perfect example of the hope I stated in the *Introduction*, that others would be motivated to write down their own memoirs in some way. Amy had to miss our final Legacy Day in November 2016, as she was expecting the birth of their second child. Her comments below are, I feel, the fitting response of someone going on to bear 'new green shoots'.

Personal highlights/challenges/lessons learned (often they are inextricably linked!)

Here are a select few of the countless highlights from my fourteen years as part of the NEO.

1. *While attending the Birmingham Cathedral Vigil in 2002, after meeting a certain Ruth Miller through a training course, I witnessed the exuberant dancing of Florence Odonga at a time when I was losing the use of my legs. She inspired me to write a song, 'In heaven I will dance', which, to cut a long story short, somehow got into the hands of Nigel Swinford, who consequently wrote to me, kindly inviting me to join the NEO Singers. By then I was a wheelchair user and had had to stop work. I had time on my hands and so…*

2. *Hearing my ex-teacher Clare McFarlane playing 'Londonderry Air' at a Vigil in London touched me deeply with its beauty, but also with sadness because I had had*

to give up my own violin playing for an extended time due to muscular ill health. When Nigel asked me to play the same piece years later it was a perfect symbol of God's restoration and my response was to offer it back in praise. However, just to stop me claiming it as 'my piece', a different illness prevented me from attending the final concert at St Peter's, Bolton, when I was looking forward to playing it again! Such are the wise but often confusing mysteries of the Lord's workings through the NEO.

3. *During a rehearsal in the Sound of Music church in Mondsee, Austria, the purity of Beth Howell's voice singing Fauré was transported via the wonderfully crafted acoustics of the building to a realm of such beauty my heart could barely contain itself. "If this is beauty on earth," I thought, "then we have just touched a corner of the hem of the garment of the glory of heaven." Who are we to have been privileged to feel that and know that the best is yet to come? Frequently with the NEO we have experienced such glimpses and it has sometimes been overwhelming for our minds and hearts, hence tears have flowed often amongst us (and the audiences!).*

4. *Many times I have been in a physical battle with health when logic and medical sense would have dictated that to come and take part in a certain tour / concert would be impossible, or plain foolhardy! There have been very few times when that battle has been lost (and maybe there has been reason for those particular incidences) but countless more when the Lord has defied the odds and lifted my strength to do something beyond even just 'coping' and transformed my frail offering into something extraordinary. On these occasions there has been no doubt that the hand of God has been the enabler.*

One example was after months of not playing (again!) due to a nerve injury in my wrist, but, Nigel still having great faith that I would make it, I had some lessening of the symptoms about two weeks before the Rome tour of 2010. I carefully practised for a maximum of ten minutes per day to pick up the Vivaldi Double Concerto I was scheduled to play with my sister Hannah during the tour. Somehow my memory kicked in and my fingers decided to work for those weeks, just enough to enable me once again to offer my playing when needed. Chris Poffley told me it was 'amazing' and I had to agree, but only because it was undoubtedly the Lord's doing! No right-minded professional would dream of standing up to perform a concerto (from memory!) in front of a thousand people in a world-famous building, after not having played for months and then only on a few minutes practice a day. This was proof that the Lord can do anything He wills if we are brave enough to let Him. After that tour I came home unable to play again for several years, until the time was right once more. Nigel and I have spoken often about this phenomenon: he can certainly relate to it because of his own significant health trials. He calls it 'special dispensation'. For anyone else (and there are many of you!) who have experienced similar happenings, it makes every note that is given to us a precious one and the offering of each one back to the Lord that much more profound.

5. *Following on from all of this, one of Nigel's themes which has carried me the most throughout the years, is the one of the woman who broke the alabaster jar to pour out her rich perfume on her Redeemer, Jesus. Her offering is one of brokenness and also extravagant sacrifice. Onlookers counted her as distasteful, inappropriate and wasteful. Instead they sought more 'practical' uses for the expensive perfume, such as giving it to the poor (though they held their own purse strings tightly). However, Jesus is the one who knew her deeply, recognised her integrity and commented that she would be remembered throughout history, and so she has been! We have gone into the NEO's work, knowing that sometimes 'logically' it doesn't make sense. It is risky, maybe even foolhardy, wasteful, impractical, but we have always sought the Lord and tried to be obedient to Him and the offerings have been sweet-smelling! We may have come home feeling spent, but never once have we regretted breaking the jars! The Lord in His goodness has refilled them for the next task...*

Bump! Back down to earth

The flip side of the privilege of having been a part of the NEO is that many of us now feel a profound loss. It hit me after the second Legacy Day, during the following morning's service at our local church. I suddenly felt very unpleasantly selfish: I, in my restricted mind, was unable to believe that the Lord would possibly use me in such a significant ministry in the future. I felt grief for losing the possibility of glimpsing God's glory in such ways, and the privilege of reaching so many spiritually needy people, and for the regular gems of Nigel's teaching, and the thought that 'no one here understands'. Could my faith look forwards and not just feed off past experience? I expect others may have entertained similar thoughts? I needed self-reprimanding not to limit our limitless God!

On that note, Rob and I have recently watched the series Band of Brothers which is a poignant, though extremely harrowing account of a US company of soldiers during World War II. The story follows their training and further postings to locations of extreme peril beyond belief (yet accurate to history). Through the series we got to know the characters and developed huge respect for their strength, sacrificial acts and humble heroism. The episodes include interviews with the surviving real-life heroes, now very old. They share with each other a comradery others will never understand. Some veterans find it near impossible to re-enter civilian life because their lives on the frontline have been way beyond the 'norm' and they can never adjust to something less extraordinary. Others chose to adapt to their new 'frontlines' and use the experiences that had shaped them, to serve those they came into contact with later. Although we cannot equate our NEO lives physically with what these young men faced (after all, eating Strudel in cafés in Salzburg is hardly comparable to losing limbs in sub-zero temperature due to frost bite or gunfire!) we have been involved in a spiritual battle together. So there is validity in that comparison: we NEO-ers must choose how we use our 'retirement'. Perish the thought that any one of us actually retires from furthering Christ's kingdom work on this earth. It's just a question of holding out this rich loaf of bread we have been given and returning it to Jesus to break and feed many others from it. Bread for the World... We look back with awe and thanks for the adventure and look forward in anticipation to the journey ahead.

Hello and Goodbye

Nigel has often said that in our music making, the NEO has wanted to say 'hello' to those to whom we are ministering. The Lord has promised that we will find Him when we seek Him and in doing this He longs to say 'hello' to us. We have doubtless all heard His 'hello', so now we can take that greeting out from the sphere of NEO's ministry and find His new ways to speak it loudly and clearly (or sometimes 'Softly and Tenderly') to the next people we encounter. Let us 'Come before the table of the Lord of hosts with all our lives in our Hands' and discover whom He invites to the table!

I say to you all, 'Au revoir', not 'Good Bye', my dear 'Band of Brothers /Sisters'!

With love from,

Amy Chidley

(Singers' Secretary, 2nd soprano and violinist)

Julie: We are delighted to say that little Guy Benedict Chidley (his middle name meaning 'blessing,' but also given in honour of our beloved Pater Benedikt) was safely delivered to his parents and elder brother Richard, on a very memorable day: 00.11 on 11.11.16! Hence, we end these memoirs with the arrival of the very youngest little green bud of the NEO tree!

Pete Desmond

That thoughtful smile!

Sarah Hatch – principal percussionist

The Family Busse

The final bow at St Peter's Halliwell, Nigel and Caro's home congregation

Appendix 1
The 'Unforgettables'

Doug Gallaher

I remember first meeting this extraordinary person at *Youthquake* in Birmingham Cathedral in the early seventies. He struck me as an enigma then. Little did I know...

Having taken over as Singers' Secretary during Ruth Miller's sabbatical, I knew that (Rev) Matthew Baynham (NEO tenor soloist) had agreed to administer bread and wine to the singers at one particular weekend rehearsal. Having recently met up again with this old friend of yesteryear,

Doug Gallaher, I thought he might appreciate joining us for the occasion, which he did. He came, shared with us accordingly and enjoyed the rest of the rehearsal – but, being an observant chap, he also noticed that I was preparing teas and coffees for the singers (as the secretary used to do in those early days!) including washing up afterwards! Since I was several months' pregnant, he thought perhaps I should consider handing this bit of the remit over to someone else, and insisted he knew exactly the right person for the job! At the next rehearsal, Doug arrived, true to his word, accompanied by one John Trow-Poole, complete with rubber gloves! This was another of many moments which should have been heralded with distant angel trumpets, but none were heard, though I expect the Lord was definitely smiling! Doug and John went on to give so much of their time, skills, care and friendship to NEO over many years (more in a moment about John) but Doug's was the insight that was to make a considerable alteration in both my life and Nigel's.

The first of his 'niggles' was that Nigel, he felt, ought to be supported by a group of people who felt willing and able to do so, out of their belief in what the Lord was accomplishing through the ministry of NEO. Doug could also see, Nigel having been a long time friend of his since the days mentioned above, that it was becoming very difficult for Nigel to fulfil all the calls NEO made on his time, whilst still holding his role as Head of Big Band Musicianship at Salford Technical College (now Salford University). To cut a long story short, a number of people stepped to the fore who were indeed willing to administrate a trust fund for Nigel, realising that Doug was quite correct in this conviction, and from the loving and faithful support given from that time on until the end of NEO by a number of friends (who remained anonymous as far as Nigel was concerned) Nigel was thereby released to work full-time for NEO.

Some considerable time later than the above account, it became apparent that Nigel needed a PA. Binnie Thompson stepped into this role very adequately for some time, but in the end was led to take a post in a school and could not manage both jobs. Doug insisted that I was the person for this – and as I was already by then functioning in the role of Central Administrator, and therefore working closely with Nigel, we eventually came to see the sense of this. The issue of there being a hundred miles of motorway between Nigel's home and mine however, was the next hurdle! Much of our work by this time could be achieved, of course, by email and many long telephone calls, but Nigel, it appeared, had paperwork all over the place at his home by this time, and it needed a good sort out and the creation of a filing system!

Doug, as ever, with the wondrous John Trow-Poole, thought up a plan to resolve this, which involved the most incredibly selfless servanthood from both of them. In short, Doug would give up his car (lovingly known as 'the Flagship' at the time) to John, to drive me to Bolton when required, usually once a fortnight. There, I was left to work with Nigel, while John would sit and rest, enjoy cups of tea and read the newspaper, and at the appropriate time we would have lunch together (often a large quiche which I would bake and take with me as Carolyn was at work) and in the evening after a final cuppa, we would drive back to Birmingham.

Meanwhile, the other half of the bargain from Doug was that he would ensure my girls arrived safely at school, that the youngest was collected at lunchtime and given lunch and returned on time – and that they would be collected and brought home in the late afternoon, where they would be treated to a meal cooked by Doug and cared for by him until Pete arrived home from work in the evening (which was usually before John and I were home). Admittedly Pete would appreciate the hot meal that awaited him, and was deeply grateful that his children were being so aptly cared for – but there were occasions when he had difficulty coping with the enormous pile of washing up which seemed to include every pot, dish, plate, cup and saucer in the house! It was also unfortunate, when our son had mislaid his key, that on arriving at the doorstep from secondary school, he found that nobody could hear him ringing the doorbell because Doug had the radio on so loud in the kitchen!

This amazing scheme went on successfully for many years – a blessing to me and Nige and probably an amusing, if not trying phase for our growing kids. Our youngest daughter recalls how embarrassing it was to be collected by someone of not much more than her own height, who insisted on dancing across the playground giving a loud rendition of 'Yer feet's too big!' She tells me he often held a steaming mug of tea in his hand, which he just couldn't bear to leave behind in the house!

Be that as it may, it was an incredible commitment on the part of both Doug and John – but astonishingly they both seemed to enjoy it and obviously felt sure it was what the Lord had asked of them.

Not only did Doug achieve the above however, but he had also been communicating for some time it appears, with those who were responsible for a 'home and away' missions fund at St John's Church. I recall that various gifts had been presented to me in this way to help cover the cost of taking our family on tour with NEO, which were a huge and unlooked for blessing, but I eventually began to find myself in receipt of regular support, which meant that I too was recognised as being a second full-time worker with NEO, something that Nigel and myself had come to realise was then a necessity, with the terrific amount of work in which we found ourselves involved, and with all the other members of our Prayer and Planning group having full-time jobs. Here I have to pay tribute to another member of St John's – John Cheatle – whom I remember first meeting via the Tuesday Talks at Birmingham Cathedral, and the Jesus Centre project which sprang into life at that time. John and his wife Adele ran a trust which took on the role of administering monies between charities, and his willingness to help in this way was foundational to the work of Nige, myself and our families. It no doubt involved a huge amount of dedicated work behind the scenes and his friendship and personal support has been immeasurable over the years.

So it was that DH Gallaher proved himself to be (as I once described him in a poem I wrote about him), 'The grit in the oyster that produces the pearl'. There is no one I know who could match Doug for nagging people to the point of irritation, until he achieved what he discerned the Lord wanted. He would often turn up on my doorstep (unbeknown to him, at precisely the right moment!) and would state, with a shrug of his shoulders, "I don't know why I'm here, but here I am!" He had a knack of being in the Spirit by default rather than by design, if you know what I mean! He knew he could at times be what he (and certainly John T-P) would term 'a pain in the neck' – in fact he used to refer to himself as 'a sweat gland in the body of Christ – obnoxious but essential!' Going back a lot further, I remember another pithy description of Doug coming from the lips of Ian Harvey, from our earliest days, who described him as 'a hod-carrier for Lego'! That was pretty mean, but Doug found it as hilarious as we all did!

Matt Baynham (aforementioned) proved a lifelong friend to Doug, even teaching him to read and write I believe, and encouraging him when he began a course in English at Hull University. Doug continued to suffer ill health unfortunately during that period, but at length obtained an honorary degree, a wonderful achievement. Together Doug and Matt and friends went on to develop a group which was at first based at the hostel in Harborne, Birmingham (Court Oak House), of which Doug served as warden for a time. This group became known as the Gospel and Culture Forum, and I believe, still holds meetings and events to address significant issues in society and has been the catalyst the publishing of some weighty books!

Doug was born with a condition known as 'Larsen's Syndrome' which accounts for one half of his body growing at a different rate from the other, and his falling prey to various other physical difficulties. In my sewing box I still affectionately keep a slip of paper which has a note of his vital statistics, as he has often brought a new pair of trousers to me to have one leg turned up the appropriate number of inches! It was always a frightening moment when I took scissors in hand, in case I turned up the wrong leg! He was a marvellous resource however on the odd occasion when I would accidentally wash a woollen jumper of Pete's on the wrong temperature and shrink it! It usually fitted Doug perfectly!

To this day, Doug is a walking miracle, considering his early years of heart trouble and various operations, plus having

to take in his stride epilepsy, a regularly dislocating shoulder joint, arthritis and a general tendency to feel unwell or in pain. As I write, he has recently celebrated his seventieth birthday, and though not as well as he would wish, is certainly as full of life and of cheek as ever! The morning after our first NEO Legacy Day in March 2016 (following our final public event on 16th January) Doug sent me the following email:

> Julie,
>
> Someone yesterday said that you have not changed since the last time she saw you many, many, many years ago and she wondered at how good you still looked; so, to keep the records straight, I gave her the name of your wig-maker, told her about the scandal concerning you and the cosmetic surgeon and about the problem recently with woodworm in your right leg. Nevertheless it was agreed that it is a God-given gift for you to have managed to look so good for so long; but we also agreed that you must keep the woodworm under control or you and your reputation will not have a leg to stand on!
>
> Always on your side, lots of love,
>
> Doug

Doug, as you see, is a very witty writer – here is one of his articles, by permission of the author, a personal favourite of mine and a taste of those heady days of 'NEO with DHG'!

Dimples

Teetering on the vulgar

A Traveller's Tale

In the early days of the NEO, the orchestra often rehearsed at a church on the outskirts of Birmingham. It was a sunny Friday morning and I was using my new, shiny estate car and trailer to transport the larger instruments from the middle of Birmingham to Sutton Coldfield. The car was stuffed with bass fiddles and cellos, leaving the trailer to proudly sport a set of kettle drums.

around the maze of Spaghetti Junction. Then a police car whizzed past on the opposite side of the motorway and returned a few seconds later from behind. It was like something out of 'Starsky and Hutch' as the car skidded to a halt. On looking quizzically at the contents of the trailer, one of the policemen exclaimed, in a tone usually kept for great moments of discovery, "Where's the animals?" "These are *** *** drums!" I explained that I must have a speech impediment and because of the noise of the traffic, the lady must have misheard what I said. This did not cut much ice. All I got was: "Well, wherever they are, this thing is a *** hazard, so we'd better get you moved in case the drums need feeding!"

At this he fixed a chain to my car and whisked us off the motorway at breakneck speed, unceremoniously depositing us at the nearest petrol station. He didn't say much after this, other than repeating "Chimps, chimps....," and I got the distinct impression he was referring to me and my passenger!

Doug Gallaher

John Trow-Poole

In my haste, I'd forgotten all about petrol and the car spluttered to a halt half way along the recently opened Aston Expressway. "Bother!" I muttered as I hurried to one of the emergency phones, as the traffic thundered past almost hitting me. I lifted the receiver and was asked by a lady in a calm and reassuring voice if she could help? "I'm sorry, but I've run out of petrol, could you please contact the A.A. for me?" "What's the number and make of the car?" was her response. I answered this, adding that the car was easy to spot as it was bright blue and was pulling a trailer. "What's in the trailer?" was her next question. As an 'orchestra man' I was not going to bother her with the common language of kettle drums etc. My reply was rather superior as I proudly intoned, "Timps!" "CHIMPS!" she screeched, "Get back to the car immediately!" At this the phone went dead!

Before you could say, 'time for a tea break', I could hear sirens, and a blue, flashing light could be seen rushing

John, as mentioned earlier, was introduced to me and to NEO by Doug, but this was not quite the first time I had heard of John, as he had a friendship with a lovely lady called Barbara, who worked for some years as receptionist at the law firm where I had started out as a legal secretary with our since life-long friend Anthony Collins as my boss. Later John himself worked on the team at the firm, proving a great help in the post room!

But back to that day in rehearsal, when he turned up with his rubber gloves and proved as good as Doug's word in taking over the job of providing drinks to thirsty singers! He little knew at that point in time, how many hundreds of teas, coffees, hot soups, hot meals, cold sandwiches etc. he would dispense to us all, both here in the UK and abroad in Austria – nor how many cars and vans he would drive, transporting instruments all over the place.

I always felt it was a particular blessing to John that the Lord drew him into this ministry, as he had a huge passion for music. He delighted in being present at rehearsals and concerts and was thrilled to soon find himself such a part of the NEO furniture, that he took part in all our away tours. Salzburg became a great favourite of his (even after he had retired from his duties with NEO) as a holiday venue for himself and perhaps his son or daughter.

John became a close friend and 'partner in crime' to me. When he finally left the post room at Anthony Collins and retired, he gave what I calculated to be a whole decade of his retirement to aiding the ministry of the NEO. There are so many stories, most of them hilarious, when I think back to my association with this man, that I find it bewildering to know which to relate! But let's have a go!

As mentioned, Doug set up the whole routine of John driving me to my Bolton days, and I still have, in my memorabilia, a whole set of cassette tapes of compilations of all kinds of old songs, or pieces by John's favourite artistes of yesteryear. He would play these in Doug's car as we drove along the M6. I drew the line at Grieg's 'Hall of the Mountain King' from 'Peer Gynt', however, as the accelerando never failed to make the speedometer rise, and by the time it reached its zenith we were going at over 90mph! Other pieces gave rise to our youngest daughter's most unusual penchant for old fashioned songs – at primary school age she could regularly be heard singing such songs as 'London in the rain' which would have totally flummoxed her peers!

My fondest memory of John being in exactly the right place, doing the right thing at the right time, requires mention of the very first programme of the six in which we were to perform during Lent 1993, entitled *People on the Way*.

Our first venue was a tiny church, literally on top of a cliff in Anglesey. We arrived in the teeth of a wind that would take your skin off, with snowflakes falling. As we stepped out of our car and pressed forward against the gale, having wrapped ourselves in scarves, hoods, gloves etc. and feeling thirsty and peckish after our long ride, behold! There in the church car park, against a backdrop of raw grey sky, in which many seagulls tried valiantly to hold their course, was dear John, stationed at the back of the van he had driven – on which he had set up the NEO tea urn, and was ready with hot drinks and – oh bliss! Hot soup too! (See Chapter 11 – *The Media Decade* for more on this remarkable set of programmes.)

John revelled in this particular series. He loved the thrill of being up with the dawn, responsible for taking a van load of instruments, including the precious harp (beloved of Sophy Cartledge) across the Irish Sea on two occasions, no matter what obstacles presented themselves in the way of missed ferries etc. He also once missed by moments, a potential marriage to one of our alto singers, Annie Routley! She found herself being driven in the van alongside John, en route to one of our Scottish venues, which entailed by-passing Gretna Green. The ensuing hilarious conversation involved John playfully popping the question, to which Annie replied that she was... "...a bit busy at the moment," and pointing out that besides this, they didn't have a ring! To which John's retort was, "What size *is* your nose anyway?"

His own fifteen minutes (or more likely seconds) of fame, came rather forlornly when we visited Lockerbie, where the programme of course featured the tragic air disaster, and those from the town who had become involved in its sad aftermath. John's previous pastor and wife had lost their daughter in this awful event, and John, usually very much behind the scenes, was interviewed, and subsequently filmed laying some roses on her grave – a moment he never forgot.

Together with Doug, John also delighted in dressing up, usually in shorts and a curly wig, in the popular Altermarkt concerts we used to perform in the afternoons on Salzburg tours, to draw in crowds for our evening concerts. These events were huge fun, and DVD footage has captured all kinds of shenanigans, ranging from one of the cellists providing a glorious juggling feat with anything from clubs to umbrellas (and threatening to use someone's violin) to the same umbrellas, fully open, being jiggled up and down to the rousing sounds of the 'Thunder and Lightning Polka'.

John was quite fussy about his outfits, and usually looked very smart – often he would ask my assistance in going to Marks and Spencer or some such, to choose a new jacket, once I recall from their 'Italian' section! (This was probably inspired by our later trips to Rome!) But there was one occasion when he had been out with friends to visit a steam railway, and had fallen foul of a dirty cloud of steam, which had peppered his favourite short-sleeved shirt with little black marks. He came to me to see if I had anything which would take them out, and though I tried valiantly, they insisted on remaining. So I gave him a choice, "We either throw it out, or I paint it!" Always up for a lark, he chose the latter, so I decided to create a garment for him, which would remind him of the war years he spent in Singapore, from which he had told me many a tale of bright-feathered

birds, exotic flowers and trees (and not a few pretty female friends). It ended up being a showcase shirt which featured from then on in the Altermarkt – sporting a bright red and blue macaw on the front, numerous flowers, palm trees and his favourite flying fish. He loved it!

One aspect of John which never failed to render me paralytic with laughter, was his inability to grasp German pronunciation! I remember him raving about having been to the opera 'Die Fledermaus', but he pronounced it 'Dye Fledermouse' and after attempting to correct him, he would say it properly several times like a good schoolboy, and then immediately lapse into the original! Similar hilarities ensued from words like the town Hallein in Austria – always pronounced by John as 'Horleen' and as for Schloss – well it inevitably came out (sometimes together with his false teeth) as 'Slosh'! That particular word cropped up often, when John, at one point in our history, used to regularly set off early for Salzburg, and gather a little team to go round the hotels (and the odd posh 'Slosh') to distribute our flyers in preparation for the tour. He used to call these his 'bombing raids' and I was forever trying to get him to find another term for them, just in case he was ever overheard by someone from GCHQ! He adored going to Salzburg and I recently watched a clip of him (at one of our 'end of tour' home brewed cabarets, in which we used to indulge) presenting an award to the babysitters, with the citation, 'For bravery above and beyond the call of duty' and the name of the award, 'The Royal Order of the Poo Poo'! The prize, handed to Nigel for presentation to them, was a large packet of Toblerone!

I shall always remember John most of all for his gift of helps. He would regularly meet me for coffee in town to find out what was coming up next and how he could assist. We had quite a few envelope-stuffing parties at our home, and he would happily haul the bags of mail off to be franked at the GPO afterwards. (Anthony Collins had trained him wonderfully!) He would collect anything that needed to be photocopied, before the days when our printers could do this for us in our home offices. He would run errands, drive me anywhere if he could get hold of a car – and if I was low for any reason, or recovering from an illness, then he would insist on taking me out for lunch. We sometimes went to the 'Bacchus' Bar of a hotel in Birmingham – which led to one of my many nicknames for John, 'The Bacchus of Beyond'! A couple of times, when he was much older and a little frail, I invited him to the Botanical Gardens in Birmingham for 'coffee'. However, to my dismay, by the second of these occasions, (his having turned up to the first with a basket over his arm, containing a clean tea towel, two highly sparkling cut glass wine glasses, and a half bottle of Champagne) I knew what would happen! We would find a nice spot with a bench in the sunshine, he would produce the drinks and we would talk and sip and sip and talk, (on a fairly empty stomach at that time in the morning) until I could clearly tell that his speech was beginning to slur – at which point I would pack everything up, sling the basket over my own arm, take John by his elbow and walk him gently to the café to treat him to lunch, in order in order to assure myself that once I'd seen him onto the bus, he would get home safely! They were happy and hilarious days!

Sadly, John lived to grieve over the loss of his son, who died suddenly and unexpectedly. We all attended his funeral as a family, and John and I shared a special moment as I accompanied him to bid his final farewell to Steve, whose coffin lay open in the front room of his mother's home (John and she had been divorced for many years). It was a difficult moment, but a privilege that he had asked me to do that small service for him. He had given so much to me.

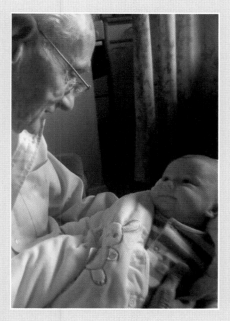

Gradually John did begin to feel his age of course, and became quite unwell. We kept in touch, and our daughter-in-law Maria (whom he referred to as either 'The Countess' or 'She who must be obeyed'!) was a wonderful companion, popping over in the car to take him anything he needed. He lived to see Luke and Maria's first child Joshua, and we have a special photo of him holding him in his arms, and the baby actually smiling up at him!

When he was finally taken into hospital after a heart attack, I was so glad to have visited him and been able to sit chatting with him and a mutual friend, Chris Winter, as, unknown to us at the time, the Lord was to take John home the very next morning. We could not help but see a ray of sunshine through the clouds however, when his daughter later wrote to inform us that John's funeral would be held on April 1st of that year! An incredible man indeed – and how heartily he would have laughed, to know we would all be gathered to celebrate his life on *April Fools' Day*! Needless to say, the most memorable card on display with the floral tributes was sent by Doug Gallaher, and in true Trow-Poole humour mode, it bore the instruction:

"Save water – drink champagne!"

Roger Knott (AKA – 'RAK')

"You need Roger Knott!" exclaimed Rev Roger Oldfield to Nigel one day at their church, "He would eat your accounts for breakfast!"

Nigel had been concerned for some time that we were in need of a treasurer, especially as we embarked on regular tours of large and popular concert halls and large amounts of money were exchanging hands. Roger Knott was the remarkable holder of that post at St Peter's Church, Halliwell, where the Swinford family had worshipped since moving to Bolton from Birmingham. He was one of God's amazing characters – with a brain capable of both vast storage capacity, and 'retrieval on demand' of huge amounts of fine detail. He had a glorious smile, white hair, an almost totally silent laugh, and a particular way of answering the telephone with his "Yes! Hello!"

Following this excellent recommendation by his vicar, he began his role in NEO with great gusto and even greater efficiency. He delighted in taking on the equally vital role of serving coffee and chocolate biscuits for Nigel and himself on the motorway. During the winter months on the M6, this entailed waiting for the point where the motorway lights began in earnest, during innumerable journeys to and from Prayer and Planning groups around the country, from Birmingham to High Legh near Knutsford, or even venturing across the Pennines to Doncaster!

Roger was a man of faith. He loved the Bible (particularly the book of Jeremiah) and he was never afraid to open the purse strings of NEO when a venture of faith required it. The rest of the time however, he was a prime example of a man who always knew the most economical way of doing anything! One of my earliest memories of Roger becoming involved in our tours to Salzburg, was of him recce-ing with Nigel. (Yes, they did several recces, tales of which do not appear in my Chapter 17 – *The Phenomenon of the 'Recce'*!) Roger was the first to locate the 'Gasthof Rechenwirt' on the outskirts of the city, in a suburb called Elsbethen, where he and Nigel would stay – and where many of us since then have been accommodated – Nigel and I on our own recces, and the married members of our teams when on tour.

He also didn't take long to find out that the local police station (at the bus stop forever engraven on our memories as 'Polizeidirektion') was the best place in town for a good dinner for just a few euros – or schillings, when we began! To this day I have no idea whether anyone actually took him up on this, but he advocated strongly it every time!

Roger actually took on a dual role, not only looking after the finances of NEO, but taking a lead in what I always referred to as 'Halls Management' i.e. negotiating all the contractual issues of staging NEO concerts in the aforementioned prestigious halls of various cities. I was hugely grateful to him for this, and we worked together quite closely as we collated the information required from Martin for orchestra, from Ruth (or indeed at times myself in the dual role of Singers' Secretary) and from Nigel, e.g. whether apron staging would be needed, or dealing with the myriad other issues that would be likely to occur. My fond memory is of the many sheets of paper with which Roger would present us, handwritten, but all very neatly printed in black ink. He must have been very busy, with all his church commitments as well as those of NEO, but he never complained, nor delivered anything late, and was always cheerful and quietly delighted to receive a gentle hug on entry to one of our homes for P & P. He often commented to Nigel that the thing he valued most about the fellowship of NEO was the 'warmth'. Knowing that Roger lived alone except for his famous dog 'Beefer', I wasn't altogether surprised by that appreciation – I do think he would have been genuinely surprised however, to learn how very fond *we* all were of *him*.

Funnily enough, Pete and I had a couple of nights away for a break just before new year 2016, and atop the rather nicely designed hotel bathroom sink I found a small motif with the initials 'RAK'. It immediately put me in mind of Roger, because I always used his initials as a quick reference, when taking notes or information from Nigel and others, which needed to be handed on to him. When I needed a longish and thorough discussion with Roger about something or other, I often put a note in the margin, "This one needs 15 minutes on the RAK!"

Roger had, as mentioned, an incredible aptitude for holding facts in his head, and we used to tease him that he knew every railway and bus timetable off by heart in any given country and not only so, but probably also what the driver had in his sandwiches!

During our 1991 tour to Salzburg with the notorious *Feast of Trumpets* production, Roger could be found sitting in an elegant room in the Residenz Palace in a quiet moment, munching an apple one minute and the next, offering it to my rather superbly 'Festival attired' lady mannequin, who stood nearby, as the moment was captured on camera!

I think the only time Nigel ever heard Roger react with full-hearted disapproval, was when someone had the temerity to suggest purchasing an item from 'PC World'. "PC World!" he exclaimed, "PC World! No one in their right mind would ever buy anything from PC World!" I gather he felt they were rather expensive, but whatever the reason, we were always careful only to submit receipts which came from elsewhere (even if we bought things from PCW privately!).

One of Nigel's remembered 'moments' with Roger, was when at the end of a busy Christmas tour, he took Nigel aside and whispered in his ear, most confidentially, that we had, by his calculation made a profit of something like forty-four pence on the tour overall! Roger took everything in his stride however, and was ready to accept with equanimity the fortunes, or lack of them, which appeared to result from our various NEO 'experiments'!

So it came about, that out of his great love of all things centred on the Lord and which involved people who were absolutely sincere in their faith, Roger had at some point, entirely without our knowledge, decided to lay his own private plans for whenever the Lord chose to call him home, which we were to find, included a special blessing for NEO.

The week I am about to describe, turned out to be a very memorable one for Nigel and his household. His own father had suffered a fall, and the ensuing complications took him quite suddenly to be with the Lord – a great shock to Nigel's mother (known to us all who love her so much as 'Grandma') and to the entire family. It was February 1999, and Nigel's birthday occurred on Monday 8th. It must already have felt like one of those occasions we all know so well, when celebration seems called upon to merge with grief in one melee of emotion. Howbeit, it was that same day that the news broke of Roger's passing away, after having been taken ill the previous evening in church, with a heart attack.

Nigel was invited to speak at Roger's funeral, which I and many others from NEO, particularly those who had been part of St Peter's congregation at some stage in their lives, attended. It was a wonderful occasion, as befits a man of God. Nigel, I remember, took up his stance at the front of the church, with one elbow affectionately leaning on Roger's coffin, as he spoke of his 'friend, Roger', and told tales of his time with us in NEO. However, it was the accolade awarded to this quiet man by others, for the many 'hidden' things he had accomplished during his lifetime, particularly ministering to the young, and undoubtedly leading many to Christ, which astonished us. We were blessed to have known all that *we* discovered in NEO about him – but this was something else!

Nigel soon received news that Roger had left a substantial legacy to NEO, which unknown to himself, was to prove a blessing, under the Lord's hand, that stayed with us for many, many years – almost literally – as with the gentle rise and fall of our finances as we followed the Lord's guidance, they always seemed to find their level back at roughly the amount Roger had left us. A very few years later, when opening my post at my desk, I was amazed to find that Roger had another little surprise in store for us, having bequeathed NEO an amount accrued from a particular policy. Even this smaller sum was as I recall in excess of £3,000 – and it made me laugh quite openly. I sat, with the letter in my hand, before ever picking up the telephone to ring Nigel, and smiled to think of Roger, with his rosy face and silent laugh, having long ago 'spiked' our future with this extra gift on top of his original legacy. What a wonderful, imaginative, caring thing to do – and how typical of him! With Roger every single detail was covered!

Yes, we were just about to get into the whole business of becoming a charity, yes, it was a bad time to lose him, yes, it was going to be hard to find someone to fill his shoes, which were 'large' indeed metaphorically speaking – but of course the Lord had His own plans ready for us in all these matters, stretching long into a future we knew nothing about at that time.

Roger was just an ordinary man, but gifted by our extraordinary God and used to redeem, assist and bless many lives and organisations. He was deeply missed at St Peter's Halliwell, and by his NEO family also – not least Nigel himself, who found in him a close and valued friend. We shall all enjoy seeing him again one day and look forward to hearing the familiar "Yes! Hello!"

Keith Buckler (and his wife Janet)

My first memory of Keith hails from my earliest involvement in singers' rehearsals at Ruth Miller's home, where for a time Keith sang with us in his deep bass voice. His main occupation however, alongside being part of the extended P & P, became the storage, administration and mail-order of NEO cassettes and later CDs and DVDs. He and Janet faithfully mailed these to purchasers on demand for years, and I cannot imagine how much space was taken up in their home by the umpteen boxes of recordings, or how many back aches were incurred from loading and unloading the car boot for all those journeys!

Another very special memory of Keith, mentioned by one of our singers, Robin Dalton, at a recent Legacy Day, was of his sweeping the stage after a downpour of rain in Salzburg, to make all safe for our dancers. I can recall this happening in my very first tour in 1985 too, when he worked alongside

Chris Bell, and much later in Spain! (Photo) This spectacle, as you can tell, was repeated quite often as Keith was and is one of those people gifted in 'seeing a need and knowing how to meet it'.

It wasn't long until I learned that Keith was a skilled surgeon, and was often to be found disappearing to some far-flung part of the globe, to minister free of charge to those who needed, but could not afford operations – sometimes in very dangerous places or circumstances. I was particularly moved, having taken part in the wonderful week we spent on tour in Cordoba, Spain at the behest of Ron Anderson of the European Christian Mission, to learn that Keith had offered to operate on Ron to remove a small piece of shrapnel that had bothered him for ages! What a gift. You will have seen 'K & J' (also mentioned in Chapter 9 – Expo '92... about our Spanish trip), as early-morning providers of breakfast to a coach full of hungry NEO members! Their talents are limitless!

Keith was one of many who are called upon to carry heavy responsibilities, but he remained totally constant to the Lord in his faith, busy to the point of excess probably, in his preaching engagements and missionary visits, and together with Janet, providing hospitality for so many. They even provided a home for some time to Nigel while he scoured the countryside around Bolton for a new home for his family – and then for the entire family when the time came to make the move from Birmingham, until their new house was ready. They are two people known for their great generosity in so many ways. They are dear friends, and we cannot express our thanks sufficiently to them for being a link over the years with fellow members of a Trust which has often supported the NEO's outreach work, home and abroad, by means of financial gifts.

So it was with huge joy that at last we heard that Keith had been included in the Honours List and was to receive an MBE – the citation, 'For services to the New English Orchestra.' This was, we think, a fitting canopy which overlaid the myriad other ministries this man had blessed, both as a medic with a big heart, and a member of the Rotary Club. He thoroughly enjoyed the day at the Palace with Janet and the family, and was presented with his award by Prince Charles, for whom he apparently left an NEO CD as a gift. (Well what else would he take?)

I shall always hold Keith and Janet dear for their warm hugs, their prayerfulness, their encouragement and their smiling efficiency at the CD sales table along with Janet and Daphne Ryland, or David and Edi Harvey, or Sue Rawlings when she acted as our Friends' Secretary.

It was a joy also to be able to hold our last *Invitation Concert* at St Mary's, Allithwaite, where Keith and Janet worship, as part of a whole series of celebratory events held in the village that year for the centenary of the church and school. It felt like an opportunity to say thank you to two of our longest serving enablers.

Despite the number of 'mature' people I know, and by no means blame, who shun modern social media – I have to say Keith soared in my estimation when I found him appearing with a smile on Facebook, where he remains my friend and where we share many a comment or greeting – usually for his part, consisting of some kind encouragement to me, often at the perfect moment! In short, Keith and Janet will always be to me and so many others, simply – unforgettable!

Erich Reischl – of the Esterbauer Riesen Coach Company, Austria!

I have to confess that I didn't know Erich personally that well. I *remember* him very well though, as the jolly person who collected us in his coaches and took us to the various mountain towns of Pfarrwerfen or Bad Hofgastein, or Sierning etc., during our tours of Salzburg.

We always had a running commentary from him about anything interesting along the way, and he would be patient

and kind, particularly when a long wait was involved before our event was over, as was the case every time in Sierning by the time we had received the presentations of gifts from Dr. Walschofer(see Chapter 3 – *Of Mountains...*) and Erich had helped load crates of beer and bananas on board as well as waiting for the last stragglers, trying to end their conversations, before we could leave!

Chris Bell of course, tells the most incredible tale of his help to the NEO in 1981 during that totally astonishing journey! He was one of the many people who seemed to 'understand' the value of this ministry fairly quickly once he became involved with it. Friendships grew, particularly with Nige and Caro, and in later years, they would visit him and his wife Anneliese and, later still, when Anneliese contacted them to say that Erich had at last passed away, they made plans to visit and comfort her. Those visits have continued whenever opportunity arises.

Throughout this entire ministry, we have been blessed with people such as Erich. There have been so many of them – people who have started out expecting us to be just like any other orchestral company, but have soon found that there is a deeper element, that they would receive smiles, conversation, friendship. Once they had experienced one of our events, it would dawn on them that this was not just a musical ensemble, but a ministry, and that at the centre of it, most undoubtedly, was the Lord Himself! I don't think we could realistically take any credit for all that, it was simply that the Lord must have said 'hello!' to them at some point (as Nigel often describes it) and from then on, we used to find that the relationship developed into something warm and lasting, and that nothing was too much trouble!

Others in NEO from its earliest days, would have far more to relate than I have here, but perhaps it's sufficient to put on record that this was one of the men of whom it could be said that for a certain length of time, 'The Lord had need'. Interesting that as I write this chapter, Palm Sunday was only a couple of weeks ago, and I learned that for a civic or religious leader, it was traditionally permissible for him to request the use of a beast of burden for a 'Triumphal Entry'. I had never heard that before. So, when Jesus requested His chosen transport, a humble donkey, it may be that for this reason, it was given without a fight. There is no doubt in my mind however, that for those blessed years in Salzburg when Erich was available to us, he was definitely providing a mode of transport 'by Royal Appointment'!

Pastor Tony Pokorny – Founder of the Austrian Bible Mission

I met Tony for the first time on our family's first visit to Salzburg in 1985. He was a very colourful character, and I liked him very much. He was short, so we could speak eye to eye, and by the time I met him that year, he was grey to white haired. He spoke excellent English and was always more than happy to display his talents at British dialects, like Yorkshire, Scottish, Welsh or Irish! He was hilarious. He was very dapper, often wearing a beautifully-tailored Austrian suit with all its trimmings; deer-horn buttons, a leather tie with silver end-clasps, the grey wool cloth edged sometimes with deeper grey or green on the jacket. He and his wife lived in the south of England in fact – but he had a missionary calling, and travelled all over Europe taking Bibles and diaries which had Scripture verses in them, to anyone who would receive them. He was always particularly concerned for refugees, and after our tours he would willingly collect any leftover tea bags, coffee, sugar, biscuits etc., for his food bank for these scattered people, of whom there have always seemed to be many in Austria, and sadly many more of course today.

Chris tells the wonderful story of how Tony came into the frame right from the very beginning in having befriended Jim Goldie, and how he was able to translate when Jim met with Archbishop Berg – to whom Nigel and the team were officially introduced on our fifth visit to Salzburg in 1985. The man the Archbishop had sent to record our concert one evening, turned out to be one Pater Schoen – who ended up making several very beautiful recordings of our work in Salzburg, which I believe Carolyn has, squirrelled away somewhere, on old 'reels' as well as cassettes! I remember listening to some of them and being very blessed. Pater Schoen was also destined to become one of the NEO's 'friends' in a special way, and thanks to the wonderful Susan Mole and Briggie Furze, found communication easy!

Tony, as you will read in those memoirs, had for a time made the decision to join the Hitler Youth Movement, from which the Lord later redeemed him! Anyone who spent any time getting to know him would find him a very strong character, not afraid to speak his mind. There were times when Chris Bell found him a challenge – as he could be very strong-willed. But he loved the NEO and believed in what we were doing, and he gave the most astonishing support in those early days, often putting a great deal of hard work into finding and setting up the venues for our tours. He was one of the Lord's 'enigmas' – capable of great achievements, and also one who shared the Gospel wherever he went. I often think the apostle Paul may have been a similar personality – astonishingly bold, and carrying God-given responsibilities, but perhaps a little unpredictable at times!

Tony's daughter, Yvonne, also became a great friend of ours and is still today. I recall on my first ever trial 'recce' with Nigel and Carolyn, in the autumn half term of 1996, which was for the most part a lovely holiday – with occasional trips into Salzburg to have important appointments – we stayed at her beautiful home in Fuchsbau in the mountains. I was in a state of bliss I recall, it was so lovely. I couldn't manage to compete with Caro's speed in climbing the local mountains, no doubt much to the bemusement of herself and Nige, (there aren't any in Birmingham unfortunately to practise on!) but the views and the beauty of the autumn leaves were a sight to behold.

Yvonne took time off from her busy accommodation business to come and visit us at our more recent concerts in Mondsee, to which she always arrived (being a talented seamstress) looking as beautifully elegant as did her father!

These are friends who have blessed us and been blessed by the Lord through our friendship too. I often wonder how many lives Tony reached with his Bible mission and his work with us and no doubt with others? I should imagine it's quite a number!

Guenther and Dorli Reinthaler

Guenther and Dorli are two more good and faithful friends of NEO, much loved by us all, and here I have asked Roger and Dawn Beasley, who have known them well for many years, to add their memoir of them! Dawn writes:

We believe our first contact with Guenther was via Pastor Pokorny above. Guenther and Dorli were involved in full-time youth work with an evangelical organisation called 'Young Life' Austria (connected to 'Young Life' in the USA) where one had to 'earn the right to be heard'. They had a very powerful ministry leading countless young people to Christ. They were already married when we met them and had a heart to encourage newlyweds to adapt to married life.

Guenther worked tirelessly alongside the NEO from our first visit to Salzburg, for many years subsequently. Guenther often acted as interpreter, including at 'The Feast of Trumpets' and 'Symphony of the Nations'. He transported us, with Nigel, to meetings to arrange venues; he managed, with his infectious personality, to cajole every police or security official to allow our van (with all the equipment) into places otherwise prohibited to the public. He helped me with any difficulties when I was secretary to Nigel for the initial years. He enabled my liaison with the hostel staff if I had a problem conveying our needs to the management at the Youth Hostel. Guenther and Dorli were there for the NEO. They greatly appreciated our visits to Salzburg because 'the spiritual atmosphere lifted' enabling the locals to personally experience God as we played and sang. Wonderful long-term supporters and enablers of the New English Orchestra!

Barbara Donovan – Administrator to the Venerable English College, Rome

As can be read in Chapter 15 – *To the Saints in Rome...*, the fairly sudden opening of our work in this amazing city came as quite a surprise, and again, we found the Lord leading us from one opportunity to another in rapid succession.

To recap, it was the Ambassador to the

Holy See, Francis Campbell (first introduced to us by our friend Peter Jennings) who kindly invited us to his residence to perform an evening concert and be entertained to a reception afterwards on his rooftop which started quite an interesting series of events. That in itself was a wonderful and memorable privilege, but as you may by now have read, the Lord had other things in mind also! Two of the guests were Monsignor Nicholas Hudson, then Rector of the Venerable English College (VEC) and his Vice Rector, Father Andrew Headon. The latter was destined to become another of our NEO friends – having decided to pop in to one of our *Recreatio* events in the beautiful Chiesa di Santa Maria sopra Minerva one day. There, he had felt significantly touched by the Lord, and as a result, he must have logged that fact, and as Nigel so often directs, 'pressed save'!

It transpired that Father Andrew was, among his other duties in the VEC, overseeing a big refurbishment project to renew their college chapel, affectionately known as the 'Jewel Box' as not only was it extremely ornate, but it contained the bones of saints in the reliquary below its altar. However, Andrew felt it would be wonderful to invite us to spend a day helping them to celebrate the re-opening of this chapel, which we subsequently did, in the October of 2009. It was around this point, that we became aware of the existence of one Barbara Donovan!

Barbara was the Administrator of the College, and having married an Italian, has lived in Rome for many years, (though herself Irish). We always have the impression that she is highly valued in the VEC. Barbara came into her own however, when Nigel and I found ourselves getting into the depths of our new relationship with Monsignor Micheletti of the Pantheon! He was such a jovial, friendly man, but we did have the most awful difficulty communicating the finer points of discussion with him as we had no Italian, and he not a great deal of English! So one day (I can't even remember when, it may have been during our many meetings with Father Andrew in London), Barbara was mentioned as someone I might contact for some information or other, and we wondered whether she might be able to help us out with this also!

I have to state quite clearly at this point (as I have often stressed to Nigel) that there is no earthly reason why this amazing lady should ever have seen the necessity to fit into her busy timetable the translation and sending of emails to priests of the Pantheon for NEO, or worse still, drop everything on a hot day, mount her trusty bicycle and ride through the ludicrous amount of city traffic, to meet us at the top of the staircase down to the Chiesa di San Vitale to act as our interpreter with Msgr Daniele Micheletti!

The fact remains however, that whenever I plucked up courage to either telephone, text or email Barbara with what for quite a while became 'the annual requests', she responded graciously, honestly and patiently. If she was really tied up, it would perhaps be a matter of a week or so before she could come through with the answer, but normally it was a couple of days! She would translate vital emails, communicating dates and times and also the latest *Recreatio* script readings to be read in Italian, and she would make appointments for us ahead of our recce trips.

She grew to have the most wonderful friendship with Msgr Micheletti – they obviously shared a similar sense of humour. On one occasion (Nigel often took a 'nice bottle of red' to these assignments but on this occasion it was a celebratory bottle of Champagne) we all sat toasting each other from plastic cups – it was a merry meeting. In fact I think it occurred when we took him as a gift, a copy of our 2014 DVD, fashioned by Paul and Julia Myles. Nigel and I would sit entranced listening to Barbara, with her rapid-fire Irish/Italian, rattling on to Msgr Micheletti, who would laugh uproariously and reply with equal speed – and though we hadn't the faintest clue what was going on, we always ended up with the right answers and the right permissions – and another happy tour would suddenly be in prospect. It was a marvellous provision from God!

I have to include the wonderful Msgr Micheletti in this account, because he too showed us the most astonishing friendship, understanding and support. He approved all our *Recreatio* scripts from the beginning, and I had some amusing emails from him, usually greeting me as "Carissima," and being short and to the point, either in Italian, or very brief English such as, "Yes, is all okay!", in answer to my question. (On occasion I *could* get away with a very short

English email of my own just to check a date!)

The Lord had again provided the perfect person for that period of time, to achieve His purposes for NEO in Rome. There was no doubt that Barbara had 'seen' the ministry and described it as beautiful. She sensed its integrity and she came whenever she could manage it to our events, having also of course witnessed our day in the College Chapel. She understood our work and her help will consequently have a share in the fruitfulness of all our Rome *Recreatio* gatherings. If even a cup of water given in the Lord's name has its reward, she will be blessed indeed!

I must also add here a record of thanks to Father Mark Harold, who was appointed to the position of Vice Rector when Father Andrew moved on. He too helped us with translation skills when we had to appeal to the great Basilica of San Giovanni in Laterano, and he also read for us along with other members of the VEC.

Father Benedikt Röck – of St Peter's Stiftskirche, Salzburg

I find myself writing these few paragraphs, very sadly, only four days after this dear friend of ours went to be with the Lord. In our bulletin to all our prayer supporters, Nigel wrote this tribute:

Pater Benedikt supported our testimony in Salzburg for around thirty years. He graciously allowed us to use St Peter's Stifstkirche as a base for our work and encouraged his fellow

monks to help us wherever they could. One of his colleagues was the wonderful Pater Petrus, who is among the finest continuo players in the region. He played with the NEO in what some regard as the best concert we ever did – the Bach evening in the Residenz during the 2005 tour. Benedikt opened the way for us at the University Church that year and also played a seminal role in getting us started in Rome. He would frequently do the readings in the Recreatios. Benedikt knew the joy of the Lord and would often eat and drink with us in the Stiftskeller. He particularly enjoyed the nickname given him by Anthony – 'Party Benedikt', and used to quote this in conversations with us. He loved the NEO and its work and came to England on two occasions to attend our concerts. He was present at the last one on January 16th in Birmingham Town Hall (2016). At this time, he was suffering with some strange symptoms to do with his vision, and soon after was diagnosed with a brain tumour. An operation swiftly followed, plus treatment. In recent weeks, he had been recovering well and on Sunday last (12th June) he was totally normal and staying with his brother Bernhardt. On Monday morning, he did not reappear for breakfast, so eventually Bernhardt went into the bedroom and found him lying there. The Lord had taken him.

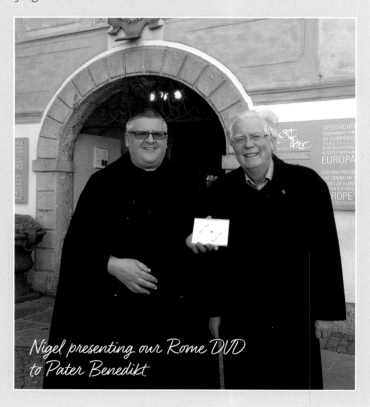

Nigel presenting our Rome DVD to Pater Benedikt

I need not say how much we loved this man of God. I can still remember the first time Nigel and I were introduced to him when he became 'Rektor' of St Peter's, responsible for all bookings, and therefore the person we needed to consult for our ongoing work at this strategic church. He was cheerful and helpful, sincere and kind. It was, unbeknown to us then, the beginning of an incredible friendship which was not only to bless both him and us, but also to oversee and bless the work we were doing in the city during our tours. Father Benedikt was of immeasurable help to us in so many ways. He would read at our Vigils in the church, he would come to the Dom and do the readings in English for our *Recreatios*, alongside the Dean, Pater Balthasar Sieberer, who read the German Bible verses. Benedikt it was, who took us across the courtyard from St Peter's, his black gown billowing out behind him, and walking with purpose and determination across to the University Church, to introduce us to Father Andreas Jakober. That opened up a new opportunity in that outstanding venue, where we held a momentous evening concert – at which I recall Sammy Lange commenting: "I think you just took the University Church!"

Benedikt also, as you will read in Chapter 15 – *To the Saints in Rome...*, was seminal in our efforts to begin working in that city – that recce was a time of amazing fellowship and not a little humour! Benedikt dearly loved a laugh, but he was also a man of deep feeling, with a pastoral heart. He wanted to minister the grace of God to the people of the Parish – to feed the sheep and the lambs. In Chapter 5 – *Whatever the weather...*, you may read of the famous 'Ash Cloud tour' where things took a turn in Benedikt's life, and he became acting Abbot of St Peter's Monastery for some time, before being again released into parish duties. We were so privileged to have been there at that time to support him, and he publicly acknowledged the blessing of NEO's presence at that strategic time. We regretted not being able to be present for the funeral, but Georg and Thea Hoelscher, our dear friends from Seekirchen near Salzburg, represented us all. No doubt Benedikt found it amusing that we fondly refer to these friends as 'G & T', which resulted in them being nicknamed 'Gin and Tonic'! A good match then with 'Party Benedikt'!

We look back with some astonishment, at the high quality of the friends, only a handful of whom are mentioned above, with which the Lord has surrounded the work of this orchestra, and we are thankful.

Dimples

When serving a snack she had made on a Birmingham, rather than a Bolton day:

Julie: 'This is very low in fat!'

Nigel: 'Oh, what a pity!'

(Just to clarify that he is also pretty unforgettable!)

Appendix 2
"By the way... what does P & P stand for?"

This is a question I have often been asked in my NEO lifetime!

I feel a need to pay tribute, on behalf of Nigel, myself and everyone in NEO, past and present, to all those who have carried out the myriad administrative duties needed to keep the NEO machine chugging along. They served faithfully as members of its *Prayer and Planning* team for their respective seasons, down through the years. We have been so blessed to know them all.

Dimples
We need to get all the beans in a row!

Nigel would explain that in principle, he doesn't tend to indulge in big sessions of public thanks to individuals, firstly because he appreciates that their work was primarily for the Lord, and secondly because the list would be huge! However, I felt that on this one occasion I should break the habit of a lifetime, firstly to give thanks to God for them all, and secondly because it's perfectly possible that there are many NEO members who never really knew who they were or what was done by whom! That in itself is probably a mark of the quality of their work.

Before I list them all however, one person has to be acknowledged before all others the amazing Carolyn Swinford(Caro) – Nige's wife, helpmeet, encourager, 'reminder', sorter of music; provider of clean shirts in hot climates, hot water bottles in cold ones, flasks of tea and coffee on demand, talking books for long European car journeys; finder of all things lost; cook of wonderful meals and sweetmeats; nurse; driver (as and when required, especially to airports at unmentionable times in the morning); source of boundless energy; mum to Lizzie and Catherine, mother-in-law to Pete White and Robin Mason, Granny to Iris, Dulcie, Jack and May; talented oboist (a regular player at the start of NEO) piano teacher beloved of so many young pupils during a long and much appreciated school career; NEO alto singer and music librarian to the end of the ministry; seamstress for endless garments for daughters and dancers; knitter of imaginative jumpers and cardigans for grandchildren, combined with an endless fascination with mountains, wild flowers, birds, stars and planets – and having developed an astonishing skill for storing innumerable scores of music for both orchestra and singers, and for the copying and distribution of CDs and DVDs! I can do no better than quote Anthony Thompson our NEO Principal Trumpet player, who, in his inimitable style, once commented during a recent tour to Rome, "I reckon an angel would look like Caro." I reckon he could be right! Here she is with the ice cream he once bought her in Rome!

The Angel Caro' with her ice cream from Anthony Thompson

Roger Beasley – long held the title 'Minister without Portfolio' – one which I found rather mystifying when I first joined the P & P! It actually meant that he held no specific role, thereby having the space to use his spiritual gifts and practical experience (not to say quirky imagination!) to contribute to the work of NEO right across the field. He did however have a long stint of working as Publicity and PR Secretary, and came up with some original designs for concert flyers! Above all this however, his outstanding contribution was as a singer/soloist, in which role he never failed (and at the time of writing, still hasn't) to be an amazing communicator of the love of God to audiences around the world.

Dawn Beasley – was the very first administrative assistant to Nigel as the ministry took off, and continued for several years, being one of three herein mentioned who gave up a job to spend more time giving her support. Together with Roger, she hosted innumerable P & P meetings and other gatherings and provided accommodation for countless people. She served as Enablers' Secretary, later as Hospitality Secretary and more recently as an enabler on the Front of House team during away tours, despite taking major surgery for cancer of the oesophagus in her stride along the way! She is a great prayer supporter of the work as a whole and individuals within it. I am personally grateful to Dawn and Roger for providing us with a lovely daughter-in-law!

Chris Bell – Chris (bass singer) was specifically appointed Central Administrator on the run up to *The Hiding Place*. He was a singular character, who learned on the job, and whose writings herein will have no doubt in one moment reduced you to tears with their poignancy, and the next cause you to cry laughing! Despite a lifetime battle with depression, Chris achieved extraordinary feats in NEO with absolutely no previous experience! His life brought testimony to the love of God, and his death was a great loss to us all, though to gather and sing at his funeral was a huge privilege.

Brian Miller – Brian (husband of Ruth who features in the present day P & P list below) functioned as an early NEO Treasurer. He was a man of great sincerity, capable of huge gentleness and sensitivity to the needs of others, and who loved praising the Lord in his role as an NEO tenor. He and Ruth hosted singers' rehearsals and P & P meetings in their home for many years and were always generous, prayerful and ready to minister to anyone in any kind of need – often opening their home to others where necessary – as Ruth still is doing today. Brian blessed us all by simply being himself.

Alison Hawcutt – Served as General Administrator/Singer for many years, providing the address via which the public could contact the NEO. I shall always remember Alison for her wonderfully warm character, her gentleness, her lovely voice, her quiet efficiency and her personal friendship to me from the start of my involvement with NEO. We had both worked as legal secretaries, and I admired the speed and accuracy of her shorthand! I especially remember her caring for and leading the small band of children in singing 'Jesus died for all the children' in 'The Horns of the Altar' movement of 'The Feast of Trumpets'!

Susan and Mike Castle – Both singers, (alto and bass respectively), the Castles' major contribution was in dance. Sue (née Hill) had known Nigel since being a pupil of his at the secondary school where he taught music in Dudley, and she came on board and worked with him alongside Marie Green, to create the unforgettably beautiful choreography for 'Symphony of the Nations' in the eighties. Whilst auditioning and recruiting dancers, she met Mike, who was destined to play the part of Jesus in this symphony, and not only did she discover in him an amazing talent for dance, but her future husband also! We were all pretty amazed when they chose to use one of our many Salzburg tours as part of their honeymoon!

Dorothy Goodliff (née Pearce) – 'Dot' was a much loved enabler and member of the extended P & P for a while, who served, along with her close friend Judi Newman, in innumerable ways over many years, catering, caring so imaginatively for the children on tours and generally being wonderful team players who were utterly faithful and reliable and added their own inimitable brand of humour and hilarity to the NEO! For quite some years, 'Dot and Judi' together were one of those amazing enigmas that made the NEO function so well. Thanks Dot and Judi – we love you!

Keith Buckler – NEO Recordings Secretary and Front of House enabler, ably assisted by Janet his wife. These are two people whom the Lord has given a heart for missionary work and outreach by any means possible, not least glorious hospitality and sincere prayer. It's a privilege to have known them. (Details in Appendix I – *The Unforgettables*)

Liz Sheppard – Alto Singer/soloist: Liz, I will always remember as a fun-filled, bubbly personality, held within a diminutive frame! Her smile and laughter was a joy to us during her time in NEO and she contributed so much with her beautiful alto voice and was the first to sing the 'Christe' from Nigel's Celebration Mass in Austria the day after a totally incredible journey – as recounted by Chris Bell!

Paul Sheppard – Bass singer and versatile instrumentalist, and also hilariously competent contributor to the Disputation Team efforts of 'YK2'! Folk who were there would remember Paul, in his stand-up comedy routine, reminding us that "All roads lead to Wolverhampton!"

Tony Trotter – For a season, Tony was our prayer letter editor and NEO Friends' Organisation's founder and first secretary, with an infectious smile and sense of humour. Tony also served on Binnie and Paul Thompson's regional P & P. We are thankful to Tony for all he spearheaded! He was a capable player too, along with Hilary his wife! My husband Pete particularly remembers being immensely grateful to Tony for 'being there' for him, helping in our first Salzburg tours when Pete had to assemble the lighting for our open air productions. Thanks for everything Tony!

Roger Knott – Finance Secretary and Halls Management for tours – you will have met him in greater detail, again in *Appendix I* – 'The Unforgettables'.

Catherine Taylor – Finance Secretary following Roger Knott's death, and Front of House Manager for a time – a dear friend and loving, conscientious person, with whom I always enjoyed spending time, and one who contributed much to NEO at a crucial time in its development as a charity. I think of Catherine as one of those people the Lord brought to us at exactly the right moment.

Kate Harrod-Wild (née Ansell) – Singer and Assistant Orchestral Secretary to Martin Lowe for a time, Kate did a good sideline as a trumpeter when required! In fact I believe she first found us when she responded to a request for extra brass when we launched 'The Feast of Trumpets'. Kate was and is always bright and vivacious. I will never forget her calm and polite stage calls to the 'Ladies and Gentlemen of the Orchestra'!

Marcus Harrod-Wild – served as NEO Front of House Manager for a time and came to agree with Scripture that, "He who finds a wife, finds a good thing!" (Proverbs 18 v 22 NKJV). They now have three boys, two of whom are twins. I have enduring memories of Marcus being baptised by (Rev) Matt Baynham from our tenor line, with a supporting cast of umpteen enthusiastic NEO members on tour in Salzburg, at the local swimming pool! A great occasion! (He was not the first to be so dunked either! There were other such memorable moments down the years! I think a young Nick Evans-Pughe (viola) once helped to set this trend!)

Paul and Kathryn Jourdan – both highly gifted members of the string section of the orchestra, they served on the P & P for a while before relocating to Edinburgh where they still live. Together they contributed so much both to NEO and to the music at St John's Harborne. Our loss is Edinburgh's gain!

Trevor Wright – Technical Enabling (PA and MCPS Secretary for NEO recordings). Trevor's wife Margaret was a founder member of the strings in NEO and was known, so Nigel tells me, for creating a particularly sweet sound. Trevor, together with Ernie Dalton, spent years 'on the road' with NEO doing heavy manual labour with speakers, cables, stands etc. to ensure we could be heard! For long years after he left his main NEO role, Trevor continued to be a huge help with copyright admin for our CDs, for which we were profoundly grateful!

Julia Myles – Dance Secretary and gifted choreographer to NEO, (along with Lizzie Swinford, Nigel's elder daughter). I have rarely met anyone so full of life and fun and displaying such a generous dose of the Holy Spirit. From the first time she danced with us, she blessed us with her huge variety of styles and the sparkle that emanated from her. She opened her home to our meetings while in Birmingham. She provided a wonderful commentary for the DVD which Paul her husband created for us (as mentioned below). She is now following her heart into the Anglican ministry.

Paul Myles – Lighting and Technical Enabling (with special remit for creation of diverse and strange 'gadgets', spanning battery powered candles for singers, ingenious kit for dispensing yards of red satin ribbon for the Feast of Trumpets (1991) to mock electric razors for dancers featured in 'The Wise and Foolish Virgins' (1992)). Much more recently Paul and Julia worked together to produce the fabulous DVD of Rome (Pantheon *Recreatio* events) and the final *40th Birthday Concert* in Birmingham Town Hall on the 16th January, 2016. Despite now living in Northumberland, Paul and Julia are still very much 'involved' NEO family!

Brenda Lowe – Childcare Secretary extraordinaire – Brenda has been beloved of all the NEO children who have grown up among us during her time of ministry. A great deal of her time was spent back 'at the ranch' in either a hostel or hotel, (caring for tiny people who needed to stay back while their parents were away performing). She thereby missed many of the performances, sometimes virtually the entire tour! Her support of Martin is also a huge part of her role, and together they have also contributed Matt and Simeon, two excellent NEO enablers, Matt developing a wonderful talent for photography, having provided some of the photographs in this book – and I shall always remember Simeon plying a cloth to dry everything in sight after our first downpour through the oculus in the Pantheon!

Luke & Maria Fry – for a period of time Head of Technical Enabling/Lighting – trained by Paul Myles from a very early age! (I believe his first major achievement was giving warning that there was a fire starting in the PA deck at a particular venue!) One of his greatest assets is a disarming smile, which always seemed to work like a charm on various vergers and 'keepers of essential keys'! Luke is married to Maria (née Beasley), who often served in child care and/or Front of House management. I recall Maria's Mum, Dawn, during our first trip to Salzburg in 1985, coming to tell me that Luke (aged five) had just upset Maria (also aged five) by pulling her hair! I know not whether this was a throw-back to the caveman instinct, but at any rate they were married many years later, and we now all share a happy extended family containing Beasleys, Frys, Smyths and Siderys! Luke used to head up a team of young and eligible NEO males, who not only served NEO fantastically well, but seemed to have a lot of fun together whilst developing future muscle. This may be attributed at least in part to regular trips to the shop for Mars Bars and Coca Cola, and the end of tour visit to the Stieglkeller at which the enablers were for many years, traditionally clapped in by an uproarious crowd of NEO rowdies, (who at other times were in fact capable of being quiet and refined!).

Sarah Richards – Sarah, herself the daughter of NEO players Peter and Shirley Richards, first appeared in NEO as a talented young soprano of soloist quality. She served on (Ext) P & P to represent our younger members, and can be seen in the final shot of our Rome DVD, being hugged by an enthusiastic tourist who had obviously enjoyed her ministry! She contributed much to NEO during her time with us, and has gone on to establish herself as a singing teacher and to use her vocal gifts in ministry. At the time of writing, she is looking forward to marrying the son of two other past members of NEO (Richard and Susan Williamson) who now work together in an established Christian music project entitled 'Epiphany', with whom she regularly sings.

Regional P & P groups

For a while, to meet the need on a regional basis, for events such as Christmas tours, Vigils etc., we appointed local groups in Manchester, Bristol and London – these were made up as follows:

Manchester

Binnie and Paul Thompson – Binnie is a great team player in NEO, beloved of us all for her fun personality. A talented singer, she and Paul (who has been a great support to Binnie and also had a turn recently at being an enabler in the heats and the rains of Rome!) also work as part of an ensemble called 'Grace Notes'. Binnie acted as PA to Nigel before I took that role, and until teaching took up more of her time, was a great help to the administration of NEO.

Tony Trotter – (mentioned above)

Lynn Attwood – part of a very gifted family! Her son Mark both sang tenor with NEO and played a mean trombone!

Liz Cassidy Pantling – one of our many beautiful and talented NEO dancers

Bristol

Carole and Graham Corpe – Carole has been from the very early years, one of our much loved singer/soloists, featured on many of our recordings. Together with Graham (bass singer) Carole made a lasting contribution to the work of NEO, along with their children, Mary (and her own husband Andrew) and Jon. At the time of writing, though not at present working within NEO, Carole is still blessing others with her singing, we are glad to hear! Carole has one of the best smiles and the bluest eyes in NEO and she and Graham helped enormously to build the strong foundations of this ministry.

Ros and Chris Gane – Ros (soprano) and I began our administrative efforts together as assistants to Ruth Miller in her Singers' Secretary role. Chris (bass singer) worked alongside her in this P & P. Both have been faithful members of the NEO singers to the end of its ministry. One feature of their work which I recall particularly was an outstandingly good event for local enablers in the Bristol area. We even met and recruited a new singer, Susan Watt, on that occasion!

Andrew Stephen – Andrew served as one of our NEO trumpeters for several years (and can be seen on various DVD shots, contributing jazz trumpet alongside the likes of Raul D'Oliveira and Pete Desmond). It was great to see him again at a recent Legacy Day!

London

Brigitte and Richard Furze – Brigitte began life with NEO as a violinist in its early history, having arrived in the UK from Switzerland. She went on to become the Leader of the orchestra for many years. Latterly she became a soprano singer also, together with her husband, a long-serving tenor, and their daughters Rachel (alto) and Miriam (soprano) who are both firmly established and popular members of the second generation of NEO Singers. Her article on how NEO changed her life appears within (Chapter 3 – *Of Mountains…*)

Nicholas and Andrea Young – Nicholas (bass) and Andrea (alto /NEO dancer) and their children Chris (enabler) and Eleanor (soprano). This is another of the many NEO families who have provided two generations of performing artistes! Andrea had a career with the Springs Dance Company, and brought her experience into NEO to its great

advantage. As a couple, she and Nicholas have had a real ministry of hospitality and encouragement as well as musicality, and Eleanor has now gone on to forge a career in Performing Arts.

Present day charitable trustees (as at 2016)

Nigel Swinford – Chairman/ Founder/ Artistic Director/Principal Conductor (Beans will have been spilled throughout about him!) I recall being very amused when on a particular car journey with him, he was munching his way through a bag of liquorice allsorts and commented, "The trouble with these Jules, is they get in your mouth!" He also writes amazing music and is a pretty mean arranger too! My theory is that when the Lord calls him home, He will simply put an arm around his shoulder and say: "Thank you Nigel that was super!"

Julie Fry – Company Secretary/Central Administrator/PA to Nigel/ soprano – living in a house in Birmingham which has a yellow door (DIY in our home standing for 'Do It Yellow'!) and is furnished with a small brass plaque stating it to be the Registered Office of the New English Orchestra. Many postmen have commented on this, and just the other week, a lovely African man who delivered some shopping, became very excited at the prospect of finding out where we would next perform, only to discover that we had held our final public event a couple of months previously! He carried all my shopping through to the kitchen whilst expressing his sympathy for me and disappointment for himself!

David Harvey – an extremely capable Finance Secretary/Front of House enabler and P & P host – David has proved invaluable in keeping us on track with pristine accounts and up to the mark with all charitable requirements. The wonderful story of how he came to be part of the NEO P & P occurs within!

Nick Gerrard – Trustee/ tenor/ Marketing Manager/original Editor of the NEO Friends' Opus magazine. Nick and his wife Nicola met one another in NEO, and, as you may by now have read, thereby became one of many such couples who somehow side-stepped the infamous NEO 'Rule 10'! (See Chapter 3 – *Of Mountains...*) Nick has not only been responsible for goodness knows how much printed publicity, but also programmes, photographs, inserts for CDs, the oversight of NEO stationery, T-shirting and NEO mug sales and generally being in charge of (pardon the phrase) 'getting bums on seats' at NEO concerts (a particularly vexing responsibility when the hall hire fee can be in excess of £11K per night!). As if that were not enough, he has on many occasions risked his voice, proclaiming outside large buildings in the heat of the day, accompanied either by a trumpeter or clarinettist, encouraging passers-by to come in! Many are the T-shirts that have needed to be changed at the last minute before he could appear, calmly transformed, in the tenor line. (I will add here that there is at times a little humorous rivalry that goes on between the tenor line and the bass line, often spearheaded by Nick, such that I once thought I might head one of these

chapters, 'Of Tenors and Men' – but I thought better of it!) My thanks Nick for your hours of help in proofreading and photographic input for this book!

Janet Ryland (with Daphne Ryland, present P & P member) – Our most recent Trustee and Joint head of Domestic Enabling (with Daphne Ryland – the latter having also been responsible for many beautifully clear renditions of the Scripture readings in our *Recreatio* events in Rome!). Together, these wonderful sisters have created the most lavish spreads and baked innumerable cakes and sweetmeats which have kept the troops on the job – especially at Singers' rehearsals. (If I forgot to mention it within, the NEO is what might be termed a 'Gastropod' – it marches on its stomach!) Moreover, Janet and Daphne faithfully served for years in caring for innumerable NEO children and young people, in the heat of Salzburg, or Rome. Even more importantly, they have been a steady source of wisdom, plain common sense and phrases like 'Stand by your beds!' applied the minute they sensed a busy challenge about to burst forth on the ranks of NEO! Janet's most recent contribution to my supreme happiness, was in helping to create the utterly beautiful flower arrangements at St John's Harborne, for our daughter Stephanie's very 'NEO' wedding to Trevor Sidery on October 8th this year!

Present day Prayer and Planning Group

All the above Trustees plus:

Martin Lowe – Orchestral Secretary and Logistics/Project Manager of UK events. Martin is an excellent bass singer/soloist – having worked with Nigel since his teens and also played clarinet in the earliest ensembles including 'Jesus Centre Jazz'. He has an incalculably wondrous gift for logistics and is generally an indispensable bod! Much has been told within about this exceptional gentleman.

Ruth Miller – Ruth was another who, along with Dawn Beasley and Chris Bell, felt called to give up their full-time employment, in her own case, to prioritise the work required to stage *The Hiding Place* many years ago, in which Ruth played the major role of Corrie Ten Boom, alongside Anne Linstrum (Betsy Ten Boom). Ruth went on to provide general administrative help, be the author of our earliest prayer letters and also serve as Singers' Secretary for many years. She continues to dispense wisdom in the P & P (often referred to by Nick Gerrard as 'Ruth Pearls', which he records in a special notebook for the purpose! We think this friendship, plus a genuine admiration of Corrie Ten Boom, may have conspired to result in Nick and Nicola naming their first daughter Corrie!). After Brian went to be with the Lord, Ruth took time first to recover, and then to prayerfully consider all her future options, and has recently been welcomed as a licensed Church of England Reader, to serve at her home church, St Germains, Edgbaston. She is also deeply committed, as she ever was, to working with or on behalf of children. Her daughter Joy was once a soprano singer with NEO, and her younger son Andrew (my own Godson) was one of Luke's enthusiastic original team!

Amy Chidley (née Monkhouse) – Singers' Secretary/soprano/violin/soloist and one of the bravest people I have had the privilege of meeting! Amy, in her gentle way, has ploughed through so many painful years with one condition or circumstance following another, and has risen to the surface every time with more to share about the love of Jesus and an obvious deepening of her faith in Him. Her playing and singing are of a rare quality, and she has given so much to the NEO family, along with her sister Hannah (alto singer and cellist, also of great quality) and her own parents, Shirley and Malcolm (who have shared our tours, acted as babysitters for their grandchildren and been a huge and supportive encouragement to NEO!) The Lord has provided some astonishing people among our ranks.

Rob Chidley – Rob served on the P & P with us for a while, contributing both generally and as Editor of the Friends' Opus magazine, writing or commissioning many wonderful articles and photographs. Rob first won our hearts however, with his commitment to supporting Amy as she took on being part of NEO at a time when she was more or less confined to a wheelchair with fibromyalgia. He commented that he wanted to do this as he felt the Lord, through this ministry, was 'healing Amy'. She stands today as a living testimony that he was right! They are now blessed with two sons, Richard and Guy.

Nicola Gerrard – Principal NEO Flautist (wife of Nick above among the Trustees) and writer of our earlier colourful and imaginative NEO Prayer Guides. Nick and Nicola's daughters, Corrie and Hannah, both contributed as performers with NEO, Corrie as a second soprano and Hannah as an NEO dancer (just once) in the Pantheon, before NEO's closure! Nicola has not shied away from being presented with the odd challenge by the Artistic Director, such as the time when she was invited to play some 'Jethro Tull' in a series of concerts. She did superbly well, and the red hat will be remembered! It also appears she can not only play Bach's 'Badinerie' between two dancers, but join in with their footwork at the same time!

Janet Fox – (soprano) responsible for dispensing much wisdom and encouragement, memorable for Bible verses texted to me while on recces abroad with Nigel, and for prayer and practical support to many. I have personally known Janet since she was thirteen years old, so we go back a long way. She is an amazing person, and one whom anyone would be glad to have on their side! She has one of the best laughs I've ever heard, has a great second soprano voice and is one of those who come alongside whenever there is a problem and do their bit to put it right! She is also 'Grade A' at hospitality and, as you may already have read, has had first-hand experience of dealing with whatever is thrown at her, when transporting members of the Fry family on tour!

Helen Friday (née Forsdike) – together with Janet above, an indefatigable team player, prepared to take on most things! Helen is a wonderful alto singer/soloist with a remarkably lovable personality. Occasionally, she has acted as Singers' Secretary in Amy's absence, but has principally taken responsibility for Singers' warm-up sessions (effective and hilarious) and both these ladies have taken it upon themselves over the years to administer large amounts of 'fun' and pastoral love wherever possible throughout the NEO family! (I always like to ask Helen to do her impression of an owl hooting the National Anthem! A skill she apparently learned as a youngster while entertaining a completely innocent couple who were sitting on a bench, whilst she was secreted behind a bush!) She has always had a remarkable ability to make our NEO warm-up sessions memorable, with phrases such as 'Benevolent Elephant' or 'Popocatepetl' being proposed as tongue-twisters to keep our lips supple (while our tongues were systematically tied in knots and our eyes streamed with tears of laughter!). Our thanks to Rob, her husband, for releasing Helen to us so often and being such a wonderful support! My immensely grateful thanks also to Helen for the final, professional proofreading of this book! It's been a mammoth task!

Nathan Laxton – NEO Web Manager/tenor – and probably due several awards for bravery in the face of combat! Nathan has a sense of humour that never fails to cheer up his comrades. He and Deb and the family allowed some of us to enjoy the hospitality of their home at the last NEO mail shot to be done by hand prior to NEO's closure! After our NEO webmail went down, Nathan manfully ensured that all our prayer supporters received their bulletins (even if it took him about eleven separate shots of email to do so!). Not for nothing is he nicknamed 'Mr. Beaver'!

Simon Johnston – occasionally serving as Logistics Assistant to Martin Lowe, Simon is a bass singer of quality and also responsible for many a prophetic observation on the P & P! Simon's wife Shelley was remarkably helpful on a Salzburg tour, in sharing her gifts as a GP when required, as well as her talent for soprano singing. Together they have succeeded in producing three beautiful children.

Ernie Dalton – Ernie and his wife Val have faithfully served NEO for years, (Val as an alto singer and percussionist). Ernie, apart from his early stints with Trevor Wright, doing just about everything, has been our main PA technician, and has, over more recent years, been responsible for capturing our events on DAT tape and producing some great recordings which have been hugely useful for rehearsals. The most pristine have been compiled into NEO 'live' CD albums. As though all that were not enough, they also contributed Steve, Jamie and Robin, all capable musicians and Steve and Jamie, capable enablers also, while Robin sings bass and plays trumpet. You will no doubt have found herein Val's memories of the first ever trip to Salzburg with NEO in 1976 (Chapter 3 – *Of Mountains...*)

Sue Rawlings – Sue served for many years as Friends of NEO Secretary – having pinpointed a need and provided the way to meet it! She has a definite ministry of helps as well as administration – even down to updating and dispensing neatly typed address labels for the Swinfords' annual Christmas card list! She is a true star when occasionally seen wielding a teapot also! Sue was not just a secretary, but a real friend to our Friends, and would reply personally to every single letter and go the extra mile to ensure everyone was informed and happy! She has been a devoted prayer warrior and encourager to us all. Thanks, Sue!

Edi Harvey – has a wonderful hospitality ministry, including being hostess of P & P meetings, which includes the provision of all sorts of cakes and biscuits, birthday treats, post-fasting day suppers (a practice begun gloriously by Nicola Gerrard in previous years) and more than one pre-Christmas meal! Pete and I met Edi many years ago, when we were all in our teens. Professionally trained in catering, she not only served at the Jesus Centre in that role, but she has always had a sincere love for the Lord and a talent extraordinaire for caring and providing imaginatively for people, no matter how large or small the group on the receiving end! Edi, we can only cry (as so many of our enthusiastic audiences have done over the years) – "More!"

When NEO was on an away tour, we would often call into the P & P the services of Matt Baynham (left), Thea and Georg Hoelscher (above) and Brigitta Hofer (top left), whose wisdom and insight, and not least practical helps were always highly valued!

And so in conclusion – that, dear friends, is what 'P & P' stands for!

Appendix 3
Their sound has gone out...

Dave Aston with Ernie Dalton & Trevor Wright

Before beginning this list, I would, on behalf of us all in NEO, like to pay tribute to two particular friends who have been faithful servants to NEO since before we even took that name!

---------------- **Dimples** ----------------

We can't have communal gasps!

As early on as the days of *Come Together,* as a teenager, Dave Aston would come along and supply our PA needs! He eventually formed the Digital Audio Co, and has been responsible for either coming to record, or editing and creating our professional recordings for the duration of this ministry, along with the editing of our Salzburg 2005 DVD filmed by John Forrest. His patience and expertise have

been hugely appreciated – he is truly someone of whom we can say, 'Once an NEO, always an NEO'!

Ernie Dalton has also recorded almost every concert since 1979! Some of these recordings have been used to produce *NEO Live!* CDs as shown and have contributed greatly to our archive, but, not least, they have been a huge help to the singers in their personal rehearsal!

Dave Aston

NEO RECORDINGS – the definitive archive

1976
Feast of Praise – Word LP now on CD
Salzburg 1976 – 2 CDs
Jesus Centre Jazz – 1 CD

1979
Recordings edited by Graham Bradburn and Roger Beasley
2 CDs
Seekirchen and Irsdorf – Ernie Dalton and Trevor Wright
2 CDs (including the 'Rodrigo Guitar Concerto' – soloist Pete White)
Official 1979 souvenir 2 CDs
The Hiding Place – 2 CDs

1981
Austria Tour souvenir recording – 2 CDs
First Performance of **'The Celebration Mass'** – 1 CD
Stand up and Live – Jesus Centre Singers + Dave Corbett (music) with lyrics by Colin Day – 1 CD
Celebrate Christmas – Nick Cuthbert, Birmingham Town Hall

1981/2
Enter His Gates – 1 CD

1982
Nottingham Albert Hall – 2 CDs

1983
Celebration Mass – 1 CD
Praise Him Alleluia! – 1 CD
Es gibt ein neues Lied im Land – 1 CD

1987
Live Classics – 1 CD

Live Worship (to be discovered!)

1988
7-29 August. *At Christmas* recorded St Philip with St Stephen, Salford

1990
Friday 24th – Monday 27th August – NEO Recording of *Among The Nations,* Manchester University Chaplaincy.
The Feast of Trumpets Tour: Monday 9th December – Westminster Central Hall (during which the recording of *The Feast of Trumpets* was made by Stephen Robbings)

1992
25th April – NEO recording of Sankey
The Feast of Trumpets cassette released

1994
24/25 Sep. Recording of *Spiritual Songs,* Edgbaston Church of England College for Girls, Edgbaston, Birmingham
29/30 Oct *Orchestral Collection* recorded in the Concert Hall at New Broadcasting House, Manchester

1995
CD *Spiritual Songs* is released along with *The Orchestral Collection* recording of Ibert, Shostakovitch and Messiaen.

1996
NEO Sings Sankey Cassette recording released

1997 30 May/1 June Vigil! CD recorded at St John's Church, Hockley, Birmingham
Director's Choice
August – launch of NEO *Vigil!* CD
At Christmas CD re-released

2000 *Jubilee – A Litany of Thanksgiving* CD launched
New European Orchestra *Stimmt an die Seiten* CD released

2001 *Among the Nations* recording re-released as CD

2004 4/6 March. *A Time to Dance* recorded at St Peter's Halliwell
Salzburg to Symphony Hall – The NEO live! CD released

2006 *NEO in Salzburg* DVD launched

2010 *Lord of the Music* Double CD launched

2012 April. *NEO Live! The Joyful Sound* – CD launched

2016 *Masses of NEO*

2016 12 CDs of NEO Legacy Days

Ernie Dalton at work

Caught on Camera!

This collection of films is quite a remarkable record of the last forty years of NEO work, and we must gratefully acknowledge the tireless efforts of Peter Mortimore, Daphne Ryland and others for capturing these historic moments for us! All the BBC recordings were given to us as a result of the television work we had been invited to do, and John Forrest (former BBC producer who now works independently) was also kind enough to give us the various clips (or 'rushes') he possessed – so we have a wonderfully broad perspective on the last four decades. Obviously much of this material is quite 'mature' now, and so the quality is not necessarily all one would wish, but nevertheless these are precious records.

I cannot leave this page however, without expressing our heartfelt thanks to Carolyn Swinford, who has worked so hard to ensure that all the old videos belonging to various NEO members were gathered together and re-created as DVDs by various means, (mainly her own battles with the Swinford computer!). She and Nigel, with the practical ministrations of Paul Myles, have been willing to spend hours creating the list of 'snippets' which we used for our Legacy Meetings throughout 2016, and which contributed a great deal in terms of awakened memories, poignancy, or just plain hilarity for all present!

List of DVDs of NEO historic footage:

1979   October. *The Hiding Place*

1985   August. *Symphony of the Nations*. Peter Mortimore

1987   August. Salzburg (Susanna Miller)

1990   *Gothenburg '90*
            December. *Still looking Forward to Christmas*

1991   August. Salzburg. Peter Mortimore
            August. Salzburg Residenz
                    The Feast of Trumpets. Peter Mortimore
                    Songs of Praise – St. Mary's Bradford. Peter Mortimore (all)
            March 10. *Songs of Praise* – Cheadle Hulme

1992   August. Spain: Cordoba – Montilla/mixture of 4 venues
            Dec 6. *Big Night Out* tour. Peter Mortimore

1993   Feb/March. *People on the Way* – Six venues
            March 9. *Songs of Praise* – Meadowhall
            August. Salzburg. Peter Mortimore
            July 10. Wells Cathedral. Peter Mortimore
            Dec 11. *Grand Christmas Tour* – Manchester, Peter Mortimore

1994	Jan.	*Vigil Tour*
	Sat 17.	Bristol
	Sat 29.	Birmingham St. Philip's
	Feb 12.	Holy Trinity, Brompton
	April 1.	*Journey to the Cross*. (Jonathan Fulford) BBC
	May 21	Lincoln Cathedral. Peter Mortimore
	Nov 11	*Yorkshire Vigil* – Linton
1995	Jan	BBC *Songs of Praise* – Sankey – Bolton
	Jan 14	*Vigil for Great Britain*: Winchester Cathedral
	Jan 21	Holy Trinity Brompton/Manchester
	Jan 28	St Philip's Birmingham Peter Mort
	Feb 2	Bradford Cathedral
	Feb 4	Manchester Cathedral
	July 3	Hereford Cathedral
	July 28	Sierning. Peter Mortimore
	August	1. *Dance Messiah* on Jedermann. Peter Mortimore
		2. Various – *Elijah*, Altermarkt etc. Peter Mortimore
		Salzburg dance. Peter Mortimore
		Various BBC *Songs of Praise* – On Ice at Blackpool
	Dec 20	*Grand Christmas Gala* – Free Trade Hall Manchester. Peter Mortimore
1996	Sept. 3	BBC *Songs of Praise 35th Anniversary*
	Dec 9	BBC *Songs of Praise,* Vienna
1997	Feb 9	*Songs of Praise*, Bournville (Cadbury's)
		Salzburg Dance. Paul Myles
1998	July 18	*Vigil for the Nation* – Centenary Square with Fireworks
2000	March	*Litany of Thanksgiving* (March) Worcester Cathedral
	October	*Fascinatin' Rhythm* (Oct)
2001		Bradford *Songs of Praise* (BBC)
2002	Feb 9	Rochester
	Feb 23	Vigil Manchester Cathedral
	Dec 25	Christmas Day – St Peter's Bolton
2003	August	Salzburg – 2 DVDs
2004	August	St. Cyprian's – *Mourning to Dancing*

2005	August	John Forrest – rushes
	August	Salzburg (Daphne Ryland)
2007	September	Rome (Daphne)
2008	August	Salzburg – 2 DVDs (Daphne)
	September	Rome – 2 DVDs (Daphne)
2009	Sept/Oct 21	Canterbury
		Rome – 2 DVDs (Daphne)
2010	August	Rome – Laterano/Pantheon/
		Papal Visit Hyde Park (Daphne)
	Sept 10	*Papal Visit to Hyde Park* (Sky News)
2013	August	Rome (Paul Myles)
2016	January 16	40th Birthday Concert, Town Hall Birmingham (Paul Myles)
2016		3 CDs of snippets created NEO Legacy Days

Peter Mortimore filming

Appendix 4
Staircase to Heaven

The compositions of Nigel Swinford:

Songs composed by Nigel Swinford with lyrics by Colin Day 1977:

> Psalm 9
>
> The Gypsy Song
>
> Marriage at Sunrise (aka 'The Bridegroom Song')
>
> Take me with you

The Hiding Place 1979

Salzburger Festmesse 1981

Symphony of the Nations 1985 (Swedish Movement added 1990)

Feast of Trumpets 1991

Jazz Parables – Wise and Foolish Virgins

Sonne der Gerechtigkeit 1999

Missa Brevis 2013

Salzburger Festmesse II 2014

Conversations for Trumpet and Orchestra 2014

Sentences from the Song of Loves 2014

Numerous songs, innumerable arrangements, and music for television

Appendix 5
The NEO Timeline

FIRST TOUR TO SALZBURG

1976

1977

Above the timeline (1976):

- **JAN 2** — The orchestra forms and takes the title: **Feast of Praise Orchestra** for first concert, Town Hall, Birmingham
- **JUL 15** — Jesus Centre choir practices began regularly on Thursdays
- **1ST SUMMER TOUR TO SALZBURG**
- **NOV** — Event at Hasbury

Above the timeline (1977):

- **JAN 1** — **The Trumpets are Sounding** Town Hall, Birmingham
- **FEB 3** — Rehearsal of **'If my People'** conducted by Val Dalton
- **FEB 26** — **Praise and Worship** New Road Baptist Church Bromsgrove
- **APR 16** — **The Trumpets are Sounding** Birmingham Cathedral with Rev David MacInnes
- **MAY 21** — **Praise and Worship** in a church in Wolverhampton
- **JUN 18** — **The Trumpets are Sounding** Birmingham Cathedral – David MacInnes. Speaking on evangelism
- **JUL 16** — **The Trumpets are Sounding** (final event with David MacInnes)
- **JUL 29** — **York Festival Concert** with orchestra and singers
- **SEP 11** — **Service at Sutton Baptist Church. Rushall Praise rally** in the evening

Below the timeline (1976):

- **JUN 25** — Singers met at Jesus Centre for prayer and discussion about Salzburg
- **JUL 22** — Concert in Birmingham Cathedral
- **SEP 18** — Duke Street 'Reunion Concert'
- **DEC 12** — Evening of worship at Chawn Hill Church

Below the timeline (1977):

- **JAN 3** — **The Trumpets are Sounding** Town Hall, Birmingham
- **FEB 5** — Cathedral follow up event to 'Trumpets are Sounding'. Conductor: Val Dalton
- **MAR 26** — **Come Alive Together** St. John's Harborne
- **MAY 3-7** — **Stoneleigh Camp** Singers and Jesus Centre Jazz group
- **MAY 28** — **Festival of the Holy Spirit** St Mary's Leamington Spa (Flower Festival)
- **JUL 9** — **Droitwich** Petertide Communion
- **JUL 24** — **Morning Worship with Jazz Band** recording
- **SEP 10** — Sutton Town Hall **Trinity Fair**
- **END OF SEP/OCT** — **Jubilee Harvest Flower Festival** St Martin's in the Bullring

298

1977 (CONTINUED)

Thanksgiving Service at venue in Bromsgrove — NOV 12

Birmingham Cathedral – lunchtime event — NOV 29

Concert at Jesus Centre — DEC 3

Praise and Glory Town Hall, Birmingham — DEC 30

NOV 19 — **Birmingham Cathedral event** – speaker Jean Darnell

NOV 29 — **Praise and Glory** Town Hall, Birmingham

DEC 12 — **Lunchtime Carols** at Tuesday Talks Birmingham Cathedral

1978

The Love Feast: 'Thanking God with Bread and Wine' at St Philip's Cathedral. 'Celebrating the Cross with Bread and Wine' – also at St Philip's Cathedral — FEB 14

Bearwood Gospel Hall — APR 12

Event at Anglican Church Kidderminster — MAR 18

Open Air at venue in Leamington Spa — SUMMER

APRIL — **'The Witness' musical** launched

APRIL — **Torch Trust event** in West Bromwich

MAY 6 — **Worcester Council of Churches/Wycliffe Bible Translators events**

DEC 30 — **Let my People Go**

1979

Rejoice Greatly Manchester, Free Trade Hall — JAN 6

Hume Street Gospel Hall — JAN 18

Bowley Park Baptist Church, Kidderminster — FEB 3

CYFA Rally Carrs Lane URC Birmingham — MAR 3

JAN 13 — Birmingham Cathedral

JAN 31 — **Concert with Anne Linstrum** – Stourport Civic Centre

FEB 11 — Westbury Chapel, Wolverhampton

MAR 31 — Event, City Road Methodist Church

1979 (CONTINUED)

APR 27 — Singers perform during rally, Birmingham Bull Ring with Juan Carlos Ortiz

APR 29 — Supported evangelistic event following Ortiz at Shirley Baptist Church

MAY 26 — Camp at Stafford Agricultural Showground – weekend arranged by Jesus Centre

JUL 8 — Event at Church in Sparkbrook

SUMMER — Goosemore Lane Residents' Association

JUL 20 TO AUG 4 — 2ND SALZBURG TOUR — Under the name of The New English Orchestra (Chris Bell becomes the Central Administrator)

SECOND TOUR TO SALZBURG

SEP 15 — Concert at Rugby Town Hall (famed for the notorious performance of the Hallelujah Chorus with two guitars which Chris' thought was awful!)

SEP 21 — Free to Serve Worcs Diocese Festival of Music at Worcester Cathedral

SEP 22 — Hosanna 79 Festival Handsworth Park with the West Indian Community

OCT 9-13 — The Hiding Place Birmingham Hippodrome

NOV 10 — Event at Bromsgrove Baptist Church

NOV 13 — Event at Pheasey Evangelical Church

DEC 18 — Birmingham Cathedral lunchtime Carol Service

DEC 20 — Carol Service in Erdington

1980

MAY 28 — Worcester Cathedral

JUL 5 — Llandaff Cathedral

1981

JAN 2 — Stand up and Live

MAR 19 — City Road Methodist, Birmingham

MAR 21 — Cannon Street Baptist Church, Handsworth

MAR 27 — Cadbury's

MAR 28 — Astwood Bank

APR 2 — Elim, Golden Hillock

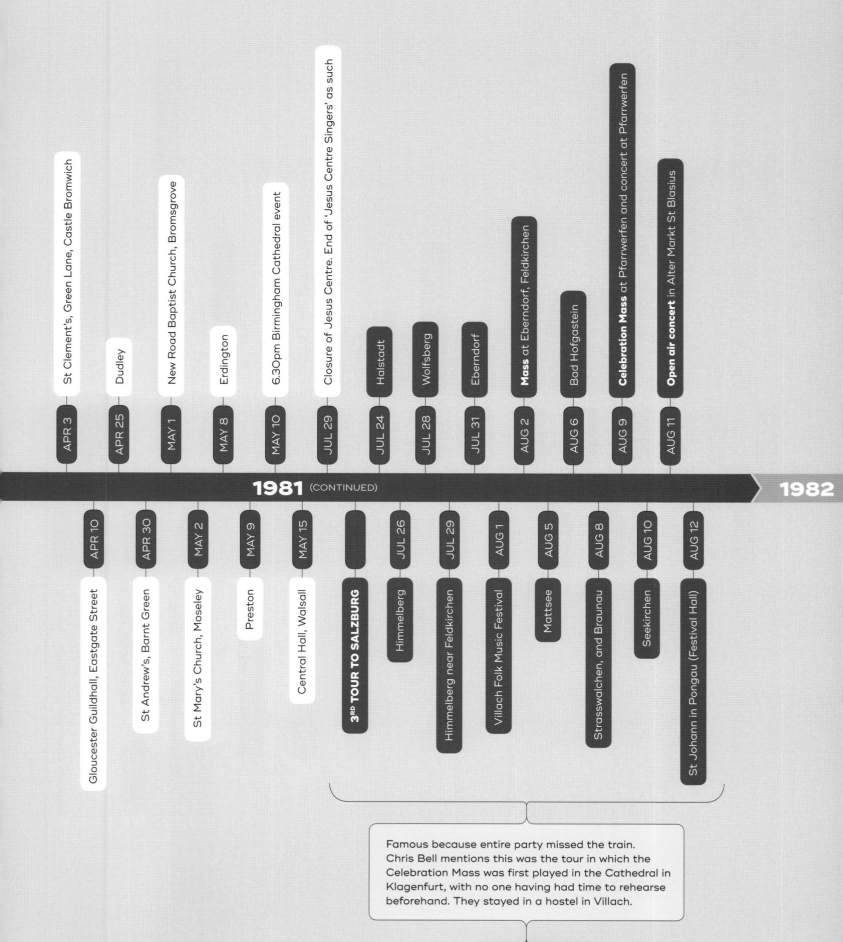

1981 (CONTINUED)

1982

APR 3 — St Clement's, Green Lane, Castle Bromwich

APR 10 — Gloucester Guildhall, Eastgate Street

APR 25 — Dudley

APR 30 — St Andrew's, Barnt Green

MAY 1 — New Road Baptist Church, Bromsgrove

MAY 2 — St Mary's Church, Moseley

MAY 8 — Erdington

MAY 9 — Preston

MAY 10 — 6.30pm Birmingham Cathedral event

MAY 15 — Central Hall, Walsall

JUL 29 — Closure of Jesus Centre. End of 'Jesus Centre Singers' as such

JUL 24 — Halstadt

JUL 26 — Himmelberg

JUL 28 — Wolfsberg

JUL 29 — Himmelberg near Feldkirchen

JUL 31 — Eberndorf

AUG 1 — Villach Folk Music Festival

AUG 2 — **Mass** at Eberndorf, Feldkirchen

AUG 5 — Mattsee

AUG 6 — Bad Hofgastein

AUG 8 — Strasswalchen, and Braunau

AUG 9 — **Celebration Mass** at Pfarrwerfen and concert at Pfarrwerfen

AUG 10 — Seekirchen

AUG 11 — **Open air concert** in Alter Markt St Blasius

AUG 12 — St Johann in Pongau (Festival Hall)

3RD TOUR TO SALZBURG

Famous because entire party missed the train.
Chris Bell mentions this was the tour in which the
Celebration Mass was first played in the Cathedral in
Klagenfurt, with no one having had time to rehearse
beforehand. They stayed in a hostel in Villach.

**THIRD
TOUR TO
SALZBURG**

1982

1983

Dudley Town Hall – including the **Celebration Mass**
JAN 1

Westminster Central Hall – including the **Celebration Mass**
FEB 6

JAN 4
Birmingham Town Hall

FEB 13
Feast of Praise Albert Hall, Nottingham

Mass Celebration Birmingham Town Hall
JAN 3

Concert St Margaret's Aspley
JAN 4

Westminster Cathedral (Catholic Charismatic Association)
APR 23

Celebration Mass Clifton Cathedral, Bristol
JUN 5

4TH TOUR TO SALZBURG

Himmelberg
JUL 30

Villach
AUG 1

Mattsee Parish Church
AUG 5

Strassvalchen Parish Hall
AUG 7

Alter Markt concert, Salzburg (St Blasius) St Peter's concert
AUG 11

Westminster Cathedral (Catholic Charismatic Association)
OCT 1

JAN 4
Mass Celebration Royal Centre Nottingham plus recording

APR 9
Ripon Cathedral

JUN 4
A Celebration Evening Colston Hall, Bristol

JUN 18
Midsummer Prom Birmingham Town Hall

JUL 28
St Veit a.d. Glan

JUL 31
Eberndorf Benedictine Church

AUG 2
Eberndorf Benedictine Church

AUG 6
Bad Hofgastein Parish Church

AUG 9
Vinzenz Pallotti Church, Lehen, morning Mass Pfarrwerfen Parish Church evening Mass followed by a concert

AUG 12
St Johann in Pongau Great Festival Hall

DEC 19
Celebrate Christmas Birmingham Town Hall

FOURTH TOUR TO SALZBURG

Timeline

1984

- **APR 28** — **Celebration Evening** Royal Centre Nottingham
- **JUN 9** — **Shout Alleluia!** Town Hall, Birmingham
- **JUL 14** — Colston Hall, Bristol

1985

- Nigel writing the **Symphony of Nations**
- **Spring Celebration** concerts
- **APR 9** — Rehearsals in Devon from April
- **APR 12** — St Mary's Bideford
- **APR 14** — St Peter's, Barnstaple
- **MAY 4** — **Symphony of the Nations premiere** Matinee and evening concerts, Town Hall, Birmingham
- **MAY 18** — Free Trade Hall, Manchester
- **MAY 19** — **Celebration Mass** Salford Cathedral
- **5TH TOUR TO SALZBURG**
- **JUL 25** — Party flew by chartered aircraft from Gatwick
- **JUL 28** — 09.00 **Celebration Mass** Lehen / 19.00 **Celebration Mass** / 20.00 Concert, Pfarrwerfen
- **JUL 29** — **Symphony of Nations** Kapitelplatz
- **JUL 30** — Parish Church, Mondsee
- **JUL 31** — 15.00 Alter Markt / 19.30 Kolpinghaus
- **AUG 1** — **Symphony of Nations** Kapitelplatz
- **AUG 2** — Free day
- **AUG 3** — **Concert** Sierning
- **AUG 4** — 11.15 Salzburg Dom **Celebration Mass** Parish Church, Bad Hofgastein / Followed by **Symphony of Nations**
- **AUG 5** — **Symphony of Nations** Kapitelplatz
- **AUG 6** — 15.00 **Open air concert** Alter Markt / 19.30 St Peter's Stiftskirche
- **AUG 7** — St Andreas

1986

Fifth Salzburg Tour with **'Symphony of Nations'**.
Our enablers built a scaffolding stage in the
Kapitelplatz for NEO Singers & Dancers.

FIFTH TOUR TO SALZBURG

303

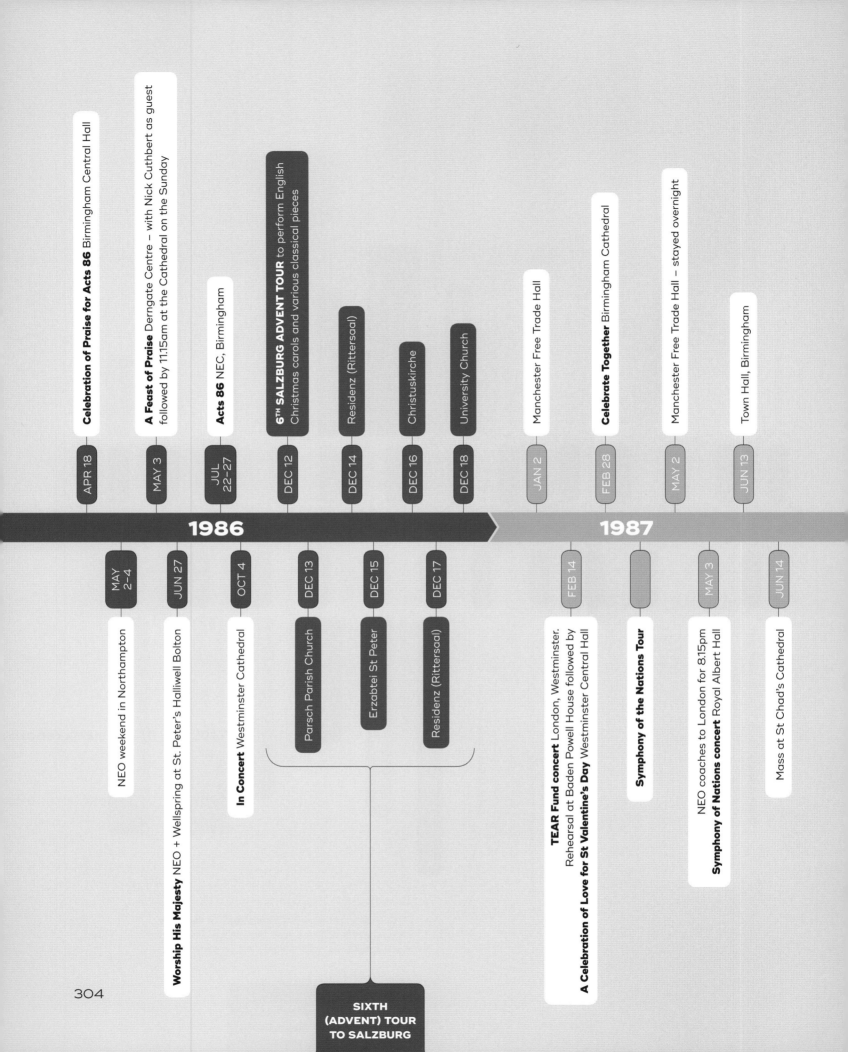

Celebration of Praise for Acts 86 Birmingham Central Hall

A Feast of Praise Derngate Centre – with Nick Cuthbert as guest followed by 11.15am at the Cathedral on the Sunday

Acts 86 NEC, Birmingham

6TH SALZBURG ADVENT TOUR to perform English Christmas carols and various classical pieces

Residenz (Rittersaal)

Christuskirche

University Church

Manchester Free Trade Hall

Celebrate Together Birmingham Cathedral

Manchester Free Trade Hall – stayed overnight

Town Hall, Birmingham

APR 18

MAY 3

JUL 22–27

DEC 12

DEC 14

DEC 16

DEC 18

JAN 2

FEB 28

MAY 2

JUN 13

1986

1987

MAY 2–4

JUN 27

OCT 4

DEC 13

DEC 15

DEC 17

FEB 14

MAY 3

JUN 14

NEO weekend in Northampton

Worship His Majesty NEO + Wellspring at St. Peter's Halliwell Bolton

In Concert Westminster Cathedral

Parsch Parish Church

Erzabtei St Peter

Residenz (Rittersaal)

TEAR Fund concert London, Westminster. Rehearsal at Baden Powell House followed by

A Celebration of Love for St Valentine's Day Westminster Central Hall

Symphony of the Nations Tour

NEO coaches to London for 8.15pm
Symphony of Nations concert Royal Albert Hall

Mass at St Chad's Cathedral

SIXTH (ADVENT) TOUR TO SALZBURG

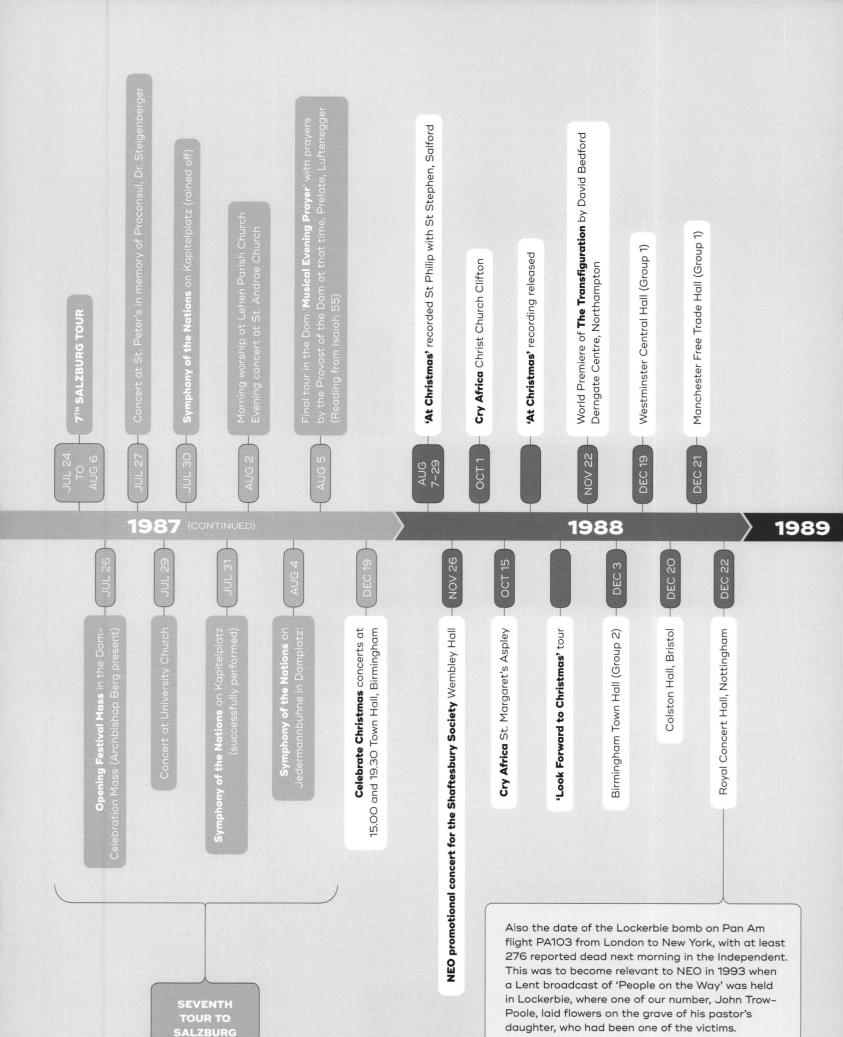

7TH SALZBURG TOUR

JUL 24 TO AUG 6

Concert at St. Peter's in memory of Proconsul, Dr. Steigenberger

JUL 27

Symphony of the Nations on Kapitelplatz (rained off)

JUL 30

Morning worship at Lehen Parish Church Evening concert at St. Andrae Church

AUG 2

Final tour in the Dom '**Musical Evening Prayer**' with prayers by the Provost of the Dom at that time, Prelate, Luftenegger (Reading from Isaiah 55)

AUG 5

'**At Christmas**' recorded St Philip with St Stephen, Salford

AUG 7–29

Cry Africa Christ Church Clifton

OCT 1

'**At Christmas**' recording released

World Premiere of **The Transfiguration** by David Bedford Derngate Centre, Northampton

NOV 22

Westminster Central Hall (Group 1)

DEC 19

Manchester Free Trade Hall (Group 1)

DEC 21

1987 (CONTINUED)   **1988**   **1989**

JUL 26

JUL 29

JUL 31

AUG 4

DEC 19

NOV 26

OCT 15

DEC 3

DEC 20

DEC 22

Opening Festival Mass in the Dom- Celebration Mass (Archbishop Berg present)

Concert at University Church

Symphony of the Nations on Kapitelplatz (successfully performed)

Symphony of the Nations on Jedermannbuhne in Domplatz!

Celebrate Christmas concerts at 15.00 and 19.30 Town Hall, Birmingham

NEO promotional concert for the Shaftesbury Society Wembley Hall

Cry Africa St. Margaret's Aspley

'**Look Forward to Christmas**' tour

Birmingham Town Hall (Group 2)

Colston Hall, Bristol

Royal Concert Hall, Nottingham

SEVENTH TOUR TO SALZBURG

Also the date of the Lockerbie bomb on Pan Am flight PA103 from London to New York, with at least 276 reported dead next morning in the Independent. This was to become relevant to NEO in 1993 when a Lent broadcast of 'People on the Way' was held in Lockerbie, where one of our number, John Trow- Poole, laid flowers on the grave of his pastor's daughter, who had been one of the victims.

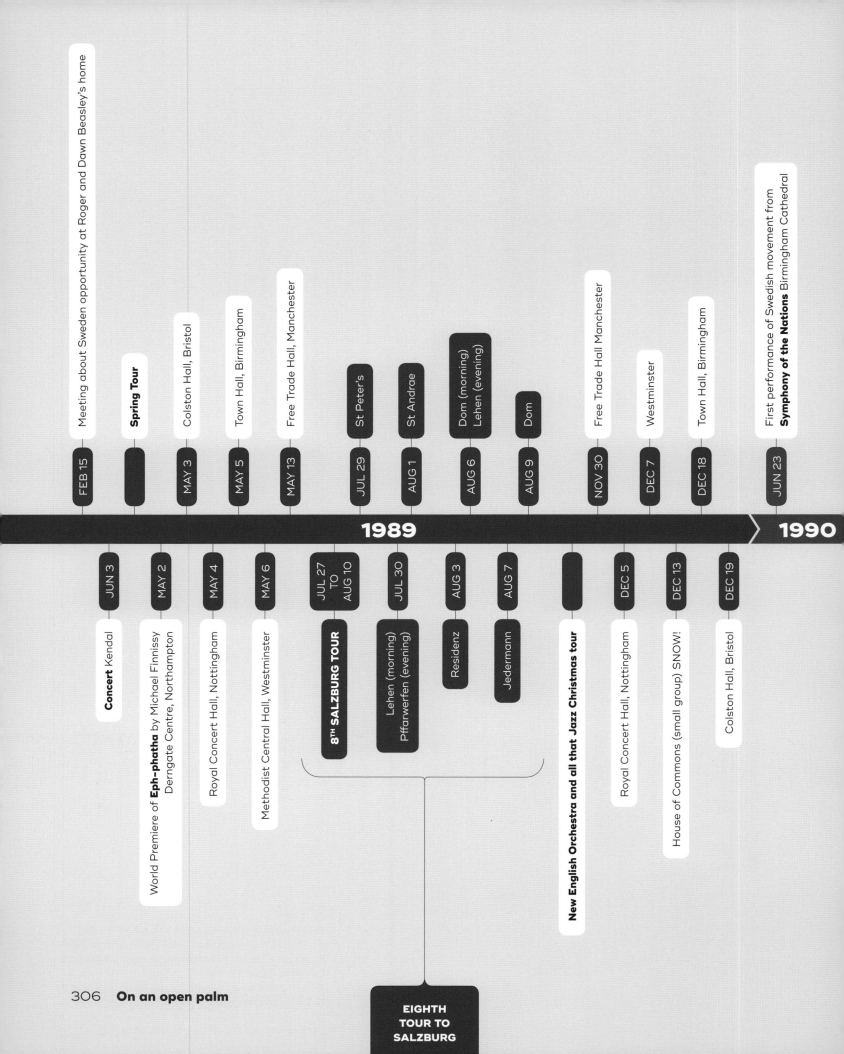

Meeting about Sweden opportunity at Roger and Dawn Beasley's home

Spring Tour

Colston Hall, Bristol

Town Hall, Birmingham

Free Trade Hall, Manchester

St Peter's

St Andrae

Dom (morning)
Lehen (evening)

Dom

Free Trade Hall Manchester

Westminster

Town Hall, Birmingham

First performance of Swedish movement from
Symphony of the Nations Birmingham Cathedral

FEB 15

MAY 3

MAY 5

MAY 13

JUL 29

AUG 1

AUG 6

AUG 9

NOV 30

DEC 7

DEC 18

JUN 23

1989

1990

JUN 3

MAY 2

MAY 4

MAY 6

JUL 27
TO
AUG 10

JUL 30

AUG 3

AUG 7

DEC 5

DEC 13

DEC 19

Concert Kendal

World Premiere of **Eph-phatha** by Michael Finnissy
Derngate Centre, Northampton

Royal Concert Hall, Nottingham

Methodist Central Hall, Westminster

8ᵀᴴ SALZBURG TOUR

Lehen (morning)
Pffarwerfen (evening)

Residenz

Jedermann

New English Orchestra and all that Jazz Christmas tour

Royal Concert Hall, Nottingham

House of Commons (small group) SNOW!

Colston Hall, Bristol

**EIGHTH
TOUR TO
SALZBURG**

Stormy start to the year – and war with Iraq broke midnight 16 January with air strikes on military targets in Iraq and Kuwait.

NINTH TOUR TO SALZBURG

Gothenburg 90

Singers to Sweden with **Symphony of the Nations**, Swedish Movement 2 Conference at the Scandinavium began that evening

Recorded BBC Choir Girl of the Year (Susan Gray) with Don Maclean

Chris Bell's funeral – NEO members sang

Still Looking Forward to Christmas Tour

Colston Hall, Bristol

BBC recording, Cheadle Hulme – Songs of Praise Hymn writing competition

BBC Songs of Praise programme from Cheadle Hulme, broadcast 6.40pm

János Czifra in London with NEO

Rehearsals followed by first concert at St Peter's

Residenz event

Second St Peter's concert

The Feast of Trumpets Jedermannbühne, Domplatz

JUL 4 · JUL 13 · AUG 29 · DEC 18 · FEB 27 · APR 14 · JUL 13–14 · JUL 26 · JUL 31 · AUG 2 · AUG 6

1990 (CONTINUED)

1991

JUL 2 · JUL 9 · AUG 24–27 · DEC 13 · DEC 19 · JUN 8 · JUL 24 · JUL 28 · AUG 1 · AUG 3

Orchestra and Dancers

Returned to Heathrow

NEO Recording of **Among The Nations**

Among the Nations cassette recording released

Christmas Concert and Reception, Manchester

Royal Theatre, Nottingham

Nigel leaves Salford University College and goes full-time with NEO supported by a Trust Fund

Nigel composes **The Feast of Trumpets**

The Feast of Trumpets Town Hall, Birmingham

Flights to Salzburg (via Munich)

Morning Mass at Dom (Missa Brevis)

Orchestra to St Gilgen

Evening: Sierning Village worship evening led by Pete & Julie Fry

Abendlob in Dom

This was the weekend that we heard of the sad death of Chris Bell.

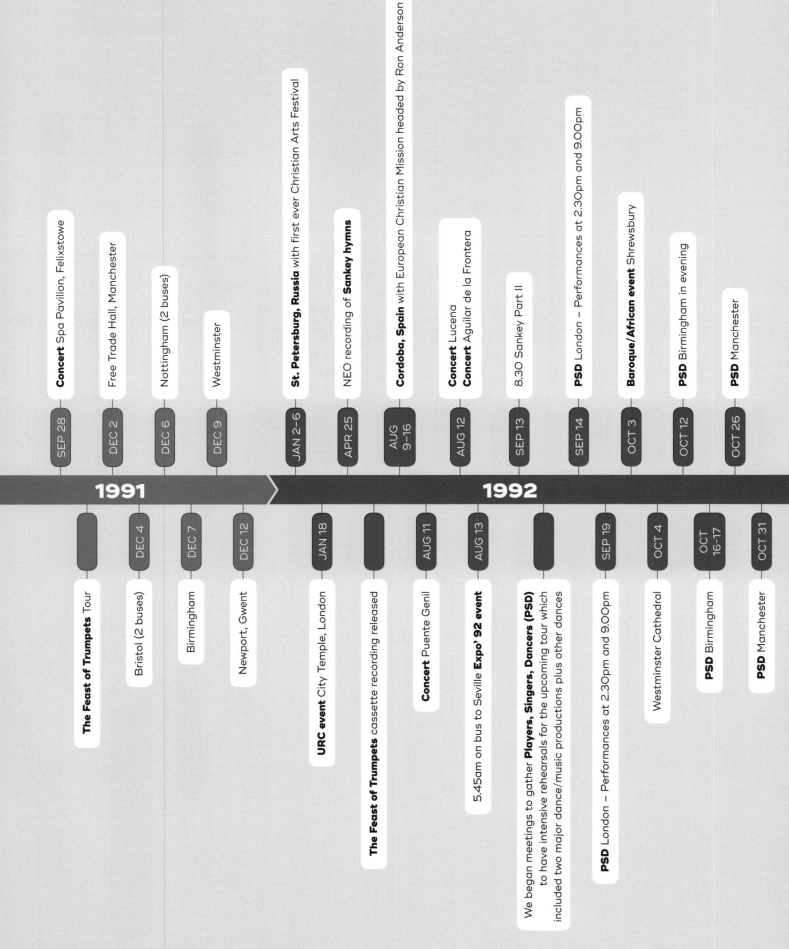

1991

Concert Spa Pavilion, Felixstowe — SEP 28

The Feast of Trumpets Tour

Bristol (2 buses) — DEC 4

Free Trade Hall, Manchester — DEC 2

Nottingham (2 buses) — DEC 6

Birmingham — DEC 7

Westminster — DEC 9

Newport, Gwent — DEC 12

1992

St. Petersburg, Russia with first ever Christian Arts Festival — JAN 2-6

URC event City Temple, London — JAN 18

NEO recording of Sankey hymns — APR 25

The Feast of Trumpets cassette recording released

Cordoba, Spain with European Christian Mission headed by Ron Anderson — AUG 9-16

Concert Puente Genil — AUG 11

Concert Lucena
Concert Aguilar de la Frontera — AUG 12

5.45am on bus to Seville Expo' 92 event — AUG 13

8.30 Sankey Part II — SEP 13

We began meetings to gather Players, Singers, Dancers (PSD) to have intensive rehearsals for the upcoming tour which included two major dance/music productions plus other dances

PSD London – Performances at 2.30pm and 9.00pm — SEP 14

PSD London – Performances at 2.30pm and 9.00pm — SEP 19

Baroque/African event Shrewsbury — OCT 3

Westminster Cathedral — OCT 4

PSD Birmingham in evening — OCT 12

PSD Birmingham — OCT 16-17

PSD Manchester — OCT 26

PSD Manchester — OCT 31

All featuring the Parable of the Wise and Foolish Virgins (composed by Nigel Swinford and choreographed by Jillian Mackrill, then of the Birmingham Royal Ballet), the Swedish Movement of Symphony of the Nations, Porgy & Bess Suite, Glen Miller, Duke Ellington, Larry Norman and Ira D. Sankey.

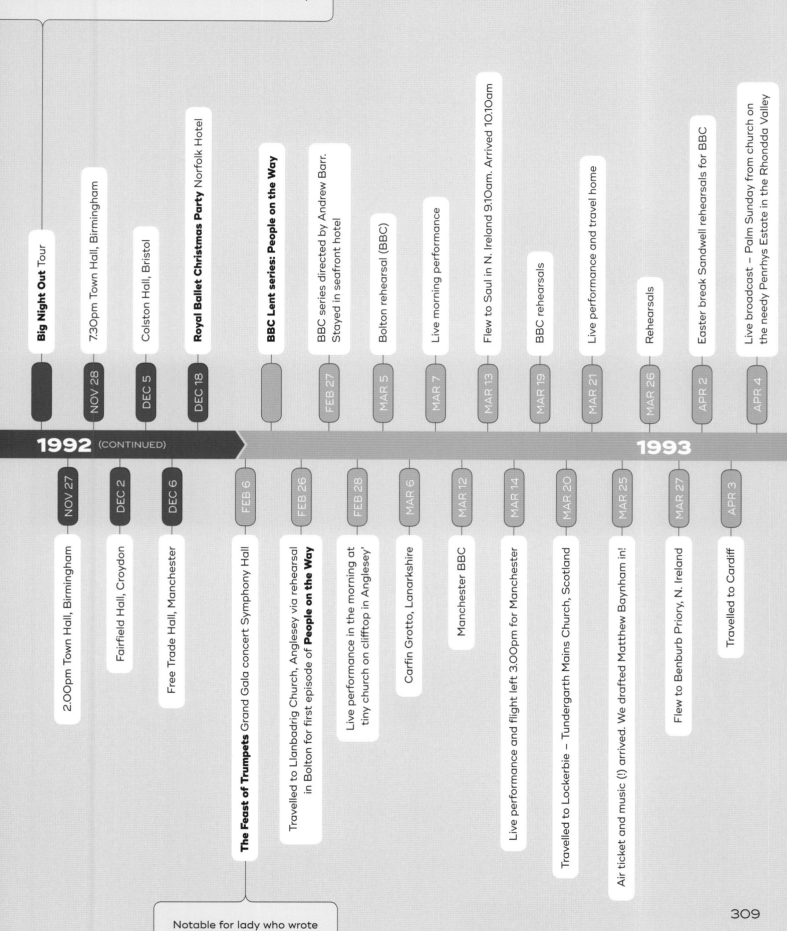

Big Night Out Tour

7.30pm Town Hall, Birmingham

Colston Hall, Bristol

Royal Ballet Christmas Party Norfolk Hotel

BBC Lent series: People on the Way

BBC series directed by Andrew Barr. Stayed in seafront hotel

Bolton rehearsal (BBC)

Live morning performance

Flew to Saul in N. Ireland 9.10am. Arrived 10.10am

BBC rehearsals

Live performance and travel home

Rehearsals

Easter break Sandwell rehearsals for BBC

Live broadcast – Palm Sunday from church on the needy Penrhys Estate in the Rhondda Valley

NOV 28

DEC 5

DEC 18

FEB 27

MAR 5

MAR 7

MAR 13

MAR 19

MAR 21

MAR 26

APR 2

APR 4

1992 (CONTINUED)

1993

NOV 27

DEC 2

DEC 6

FEB 6

FEB 26

FEB 28

MAR 6

MAR 12

MAR 14

MAR 20

MAR 25

MAR 27

APR 3

2.00pm Town Hall, Birmingham

Fairfield Hall, Croydon

Free Trade Hall, Manchester

The Feast of Trumpets Grand Gala concert Symphony Hall

Travelled to Llanbadrig Church, Anglesey via rehearsal in Bolton for first episode of **People on the Way**

Live performance in the morning at tiny church on clifftop in Anglesey'

Carfin Grotto, Lanarkshire

Manchester BBC

Live performance and flight left 3.00pm for Manchester

Travelled to Lockerbie – Tundergarth Mains Church, Scotland

Air ticket and music (!) arrived. We drafted Matthew Baynham in!

Flew to Benburb Priory, N. Ireland

Travelled to Cardiff

Notable for lady who wrote to Julia 3 months later so far healed of panic attacks.

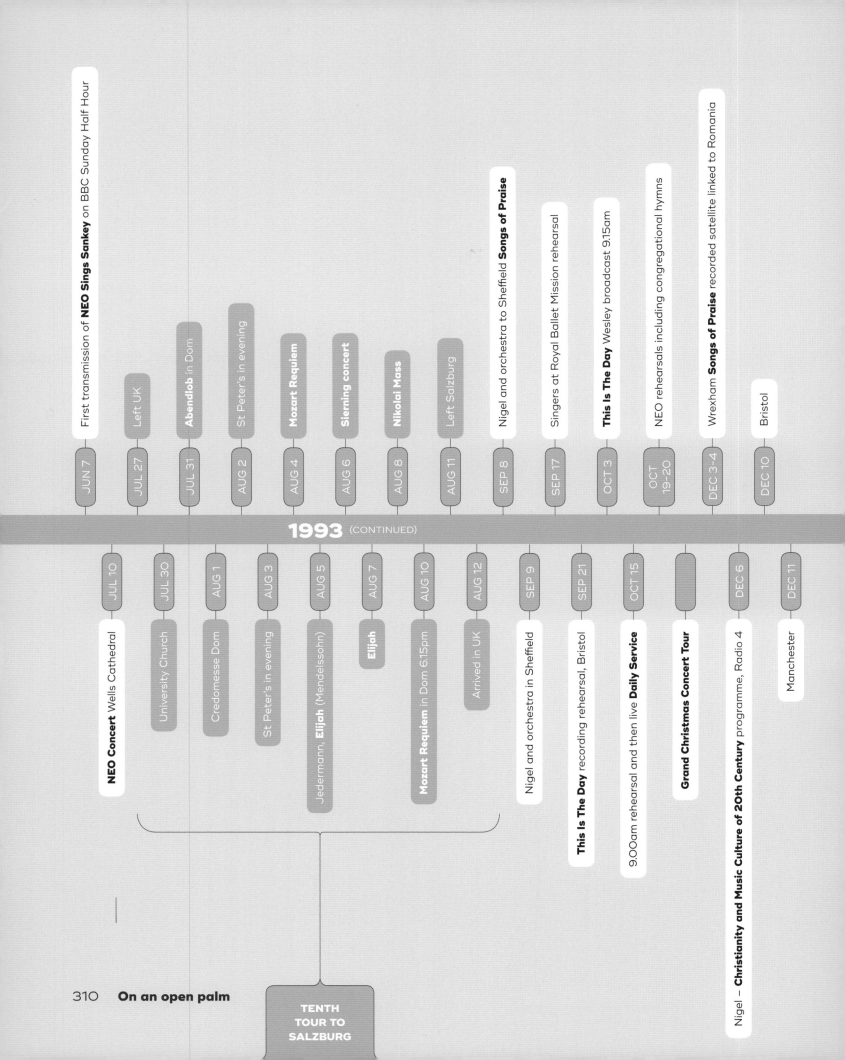

First transmission of **NEO Sings Sankey** on BBC Sunday Half Hour — JUN 7

Left UK — JUL 27

Abendlob in Dom — JUL 31

St Peter's in evening — AUG 2

Mozart Requiem — AUG 4

Sierning concert — AUG 6

Nikolai Mass — AUG 8

Left Salzburg — AUG 11

Nigel and orchestra to Sheffield **Songs of Praise** — SEP 8

Singers at Royal Ballet Mission rehearsal — SEP 17

This Is The Day Wesley broadcast 9.15am — OCT 3

NEO rehearsals including congregational hymns — OCT 19–20

Wrexham **Songs of Praise** recorded satellite linked to Romania — DEC 3–4

Bristol — DEC 10

1993 (CONTINUED)

JUL 10 — **NEO Concert** Wells Cathedral

JUL 30 — University Church

AUG 1 — Credomesse Dom

AUG 3 — St Peter's in evening

AUG 5 — Jedermann, **Elijah** (Mendelssohn)

AUG 7 — **Elijah**

AUG 10 — **Mozart Requiem** in Dom 615pm

AUG 12 — Arrived in UK

SEP 9 — Nigel and orchestra in Sheffield

SEP 21 — **This Is The Day** recording rehearsal, Bristol

OCT 15 — 9.00am rehearsal and then live **Daily Service**

DEC 6 — **Grand Christmas Concert Tour**

DEC 11 — Manchester

Nigel – **Christianity and Music Culture of 20th Century** programme, Radio 4

TENTH TOUR TO SALZBURG

1994

Above the timeline:

- **DEC 12** — Orchestra to London Palladium to lead Charity show, **Sign of the Son** featuring Roy Castle in possibly his last performance
- **DEC 15** — Central Hall, London
- **DEC 20** — Third of Nigel's **Music Culture** radio talks
- **Vigil Tour**
- **JAN 19** — **Big Band Songs of Praise** recording London
- **JAN 29** — St Philip's Cathedral, Birmingham
- **FEB 12** — **Vigil** Holy Trinity Brompton, London
- **MAR 18** — Rehearsal for Care event
- **APR 1** — Good Friday broadcast 11 a.m. BBC 1 featuring Allegri Miserere (J. Fulford producer)
- **EARLY SUMMER** — Nigel wrote incidental music for **This is the Day** programmes on BBC1 featuring Liz Davidson and Kirsten Hellier multitasking on violin, harp, tin whistle and drum and following a canal boat journey
- **SEP 24–25** — Recording of **Spiritual Songs**, Edgbaston Church of England College for Girls, Edgbaston, Birmingham
- **OCT 16** — **World of Faith** broadcast on BBC Radio 2

Below the timeline:

- **DEC 13** — Second **Music Culture** radio programme Evening: Symphony Hall, Birmingham
- **DEC 18** — Small group to London Athenaeum Club in Pall Mall for Christmas Carols and lunch
- **NEO Friends** organisation is formed
- **JAN 15** — **Vigil** Bristol Cathedral
- **JAN 28** — St Chad's Cathedral, Birmingham
- **FEB 5** — **Vigil** Manchester Cathedral
- In March, Nigel records first **Seeds of Faith** Radio 4 programme, with the second a couple of days later
- **MAR 21–22** — Recording/Care event at Aston University promoting Rob Parsons' book **Loving Against the Odds**
- **MAY 21** — Lincoln Cathedral (and Royal Ballet dancers)
- **SEP 15** — St Philip's Cathedral, Birmingham with Anthony Collins (21st)
- **OCT 3** — **World of Faith** recording for BBC, London
- **OCT 29–30** — **Orchestral Collection** recorded in the Concert Hall at New Broadcasting House, Manchester

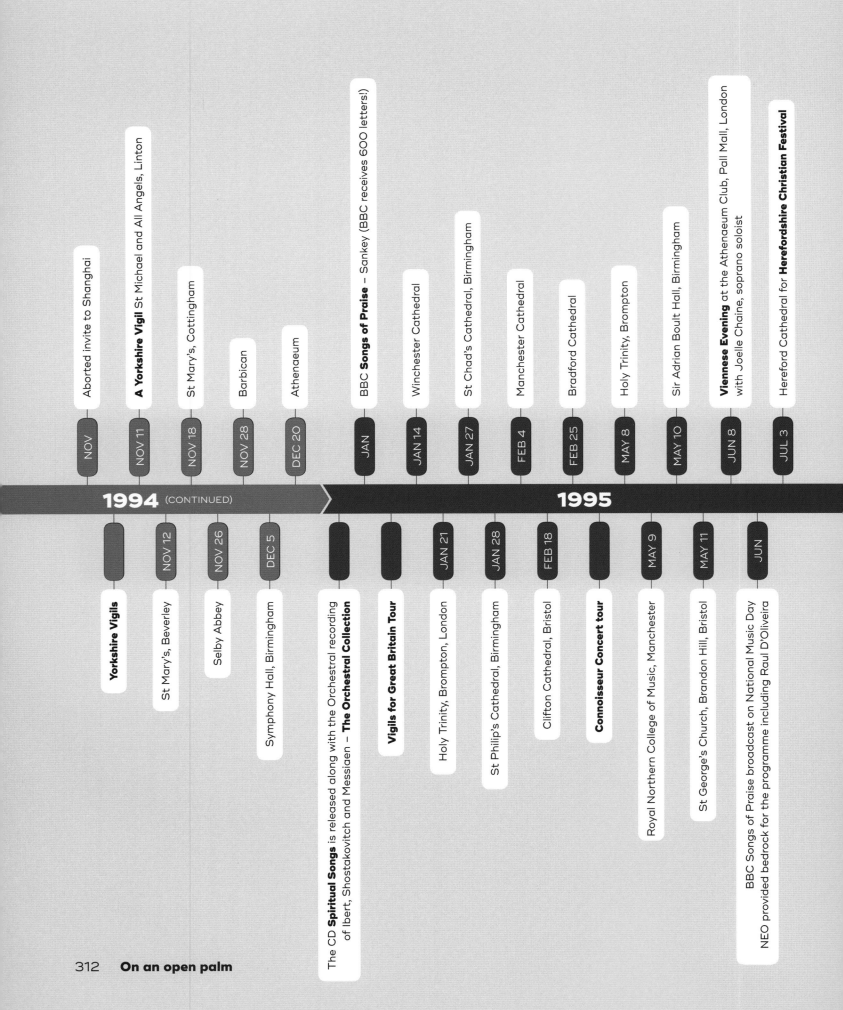

Aborted invite to Shanghai

A Yorkshire Vigil St Michael and All Angels, Linton

St Mary's, Cottingham

Barbican

Athenaeum

BBC **Songs of Praise** – Sankey (BBC receives 600 letters!)

Winchester Cathedral

St Chad's Cathedral, Birmingham

Manchester Cathedral

Bradford Cathedral

Holy Trinity, Brompton

Sir Adrian Boult Hall, Birmingham

Viennese Evening at the Athenaeum Club, Pall Mall, London with Joelle Chaine, soprano soloist

Hereford Cathedral for **Herefordshire Christian Festival**

NOV

NOV 11

NOV 18

NOV 28

DEC 20

JAN

JAN 14

JAN 27

FEB 4

FEB 25

MAY 8

MAY 10

JUN 8

JUL 3

1994 (CONTINUED)

1995

Yorkshire Vigils

St Mary's, Beverley

Selby Abbey

Symphony Hall, Birmingham

The CD **Spiritual Songs** is released along with the Orchestral recording of Ibert, Shostakovitch and Messiaen – **The Orchestral Collection**

Vigils for Great Britain Tour

Holy Trinity, Brompton, London

St Philip's Cathedral, Birmingham

Clifton Cathedral, Bristol

Connoisseur Concert tour

Royal Northern College of Music, Manchester

St George's Church, Brandon Hill, Bristol

BBC Songs of Praise broadcast on National Music Day NEO provided bedrock for the programme including Raul D'Oliveira

NOV 12

NOV 26

DEC 5

JAN 21

JAN 28

FEB 18

MAY 9

MAY 11

JUN

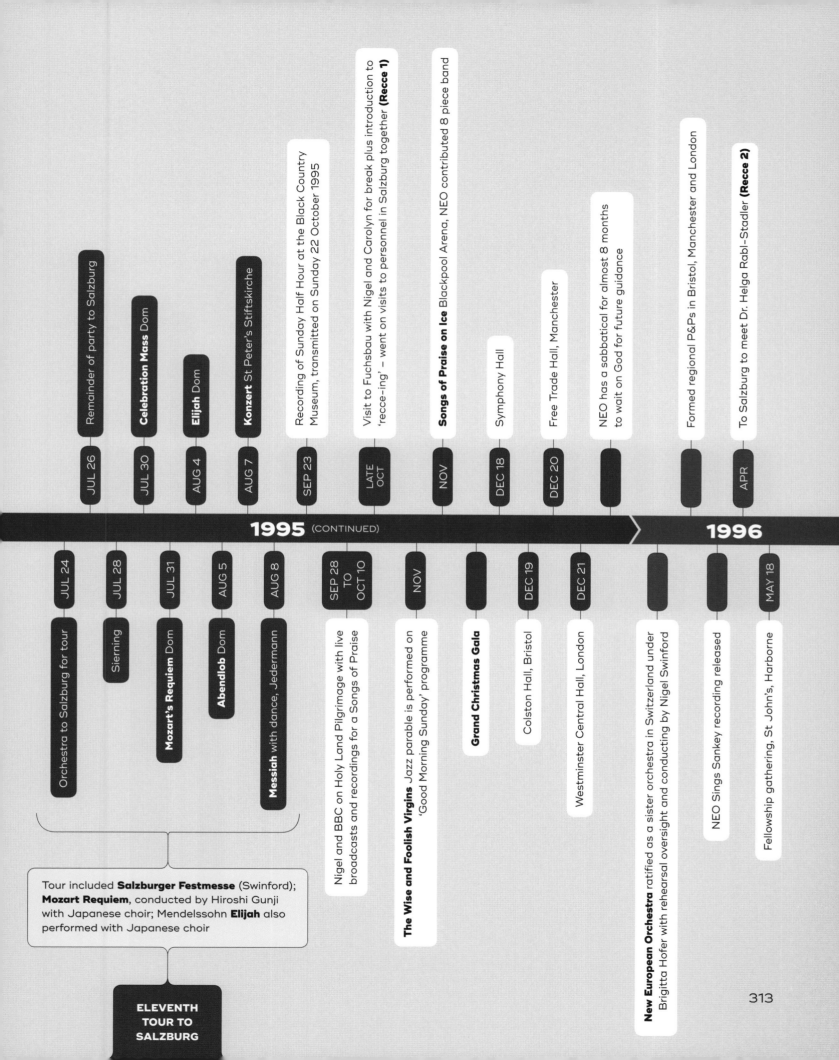

1995 (CONTINUED)   **1996**

Above timeline:

- JUL 26 — Remainder of party to Salzburg
- JUL 30 — **Celebration Mass** Dom
- AUG 4 — **Elijah** Dom
- AUG 7 — **Konzert** St Peter's Stiftskirche
- SEP 23 — Recording of Sunday Half Hour at the Black Country Museum, transmitted on Sunday 22 October 1995
- LATE OCT — Visit to Fuchsbau with Nigel and Carolyn for break plus introduction to 'recce-ing' – went on visits to personnel in Salzburg together **(Recce 1)**
- NOV — **Songs of Praise on Ice** Blackpool Arena, NEO contributed 8 piece band
- DEC 18 — Symphony Hall
- DEC 20 — Free Trade Hall, Manchester
- NEO has a sabbatical for almost 8 months to wait on God for future guidance
- Formed regional P&Ps in Bristol, Manchester and London
- APR — To Salzburg to meet Dr. Helga Rabl-Stadler **(Recce 2)**

Below timeline:

- JUL 24 — Orchestra to Salzburg for tour
- JUL 28 — Sierning
- JUL 31 — **Mozart's Requiem** Dom
- AUG 5 — **Abendlob** Dom
- AUG 8 — **Messiah** with dance, Jedermann
- SEP 28 TO OCT 10 — Nigel and BBC on Holy Land Pilgrimage with live broadcasts and recordings for a Songs of Praise
- NOV — **The Wise and Foolish Virgins** Jazz parable is performed on 'Good Morning Sunday' programme
- **Grand Christmas Gala**
- DEC 19 — Colston Hall, Bristol
- DEC 21 — Westminster Central Hall, London
- **New European Orchestra** ratified as a sister orchestra in Switzerland under Brigitta Hofer with rehearsal oversight and conducting by Nigel Swinford
- NEO Sings Sankey recording released
- MAY 18 — Fellowship gathering, St John's, Harborne

Tour included **Salzburger Festmesse** (Swinford); **Mozart Requiem**, conducted by Hiroshi Gunji with Japanese choir; Mendelssohn **Elijah** also performed with Japanese choir

ELEVENTH TOUR TO SALZBURG

313

1996 (CONTINUED)

JUN 22 — Coventry Cathedral with Sir David Wilcox (Nigel not present)

JUN / JUL — Nigel visits Africa to record Radio 2 arts programme

SEP 3 — **BBC Songs of Praise 35th Anniversary** Symphony Hall

OCT 19 — Broadcast of Radio 2 arts programme from Africa – nominated for an award for Racial Equality

DEC 5 — NEO at Hereford Cathedral (2nd visit) under auspices of the Hereford Cathedral Perpetual Trust to celebrate the 150th anniversary of Russell, Baldwin & Bright, Auctioneers

DEC 6-7 — Nigel and Keith Buckler fly to Vienna for rehearsals of **BBC Songs of Praise from Vienna** (Doug Gallaher and John Trow-Poole had already arrived to get all ready for weekend's refreshments)

DEC 9 — BBC **Songs of Praise from Vienna** recording takes place featuring Maria Brummer of Finland, discussing 'Cellos and Christianity' with Viennese Cello-maker

DEC 29 — Broadcast of BBC **Songs of Praise from Vienna**

1997

JAN / FEB — **Vigil 97** with extended choirs from local singers with NEO featuring Allegri Miserere

JAN 25 — **Vigil** Bristol Cathedral

FEB 1 — **Vigil** Manchester Cathedral

FEB 2 — Manchester Fellowship meeting at Cheadle Hulme Methodist Church

FEB 9 — **Songs of Praise** Bournville

FEB 15 — **Vigil** Bradford Cathedral

FEB 16 — Fellowship meeting at St Peter's, Shipley

FEB 19 — **Songs of Praise** Clitheroe

FEB 28 — **Vigil** St Chad's Cathedral, Birmingham

MAR 1 — **Vigil** St Philip's Cathedral, Birmingham

MAR 2 — Fellowship meeting, St Martin's in the Bullring

MAR 21 — Small group visit to Salzburg for Kapitelsaal concerts

MAR 22 — Concert Kapitelsaal

MAR 23 — Main party returns to UK – Nigel and Julie stay for meetings with church leaders on Mar 24, returning Mar 25

MAY 5-10 — Salzburg – Discussions for Mozarteum 21st Birthday **(Recce 3)**

MAY 30 TO JUN 1 — **Vigil CD** recorded at St John's Church, Hockley, Birmingham

TWELFTH WEEKEND TOUR TO SALZBURG

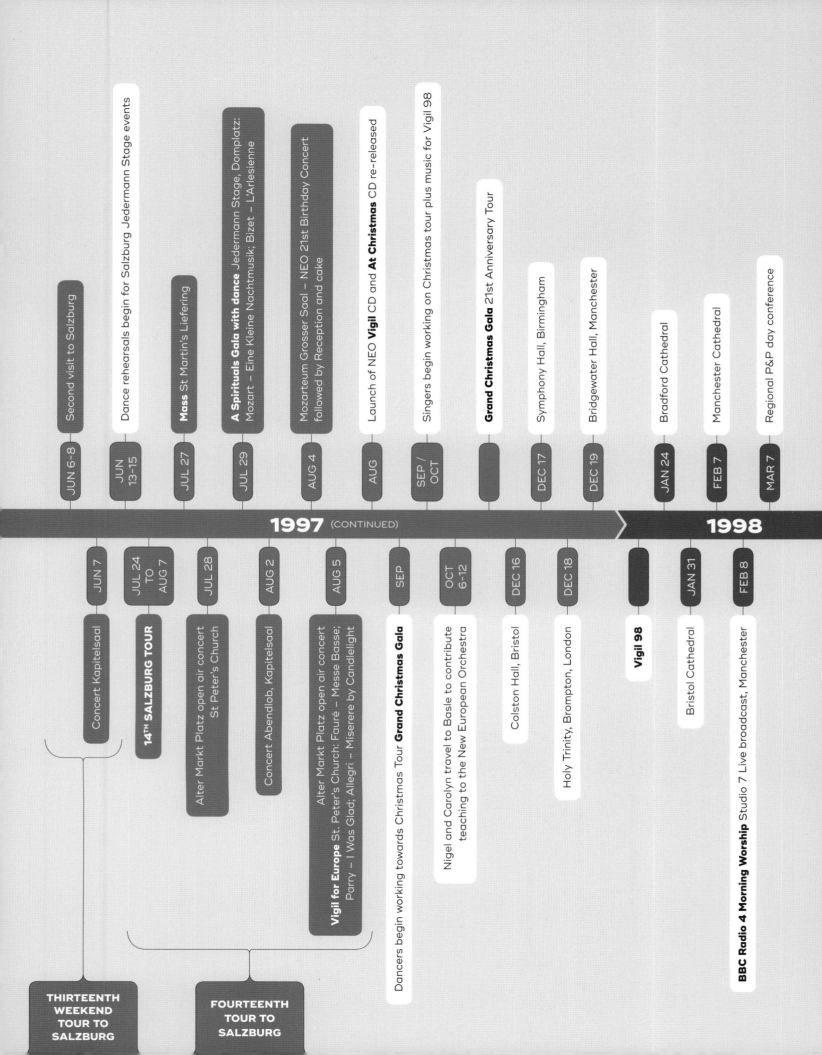

Above the timeline (1997):

Second visit to Salzburg — JUN 6-8

Dance rehearsals begin for Salzburg Jedermann Stage events — JUN 13-15

Mass St Martin's Liefering — JUL 27

A Spirituals Gala with dance Jedermann Stage, Domplatz: Mozart – Eine Kleine Nachtmusik; Bizet – L'Arlesienne — JUL 29

Mozarteum Grosser Saal – NEO 21st Birthday Concert followed by Reception and cake — AUG 4

Launch of NEO **Vigil** CD and **At Christmas** CD re-released — AUG

Singers begin working on Christmas tour plus music for Vigil 98 — SEP / OCT

Grand Christmas Gala 21st Anniversary Tour — (1998)

Symphony Hall, Birmingham — DEC 17

Bridgewater Hall, Manchester — DEC 19

Above the timeline (1998):

Bradford Cathedral — JAN 24

Manchester Cathedral — FEB 7

Regional P&P day conference — MAR 7

Timeline:

1997 (CONTINUED) ➤ **1998**

Below the timeline (1997):

Concert Kapitelsaal — JUN 7

14TH SALZBURG TOUR — JUL 24 TO AUG 7

Alter Markt Platz open air concert St Peter's Church — JUL 28

Concert Abendlob, Kapitelsaal — AUG 2

Vigil for Europe St. Peter's Church: Fauré – Messe Basse; Parry – I Was Glad; Allegri – Miserere by Candlelight / Alter Markt Platz open air concert — AUG 5

Dancers begin working towards Christmas Tour **Grand Christmas Gala** — SEP

Nigel and Carolyn travel to Basle to contribute teaching to the New European Orchestra — OCT 6-12

Colston Hall, Bristol — DEC 16

Holy Trinity, Brompton, London — DEC 18

Below the timeline (1998):

Vigil 98 — (JAN)

Bristol Cathedral — JAN 31

BBC Radio 4 Morning Worship Studio 7 Live broadcast, Manchester — FEB 8

Bottom brackets:

THIRTEENTH WEEKEND TOUR TO SALZBURG

FOURTEENTH TOUR TO SALZBURG

Jason McCauley, trumpeter and founder of the New Scottish Orchestra, played on this occasion.

Nigel in Basle to conduct rehearsals

Nigel conducts concert at Wadenswil

BBC 1 **Easter Service** from Arundel

NEuO – Hamburg

Nigel in Wurzburg

Nigel in Basle to conduct rehearsals

Nigel in Wurzburg

BBC Manchester and on to Edinburgh Carruber's Christian Centre Royal Mile for Roger Royle and Sunday Half Hour – Sankey hymns (16 singers)

Nigel in St Gallen

Carols and Classics Christmas Tour

HM Theatre Haymarket, London

Colston Hall, Bristol

NEO to become a charity – Julie consults Anthony Collins Solicitors on behalf of NEO

NEO becomes a registered company, no. 3847975

| MAR 22–28 | MAR 29 | APR 12 | MAY | JUL 11 | AUG 21–23 | | OCT 30 TO NOV 1 | NOV 20–23 | | DEC 13 | DEC 15 | | SEP 24 |

1998 (CONTINUED)

1999

| MAR 28 | APR 11 | APR 26 | | JUL 19 | SEP 27 | OCT 16–19 | NOV 15–22 | DEC 6 | DEC 11 | DEC 14 | FEB 8 |

First New European Orchestra (NEuO) **concert in Basle**

Nigel to rehearsal for Easter Service

Vigil for Shaftesbury Sunday Southwark Cathedral, London

Nigel involved in Daily Services on radio and visits to work with NEuO

Vigil for the Nation in Centenary Square, Birmingham 8.45pm

Nigel in Wurzburg

Nigel in Basle

Sunday Half Hour broadcasts

The NEO and Kennedy Stratford upon Avon – event to celebrate the testimonial year of the Warwickshire and England fast bowler, Tim Munton – whose friend Nigel Kennedy agreed to play at this event

Bridgewater Hall, Manchester

Symphony Hall, Birmingham

Roger Knott went to be with the Lord

FIFTEENTH
TOUR TO
SALZBURG

1999 (CONTINUED)   **2000**

Above the timeline (1999):

OCT 16 — Bradford Cathedral

NOV 13 — Manchester Cathedral

15TH SALZBURG ADVENT TOUR Second group performing Advent (Christetag) with members of the NEuO in Salzburger Dom, featuring a new piece by Nigel based on the hymn 'Sun of Righteousness'

DEC 3 — **Millennium Farewell Concert** Hereford Cathedral

Above the timeline (2000):

JAN 21-23 — All off to NEO rehearsals at The Gaines

FEB 11-13 — Second Gaines weekend with all concerned, i.e. Singers, Orchestra & Disputation Team (Chrissy Joynes/Robin Mason/Paul Sheppard)

Jubilee: Litany of Thanksgiving Tour with 'Watch' service (Gerrards)

MAR 3 — Catherine Swinford married Peter White

MAR 11 — Manchester Cathedral

BBC Radio 2 recording to be broadcast on June 4

APR 8 — Rochester Cathedral

MAY — Evenings at St.Peter's Halliwell and Parbold (22nd May)

Below the timeline (1999):

Vigil for the Millennium Tour

NOV 6 — Bristol Cathedral

NOV 27 — Group at Linton Parish Church, near Grassington, Yorkshire

DEC 1 — NEO becomes a registered charity

DEC 4 — Hull Methodist Central Hall

Below the timeline (2000):

FEB 3 — NEO logo registered as a trademark

FEB 16 — **First Trustees' Meeting of NEO** 8.30pm

FEB 26 — Bristol Cathedral

MAR 4 — St Philip's Cathedral, Birmingham

MAR 18 — Worcester Cathedral – including **Site-Specific Dance** choreographed by Lizzie Swinford and danced by herself and Sarah Christopher to Bach and Britten cello suites played by Christopher Poffley

APR 1 — Bradford Cathedral

APR — New English Micro-Orchestra born

JUN 4 — BBC Radio 2 Broadcast of **Worcester Jubilee**

317

SIXTEENTH TOUR TO SALZBURG

2000 (CONTINUED)

JUL 29 — Tour begins

JUL 30 — Rehearsals

JUL 31 — Rehearsals

AUG 1 — Rehearsals and evening fellowship with local Christians

AUG 2 — Kapitelplatz – permits not allowed for Alter Markt

AUG 3 — Morning rehearsals p.m free/ Jedermannbuhne in evening

AUG 4 — Rehearsals / St Peter's

AUG 5 — Lobpreis

AUG 6 — Mass 10.00am then free

AUG 7 — Coach to Hallein 6.30pm

AUG 8 — Free day

AUG 9-10 — Recording of **Stimmt an die Seiten** CD (New European Orchestra) by ERF in Hallein, Salzburg

AUG 11 — Concert 8.30pm

AUG 12 — Returned to UK (flights)

Fascinatin' Rhythm tour — A unique evening of music, comedy and conversation

SEP 22-24 — Third Gaines weekend. Nigel in hospital – weekend run by Martin Lowe and Pete Desmond. Mock Disputation took place

OCT 7 — Grand Moat House Hotel, Birmingham

OCT 14 — Jarvis Piccadilly Hotel, Manchester

OCT 21 — Jarvis International Hotel, Bristol

OCT 28 — Denbies Wine Estate, Dorking

New European Orchestra **Stimmt an die Seiten** CD released

NOV 9 — Nigel's major surgery

Looking Forward to Christmas tour — Conducted by Pete' Desmond and Martin Lowe in Nigel's absence

DEC 1 — Bridgewater Hall, Manchester

DEC 2 — Colston Hall, Bristol

DEC 5 — Symphony Hall, Birmingham

DEC 8 — St Paul's Church, Hammersmith, London

2001

Above the timeline:

- JAN 11 — Nigel rehearsing for **Songs of Praise**
- JAN 26 — Nigel begins radiotherapy treatment
- NOV 19 — Recce to Salzburg **(Recce 4)**
- **Vigil series** with Rev. Bob Dunnett in response to events of last year in USA
- FEB 2 — Bristol Cathedral
- FEB 9 — Rochester Cathedral
- FEB 23 — St Mary's, Watford
- MAR 2 — Worcester Cathedral
- APR 24 — Rehearsals, Manchester
- JUL 7 — Open air **Songs of Praise** in Bolton conducted by Nigel Swinford
- NOV 1-3 — Fireworks at the Gaines (NEO family event)
- NOV 23 — Rehearsal for Christmas Day service at St Peter's Halliwell
- DEC 25 — Christmas Day **No Room at the Inn** live BBC 1 broadcast at St Peter's Halliwell
- JAN 19 — P&P meet at Mark and Iona Birchall's home at Cotswold Farm

Below the timeline:

- JAN 16-17 — Nigel recording **Songs of Praise**
- SEP 11 —
- **Among the Nations** recording re-released as CD
- JAN 26 — Great St Mary's, Cambridge
- FEB 7 — Day of Prayer and Fasting for Vigils / Bob Dunnett
- FEB 16 — Bradford Cathedral
- MAR 1 — St Philip's Cathedral, Birmingham
- MAR 16 — Manchester Cathedral
- APR 25 — BBC recording of **A Deep But Dazzling Darkness** recorded at Lowry Centre, Salford Quays.
- SEP 6-12 — Recce to Salzburg **(Recce 5)**
- NOV 8-10 — Karlsruhe Conference with Nigel and Carolyn **(Recce 6)** NEuO
- DEC 12 — NEO micro Christmas Carol Concert at Manchester Cathedral in aid of National Children's Home
- JAN 18 — Enablers' meeting in Bristol with Ros Gane

2002

2003

Events in America involving terrorist attacks on Twin Towers.

2003 (CONTINUED)

Timeline (upper entries)

- **JAN 20** — Nigel recorded for Holocaust Broadcast – Arvo Pärt
- **JAN 27** — Nigel and Julie recce to Salzburg via Munich **(Recce 7)**
- **JAN 29** — Met with János Czifra
- **FEB 7** — Big Band group and Baroque orchestra met to rehearse
- **FEB 26** — Bridgewater Hall, Manchester
- **MAR 8** — Colston Hall, Bristol
- **MAR 12** — Micro event York and Georg Hoelscher
- **APR 12** — **A Manchester Vigil** at Manchester Cathedral with CD 'Lamentations' by Alex Robertson on sale, 2 pieces having been featured during the Vigil
- **MAY 27** — Nigel and Carolyn to Seewis
- **JUN 11** — 10.30am met with Karen Buckauer 11.30am met with János Czifra
- **JUL 22** — Travel to Salzburg
- **JUL 26** — Rehearsals with János Czifra, Domkappelmeister
- **JUL 29** — 3.00pm Altermarkt concert St Peter's contemplation evening with Georgs Pelecis' piece **'Nevertheless'** Georgs and Marina stayed in a hotel as guests of the NEO

Timeline (lower entries)

- **JAN 23** — Day of prayer and fasting
- **JAN 28** — Met with Prof. Winter
- **JAN 31** — Travelled back to UK
- **Big Band Baroque tour** with indoor fireworks
- **FEB 27** — Symphony Hall, Birmingham
- **MAR 10** — Micro event Rhyll and Georg Hoelscher
- **MAR 21–23** — P&P weekend in Cotswolds
- **MAY 8** — St Philip's Cathedral, Birmingham, celebration of 30th Anniversary of Anthony Collins Solicitors
- **JUN 8–13** — Nigel and Julie recce to Salzburg **(Recce 8)** for Pelecis Visit
- **Festival of Spiritual Music**
- **JUL 25** — Concert in Alter Markt. St Peter's Stiftskirche in evening
- **JUL 27** — Dom 11.30am Mass for opening of Salzburg Music Festival
- **JUL 30** — Day off for most personnel, but 11.00am–12.00pm Press Conference in Romanischer Saal for P&P members and some players

Julie was his Secretary between June 1974 – November 1980 and he remains a great supporter of NEO.

SEVENTEENTH TOUR TO SALZBURG

2003 (CONTINUED)

JUL 31 — 6.00-7.00pm Lecture

AUG 4 — St Peter's Vigil in evening

AUG 6 — Return to UK

SEP 4 — **Songs of Praise** recording in Letchworth – recorded 'Give me Oil in my Lamp' around 40 odd times!

SEP 21 — **Songs of Praise** broadcast featuring 'Give me Oil in my Lamp' with an abridgement!

NOV 22 — Nigel and Julie to Luton for 12 noon flight via Zurich for recce to Salzburg **(Recce 9)**

NOV 27 — Returned to UK

2004

JAN 31 — **From Mourning into Dancing Vigil** at St Cyprian's Church, London

FEB 7 — 10.30am – 4.00pm Small group rehearsal for Cambridge **Festival of Spiritual Music**

FEB 21 — 4.00 – 6.00pm Small group for Cambridge

FEB 26 — Cambridge Michaelhouse

FEB 27 — Cambridge Michaelhouse

FEB 28 — Cambridge St Giles

MAR 4-6 — Recorded **A Time to Dance** CD at St Peter's Halliwell

MAR 13 — Rehearsals for BBC Recording (Billy Graham)

MAY 19–25 — Nigel and Julie recce to Salzburg **(Recce 10)**

JUN 17 — Day of prayer and fasting

JUL 4 — BBC Sunday Half Hour broadcast featuring NEO singers

JUL 31 — New English Micro Orchestra to Salzburg with new **Recreatio** Genre

AUG 2 — **Salzburg to Symphony Hall – The NEO live!** CD released. **Time to Dance** CD released

AUG 2 — **Recreatio** in Dom (premiere)

AUG 3 — **Recreatio** in Dom

AUG 4 — **Recreatio** in Dom Concert in St Peter's

AUG 5 — **Recreatio** in Dom

AUG 6 — **Recreatio** in Dom Concert in St Peter's

2004 (CONTINUED) — 2005

Above the timeline:

- **SEP 16** — Nigel and Julie recce to Salzburg (**Recce 11**)
- **SEP 20** — 2.00pm met at Residenz
- **SEP 22** — University Church
- **DEC 5** — BBC 1 Advent Series featuring NEO
- **FEB 19** — Colston Hall, Bristol
- **FEB 22** — Bridgewater Hall, Manchester
- **MAY 14** — Salzburg rehearsal plus extension for Cornerstone event
- **JUN 12–16** — Recce to Salzburg (**Recce 12**)
- **JUN 14** — Went to Hostel and to Billroth Hotel (to see Herr Lietinger).
- **JUN 16** — Returned to UK straight to P&P High Legh
- **JUL 27** — 12.30pm **Recreatio** Dom / 8.00pm St Peter's Church
- **JUL 29** — 12.30pm **Recreatio** Dom / 8.00pm St Peter's Church
- **AUG 1** — 12.30pm **Recreatio** Dom / 8.00pm Residenz

Below the timeline:

- **SEP 17** — 9.00am met Baltashar Sieberer / Met Pater Benedikt in afternoon
- **SEP 21** — Benedikt and Thea Hoelscher at St Peter's
- **NOV 20** — Recording of BBC Advent series **Down to Earth** at St Mary's, Chesham
- **Big Band Baroque and other Animals**
- **FEB 21** — Symphony Hall, Birmingham (light snow!)
- **MAY 11** — Salzburg rehearsal
- **MAY 25** — **Cornerstone 25 Year Celebration event** at Symphony Hall, Birmingham
- **JUN 13** — 11.00am met Pater Sieberer
- **JUN 15** — Breakfast with Georg & Thea Hoelscher
- **JUN 22 TO AUG 6** — **19TH SALZBURG TOUR**
- **JUL 28** — 12.30pm **Recreatio** Dom
- **JUL 30** — Day off at Georg and Thea Hoelscher
- **AUG 2** — 12.30pm Recreatio Dom

NINETEENTH TOUR TO SALZBURG

That Christmas saw the awful Boxing Day Tsunami in Thailand, etc.

2005 (CONTINUED)

2006

AUG 3 — 12.30pm **Recreatio** Dom 8.00pm St Peter's Church

AUG 4 — Day off

AUG 5 — 8.00pm University Church

AUG 6 — Main party returned to UK

NOV 22 — Small group at Castleford Salvation Army Church

DEC

FEB 17 — Recce to Salzburg **(Recce 13)** Snow!

FEB 23 — Returned to UK in extremely cold weather!

Spring Tour to Switzerland

MAR 3–6 — First weekend of events Switzerland

MAR 4 — Friedenskirche, Olten

MAR 5 — Katholische Kirche, Peter and Paul, Aarau

MAR 24–27 — Second weekend in Switzerland

MAR 25 — Reformed Church Hall, Oberentfelden

MAR 26 — Theodorskirche, Basle

APR 10 — Nigel and Julie to Lindfield to do site visit at church for first of new genre of Invitation Concerts

APR 11 — Nigel and Julie to St. Mary Bredin, Canterbury

MAY 14–17 — First recce to Rome! **(Recce 14)** Met Pater Benedikt

MAY 15 — J Sabbatical discussions

MAY 20 — **Consideration Evening** at St. John's for singers

MAY 25 — Nigel to Switzerland

MAY 26 — All flew to Switzerland

MAY 27 — Morning rehearsals – wonderful evening concert in Barenmatte – Saal, Suhr

MAY 28 — Cleaned the entire hostel together and travelled to Basle for lunch, saw Cathedral then made journey home

MAY 31 — Site visit to a church in Hall Green for Invitation Concert

JUN 5 — Our dear friend and trombone player Russell, Baldwin died on this day of cancer

323

Timeline

2006 (CONTINUED) — 2007

SEP 23 — St John's, Harborne – NEO Advent

SEP 25 — Collected music from the Royal Ballet for Nigel

SEP 26 — A Nigel in London

SEP 28 — Day of prayer and fasting and P&P at High Legh

NOV 5 — NEO Friend, Michael Warren went to be with the Lord

NOV 11 — **First Invitation Concert** at All Saints, Lindfield, West Sussex

NOV 26 — Nigel in **'Cricket'** programme

DEC 2 — **Advent Invitation Concert** St. Mary Bredin, Canterbury

DEC 8 — **Advent Invitation Concert** Liverpool Hope University Hall

DEC 9 — **Advent Invitation Concert** St Peter's Halliwell

NEO in Salzburg DVD launched

JAN 12 — Recce to Salzburg **(Recce 15)** with Nigel Visited University Church and St Peter's

JAN 13 — Worked on planning at Stein and had lunch at echenwirt with Georg & Thea Hoelscher

JAN 15 — Breakfast at Tomaselli's (Ruhetag at Rechenwirt!) 9.00am meeting with Pater Benedikt 3.00pm meeting at Offener Himmel (shop)

JAN 16 — Visited Aula (Herr Lietinger at Europa Kolleg also), Kajetanerkirche (in hope of venue for a Recreatio about healing) 8.15pm met Pater Benedikt at St. Peter's

JAN 17 — Met Franz/Petrus for playing and AKM (PRS) help

JAN 18 — Flew to UK and spent night in Bolton

JAN 19 — Recce to Rome **(Recce 16)**

JAN 20 — Meeting with Father Paciolla at Trevi

JAN 21 — Discussion and planning – viewed St. Peter's Square

JAN 22 — Discussion of possible rooms for small party in September at the Lancelot

JAN 23 — Rooms booked at the Lancelot for prospective tour

JAN 24 — Return to UK

FEB 2 — Nigel to Basle

Lent Invitation Concerts

MAR 17 — Hall Green Baptist Church, Birmingham

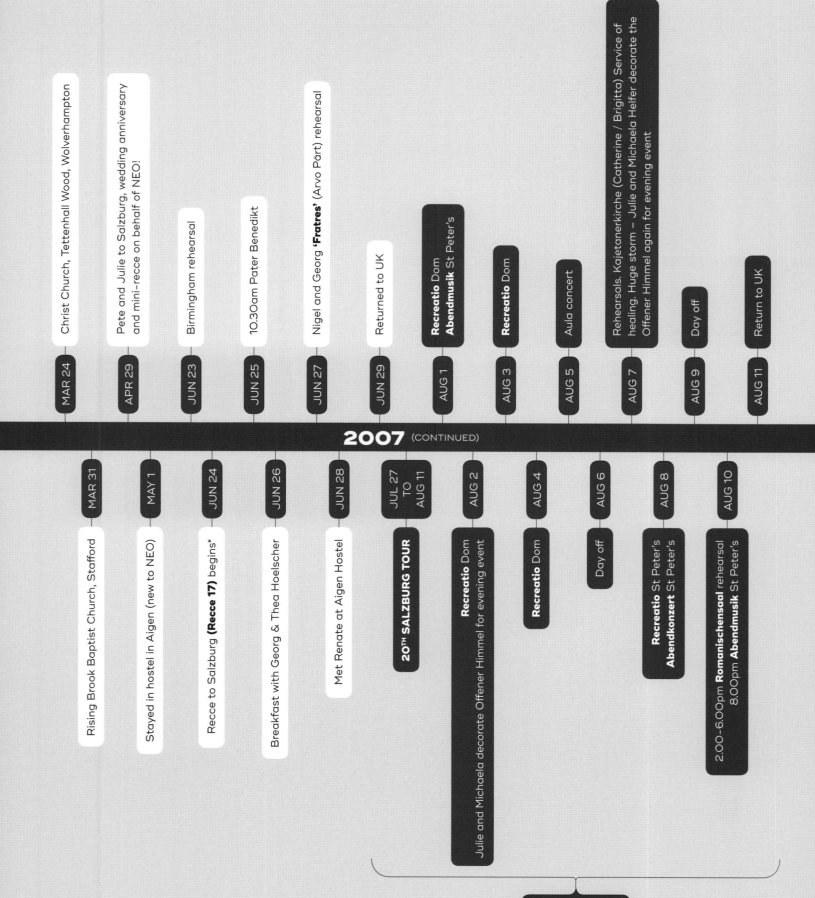

2007 (CONTINUED)

MAR 24 — Christ Church, Tettenhall Wood, Wolverhampton

MAR 31 — Rising Brook Baptist Church, Stafford

APR 29 — Pete and Julie to Salzburg, wedding anniversary and mini-recce on behalf of NEO!

MAY 1 — Stayed in hostel in Aigen (new to NEO)

JUN 23 — Birmingham rehearsal

JUN 24 — Recce to Salzburg **(Recce 17)** begins*

JUN 25 — 10.30am Pater Benedikt

JUN 26 — Breakfast with Georg & Thea Hoelscher

JUN 27 — Nigel and Georg **'Fratres'** (Arvo Pärt) rehearsal

JUN 28 — Met Renate at Aigen Hostel

JUN 29 — Returned to UK

JUL 27 TO AUG 11 — **20TH SALZBURG TOUR**

AUG 1 — **Recreatio** Dom **Abendmusik** St Peter's

AUG 2 — **Recreatio** Dom Julie and Michaela decorate Offener Himmel for evening event

AUG 3 — **Recreatio** Dom

AUG 4 — **Recreatio** Dom

AUG 5 — Aula concert

AUG 6 — Day off

AUG 7 — Rehearsals. Kajetanerkirche (Catherine / Brigitta) Service of healing. Huge storm – Julie and Michaela Helfer decorate the Offener Himmel again for evening event

AUG 8 — **Recreatio** St Peter's **Abendkonzert** St Peter's

AUG 9 — Day off

AUG 10 — 2.00-6.00pm **Romanischensaal** rehearsal 8.00pm **Abendmusik** St Peter's

AUG 11 — Return to UK

TWENTIETH TOUR TO SALZBURG

325

2007 (CONTINUED)

SEP 23 — 3 **Recreatios** at Chiesa de San Anastasio e Vicenzo with readings by Rev. Roger and Ruth Oldfield

SEP 24 — 3 **Recreatios** at Chiesa de San Anastasio e Vicenzo

SEP 25 — 3 **Recreatios** at Chiesa de San Anastasio e Vicenzo Ambassador to Holy See' Residenz

SEP 27 — Returned home to UK

OCT 5 — To Dunblane for wedding of Richard Turner & Julie Morrin

OCT 6 — Wedding service at which an NEO group sang Ceilidh / concert items from Catherine and Nigel etc. in evening

OCT 13 — **Invitation Concert** Ottery St. Mary, Devon

NOV 1-12 — Nigel to Salzburg for various meetings including János Czifra and Pater Benedikt and on to Basle on November 9

NOV 14 — Nigel and Julie to Guildford for discussions with Julian Briscoe and vicar (David Bracewell) of St. Saviour's Church with a view to a Recreatio concert

DEC 8 — **Invitation Concert** St Mary Magdalene, Stoke Bishop, Bristol

DEC 18 — Julie admitted to Hospital for leg operation

2008

JAN 18-25 — Nigel and Julie recce to Rome **(Recce 18)**

FEB 23 — St John's NEO Get Together Fellowship Meeting

MAR 14 — Nigel and Julie recce to Rome **(Recce 19)**

MAR 15 — Father Ballicu of Chiesa di Santa Maria sopra Minerva, (with the recommendation of Cardinal Cormack Murphy O'Connor, whose titular church this is).

MAR 17 — 9.00am met Father Raniero Cantalamessa

MAY 10 — **A Recreatio for Pentecost** St Saviour's, Guildford

JUN 23 — Nigel and Julie recce to Rome **(Recce 20)**
12 noon meeting with Nicoletta Vanuccini at Santa Maria Sopra Minerva

JUN 24 — 12 noon meeting with Monsignor Micheletti (Pantheon) and Philippa Hitchen of Vatican Radio (Davide his assistant met us instead! Philippa interpreted)

JUN 25 — Returned to UK

JUN 26-27 — Swinford Family to Switzerland for NEuO concerts

JUN 28 — Arrau

JUN 29 — Wetzikon

JUN 30 — Returned to UK

JUL 23 — Guildford planning visit (Nigel and Julie)

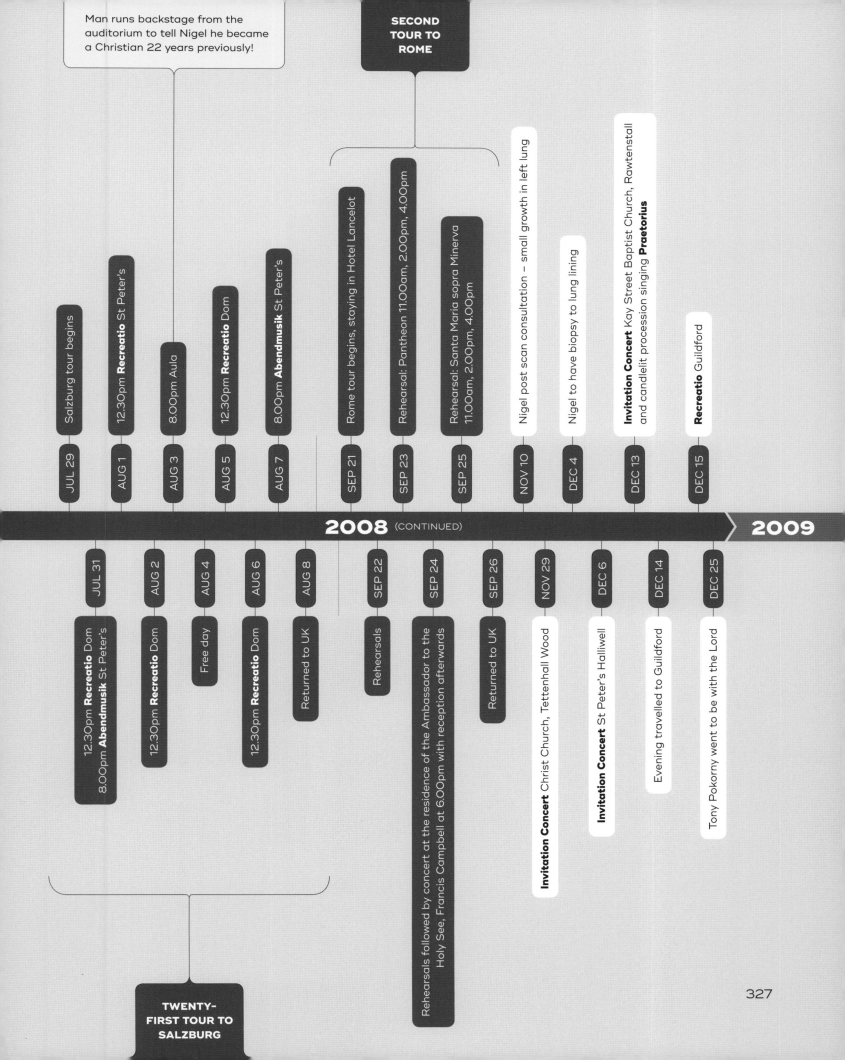

Man runs backstage from the auditorium to tell Nigel he became a Christian 22 years previously!

SECOND TOUR TO ROME

Salzburg tour begins — **JUL 29**

12.30pm **Recreatio** St Peter's — **AUG 1**

8.00pm Aula — **AUG 3**

12.30pm **Recreatio** Dom — **AUG 5**

8.00pm **Abendmusik** St Peter's — **AUG 7**

Rome tour begins, staying in Hotel Lancelot — **SEP 21**

Rehearsal: Pantheon 11.00am, 2.00pm, 4.00pm — **SEP 23**

Rehearsal: Santa Maria sopra Minerva 11.00am, 2.00pm, 4.00pm — **SEP 25**

Nigel post scan consultation – small growth in left lung — **NOV 10**

Nigel to have biopsy to lung lining — **DEC 4**

Invitation Concert Kay Street Baptist Church, Rawtenstall and candlelit procession singing **Praetorius** — **DEC 13**

Recreatio Guildford — **DEC 15**

2008 (CONTINUED)

2009

JUL 31 — 12.30pm **Recreatio** Dom / 8.00pm **Abendmusik** St Peter's

AUG 2 — 12.30pm **Recreatio** Dom

AUG 4 — Free day

AUG 6 — 12.30pm **Recreatio** Dom

AUG 8 — Returned to UK

SEP 22 — Rehearsals

SEP 24 — Rehearsals followed by concert at the residence of the Ambassador to the Holy See, Francis Campbell at 6.00pm with reception afterwards

SEP 26 — Returned to UK

NOV 29 — **Invitation Concert** Christ Church, Tettenhall Wood

DEC 6 — **Invitation Concert** St Peter's Halliwell

DEC 14 — Evening travelled to Guildford

DEC 25 — Tony Pokorny went to be with the Lord

TWENTY-FIRST TOUR TO SALZBURG

2009

Above timeline:

JAN 17 — **Recreatio** Town Hall, Birmingham (loud Gaza conflict demo' outside!)

FEB 18–23 — Nigel and Julie recce to Rome **(Recce 21)** – painful for Nigel this time!

FEB 19 — Meeting with Father Andrew Headon of VEC – invited to celebrate in October re-opening of refurbished chapel and stay at Palazolla

Nigel and David MacDonald meet the Dean of Canterbury Cathedral (Rev. Canon Robert Willis ex of Worcester Cathedral)

JUN 1–5 — Recce to Salzburg **(Recce 22)**

The Canterbury Vigils

JUL 4 — **Vigil** Wye Parish Church, Kent

SEP 19 — **Invitation Concert** St Swithins, Bath

SEP 30 — Rehearsal: Santa Maria sopra Minerva 11.00am, 2.00pm, 4.00pm

OCT 10 — **The Maidstone Vigil** St Luke's Church, Maidstone

NOV 21 — Culmination of **Vigils** in Canterbury Cathedral

JAN 16 — **Recreatio** Town Hall, Birmingham

MAR 1–5 — Recce to Salzburg **(Recce 24)** Met Abbot Bruno at St Peter's

Below timeline:

JAN 19 — Nigel's operation at Manchester Royal Infirmary

FEB 18 — Met with Mons. Micheletti to discuss 29 September. Recreatios in year celebrating 1400 years since The Pantheon (temple to all the gods) was consecrated as a church 'St Mary and the Martyrs'

During this period Nigel is scheduled for radiotherapy beginning 23 March

MAR 27 — Voting for the new Abbot of St Peter's in Salzburg

JUN 14–18 — Recce to Rome **(Recce 23)**

JUN 13 — **Vigil** St Saviour's, Guildford

JUL 18 — **Invitation Concert** St Mary's, Pembridge

SEP 29 — Rehearsal: Pantheon 11.00am, 2.00pm, 4.00pm

OCT 1 — Concert at British Embassy to Vatican 3 **Recreatios** Venerable English College

NOV 7 — **Vigil** Holy Trinity Church, Margate

Lord of the Music CD launched

FEB 6 — **Invitation Concert** St Peter's Church, Harold Wood, Essex

THIRD TOUR TO ROME

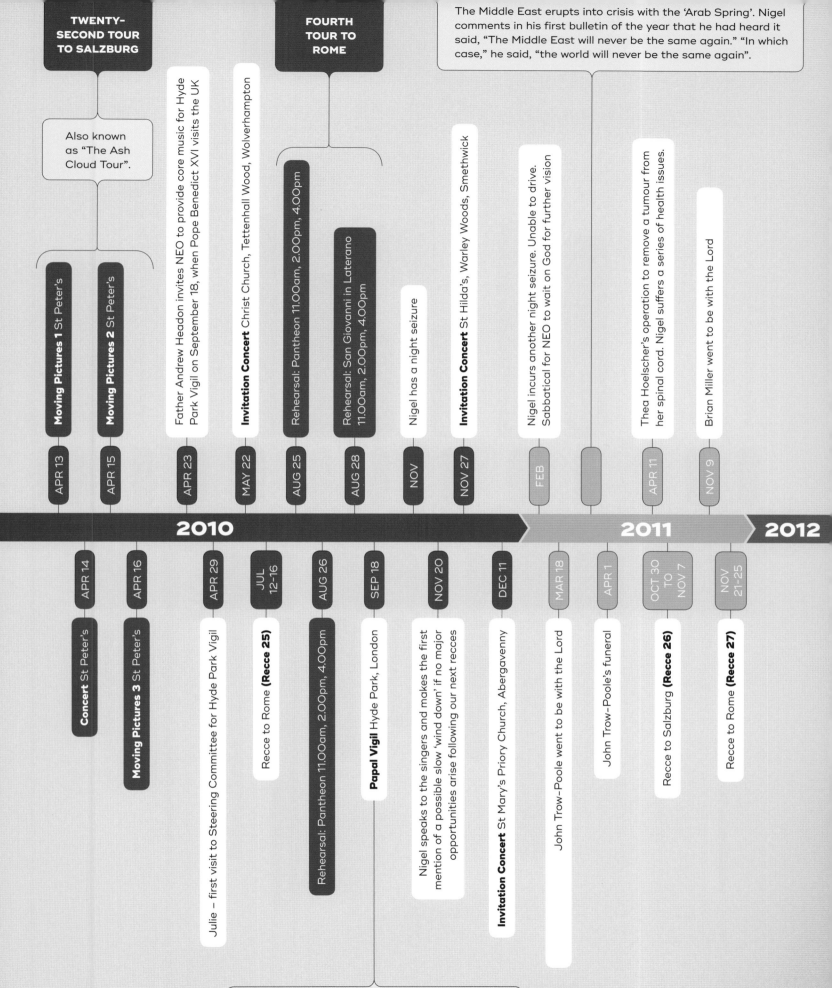

TWENTY-SECOND TOUR TO SALZBURG

Also known as "The Ash Cloud Tour".

FOURTH TOUR TO ROME

The Middle East erupts into crisis with the 'Arab Spring'. Nigel comments in his first bulletin of the year that he had heard it said, "The Middle East will never be the same again." "In which case," he said, "the world will never be the same again".

Moving Pictures 1 St Peter's — **APR 13**

Moving Pictures 2 St Peter's — **APR 15**

Father Andrew Headon invites NEO to provide core music for Hyde Park Vigil on September 18, when Pope Benedict XVI visits the UK — **APR 23**

Invitation Concert Christ Church, Tettenhall Wood, Wolverhampton — **MAY 22**

Rehearsal: Pantheon 11.00am, 2.00pm, 4.00pm — **AUG 25**

Rehearsal: San Giovanni in Laterano 11.00am, 2.00pm, 4.00pm — **AUG 28**

Nigel has a night seizure — **NOV**

Invitation Concert St Hilda's, Warley Woods, Smethwick — **NOV 27**

Nigel incurs another night seizure. Unable to drive. Sabbatical for NEO to wait on God for further vision — **FEB**

Thea Hoelscher's operation to remove a tumour from her spinal cord. Nigel suffers a series of health issues. — **APR 11**

Brian Miller went to be with the Lord — **NOV 9**

2010 / 2011 / 2012

Concert St Peter's — **APR 14**

Moving Pictures 3 St Peter's — **APR 16**

Julie – first visit to Steering Committee for Hyde Park Vigil — **APR 29**

Recce to Rome **(Recce 25)** — **JUL 12–16**

Rehearsal: Pantheon 11.00am, 2.00pm, 4.00pm — **AUG 26**

Papal Vigil Hyde Park, London — **SEP 18**

Nigel speaks to the singers and makes the first mention of a possible slow 'wind down' if no major opportunities arise following our next recces — **NOV 20**

Invitation Concert St Mary's Priory Church, Abergavenny — **DEC 11**

John Trow-Poole went to be with the Lord — **MAR 18**

John Trow-Poole's funeral — **APR 1**

Recce to Salzburg **(Recce 26)** — **OCT 30 TO NOV 7**

Recce to Rome **(Recce 27)** — **NOV 21–25**

NEO embarks on the biggest single event of its history, the **Vigil for Young People** in Hyde Park, London during the visit of Pope Benedict XVI.

329

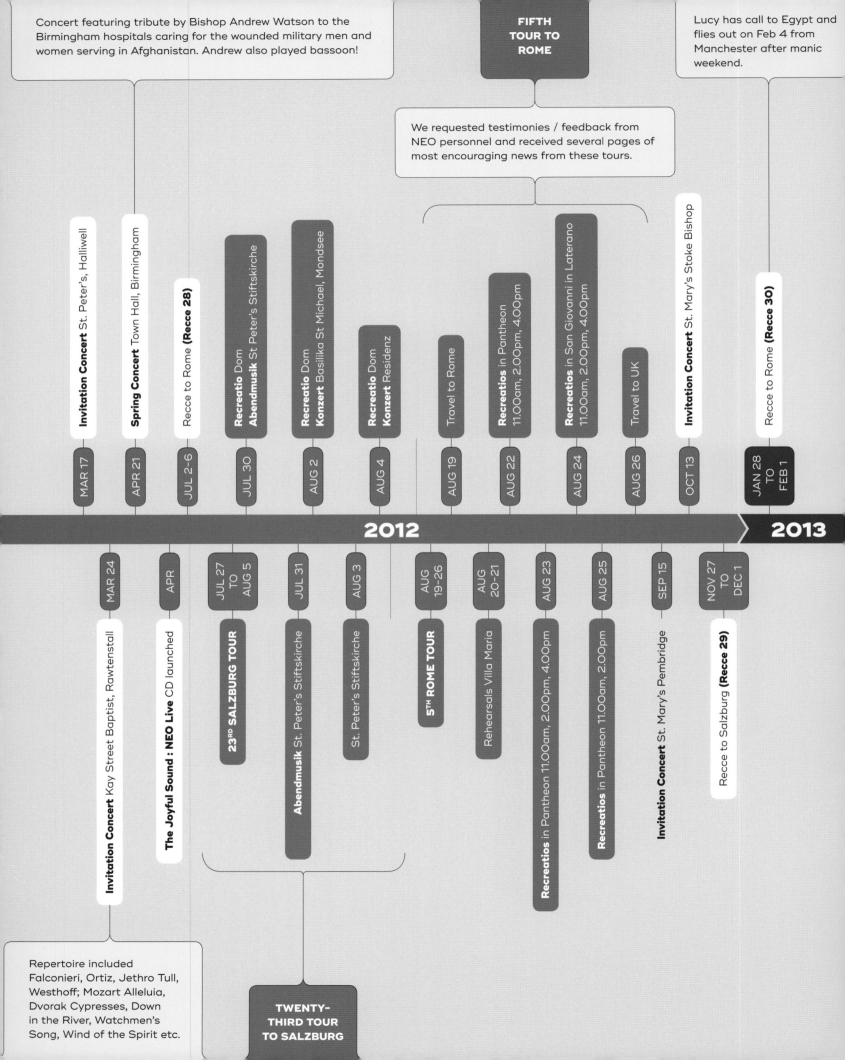

Concert featuring tribute by Bishop Andrew Watson to the Birmingham hospitals caring for the wounded military men and women serving in Afghanistan. Andrew also played bassoon!

FIFTH TOUR TO ROME

Lucy has call to Egypt and flies out on Feb 4 from Manchester after manic weekend.

We requested testimonies / feedback from NEO personnel and received several pages of most encouraging news from these tours.

Invitation Concert St. Peter's, Halliwell

Spring Concert Town Hall, Birmingham

Recce to Rome **(Recce 28)**

Recreatio Dom **Abendmusik** St Peter's Stiftskirche

Recreatio Dom **Konzert** Basilika St Michael, Mondsee

Recreatio Dom **Konzert** Residenz

Travel to Rome

Recreatios in Pantheon 11.00am, 2.00pm, 4.00pm

Recreatios in San Giovanni in Laterano 11.00am, 2.00pm, 4.00pm

Travel to UK

Invitation Concert St. Mary's Stoke Bishop

Recce to Rome **(Recce 30)**

MAR 17

APR 21

JUL 2-6

JUL 30

AUG 2

AUG 4

AUG 19

AUG 22

AUG 24

AUG 26

OCT 13

JAN 28 TO FEB 1

2012

2013

MAR 24

APR

JUL 27 TO AUG 5

JUL 31

AUG 3

AUG 19-26

AUG 20-21

AUG 23

AUG 25

SEP 15

NOV 27 TO DEC 1

Invitation Concert Kay Street Baptist, Rawtenstall

The Joyful Sound : NEO Live CD launched

23RD SALZBURG TOUR

Abendmusik St. Peter's Stiftskirche

St. Peter's Stiftskirche

5TH ROME TOUR

Rehearsals Villa Maria

Recreatios in Pantheon 11.00am, 2.00pm, 4.00pm

Recreatios in Pantheon 11.00am, 2.00pm

Invitation Concert St. Mary's Pembridge

Recce to Salzburg **(Recce 29)**

Repertoire included Falconieri, Ortiz, Jethro Tull, Westhoff; Mozart Alleluia, Dvorak Cypresses, Down in the River, Watchmen's Song, Wind of the Spirit etc.

TWENTY-THIRD TOUR TO SALZBURG

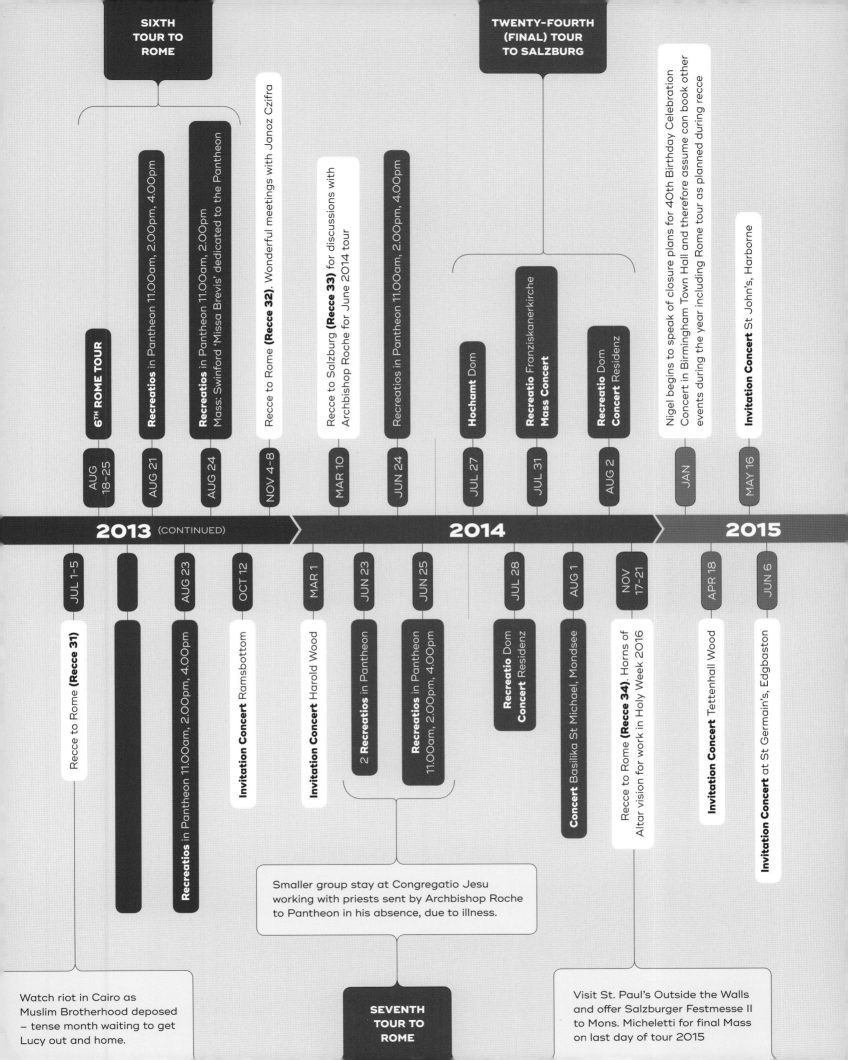

SIXTH TOUR TO ROME

TWENTY-FOURTH (FINAL) TOUR TO SALZBURG

Recreatios in Pantheon 11.00am, 2.00pm, 4.00pm

Recreatios in Pantheon 11.00am, 2.00pm
Mass: Swinford 'Missa Brevis' dedicated to the Pantheon

Recce to Rome **(Recce 32)**. Wonderful meetings with Janoz Czifra

Recce to Salzburg **(Recce 33)** for discussions with Archbishop Roche for June 2014 tour

Recreatios in Pantheon 11.00am, 2.00pm, 4.00pm

Hochamt Dom

Recreatio Franziskanerkirche **Mass Concert**

Recreatio Dom **Concert** Residenz

Nigel begins to speak of closure plans for 40th Birthday Celebration Concert in Birmingham Town Hall and therefore assume can book other events during the year including Rome tour as planned during recce

Invitation Concert St John's, Harborne

6TH ROME TOUR

AUG 18–25

AUG 21

AUG 24

NOV 4–8

MAR 10

JUN 24

JUL 27

JUL 31

AUG 2

JAN

MAY 16

2013 (CONTINUED)

2014

2015

JUL 1–5

AUG 23

OCT 12

MAR 1

JUN 23

JUN 25

JUL 28

AUG 1

NOV 17–21

APR 18

JUN 6

Recce to Rome **(Recce 31)**

Recreatios in Pantheon 11.00am, 2.00pm, 4.00pm

Invitation Concert Ramsbottom

Invitation Concert Harold Wood

2 **Recreatios** in Pantheon

Recreatios in Pantheon 11.00am, 2.00pm, 4.00pm

Recreatio Dom **Concert** Residenz

Concert Basilika St Michael, Mondsee

Recce to Rome **(Recce 34)**. Horns of Altar vision for work in Holy Week 2016

Invitation Concert Tettenhall Wood

Invitation Concert at St Germain's, Edgbaston

Smaller group stay at Congregatio Jesu working with priests sent by Archbishop Roche to Pantheon in his absence, due to illness.

Watch riot in Cairo as Muslim Brotherhood deposed – tense month waiting to get Lucy out and home.

SEVENTH TOUR TO ROME

Visit St. Paul's Outside the Walls and offer Salzburger Festmesse II to Mons. Micheletti for final Mass on last day of tour 2015

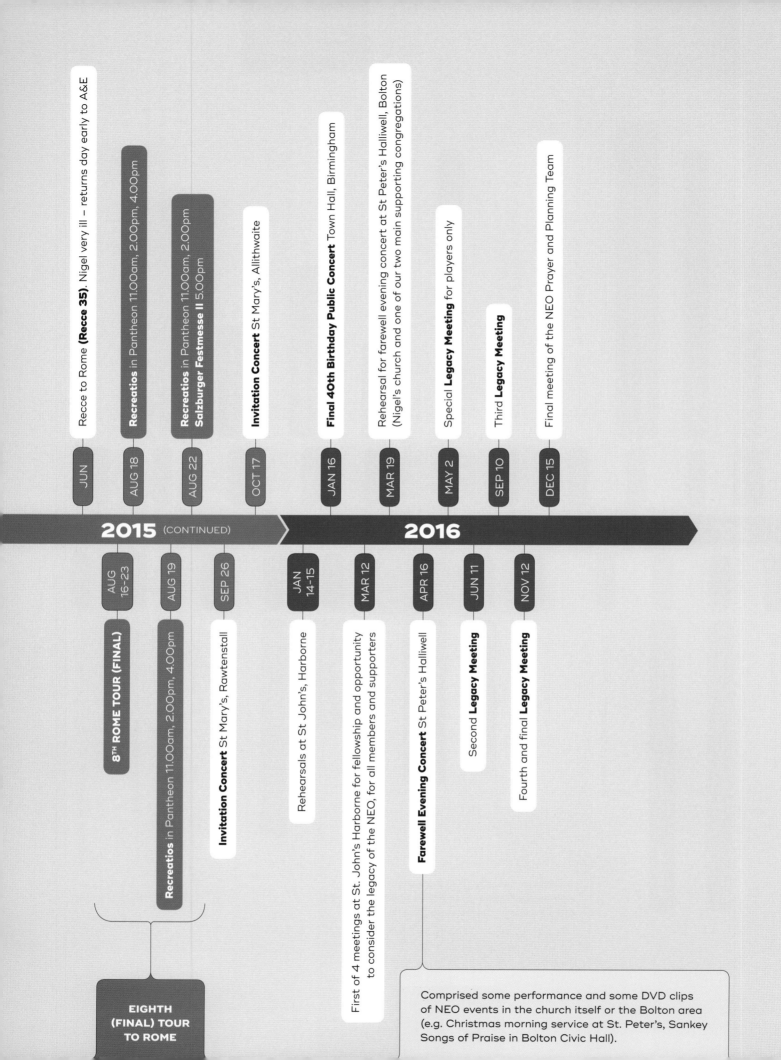

Recce to Rome **(Recce 35)**. Nigel very ill – returns day early to A&E

Recreatios in Pantheon 11.00am, 2.00pm, 4.00pm

Recreatios in Pantheon 11.00am, 2.00pm **Salzburger Festmesse II** 5.00pm

Invitation Concert St Mary's, Allithwaite

Final 40th Birthday Public Concert Town Hall, Birmingham

Rehearsal for farewell evening concert at St Peter's Halliwell, Bolton (Nigel's church and one of our two main supporting congregations)

Special **Legacy Meeting** for players only

Third **Legacy Meeting**

Final meeting of the NEO Prayer and Planning Team

JUN

AUG 18

AUG 22

OCT 17

JAN 16

MAR 19

MAY 2

SEP 10

DEC 15

2015 (CONTINUED)

2016

AUG 16-23

AUG 19

SEP 26

JAN 14-15

MAR 12

APR 16

JUN 11

NOV 12

8TH ROME TOUR (FINAL)

Recreatios in Pantheon 11.00am, 2.00pm, 4.00pm

Invitation Concert St Mary's, Rawtenstall

Rehearsals at St John's, Harborne

First of 4 meetings at St. John's Harborne for fellowship and opportunity to consider the legacy of the NEO, for all members and supporters

Farewell Evening Concert St Peter's Halliwell

Second **Legacy Meeting**

Fourth and final **Legacy Meeting**

EIGHTH (FINAL) TOUR TO ROME

Comprised some performance and some DVD clips of NEO events in the church itself or the Bolton area (e.g. Christmas morning service at St. Peter's, Sankey Songs of Praise in Bolton Civic Hall).

Great solo by Bob McKay!

Helen Shillito on horn

Will Napier on saxophone

Nick Parrans-Smith

Pete Desmond, Raul D'Oliveira, Nick P-S and Mark Attwood

NEO Big Band boys and girls!

Adam Kishtainy, guitar & James Manson, bass

Our dear friend Keith Entwistle, now with the Lord

Rare pic of the lovely Stephanie Blanchard!

Nicola sorting the orchestral folders!

Catherine and Lesley, two of our lovely soloists

Lesley Thompson misbehaving!

Catherine Swinford-White

BiGBAND

NEW ENGLISH orCHeStra
and Singers

BAROQUE
and other animals

Director – Nigel Swinford

Highlights include:

Jazz classics by: Tommy Dorsey, Woody Herman, Count Basie, Fletcher Henderson and Stan Kenton

Bach: Brandenburg Concerto No 2
Saint-Saëns: Carnival of the Animals
Handel: Worthy is the Lamb from Messiah
Handel: Fireworks Music – La Réjouissance

NEO sings Gospel

NEO sings Gospel!

Venues

Colston Hall, Bristol
Saturday 19th February 2005, 7.30pm
Box Office 0117 922 3686
www.colstonhall.org

Symphony Hall, Birmingham
Monday 21st February 2005, 7.30pm
Box Office 0121 780 3333
www.symphonyhall.co.uk/boxoffice

The Bridgewater Hall, Manchester
Tuesday 22nd February 2005, 7.30pm
Box Office 0161 907 9000
www.bridgewater-hall.co.uk

Tickets for all venues Freephone: 0800 018 2695 (booking fee)

PLUS
a spectacular
indoor firework
display

NEW ENGLISH ORCHESTRA

Director – Nigel Swinford

The NEO returns with its stunning varied concert format (first introduced in 2003) where the pounding rhythm and blazing brass of Big Band music vie with the speed, delicacy, dance beats and rippling virtuosity of the Baroque, and the ever popular Carnival of the Animals. The performance is bound together by the vibrant NEO Singers performing a wide range of Gospel music and a joyous evening of celebration climaxes with a spectacular indoor firework display in three of the country's major concert halls.

A superb evening is guaranteed as witnessed by comments about previous NEO performances:

"I had the time of my life"

"The concert at Symphony Hall was just awesome!"

"We didn't want to leave"

"The NEO has triumphed again"

"Much more than just an evening of entertainment"

"Consummate professionalism"

The **New English Orchestra** is noted for its innovative approach to performance aiming to bring a specifically Christian emphasis to a broad range of music. The NEO has visited The Bridgewater, Symphony and Colston Halls many times in the last decade and has also performed in major venues across Europe, notably in Salzburg.

Based in England, the NEO, founded in 1976, is composed of high quality instrumentalists and is adaptable in size from a small chamber group to a jazz band to a full symphony orchestra.

The **NEO Singers** are a polished and versatile group with an extensive repertoire ranging from choral classics to contemporary works. A key feature of their lively and enthusiastic style is the ability to communicate effectively with their audience, an approach which is aided by their memorising all that they sing.

New English Orchestra – a registered charity no 1078424

www.newenglishorchestra.org

Designed and Produced by Q2 Creative